Educational Linguistics

Volume 45

Educational Linguistics is dedicated to innovative studies of language use and language learning. The series is based on the idea that there is a need for studies that break barriers. Accordingly, it provides a space for research that crosses traditional disciplinary, theoretical, and/or methodological boundaries in ways that advance knowledge about language (in) education. The series focuses on critical and contextualized work that offers alternatives to current approaches as well as practical, substantive ways forward. Contributions explore the dynamic and multi-layered nature of theory-practice relationships, creative applications of linguistic and symbolic resources, individual and societal considerations, and diverse social spaces related to language learning.

The series publishes in-depth studies of educational innovation in contexts throughout the world: issues of linguistic equity and diversity; educational language policy; revalorization of indigenous languages; socially responsible (additional) language teaching; language assessment; first- and additional language literacy; language teacher education; language development and socialization in non-traditional settings; the integration of language across academic subjects; language and technology; and other relevant topics.

The *Educational Linguistics* series invites authors to contact the general editor with suggestions and/or proposals for new monographs or edited volumes. For more information, please contact the Editor: Natalie Rieborn, Van Godewijckstraat 30, 3300 AA Dordrecht, The Netherlands.

All proposals and manuscripts submitted to the Series will undergo at least two rounds of external peer review.

More information about this series at http://www.springer.com/series/5894

Zhongfeng Tian • Laila Aghai
Peter Sayer • Jamie L. Schissel

Editors

Envisioning TESOL through a Translanguaging Lens

Global Perspectives

 Springer

Editors
Zhongfeng Tian (iD)
Department of Bicultural-Bilingual Studies
The University of Texas at San Antonio
San Antonio, TX, USA

Peter Sayer (iD)
College of Education and Human Ecology
The Ohio State University
Columbus, OH, USA

Laila Aghai
Department of Teaching, Leadership &
Professional Practice
University of North Dakota
Grand Forks, ND, USA

Jamie L. Schissel
Department of Teacher Education and
Higher Education
University of North Carolina at Greensboro
Greensboro, NC, USA

ISSN 1572-0292   ISSN 2215-1656   (electronic)
Educational Linguistics
ISBN 978-3-030-47030-2   ISBN 978-3-030-47031-9   (eBook)
https://doi.org/10.1007/978-3-030-47031-9

This Springer imprint is published by the registered company Springer Nature Switzerland AG
The registered company address is: Gewerbestrasse 11, 6330 Cham, Switzerland

Foreword: Cutting Through the Monolingual Grip of TESOL Traditions – The Transformative Power of the Translanguaging Lens

Since the publication of García and Li Wei's seminal work *Translanguaging* in 2014, translanguaging has become a buzzword in TESOL and Applied Linguistics conferences and an intellectual and pedagogical movement among language education communities. The 17 chapters collected in this book have further provided empirical evidence that the translanguaging lens can offer pedagogical affordances and a renewed sense of agency among both teachers and students. A social justice concern is also central to translanguaging pedagogies (see Sembiante and Tian; Robinson et al., and many other chapters in this volume). The authors in this book have spoken on a wide range of contexts and issues: from *translanguaging* [used as a transitive verb here] TESOL pedagogies, to *translanguaging* TESOL assessment design, to *translanguaging* TESOL/ESL/EFL teacher education courses.

Yet, some chapters in this book also documented some challenges facing the translanguaging intellectual and pedagogical movement, among which are the resistance, confusion, lack of confidence and strategies in trying out translanguaging pedagogies among some teachers, the rigidity and hegemony of (dominant forms of) English in high-stakes tests (e.g. IELTS, TOEFL), and the deep-rooted ideologies shaping teachers' orientation or stance towards translanguaging.

As Lau cautions:

> Researchers on international development also need to exercise vigilance and humility in our understanding of what decolonization means to local communities (Darroch & Giles, 2014) and how our new theories and insights on language and language education might facilitate or hinder local agentive efforts to find creative solutions to make do with varied severe socio-political and economic demands. (Lau, this volume)

However, when local researchers and teachers themselves (e.g. the teacher in Seltzer and García's study, this volume) contribute to translanguaging theory and practice and speak to the agency that the translanguaging lens can afford them and their students in their own contexts, then it is not about some foreign experts imposing 'new' theories and pedagogies on other people, but about how local communities in different contexts begin to use the translanguaging lens to speak back to traditional TESOL theory and to bring back a focus on social justice, which has been so sorely missing in the monolingual, monoglossic grip of the TESOL tradition for too long. When Sembiante and Tian (this volume) re-position the 'E', 'SOL' and 'T' through the translanguaging lens, they also start to break through this grip by using the translanguaging lens as a diamond that cuts through the mythologies/ideologies that have beset TESOL like an invisible curse (Lin & Motha, 2019).

⌐While there is an emerging body of research studies contributing to the development of translanguaging theory and pedagogies, there have also been queries about the transformative power of translanguaging (Jaspers, 2018). Lin, Wu, and Lemke (2020) have summarized these queries heard among some critics and teachers as follows:

1. 'What are the differences between translanguaging and code-switching/code-mixing or code alternation?'
2. 'I cannot wrap my mind around the notion that there are no boundaries among languages; that a speaker only has one holistic repertoire and there are no internal differentiations in this repertoire. It goes against my gut feeling that I am speaking different languages... How does translanguaging theory explain the fact that I do feel that I am speaking different languages?'
3. 'Translanguaging pedagogy is similar to existing pedagogical approaches that argue for the importance of valuing students' familiar linguistic and cultural resources (Cook, 2001; Cummins, 2007) and sociocultural theories of "funds of knowledge" (González, Moll, & Amanti, 2005); what's new about it?'
4. 'There is limiting potential of translanguaging to disrupt the hierarchy of languages: many of the translanguaging examples in conference presentations sound so much like previous examples of using L1 to scaffold the learning of the target language; the hierarchy is still there.'
5. 'Translanguaging theory argues that the language boundaries are porous and that named languages are historical, social, political, institutional constructions. This idea cannot help minoritized linguistic and cultural groups who want to revive, maintain and uphold their heritage languages and linguistic identities. This is especially worrying in situations where minority groups want to revive their endangered languages under the domination of an institutionally powerful language (e.g. English).' (Extracted from Lin et al., 2020)

In Lin et al. (2020), some possible responses to the above questions are explored and offered. One key to appreciating the paradigm shifting power of the translanguaging lens is to understand the different ontologies underpinning the translanguaging view and the traditional code view. As Seltzer and García put it:

> Translanguaging also bridges understandings of language diversity for different types of students—those who are said to be bilingual and those considered to be multidialectal. *By focusing on linguistic features, and not language as an autonomous structure*, translanguaging theory makes it possible for African American and Latinx students to understand their language development as being part of the same process, despite the socio-political differences between what are seen as "varieties of English" and "different languages." In so doing, students become better listeners for one another, engaging in developing each other's repertoires without regard of whether students are said to be "bilingual" or "multidialectal." (Seltzer and García, this volume; italics added)

In Fig. 1, I attempt to construe and visualize (albeit with some theoretical simplification) two different views of language learning. The traditional code view focuses on learning languages as bounded autonomous structures in compartmentalized spaces ('parallel monolingualisms') whereas the translanguaging lens embraces a *languaging* (dynamic meaning-making process) view of language learning.

To conclude this foreword, I want to outline some urgent directions for research in the emerging field of translanguaging in TESOL:

1. If translanguaging performances can be conceptualized as including complex performances of trans-semiotizing (Lin, 2015; Wu & Lin, 2019), trans-registering, trans-styling, or trans-featuring even by 'monolinguals', how can we explore and describe the characteristics, structuring and patterning, and meanings of these complex dynamic performances? What would be the research methodological approaches to move the field forward?

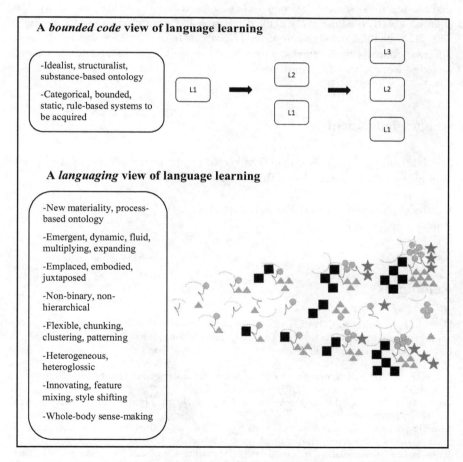

Fig. 1 Construing two different views of language learning. (Adapted from Lin, 2017)

2. How to *translanguage* TESOL assessment at different levels (e.g. K-12, tertiary)? What are the theoretical, implementational and policy advocacy issues involved? How to tackle them?
3. How to *translanguage* TESOL teacher education? What are the possible processes that can lead to changes in some of the deep-rooted beliefs, stances and orientations among teachers, students, parents and school administrators?
4. Drawing on Janks' (2000) question: "How does one provide access to dominant forms, while at the same time valuing and promoting the diverse languages and literacies of our students?" (p.176). What are the ways in which translanguaging pedagogies can disrupt the hierarchy of languages while providing access to dominant forms that will enable students to survive the monolingual high-stakes tests?

As the saying goes, 'It takes a village to research a village', it would take different parties (e.g. researchers across different disciplines and generations, policy makers, teachers, students, parents, school administrators), voices and viewpoints (Lemke, 2000) co-contributing to the discussion and research on translanguaging in TESOL. I see this book that comprises 17 chapters from over 25 authors working in different contexts in different continents of the world as a breathtaking, groundbreaking work in this direction.

Acknowledgement

Special thanks go to Dr. Peichang (Emily) He for her invaluable assistance in construing and visualizing the two different views in Fig. 1.

Faculty of Education, Simon Fraser University   Angel M. Y. Lin
Burnaby, BC, Canada

References

Darroch, F., & Giles, A. (2014). Decolonizing health research: Community-based participatory research and postcolonial feminist theory. *Canadian Journal of Action Research, 15*(3), 22–36.

Cook, V. (2001). Using the first language in the classroom. *The Canadian Modern Language Review, 57*(3), 402–421.

Cummins, J. (2007). Rethinking monolingual instructional strategies in multilingual classrooms. *Canadian Journal of Applied Linguistics, 10*(2), 221–240.

García, O., & Li Wei. (2014). *Translanguaging: Language, bilingualism and education.* New York, NY: Palgrave Macmillan.

González, N., Moll, L. C., & Amanti, C. (Eds.). (2005). *Funds of knowledge: Theorizing practices in households, communities, and classrooms.* Mahwah, NJ: Lawrence Erlbaum Associates.

Janks, H. (2000). Domination, access, diversity and design: A synthesis for critical literacy education. *Educational Review, 52*(2), 175–186.

Jaspers, J. (2018). The transformative limits of translanguaging. *Language & Communication,* *58*, 1–10.

Lemke, J. L. (2000). Across the scales of time: Artifacts, activities, and meanings in ecosocial systems. *Mind, Culture, and Activity, 7*(4), 273–290.

Lin, A. M. Y. (2015). Egalitarian bi/multilingualism and trans-semiotizing in a global world. In W. E. Wright, S. Boun, & O. García (Eds.), *The handbook of bilingual and multilingual education* (pp. 19–37). West Sussex, UK: Wiley Blackwell.

Lin, A. M. Y. (2017, December 21). *Translanguaging and different ontological views of language.* Research notes presented at the Academic Literacies Research Study Group, Faculty of Education, The University of Hong Kong.

Lin, A. M. Y., & Motha, S. (2019). "Curses in TESOL": Postcolonial desires for colonial English. In R. Arber, M. Weinmann, & J. Blackmore (Eds.), *Rethinking languages education*: *Directions, challenges and innovations.* New York, NY: Routledge.

Lin, A. M. Y., Wu, Y., & Lemke, J. L. (2020). 'It takes a village to research a village': Conversations between Angel Lin and Jay Lemke on contemporary issues in translanguaging. In S. M. C. Lau & S. Van Viegen. (Eds.), *Plurilingual Pedagogies: Critical and Creative Endeavors for Equitable Language in Education* (pp. 47–74), Cham: Springer International Publishing.

Wu, Y., & Lin, A. M. Y. (2019). Translanguaging and trans-semiotizing in a CLIL biology class in Hong Kong: Whole-body sense-making in the flow of knowledge co-making. *Classroom Discourse, 10*(3–4), 252–273.

Preface

Our aim is to open a critical conversation about English teaching and learning by re-examining TESOL through a translanguaging lens. The contributions reflect diverse views in TESOL scholarship from five continents. The authors respond to the multilingual turn in language education and challenge the monolingual orthodoxy and the native-speakerism paradigm by valuing the linguistic resources or repertoires of individuals holistically. Through bringing theoretical and pedagogical orientations of translanguaging into TESOL, teachers and learners' full linguistic repertoires become integral to the teaching and learning of English. This shift serves to transform the roles of teachers and learners in TESOL.

This book is intended for educators and language teachers in the fields of TESOL and foreign language education. Additionally, this book is intended for graduate and undergraduate students seeking a degree in second language teaching, teaching English as a second and foreign language, and applied linguistics.

The conceptualization of this volume was particularly inspired by the thinking and work of Ofelia García. Her theorization of the notion of translanguaging was instrumental in our own thinking of how to envision the possibilities of TESOL classrooms, and beyond the citations, the imprint of her ideas is everywhere across the chapters. We would also like to thank Francis Hult, the Educational Linguistics series editor at Springer, for his supporting in moving the idea for this book forward. Finally, we want to thank the contributing authors. The overwhelming response we received from the call for proposals convinced us that this topic had struck a chord, and we greatly appreciate the authors' hard work and timeliness in making this volume possible.

San Antonio, TX, USA   Zhongfeng Tian
Grand Forks, ND, USA   Laila Aghai
Columbus, OH, USA   Peter Sayer
Greensboro, NC, USA   Jamie L. Schissel

Contents

Contributors

Laila Aghai College of Education and Human Development, Department of Teaching, Leadership & Professional Practice, University of North Dakota, Grand Forks, ND, USA

Elena Andrei College of Education and Human Services, Cleveland State University, Cleveland, OH, USA

Madeline Ash School of Linguistics and Applied Language Studies, Victoria University of Wellington, Wellington, New Zealand

Elie Crief University of Pennsylvania, Philadelphia, PA, USA

Peter I. De Costa Department of Linguistics and Languages, Michigan State University, East Lansing, MI, USA

Department of Teacher Education, Michigan State University, East Lansing, MI, USA

Mirjam Günther-van der Meij Research group on Multilingualism & Literacy, Department of Primary Teacher Education, NHL Stenden University of Applied Sciences, Leeuwarden, The Netherlands

Matthew R. Deroo Department of Teaching and Learning, School of Education and Human Development, University of Miami, Coral Gables, FL, USA

Joana Duarte Research group on Multilingualism & Literacy, Department of Primary Teacher Education, NHL Stenden University of Applied Sciences, Leeuwarden, The Netherlands

Christian Fallas-Escobar Department of Bicultural and Bilingual Studies, University of Texas at San Antonio, San Antonio, TX, USA

Angelica Galante McGill University, Montreal, QC, Canada

Ofelia García The Graduate Center, City University of New York, New York, NY, USA

Graham Hall English Language and Linguistics, Department of Humanities, Lipman Building, Northumbria University, Newcastle upon Tyne, UK

Amanda K. Kibler College of Education, Oregon State University, Corvallis, OR, USA

Somin Kim Department of Teaching and Learning, College of Education and Human Ecology, The Ohio State University, Columbus, OH, USA

Sunny Man Chu Lau Bishop's University, Sherbrooke, QC, Canada

Angel M. Y. Lin Faculty of Education, Simon Fraser University, Burnaby, BC, Canada

Maíra Lins Prado Faculdade de Direito de São Bernardo do Campo, São Bernardo do Campo, SP, Brazil

Mario López-Gopar Universidad Autónoma Benito Juárez de Oaxaca, Oaxaca, México

Julio Morales Universidad Autónoma Benito Juárez de Oaxaca, Oaxaca, México

Jonathan Newton School of Linguistics and Applied Language Studies, Victoria University of Wellington, Wellington, New Zealand

Bao Trang Thi Nguyen Faculty of English, University of Foreign Languages, Hue University, Hue, Vietnam

Christina M. Ponzio Curriculum, Instruction and Teacher Education, Michigan State University, East Lansing, MI, USA

Elizabeth Robinson Suffolk University, Boston, MA, USA

April S. Salerno School of Education and Human Development, University of Virginia, Charlottesville, VA, USA

Peter Sayer College of Education and Human Ecology, The Ohio State University, Columbus, OH, USA

Jamie L. Schissel School of Education, University of North Carolina at Greensboro, Greensboro, NC, USA

Corinne A. Seals School of Linguistics and Applied Language Studies, Victoria University of Wellington, Wellington, New Zealand

Brian Seilstad American College Casablanca, Casablanca, Morocco

Kate Seltzer College of Education, Department of Language, Literacy and Sociocultural Education, Rowan University, Glassboro, NJ, USA

Sabrina F. Sembiante College of Education, Department of Curriculum, Culture, and Educational Inquiry, Florida Atlantic University, Boca Raton, FL, USA

Zhongfeng Tian College of Education and Human Development, Department of Bicultural-Bilingual Studies, The University of Texas at San Antonio, San Antonio, TX, USA

Marianne Turner Monash University, Clayton, VIC, Australia

Mary Lou Vercellotti Department of English, Ball State University, Muncie, IN, USA

Chapter 1
Envisioning TESOL through a Translanguaging Lens in the Era of Post-multilingualism

Zhongfeng Tian ⓘ, Laila Aghai, Peter Sayer ⓘ, and Jamie L. Schissel

Abstract While the arrival of the post-multilingualism era has catalyzed linguistic diversity and fluidity across physical and ideological borders, the profession of TESOL continues to promote English teaching and learning with entrenched mono-lingual bias across language-minoritized communities and diasporas. To counteract this trend, we, as the editors of this volume, offer one possibility – *envisioning TESOL through a translanguaging lens*. We explicate translanguaging as a multi-faceted lens in three interrelated aspects: a descriptive, theoretical, and pedagogical lens with strong social justice implications; we see that it could provide a promising path to dismantle "English" as a monolithic entity, "native-speakerism" as a pervasive ideology, and "English-only" as a pedagogical orientation. Built around this theme, this volume invites scholars from five continents offering complex global perspectives on theorizing, integrating, and implementing translanguaging in TESOL teacher education and classroom instruction and assessment. It consists of 15 chapters (organized into three parts) and brings theory, practice, and pedagogy together to reimagine a "translanguaged TESOL profession". Through this volume, we aim to call upon different educational stakeholders to jointly reflect on the opportunities and challenges of applying a translanguaging lens in TESOL.

Z. Tian (✉)
College of Education and Human Development, Department of Bicultural-Bilingual Studies, The University of Texas at San Antonio, San Antonio, TX, USA
e-mail: zhongfeng.tian@utsa.edu

L. Aghai
College of Education and Human Development, Department of Teaching, Leadership & Professional Practice, University of North Dakota, Grand Forks, ND, USA
e-mail: laila.aghai@und.edu

P. Sayer
College of Education and Human Ecology, The Ohio State University, Columbus, OH, USA
e-mail: sayer.32@osu.edu

J. L. Schissel
School of Education, University of North Carolina at Greensboro, Greensboro, NC, USA
e-mail: jlschiss@uncg.edu

© Springer Nature Switzerland AG 2020
Z. Tian et al. (eds.), *Envisioning TESOL through a Translanguaging Lens*,
Educational Linguistics 45, https://doi.org/10.1007/978-3-030-47031-9_1

Keywords Translanguaging · TESOL · Post-multilingualism · Monolingual Bias · Native speakerism · Social justice

1 Introduction

The first part of the twenty-first century has witnessed the formation and expansion of a complex linguistic landscape. Due to increased spatial and social mobilities, numerous conflict zones, technological advances, and other socio-political factors, we are entering what Li Wei (2016, 2018a) has characterized a *post-multilingualism era*. The field of applied linguistics/TESOL (TESOL refers to "Teaching English to Speakers of Other Languages" in this chapter and throughout this whole volume) is experiencing this shift directly, where "multiple ownerships and more complex interweaving of languages and language varieties" have become more communally recognized and welcomed, and "where boundaries between languages, between languages and other communicative means and the relationship between language and the nation-state are being constantly reassessed, broken or adjusted" (Li Wei, 2018a, p. 22). Research in applied linguistics is increasingly affirming the phenomenon of dynamic and fluid language contact and development. These shifts in perspectives are reflective of decades of work arguing against biases in research that view forms of multilingualism as limiting cognitive skills (see Hakuta, 1986 for a review of this history). Further, these perspectives are grounded in the multilingual realities of individuals, and research reflective of this orientation actively works to dismantle language ideologies privileging monolingualism and elite bilingualism steeped in monolingual/monoglossic ideologies (Flores & Rosa, 2015). We are all (active or forced) social participants of this process, regardless of birthright or geographical location, who manipulate our ever-expanding linguistic repertoires in agentive, critical, and creative ways.

While the arrival of the post-multilingualism era has catalyzed linguistic diversity and fluidity across physical and ideological borders, English (or more precisely, the standardized variety of English) remains its hegemonic role on a global scale when considering power imbalances in different contact zones (Pratt, 1999). The profession of TESOL continues to promote English teaching and learning with entrenched monolingual bias (Ortega, 2014, 2019) across language-minoritized communities and diasporas. The field of TESOL has not yet fully moved away from the comparative fallacy (Bley-Vroman, 1983) – the untenable comparison of additional language learners' linguistic systems to the target language norm – which manifests as the privileging of linguistic purism, the differential idealization of native over nonnative speakers (e.g., Absillis & Jaspers, 2016; Aneja, 2016), and the suppression of speakers' "other languages" in favor of the idealized target language norms (e.g., Kamwangamalu, 2010; Zhao & Macaro, 2016), to name a few. However, tensions arise for language users that are "hardly any monolingual speaker[s] in the community who has ever had an entirely monolingual experience" (Li Wei, 2018a,

p. 22): the traditional nomenclature such as L1, L2, EFL/ESL, native/nonnative dichotomy is insufficient to describe individuals' complex linguistic profiles and environment. Furthermore, additional language learning goals "[do] not mean accepting the cultural values and ideologies that the language typically symbolizes; on the contrary, [they are] often aimed at achieving a better understanding of the values, ideologies and practices, in order to challenge them" (Li Wei, 2018a, p. 23). Canagarajah (2014) also points out that teaching English as an international language in the current age should aim to develop students' complex language awareness, rhetorical sensitivity, and negotiation strategies, building upon their extant multilingual resources, to foster their linguistic dexterity and a clear sense of identity and subjectivity for flexible, effective, and strategic adaptation in different communicative contexts – students "not only recognize the contexts where they can be creative but also the contexts where they have to be observant of established norms" (p. 782). This volume therefore takes on the task to question, challenge, and deconstruct the underlying monolingual orthodoxy (Valdés, 2020) in the post-multilingualism era. It urges the field of TESOL to continuously seek ways to embrace multilingualism and multiculturalism as central rather than auxiliary and to be culturally and linguistically sustaining instead of dominating (Paris, 2012; Paris & Alim, 2014, 2017).

We, as the editors of this volume, offer one possibility – **envisioning TESOL through a translanguaging lens** to foster individuals' linguistic fluidity, dexterity, and identity while expanding their linguistic repertoire to include English features reflecting a post-multilingualism view. We have specifically chosen translanguaging due to its multifaceted nature which has both theoretical and pedagogical insights (Leung & Valdés, 2019) inclusive of policies and assessments (Cenoz & Gorter, 2017) with strong social justice implications (García & Li Wei, 2014; Tian & Link, 2019); we see that it could provide a promising path which not only reconceptualizes the traditional notion of language (or more specifically "English") and problematizes the so-called native speakerism paradigm, but also dismantles monolingual approaches in instruction and assessment in TESOL.

We would like to be clear that our take-up of translanguaging lens does not necessarily replace, criticize, or reject other extant theoretical orientations and pedagogical philosophies to counteract monolingualism to (re)imagine the future of English teaching and learning. Overlapping scholarship focusing on bi−/multilingualism broadly (Blackledge & Creese, 2010) and within the framework of translingualism (Canagarajah, 2013; Lee, 2017), polylanguaging (Jørgensen, 2008), and metrolingualism (Otsuji & Pennycook, 2010) specifically contribute to our similar aims and goals with this edited volume on translanguaging. Further, we acknowledge that the development of translanguaging research is built upon and will continue to enrich the long-held dialogues/debates about home and community languages and embracing a multilingual TESOL. Through this volume we aim to open critical conversations on how to conceptualize and implement translanguaging in TESOL teacher education and classrooms of various contexts. We aim to call upon different educational stakeholders from different parts of the world to jointly reflect upon the opportunities and challenges of applying a translanguaging lens for cultural and linguistic pluralism in TESOL. Ultimately, we aim to contribute to generating authentic, sustainable, and contextualized knowledge for the whole field for curricular and pedagogical improvements and new theoretical understandings on translanguaging in TESOL.

2   What is a Translanguaging Lens?

Until now, you might be wondering "so what is a translanguaging lens?" As illustrated above, we see translanguaging as a "multifaceted and multilayer polysemic" lens (Leung & Valdés, 2019, p. 12). It has been defined in a number of different ways to date and has continuously been expanding its notion drawing from contemporary perspectives on critical applied linguistics and multilingualism since the "multilingual turn" (e.g., May, 2014; Ortega, 2013, 2014); it has also captured people's imagination to apply in related disciplines, such as bilingual education (e.g., Gort, 2015, 2018; Kirsch, 2018; Palmer, Martínez, Mateus, & Henderson, 2014; Young, 2014), content and language integrated learning (CLIL – e.g., Lin & He, 2017; Lin & Lo, 2017; Mazak & Carroll, 2016; Vaish & Subhan, 2015), translation studies (e.g., Baynham & Lee, 2019), everyday social communication studies (e.g., Mazzaferro, 2018), and TESOL (e.g., García, 2014a and we are one of them). A comprehensive review of the term translanguaging is beyond the scope of this chapter (for a full review see e.g., Blackledge & Creese, 2014; Conteh, 2018; Li Wei & García, 2016; Poza, 2017; Vogel & García, 2017). We explicate how we take up this lens based on the extant literature and our understanding. We draw on momentum of translanguaging work, which has become prolific in particular connected to the foundational scholarship from García and Li Wei and together, separately, and in collaboration with colleagues.

Li Wei has repeatedly stated that "translanguaging is not an object to describe and analyse" (2018a, p. 23) or "[it] is not a thing in itself" (2019). Rather translanguaging is more like an emerging perspective or lens that could provide new insights to understand and examine language and language (in) education. Echoing with this, we adopt the term *translanguaging lens* and see this lens as "transmutable", "multifaceted" (Leung & Valdés, 2019, p. 11–12) in three aspects: a descriptive lens, a theoretical lens, and a pedagogical lens. However, we do recognize that these three lenses are interrelated to one another and have no clear-cut boundaries; this categorization only serves to make our following explanation clearer.

2.1 Translanguaging as a Descriptive Lens

A descriptive lens for translanguaging focuses on multilingual speakers' readily observable *practices* and their meaning-making *process* – how they actually "do" multilingualism[1] using the totality of their communicative repertoire in different social contexts. García (2009) sees translanguaging as "*multiple discursive practices* in which bilinguals engage in order to *make sense of their bilingual worlds*" (p. 45, emphasis in original) to describe the complex ways in which bilinguals move fluidly among multiple languages, language varieties, and modalities in their everyday interactions. Similarly, Li Wei (2011) uses this lens to capture the dynamic process whereby multilingual language users harness their linguistic and semiotic resources in a strategic and functionally integrated manner to gain and construct knowledge, to make sense, to articulate and communicate one's thoughts, and to perform their identities in social settings. Li Wei (2018a, 2018b) posits that "language" in this sense is a verb (not a noun) and "languag-*ing*" indicates meaning making is an ongoing negotiation process enacted by individuals as a result of social interaction. "*Trans*-languaging" further indicates that for multilinguals, their knowledge construction and sense-making process not just simply goes between languages and cognitive and semiotic systems, but goes *beyond* them (i.e., transcending) – it is a process that goes beyond narrowly defined linguistic cues and transcends the culturally and politically defined language boundaries as well as the traditional divides between language and non-language cognitive and semiotic systems.

Accordingly, this descriptive lens emphasizes the active role or agency of multilingual speakers/users and defines language practices and languaging process on their own terms (instead of being confined to monolingual norms). As Li Wei (2011) describes, multilingual individuals "[bring] together different dimensions of their personal history, experience and environment, their attitude, belief and ideology, their cognitive and physical capacity into one coordinated and meaningful performance" (p. 1223). They create a *translanguaging space* and this space has its own transformative power because it affords multilingual speakers the opportunity to become *creative* and *critical* language users (creativity refers to the ability to follow or flout norms of language use while criticality is the ability to use evidence to question, problematize, or express views). This lens therefore provides an insightful way to understand and depict the complex, dynamic, fluid linguistic phenomena in the post-multilingualism era: translanguaging is a normative act of multilingual speakers "and cannot be compared to a prescribed monolingual use" (García, 2009, p. 51); it is characterized by multilingual, multimodal, multisemiotic, and multisensory performance (Li Wei, 2018b) that integrates diverse languaging and literacy practices to maximize communicative potential and indicate sociocultural

---

[1] We acknowledge that there are some important distinctions and that terminology is important; however, for our purposes here we use the term *multilingualism* to encompass various related terms: *bilingualism, bi/multilingualism, plurilingualism.*

identities, positionings, and values in different social contexts. It challenges the traditional boundaries between named languages and argues for more complex, fluid understandings of language as a social practice and process.

2.2 Translanguaging as a Theoretical Lens

Secondly, translanguaging also provides a theoretical lens with a new epistemological stance to reexamine language and multilingualism. Vogel and García (2017) succinctly summarize the three core premises that undergird translanguaging theory:

1. It posits that individuals select and deploy features from a unitary linguistic repertoire in order to communicate.
2. It takes up a perspective on bi- and multilingualism that privileges speakers' own dynamic linguistic and semiotic practices above the named languages of nations and states.
3. It still recognizes the material effects of socially constructed named language categories and structuralist language ideologies, especially for minoritized language speakers. (p. 4)

To elaborate, translanguaging as a linguistic theory (García & Lin, 2017; Li Wei, 2018b) questions the notion of language as static systems of discrete, prescribed structures. Multilingual speakers in this sense do not have two or more separate, bounded linguistic and semiotic entities but only one unitary repertoire composed of meaning-making features that are selected and deployed in different contexts (García & Kleyn, 2016; García & Li Wei, 2014). Translanguaging theory therefore stands from the point of view of speakers themselves to describe bilinguals' flexible and fluid use of language features "without regard for watchful adherence to the socially and politically defined boundaries of named (and usually national and state) languages" (Otheguy, García, & Reid, 2015, p. 283). Although translanguaging theory does recognize the existence of named languages because they have material and consequential effects on multilinguals (e.g., standardized testing), these socially or externally constructed categories are not linguistic facts (Vogel & García, 2017) and does not reflect psycholinguistic realities[2] (Li Wei, 2019). Moreover, this theory seeks "to dismantle named language categories and counters ideologies that position particular languages as superior to others and the language practices of monolinguals as superior to those who are said to speak with linguistic resources that go beyond the strict boundaries of named languages" (Vogel & García, 2017, p. 6). In other words, the central goal of translanguaging theory is to challenge colonial and modernist-era structuralist ideologies of language standardization (Makoni &

---

[2] We do recognize that there are conflicting perspectives regarding the notion of "unitary repertoire" and its relation to named languages in the current field. To learn more about the debates, see Otheguy et al. (2015), MacSwan (2017), Otheguy, García, and Reid (2018), and Lin, Wu, and Lemke (2020).

Pennycook, 2007) by liberating and privileging language-minoritized speakers' multilingual performances and legitimizing all their linguistic varieties.

2.3   Translanguaging as a Pedagogical Lens

Building on its descriptive and theoretical lenses, translanguaging has been extended by García (2009) from its pedagogical origins as language input and output alternation in Welsh and English bilingual context, into a pedagogical lens to transform teaching and learning. Generally speaking, translanguaging as pedagogy refers to "the ways in which bilingual students and teachers engage in complex and fluid discursive practices that include, at times, the home language practices of students in order to 'make sense' of teaching and learning, to communicate and appropriate subject knowledge, and to develop academic language practices" (García, 2014b, p. 112). In a translanguaging classroom, teachers acknowledge multilingualism as a resource and strategically incorporate learners' familiar cultural and language practices (or funds of knowledge) in academic learning while also showing students "when, where, and why to use some features of their repertoire and not others, enabling them to also perform according to the social norms of named languages as used in schools" (García & Kleyn, 2016, p. 15). Therefore, translanguaging pedagogy calls upon teachers to grapple with both perspectives: on the one hand, teachers should make heteroglossic spaces that leverage students' bilingualism and bilingual ways of knowing and that support their socio-emotional development and bilingual identities; on the other hand, teachers should provide opportunities to expand students' linguistic repertoires to include new "academic" features so they may successfully navigate different contexts of school-based literacies and subject-matter knowledge (García, Johnson, & Seltzer, 2017).

García and Kleifgen (2018) emphasize that "a translanguaging pedagogy is not simply a series of strategies and scaffolds, but also *a philosophy of language and education* that is centered on a bilingual minoritized community" (p. 80, emphasis added). This pedagogical lens is positioned as a vehicle for "liberating the voices of language minoritized students" (García & Leiva, 2014, p. 200), calling attention to bilingual students' agency, criticality, and creativity in communicative and meaning-making acts while questioning the social hierarchies that would curtail such traits (Li Wei & Wu, 2009; Tian & Link, 2019). Translanguaging has the potential to "transform relationships between students, teachers, and the curriculum" (Vogel & García, 2017, p. 10) to necessitate a co-learning space (Li Wei, 2013) where teachers and students learn from each other, and all language practices are equally valued, and ultimately to advance social justice to ensure that all students are educated deeply and justly (García, Seltzer, & Witt, 2018).

In summary, we see translanguaging as a multifaceted lens in three aspects: to describe multilinguals' language practice and process as "transcend[ing] the boundaries between named languages and between language and other cognitive and semiotic systems" (Li Wei, 2019), to theorize "language as bundles of lexical, syntactic, phonological, and orthographic features in use in specific places and times" instead of static, even fixed and separate entities (Leung & Valdés, 2019, p. 16), and to provide a pedagogical approach which leverages students' entire linguistic repertoires in academic tasks. All these three lenses share one important common theme – they are all critical with strong social justice implications: as a descriptive lens, translanguaging aims to normalize multilinguals' transgressive performances as natural communicative act; as a theoretical lens, translanguaging aims to legitimize all linguistic varieties (e.g., "Spanglish" and "Chinglish" with negative connotations in a traditional sense); and as a pedagogical lens, translanguaging aims to validate language-minoritized students' home and community languages and cultures in classroom settings. As García and Li Wei (2014) argue, "Translanguaging for us … is part of a moral and political act that links the production of alternative meanings to transformative social action. As such, translanguaging contributes to the social justice agenda. This in itself distinguishes our concept from many others" (p. 37). This is also one reason that we have chosen translanguaging as a particular lens in this volume because of our shared commitment to social justice; we would like to see what translanguaging could bring to TESOL, both promises and tensions, to transform English teaching and learning in the post-multilingualism era.

[margin note: define?]

3   When Envisioning TESOL through a Translanguaging Lens

As "monolingual bias" continues to dominate the TESOL field, which manifests in three main aspects – "English" as a monolithic entity, "native-speakerism" as a pervasive ideology, and "English-only" as monolingual approaches, a translanguaging lens introduces a marked shift in re-examining these issues and provides a potentially transformative path from three orientations – descriptive, theoretical, and pedagogical ones.

3.1   Recognizing Englishes and English-ing

We would like to briefly explain how a translanguaging lens could counteract the three major manifestations of "monolingual bias" in TESOL. This idea is further developed through the conceptual discussions in Part I "Theorizing Translanguaging in TESOL." Firstly, a descriptive lens with an emphasis on practice and process shifts away from privileging of English as a prescribed, static system of grammatical and pragmatic rules. Instead, it recognizes the heterogeneous nature of English or Englishes – how people actually "do" or "practice" English in the post-multilingualism era – and focuses on English as an emergent social process within and across different contexts or English-*ing*.

To elaborate, the *languaging* part of translanguaging captures the notion that language is situated social practice. From a translanguaging perspective, language structures are created in moment-to-moment interactions, as meanings are negotiated and employing mutually recognizable linguistic forms drawn from language users' linguistic repertoires. The specific choice of forms, what constitutes an "appropriate" use of language in a given situation, is mediated by individuals' identities and through the broader circulating ideologies of language. A translanguaging lens sees "English" not as a stable box belonging to a specific nation/state composed of pre-formulated rules; rather it conceptualizes "English" as socially constructed with emergent characteristics in real-life communicative contexts. When multilingual individuals select English features from their linguistic and semiotic repertoire to convey their thoughts or to make meaning, they also bring together "different dimensions of their personal history, experience and environment; their attitude, belief, and ideology; and their cognitive and physical capacity ... making language use into a lived experience" (Li Wei, 2018a, p. 25). During the process, they co-construct different varieties of Englishes with their agency (including criticality and creativity) that transcend the established, named "English" (Canagarajah, 2014); they are Englishing in a translanguaging space where "different identities, values, and practices simply co-exist, but combine together to generate new identities, values, and practices" (Li Wei, 2018a, p. 25). In this sense, English is no longer a monolithic entity; it is always in a fluid state of being and becoming "with multiple grammars, vocabulary, accents, and pragmatic discourse conventions" (Marlina, 2014, p. 7). A descriptive lens thus recognizes the complex, dynamic, and diverse nature embedded in English as a social practice and process.

3.2   Dismantling the "Native vs. Non-native" False Dichotomy

Secondly, with an understanding of English as a diverse practice and emergent process, a theoretical lens further grapples with the power imbalance of how Englishes are named and understood or accepted as varieties. While Englishes are developed and created in social contact zones, only some standardized varieties (e.g., standardized American or British English) are privileged due to socio-historical-political processes, keeping the power in the hands of a few – "native speakers" which usually is defined around white supremacist, imperialistic or colonial standards that favor White, middle or upper-class, cis, heterosexual, Christian male monolingual English speakers. There has been long-held ideology that has been reflected in lines of research as well that upholds native speakers as the ideal model and their produced linguistic form of standardized English as the golden standard while other English varieties such as AAVE (African-American Vernacular English) or Spanglish are seen as needing remediation. Translanguaging as theory aims to combat the ideology of "native-speakerism" by problematizing the false dichotomy of "native vs. non-native" (García, 2014a), questioning structuralist ideologies of language standardization, and legitimizing English-ing. This theoretical lens does not deny the material and consequential roles of standardized English varieties such as views that academic English literacy skills connect with upward mobility in English-dominated societies. Rather, it emphasizes fostering a critical consciousness toward these constructs and further disrupting them. As such, "Standardized English", "academic English" and other related concepts are understood to be socio-politically constructed entities to maintain certain groups' power and interests that are by no means superior or more efficient, effective, sophisticated, nor articulate forms of communication.

3.3   Counteracting "English-only" Monolingual Approaches

Finally, translanguaging as a pedagogical lens holds great promises to counteract "English-only" monolingual approaches. Specifically speaking, in a translanguaged TESOL classroom, language learners are not situated as deficient non-natives lacking of English proficiency but as resourceful agents with complete multilingual repertoires and abilities (García & Kleifgen, 2018). Teachers purposefully and strategically create safe, inclusive, and heterogeneous educational spaces (instead of policing an English-only zone) to value, leverage, and even sustain students' home/community languages, cultures, and identities while expanding their repertoire to include certain "English" features. Teachers also "become [co-]learners with our students – learning new varieties of English, new genres of communication, and new modes of negotiating language diversity" (Canagarajah, 2014, p. 783), encouraging students to develop their multilingual awareness and linguistic dexterity in the post-multilingualism era. This means that students not only recognize standard English varieties and their normative usage and can adjust their language practice accordingly, but can also be creative with and critical of language forms, indicating their values, ideologies, and identities and transcending the dominant structures. The goal of English teaching and learning in the post-multilingual era is no longer acquiring the native-like form of English and becoming another monolingual, but becoming a competent, multilingual language user who are aware of and sensitive to the context and could perform fluid, dynamic, and complex language practices with creativity and criticality to achieve their expressive and communicative needs. As Li Wei (2018b) writes,

> [b]y deliberately breaking the artificial and ideological divides between indigenous versus immigrant, majority versus minority, and target versus mother tongue languages, Translanguaging empowers both the learner and the teacher, transforms the power relations, and focuses [on] the process of teaching and learning on making meaning, enhancing experience, and developing identity. (p. 7)

Translanguaging as pedagogy also challenges the hegemony of standardized English by fostering culturally and linguistically sustaining practices to educate students from language-minoritized communities in a more socially just and equitable way.

To summarize, we see translanguaging as a multifaceted lens that can overtly challenge the monolingual orthodoxy which dominates the TESOL field (Flores & Aneja, 2017; Valdés, 2020) – "English" as a monolithic entity, "native-speakerism" as a pervasive ideology, and "English-only" as pedagogical orientations. García (2014a) emphasizes the potential positive impacts of translanguaging within the field of TESOL:

> TESOL translanguaged holds the promise of developing the English language practices of emergent bilinguals that would enable them to be successful in academic tasks, while supporting a social justice agenda that holds emergent bilinguals as knowers, thinkers, and imaginative meaning-makers. (p. 8)

A translanguaging lens could thereby offer promising possibilities to reimagine the roles of teachers and learners, the process and goals of teaching and learning, as well as the future directions of the TESOL profession.

4   Book Organization: Three Parts

The current book aims to discuss the promises and challenges of translanguaging as a descriptive, theoretical, and pedagogical lens in TESOL. The volume consists of contributions from around the world. The 15 chapters (from Chaps. 2, 3, 4, 5, 6, 7, 8, 9, 10, 11, 12, 13, 14, 15 and 16) altogether offer complex global perspectives – with contributions from five continents – to open conversations on how to conceptualize and implement translanguaging in teacher education and classrooms of various contexts. While translanguaging has garnered much attention in bilingual and multilingual education, we attempt to offer a critical examination of translanguaging with a particular eye toward TESOL. The contributors exhibit a shared commitment to transforming TESOL profession that values teachers and learners' full linguistic repertoires.

The volume has been organized around three parts: Part I "Theorizing translanguaging in TESOL", Part II "Translanguaging in TESOL teacher education", and Part III "Translanguaging in TESOL classrooms". We have developed this structure because we see that it mirrors the development of translanguaging in TESOL – how different stakeholders (specifically researchers, teacher educators, teachers/practitioners) in the TESOL profession could collaborate together to push the field forward.

As shown in Fig. 1.1, at an early stage, the development of translanguaging in TESOL follows a *top-down* pattern. Through researchers' exploring the affordances and constraints of translanguaging theory in TESOL conceptually, teacher educators may be aware of its promises and start to introduce it to pre- and in-service teachers in teacher education. This may further facilitate TESOL teachers' interest

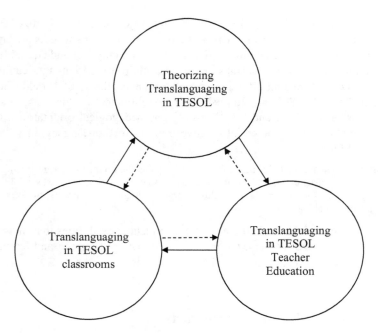

Fig. 1.1 The development of translanguaging in TESOL

in designing and implementing translanguaging instruction and assessment in actual classrooms to test its feasibility, practicality, and effectiveness. In the meantime, this development also follows a *bottom-up* process. Through experimenting with translanguaging as pedagogy in classrooms of different contexts, teachers may offer new insights regarding its transformative potential. This may in turn call for more discussions and training to occur in teacher education to critically examine the translanguaging approach and further generate new theoretical understandings for researchers.

With the growing attention of translanguaging in the TESOL field, we envision that this earlier-on linear development will gradually become more dynamic, non-linear, fluid, and complex; the three areas of inquiry will become more closely connected and porous, and should follow an iterative and reciprocal process. Different stakeholders from each inquiry circle will transgress the boundaries and collaborate with each other to achieve a "holistic, professional, TESOL researcher-practitioner perspective" (McKinley, 2019, p.6) to jointly reimagine and reshape a "translanguaged TESOL profession" (García, 2014a, p. 8) with a social justice agenda. New opportunities and challenges will be further emergent from the developmental process to illuminate the possibilities of translanguaging in TESOL.

As Lin et al. (2020) indicate in their article, "It takes a village to research a village", the current volume would not be possible without "a village" of emerging, junior, and senior scholars around the world who have taken initiatives and efforts in conducting research on the "village" – translanguaging in TESOL. Part I focuses on conceptual discussions to showcase the possibilities of translanguaging in destabilizing the monolingual grip of TESOL. Parts II and III further provides empirical studies to shed light on the transformative potential of translanguaging in TESOL, in both teacher education and classrooms of various contexts. All the parts bring theory, practice, and pedagogy together in a holistic and dynamic manner to chart the current as well as the future landscape of TESOL through a translanguaging lens in the post-multilingualism era.

5 Chapter Overview: Bring Global Perspectives Together

In Part I, we present three in-depth theoretical discussions on translanguaging in TESOL. First, **Seltzer** and **García** revisit a question posed by García (2014a): "what does a shift to translanguaging mean for TESOL?" Drawing on examples from a teacher's translanguaging instructional design adopting multilingual and multimodal texts in a high school English Language Arts classroom in New York, U.S., they illustrate that translanguaging theory can transform the teaching for English to *all* language-minoritized learners because it re-sees language-minoritized students as speakers and writers who use their agency to shape "English" in creative and critical ways.

Next, **Sembiante** and **Tian** focus on the need for translanguaging in TESOL given its unique social justice-oriented practice and theoretical stance. They reposition what "E (English)", "SOL (Speakers of Other Languages)", and "T (Teaching)" means for TESOL through a translanguaging lens, and urge that the TESOL International Association must heed the incessant call throughout its history to shift its macro-discourse and embrace an identity that advocates for English teaching and learning through support of multilingualism. Then, **Hall** argues that while the extant literature surrounding TESOL has promoted monolingual, English-only approaches in the classroom, the deployment of multilingual resources and repertoires (i.e., translanguaging practices) has long been a reality in many TESOL contexts around the world. The lack of recognizing localized communities of practice in the literature leads to the disjunction between TESOL "theory" and "practice". To narrow down this gap, he suggests that professional discussion of translanguaging needs to occur particularly during teacher training and education programs and teacher conferences to facilitate teachers' professional development and support their multilingual classroom practice.

In Part II, we examine the introduction and integration of translanguaging in TESOL teacher education for pre- and in-service teachers. The six studies in this part come from different geographical contexts (including U.S., México, Australia, and Malawi) and adopt various methodologies to investigate the tensions and opportunities emerging from the process for different stakeholders. The first three studies look at the U.S. context. First, using narrative inquiry, **Andrei**, **Kibler**, and **Salerno** document one teacher educator (Andrei)'s difficult experiences in her initial effort at introducing translanguaging to pre-service teachers in a second language learning course: tensions arose when the students and the teacher showed strong disagreements on translanguaging and its relationship to code-switching. This study raises important questions about the relationship between scholarly and practitioner communities in the language education field and offers viable suggestions for teacher educators who embark on teaching new concepts. Second, **Deroo**, **Ponzio**, and **De Costa** present two case studies of one pre-service teacher and one in-service teacher and look at particularly how they develop a translanguaging stance to make sense of translanguaging as theory and pedagogy. Their data reveal that the integration of coursework and field experiences was essential for connecting the teachers' theoretical understanding to practice, problematizing their personal language ideologies, and recognizing the system barriers for translanguaging implementation. They conclude with concrete recommendations for (re)structuring course and fieldwork and integrating a translanguaging lens across the teacher education curriculum to prepare culturally and linguistically competent teachers for TESOL education. Then, **Robinson**, **Tian**, **Crief** and **Lins Prado** conduct a collaborative qualitative inquiry to investigate to what extent the social justice orientations of translanguaging could be achieved by the pre-service teachers in a TESOL Certificate course. The teachers' coursework and micro-teaching videos showed their critical understanding of translanguaging in relation to language, culture, and power, though they still struggled with embodying translanguaging in their teaching practice. This research illuminates the possibilities of adopting a translanguaging lens to prepare teachers to teach English for justice.

Moving from the U.S. context, the next chapter by **Morales**, **Schissel**, and **López-Gopar** look at how translanguaging can be integrated into instruction and assessment in a university TESOL classroom in Oaxaca, México for pre-service teachers who are both learning English and learning how to be language teachers. This is a participatory action research (PAR) project in which the course instructor (Morales) worked together with a research team (Schissel and López-Gopar): they collaboratively contributed to the process of creating translanguaging approaches to classroom language assessment. This project highlights the importance of creating contextually relevant assessments drawing from the extant multilingual resources in the classroom, university, and the wider community, and also suggests that the students performed better on the translanguaging tasks than on the English-only tasks.

Turner then takes us to Australia to examine a professional learning of seven in-service generalist teachers. This study adopts the form of design-based research (DBR) which follows a three-day iterative process. Teachers attended an initial seminar day in which they were introduced to translanguaging and learned how to conduct a language mapping lesson sequence to get linguistic data from their students. After delivering this sequence of lessons, teachers regrouped with the researcher to discuss and plan how to leverage their students' language practices with planned curriculum objectives. Then the teachers implemented this second lesson sequence, and came together once more to do reflections. Findings demonstrate that the professional learning was found to have a marked influence on teachers' understanding of what it means to be multilingual and on their perceived capacity to leverage students' linguistic repertoires for specific learning objectives.

Finally, **Lau** presents us an action research study that was on a professional development (PD) course for a group of primary school teachers in a rural Malawian community. In this postcolonial context, the enduring symbolic dominance of English had led local educators to believe that strict adherence to English only would ensure school success, which has, however, caused much shame and drainage of multilingual resources and identities for more meaningful and complex learning. Through the PD course on critical language pedagogy, the local teachers came to a nuanced understanding of translanguaging as a legitimate approach which positions teachers and students as agentive knowledge-makers and (re)affirms their own ethnolinguistic identities. This study shows certain promises of translanguaging to "decolonize" language and knowledge; however, Lau reminds us that researchers need to exercise vigilance and humility in understanding what decolonization means to local communities.

Moving to Part III "Translanguaging in TESOL Classrooms", we specifically showcase six empirical studies representing a wide range of teaching and learning contexts: different geographical locations including U.S., Canada, the Netherlands, Vietnam, and Costa Rica and different student age groups from K-16 (kindergarten to post-secondary education) with various English learning goals. These studies aim to illuminate the possibilities of translanguaging in actual TESOL classrooms across contexts to strengthen theory-practice nexus; they also urge us to take a contextual look at the implementation of translanguaging and its transformative potential. We need to bear in mind that translanguaging is not a one-size-fits-all approach and it needs to be strategically and purposefully planned in instruction and assessment considering multiple contextual factors at different scales (macro, meso, and micro levels), such as imbalanced power dynamics among languages, learner background, teachers' language ideologies, program ecologies, and lesson/unit goals. As you will see in this part, each chapter adopts and adapts the translanguaging lens to suit their own contexts, which lead to different opportunities and challenges. We hope that these complex global perspectives could offer many pockets of hope and significant pedagogical implications for the field of TESOL.

First, **Günther-van der Meij** and **Duarte** present two DBR research projects investigating English learning at the kindergarten and elementary school level in the context of the officially bilingual Province of Friesland, the Netherlands. The teachers designed a series of multilingual activities based on a holistic model for multilingual education (Duarte, 2017) which integrated a translanguaging approach. Their study shows that the teachers' use of different languages (pedagogical translanguaging) in classroom interactions can serve different functions to enhance the content and language learning of the pupils. It also highlights that the framework of DBR could provide the necessary support for teachers to progressively operationalize the concept of translanguaging for their own contexts. Next, **Seilstad** and **Kim** direct us to an adolescent newcomer program in Central Ohio, U.S. They specifically look at a tenth grade biology project, "Bilingual Biomes", which purposefully engaged students to use their multilingual and multimodal resources during research and final presentation. Drawing from classroom discourse analysis, they propose a new metaphor, "*colibrí*" 'hummingbird' which arose from a specific moment during the project presentations, to exemplify the potential of translanguaging as theory and practice to destabilize national/named borders between languages, create opportunities for shared understanding, and evoke unimagined moments of joy.

Seals, **Newton**, **Ash**, and **Nguyen** then explores what possible synergies exist theoretically and empirically for Task Based Language Teaching (TBLT) and translanguaging. They revisit data from a study carried out in EFL classrooms at a secondary school in Hanoi, Vietnam. Although the original purpose of the study was to understand how the teachers utilized TBLT in the speaking lessons and how learners engaged with the task, their re-analysis finds many examples demonstrating translanguaging behaviors. They conclude that translanguaging has the potential to bring positive gains to TBLT because it could empower learners during the task rehearsal phase, and allow teachers and learners to be more fully able to realize the meaning making goals of TBLT, freed from the constraint of only making meaning in the target language.

In the next study, **Galante** adopts mixed methods to examine whether translanguaging has positive effects on academic vocabulary knowledge compared to a traditional teaching approach that follows monolingual ideologies in an English for Academic Purposes (EAP) program for international students (adult learners) in Toronto, Canada. Both treatment (translanguaging) and comparison (monolingual) groups followed the same curriculum with three similar vocabulary tasks but with different pedagogical orientations. Quantitative results show that students in the treatment group had significantly higher scores in academic vocabulary tests compared to students in the comparison group. Qualitative analysis indicates that students took an active role in meaning making across languages. She calls for a shift in language pedagogy to infuse translanguaging in the curriculum.

The last two studies concern teachers' language ideologies and translanguaging in TESOL classrooms. **Fallas Escobar** conducts a case study with three instructors from an EFL department in a Costa Rican university. He organized a series of critical dialogue sessions with them to learn about their ambivalent postures and stances toward translanguaging. Drawing upon theories on language ideologies, he illustrates that critical dialogues on translanguaging could help teachers build agency to dismantle broader ideologies and to start to resist the institutionalized monolingual ideologies. Similarly, **Aghai**, **Sayer**, and **Vercellotti** focus on teachers who work at the university level. They explore three ESL teachers' language ideologies and their language policies (whether they encourage or restrict the use of translanguaging) in their intensive English program (IEP) classes in U.S. Their findings reveal that the teachers held three different views toward students' translanguaging: *translanguaging-as-a-problem*, *translanguaging-as-a-natural-process*, and *translanguaging-as-a-resource*, and these orientations are influenced by their language ideologies. These two studies further prove the importance of unpacking teachers' language ideologies and engaging them in critical reflections to develop their translanguaging stance (García et al., 2017) in order to fulfill the promise of translanguaging pedagogy.

6   Final Remarks

This volume constitutes a challenge to the entrenched monolingual, native speaker-ism paradigm in the field of TESOL through a translanguaging lens in response to the new challenges of the post-multilingualism era. It brings together a large group of scholars from different continents offering complex global perspectives on theorizing, integrating, and implementing translanguaging in TESOL teacher education and classrooms. We believe that this is the first volume to apply a translanguaging lens to TESOL from an array of learning contexts across the lifespan. We hope that this volume should prove a valuable resource for students, teachers, teacher educators, and researchers interested in English teaching and learning, applied linguistics, second language acquisition, and social justice. As you are about to embark on this reading journey, we sincerely look forward to having conversations with you.

References

Absillis, K., & Jaspers, J. (2016). Reconsidering purism: The case of Flanders. In K. Horner & R. Gijsbert (Eds.), *Metalinguistic perspectives on Germanic languages: European case studies from past to present* (pp. 105–129). New York, NY: Peter Lang.

Aneja, G. A. (2016). (Non)native speakered: Rethinking (non)nativeness and teacher identity in TESOL teacher education. *TESOL Quarterly, 50*(3), 572–596.

Baynham, M., & Lee, T. K. (2019). *Translation and translanguaging.* London, UK: Routledge.

Blackledge, A., & Creese, A. (2010). *Multilingualism: A critical perspective.* London, UK: Continuum.

Blackledge, A., & Creese, A. (Eds.). (2014). *Heteroglossia as practice and pedagogy.* Dordrecht, The Netherlands: Springer.

Bley-Vroman, R. (1983). The comparative fallacy in interlanguage studies: The case of systematicity. *Language Learning, 33*(1), 1–17.

Canagarajah, A. S. (2013). *Translingual practice: Global Englishes and cosmopolitan relations.* London, UK/New York, NY: Routledge.

Canagarajah, A. S. (2014). In search of a new paradigm for teaching English as an international language. *TESOL Journal, 5*(4), 767–785.

Cenoz, J., & Gorter, D. (2017). Minority languages and sustainable translanguaging: Threat or opportunity? *Journal of Multilingual and Multicultural Development, 38*(10), 901–912.

Conteh, J. (2018). Translanguaging as pedagogy – A critical review. In A. Creese & A. Blackledge (Eds.), *The Routledge handbook of language and superdiversity* (pp. 473–487). New York, NY: Routledge.

Duarte, J. (2017). *Project proposal 3M project (Meer Kansen Met Meertaligheid).* Leeuwarden, The Netherlands: NHL Stenden University of Applied Sciences.

Flores, N., & Aneja, G. (2017). "Why needs hiding?" Translingual (re)orientations in TESOL teacher education. *Research in the Teaching of English, 51*(4), 441–463.

Flores, N., & Rosa, J. (2015). Undoing appropriateness: Raciolinguistic ideologies and language diversity in education. *Harvard Educational Review, 85*(2), 149–171.

García, O. (2009). *Bilingual education in the 21st century: A global perspective.* Malden, MA: Wiley/Blackwell.

García, O. (2014a). TESOL translanguaged in NYS: Alternative perspectives. *NYS TESOL Journal, 1*(1), 2–10.

García, O. (2014b). Countering the dual: Transglossia, dynamic bilingualism and translanguaging in education. In R. Rubdy & L. Alsagoff (Eds.), *The global-local interface and hybridity: Exploring language and identity* (pp. 100–118). Bristol, UK: Multilingual Matters.

García, O., Johnson, S. I., & Seltzer, K. (2017). *The translanguaging classroom: Leveraging student bilingualism for learning*. Philadelphia, PA: Calson.

García, O., & Kleifgen, J. A. (2018). *Educating emergent bilinguals: Policies, programs, and practices for English learners* (2nd ed.). New York, NY: Teachers College Press.

García, O., & Kleyn, T. (Eds.). (2016). *Translanguaging with multilingual students: Learning from classroom moments*. New York, NY: Routledge.

García, O., & Leiva, C. (2014). Theorizing and enacting translanguaging for social justice. In A. Creese & A. Blackledge (Eds.), *Heteroglossia as practice and pedagogy* (pp. 199–216). New York, NY: Springer.

García, O., & Li Wei. (2014). *Translanguaging: Language, bilingualism and education*. New York, NY: Palgrave Macmillan.

García, O., & Lin, A. M. Y. (2017). Translanguaging in bilingual education. In O. García, A. M. Y. Lin, & S. May (Eds.), *Bilingual and multilingual education* (pp. 117–130). Cham, Switzerland: Springer.

García, O., Seltzer, K., & Witt, D. (2018). Disrupting linguistic inequalities in US urban classrooms: The role of translanguaging. In S. Slembrouck, K. Van Gorp, S. Sierens, K. Maryns, & P. Van Avermaet (Eds.), *The multilingual edge of education* (pp. 414–456). Oxford, UK: Palgrave Macmillan UK.

Gort, M. (Ed.). (2015). *International Multilingual Research Journal, 9*(1).

Gort, M. (Ed.). (2018). *The complex and dynamic languaging practices of emergent bilinguals. Translanguaging across diverse educational and community contexts*. New York, NY: Taylor and Francis.

Hakuta, K. (1986). *Mirror of language: The debate on bilingualism*. New York, NY: Basic Books.

Jørgensen, J. N. (2008). Polylingual languaging around and among children and adolescents. *International Journal of Multilingualism, 5*(3), 161–176.

Kamwangamalu, N. (2010). Multilingualism and code-switching in education. In N. Hornberger & S. McKay (Eds.), *Sociolinguistics and language education* (pp. 116–142). Clevedon, UK: Multilingual Matters.

Kirsch, C. (2018). Young children capitalising on their entire language repertoire for language learning at school. *Language, Culture and Curriculum, 31*(1), 39–55.

Lee, J. W. (2017). *The politics of translingualism: After Englishes*. New York, NY: Routledge.

Leung, C., & Valdés, G. (2019). Translanguaging and the transdisciplinary framework for language teaching and learning in a multilingual world. *The Modern Language Journal, 103*(2), 348–370.

Li Wei. (2011). Moment analysis and translanguaging space: Discursive construction of identities by multilingual Chinese youth in Britain. *Journal of Pragmatics, 43*(5), 1222–1235.

Li Wei. (2013). Who's teaching whom? Co-learning in multilingual classrooms. In S. May (Ed.), *The multilingual turn: Implications for SLA, TESOL and bilingual education* (pp. 167–190)). New York, NY: Routledge.

Li Wei. (2016). New Chinglish and the post-multilingualism challenge: Translanguaging ELF in China. *Journal of English as a Lingua Franca, 5*(1), 1–25.

Li Wei. (2018a). Linguistic (super)diversity, post-multilingualism and translanguaging moments. In A. Creese & A. Blackledge (Eds.), *The Routledge handbook of language and superdiversity* (pp. 16–29). New York, NY: Routledge.

Li Wei. (2018b). Translanguaging as a practical theory of language. *Applied Linguistics, 39*(1), 9–30.

Li Wei. (2019). *Translanguaging learning*. Speech given at the ECIS Multilingual Learning in International Education (MLIE) conference in London, UK.

Li Wei, & García, O. (2016). From researching translanguaging to translanguaging research. In K. King, Y. J. Lai, & S. May (Eds.), *Research methods in language and education* (3rd ed., pp. 227–240). Cham, Switzerland: Springer.

Li Wei, & Wu, C. J. (2009). Polite Chinese children revisited: Creativity and the use of codeswitching in the Chinese complementary school classroom. *International Journal of Bilingual Education and Bilingualism, 12*(2), 193–211.

Lin, A. M. Y., & He, P. (2017). Translanguaging as dynamic activity flows in CLIL Classrooms. *Journal of Language, Identity and Education, 16*(4), 228–244.

Lin, A. M. Y., & Lo, Y. Y. (2017). Trans/languaging and the triadic dialogue in Content and Language Integrated Learning (CLIL) classrooms. *Language and Education, 31*(1), 26–45.

Lin, A. M. Y., Wu, Y., & Lemke, J. L. (2020). 'It takes a village to research a village': Conversations between Angel Lin and Jay Lemke on contemporary issues in translanguaging. In: S. M. C. Lau & S. Van Viegen (Eds.), *Plurilingual pedagogies: critical and creative endeavors for equitable language in education* (pp. 47–74). Switzerland: Springer International Publishing.

MacSwan, J. (2017). A multilingual perspective on translanguaging. *American Educational Research Journal, 54*(1), 167–201.

Makoni, S., & Pennycook, A. (2007). *Disinventing and reconstituting languages*. In S. Makoni & A. Pennycook (Eds.), *Disinventing and reconstituting languages* (pp. 1–41). Clevedon, UK: Multilingual Matters.

Marlina, R. (2014). The pedagogy of English as an international language (EIL): More reflections and dialogues. In R. Marlina & R. A. Giri (Eds.), *Pedagogy of English as an international language: Perspectives from scholars, teachers and students* (pp. 1–19). New York, NY: Springer.

May, S. (Ed.). (2014). *The multilingual turn: Implications for SLA, TESOL, and bilingual education*. New York, NY: Routledge.

Mazak, C. M., & Carroll, K. S. (Eds.). (2016). *Translanguaging in higher education: Beyond monolingual ideologies*. Buffalo, NY/Bristol, UK: Multilingual Matters.

Mazzaferro, G. (Ed.). (2018). *Translanguaging as everyday practice*. Cham, Switzerland: Springer.

McKinley, J. (2019). Evolving the TESOL teaching-research nexus. *TESOL Quarterly, 53*(3), 875–884.

Ortega, L. (2013). SLA for the 21st century: Disciplinary progress, transdisciplinary relevance, and the bi/multilingual turn. *Language Learning, 63*(Suppl.1), 1–24.

Ortega, L. (2014). Ways forward for a bi/multicultural turn in SLA. In S. May (Ed.), *The multilingual turn. Implications for SLA, TESOL, and bilingual education* (pp. 32–53). New York, NY: Routledge.

Ortega, L. (2019). SLA and the study of equitable multilingualism. *The Modern Language Journal, 103*(Suppl.1), 23–38.

Otheguy, R., García, O., & Reid, W. (2015). Clarifying translanguaging and deconstructing named languages: A perspective from linguistics. *Applied Linguistics Review, 6*(3), 281–307.

Otheguy, R., García, O., & Reid, W. (2018). A translanguaging view of the linguistic system of bilinguals. *Applied Linguistics Review, 0*(0), 1–22.

Otsuji, E., & Pennycook, A. (2010). Metrolingualism: Fixity, fluidity and language in flux. *International Journal of Multilingualism, 7*(3), 240–254.

Palmer, D. K., Martínez, R. A., Mateus, S. G., & Henderson, K. (2014). Reframing the debate on language separation: Toward a vision for translanguaging pedagogies in the dual language classroom. *The Modern Language Journal, 98*(3), 757–772.

Paris, D. (2012). Culturally sustaining pedagogy: A needed change in stance, terminology, and practice. *Educational Researcher, 41*(3), 93–97.

Paris, D., & Alim, S. H. (2014). What are we seeking to sustain through culturally sustaining pedagogy? A loving critique forward. *Harvard Educational Review, 84*(1), 85–100.

Paris, D., & Alim, S. H. (2017). *Culturally sustaining pedagogies: Teaching and learning for justice in a changing world*. New York, NY: Teachers College Press.

Poza, L. E. (2017). Translanguaging: Definitions, implications, and further needs in burgeoning inquiry. *Berkeley Review of Education, 6*(2), 101–128.

Pratt, M. L. (1999). Arts of the contact zone. In D. Bartholomae & A. Petrovsky (Eds.), *Ways of reading* (5th ed.). New York, NY: Bedford/St. Martin's Press.

Tian, Z., & Link, H. (Eds.). (2019). Positive synergies: Translanguaging and critical theories in education. *Translation and Translanguaging in Multilingual Contexts 5*(1).

Vaish, V., & Subhan, A. (2015). Translanguaging in a reading class. *International Journal of Multilingualism, 12*(3), 338–357.

Valdés, G. (2020). Sandwiching, polylanguaging, translanguaging, and codeswitching: Challenging monolingual dogma in institutionalized language teaching. In J. MacSwan & C. J. Faltis (Eds.), *Codeswitching in the classroom: Critical perspectives on teaching, learning, policy, and ideology* (pp. 114–147). New York, NY: Routledge.

Vogel, S., & García, O. (2017). Translanguaging. In G. Noblit (Ed.), *Oxford research encyclopedia of education* (pp. 1–21). Oxford, UK: Oxford University Press.

Young, A. S. (2014). Unpacking teachers' language ideologies: Attitudes, beliefs, and practiced language policies in schools in Alsace, France. *Language Awareness, 23*(1–2), 157–171.

Zhao, T., & Macaro, E. (2016). What works better for the learning of concrete and abstract words: Teachers' L1 use or L2-only explanations? *International Journal of Applied Linguistics, 26*(1), 75–98.

Part I
Theorizing Translanguaging in TESOL

Chapter 2
Broadening the View: Taking up a Translanguaging Pedagogy with All Language-Minoritized Students

Kate Seltzer and Ofelia García

Abstract This chapter revisits a question posed by García (NYS TESOL J 1(1):2–10, 2014): what does a shift to translanguaging English mean for TESOL? To address this question, this chapter applies a translanguaging lens to the teaching of English, in the TESOL classroom *and beyond*. We first lay out the theoretical perspectives of a translanguaging approach, which include a series of paradigm shifts, ranging from a reimagining of English as a named language (Otheguy R, García O, Reid W, Applied Linguistics Review 6(3):281–307, 2015; Appl Linguist Rev. https://doi.org/10.1515/applirev-2018-0020, 2018) to a "re-seeing" of language-minoritized students as speakers and writers who use their agency to shape "English" in creative and critical (Li Wei, J Pragmat 43:1222–1235, 2011) ways. Our chapter draws on examples from a high school English Language Arts classroom made up of bilingual students as well as those traditionally viewed as monolingual, namely African American students. We describe how one teacher enacted a translanguaging pedagogy (García O, Johnson S, Seltzer K, The translanguaging classroom. Leveraging student bilingualism for learning. Caslon, Philadelphia, 2017) by (1) embracing a translanguaging *stance* regarding the "acquisition" of English, (2) centering her translanguaging *design* around texts that challenge monoglossic "native speaker" and "standard language" expectations and engage students in critical discussions about English itself, and (3) making translanguaging *shifts* that destabilize the role of the English teacher as linguistic expert.

Keywords Translanguaging · Language ideologies · Language-minoritized students · English Language Arts · TESOL

K. Seltzer (✉)
College of Education, Department of Language, Literacy and Sociocultural Education, Rowan University, Glassboro, NJ, USA
e-mail: seltzerk@rowan.edu

O. García
The Graduate Center, City University of New York, New York, NY, USA
e-mail: ogarcia@gc.cuny.edu

Z. Tian et al. (eds.), *Envisioning TESOL through a Translanguaging Lens*, Educational Linguistics 45, https://doi.org/10.1007/978-3-030-47031-9_2

1   Introduction

On the very first day of their 11th grade English Language Arts (ELA) class, Ms. Winter[1] poses several essential questions that she tells her students they will investigate that year. She directs their attention to a bulletin board in front of the classroom where, written in neat, colorful handwriting, are the following questions:

1. How can I integrate multiple language practices and elements of voice into my creative work?
2. How can language be used to open and close doors?
3. How does the way I communicate connect with my identity and who I am?
4. What does it mean for us to have and use multiple language practices in our society today?

At their square tables where they sit in groups of four, students – all multilingual, multidialectical teenagers, almost all of whom are Latinx[2] and African American – read the questions to themselves and discuss them. They ask about the phrase "language practices." They discuss what "doors" might be opened or closed by language. One student, looking around the brightly decorated room, remarks upon the quotes by famous writers and thinkers posted around the room in a variety of languages. Between the discussion of these essential questions about language in their lives, the multilingual ecology of the classroom, and the first day's reading – an interview with a famous bilingual author about the process of translating his book from English into Spanish – students were introduced to a very different kind of *English[3] classroom. As Ms. Winter tells her students right before the bell rings, "this is English, but it's also English Language Arts."

Ms. Winter's organization of that first day of class – just one of her thoughtful and purposeful decisions about the physical and curricular design of her classroom – emerges out of her desire to emphasize the *language arts* that so often lie beneath the surface of the so-called English classroom (Gutiérrez, 2001; Martínez, 2012). And though Ms. Winter's classroom is officially designated an ELA classroom with "push-in" English as a New Language (ENL) services,[4] her approach – which Seltzer (2017, 2019) has referred to as a *critical translingual approach* – is rooted in a question that García (2014) once asked about the field of TESOL: what would it mean to shift from "merely teaching English to translanguaging English" (p.3)?

---

[1] All names of participants are pseudonyms.

[2] We use the term Latinx as a gender-neutral way of referring to Latinos/as.

[3] We follow Lippi-Green's (2012) use of an asterisk next to *Standard American English "to refer to that mythical beast, the idea of a homogenous, standard American English" (p.62) when we write about the ideological named language of *English.

[4] In New York State, students labeled "English Language Learners" receive mandated service hours through several program structures, including "push-in" English as a New Language (ENL) services. In "push-in" programs, a certified ENL teacher comes into a general education classroom to provide support for emergent bilinguals.

In this chapter, we consider what translanguaging theory could contribute to the teaching of *English to language-minoritized students whose language practices are different from those legitimated in traditional English curricula. Although we focus on the ways in which translanguaging has the potential to transform TESOL instruction, we consider here the reality of many urban high school classrooms, where African American students and bilingual students, especially Latinx, who fall along all points of the bilingual continua (Hornberger, 2003) are taught jointly. To address the TESOL profession explicitly, we revisit García's (2014) discussion of "TESOL translanguaged," focusing on "major misconstructions about English, its speakers, the learning of English, bilingualism, and the teaching of English" (p.4). By revisiting these misconstructions through a translanguaging lens, we offer an approach to instruction in the English-medium classroom – be it TESOL, ELA, or another content-area class – that views students not merely as "English learners," but as speakers and writers who bring creative and critical (Li Wei, 2011) perspectives and language practices and use their agency to shape the learning of *English.

The education of bilingual students, and especially those labeled "English Language Learners," but whom we refer to as emergent bilinguals, is often studied separately from the reality in which it occurs. That is, in focusing only on TESOL education, we miss what goes on when emergent bilinguals, alongside other language-minoritized students, are taught by an English teacher or a content-area teacher, often with little understandings of bilingual development. It is the purpose of this chapter to show how leveraging translanguaging in a "general education" ELA classroom can bridge the ways in which bilingual, and specifically Latinx emergent bilingual, students and students who speak minoritized varieties of *English perform *English. This is a most important contribution, for Latinx and African Americans often live in the same communities, attend the same schools, and spend most of the time in the same classrooms. Although educators who focus on "second language" development and bilingualism are highly important for emergent bilingual students, *all* general education teachers, and especially those whose role is to develop *English, must understand the potential of translanguaging for *all* students.

Translanguaging also bridges understandings of language diversity for different types of students – those who are said to be bilingual and those considered to be multidialectal. By focusing on linguistic features, and not language as an autonomous structure, translanguaging theory makes it possible for African American and Latinx students to understand their language development as being part of the same process, despite the socio-political differences between what are seen as "varieties of English" and "different languages." In so doing, students become better listeners for one another, engaging in developing each other's repertoires without regard to whether they are said to be "bilingual" or "multidialectal." This development of what Martínez (2017) calls linguistic solidarity between these two populations of students offers the opportunity "to incite transformative learning experiences for youth who often do not have a language to express their own frustration, anger, and sadness about their collective experiences" (p.182).

To make tangible this kind of approach, we step into Ms. Winter's ELA class-room and describe the three strands of what we have termed a translanguaging ped-agogy: the *stance*, or the philosophy that teachers bring into their work with emergent bilinguals; the *design*, or the organization of both the physical space and the curriculum, instruction and assessment that is informed by the teachers' stance; and the *shifts*, or the unplanned, moment-by-moment "moves" that teachers make within a translanguaging design that allow for students' language practices, inter-ests, and needs to take center stage (García, Johnson & Seltzer, 2017). We will show how Ms. Winter enacted a translanguaging *stance* regarding the "acquisition" and development of *English, centered her translanguaging *design* around multilingual, multidialectal, multimodal texts that challenge monoglossic "native speaker" and "standard language" ideals and expectations and engage students in critical discus-sions about *English itself, and made translanguaging *shifts* that destabilized her own role as the linguistic expert and instead positioned her as a co-learner, allied with students in resisting oppressive language ideologies.

2   *English with an Asterisk: Translanguaging English

The teaching of what is said to be English to today's learners with highly diverse language practices cannot rely on traditional understandings of language, but must incorporate critical post-structuralist sociolinguistic understandings (García, Flores & Spotti, 2017). In this section we explore how translanguaging theory disrupts traditional understanding about English, and the consequences that this might have for teaching language-minoritized students.

With regards to the *English language, scholars working with translanguaging theory have posited three principles that must be fully understood by all educators:

1. *English is not simply a closed and autonomous system of lexical, morphologi-cal, syntactic and phonological features that correspond to what is named as English.

    Although *English is an important social construct that has had real and material effects, it does not have psycholinguistic reality. That is, what we call *English is not what anyone actually speaks; it is what has been "invented" (Makoni & Pennycook, 2007; Otheguy, García, & Reid, 2015) for purposes of nation-building and colonialism. It is this invented, homogeneous "standard English" that is then presented as *English in schools.

2. All speakers engage in *languaging*, a series of social practices that they perform as semiotic beings, as they are given opportunities to interact with listening sub-jects who legitimate their practices (or do not). To do so, speakers assemble a wide range of linguistic, multimodal, social, semiotic and environmental resources. This languaging is different from the "English" or "Spanish" or "Chinese" that is legitimated in schools.

3. The linguistic, cognitive, social and emotional components of speakers' languaging are inseparable. All speakers perform their languaging with a *unitary repertoire of features* which they assemble, and that reflects the languaging opportunities that they have had, and the interlocutors and listening subjects with whom they have come into contact. It is from this "assemblage" (Pennycook, 2017) that speakers select the features that offer the best "hints" to engage with their listeners.

These three positions on language clearly support the idea that *all* speakers engage in selecting features from a unitary repertoire that they have constructed in social interaction. Those considered to speak *English "appropriately" (Flores & Rosa, 2015) are those whose language practices and other semiotic features match those of powerful speakers legitimated in institutions like schools. Many language-minoritized students – some who are called "bi/multilingual" and others who are called "multidialectical" – have a semiotic repertoire that is much more extensive than those authorized in institutions, but many of their linguistic and multimodal features have never been legitimated in schools.

It is the inability to consider the languaging of *all* language-minoritized students as "appropriate" for their education that has led to their extensive failure in schools. And it is the inability to understand their language practices from this translanguaging perspective that has led to the complete separation of educational programs to teach *English to "multidialectal" African American students, "bilingual" Latinx students, and Latinx "English Language Learners." We explore in the study below how English Language Arts instruction steeped in translanguaging theory has the potential to expand the linguistic repertoire of all language-minoritized students, while paying attention to the different sociolinguistic realities of African American and Latinx bilingual students, and especially those labeled English Language Learners.

It is important, of course, for all teachers to understand how *bilingualism* operates in the world, and especially in contexts where *English is dominant; for despite the understandings that *English has been invented, it exists as a social reality with many material effects. For example, high school students are asked to perform in assessments with features considered "standardized English." When bilingual Latinx students use features considered "Spanish" in such assessments, they are penalized. Translanguaging provides a way to view bilingualism without reference to the dichotomies that have been essentialized – that bilingualism refers to the presence of a first and a second language (an L1 and L2), and that it is either additive or subtractive (Lambert, 1974). Instead, translanguaging theory acknowledges that bilingualism, like all languaging, is dynamic (De Bot, Lowie, & Verspoor, 2005; García, 2009; Larsen-Freeman & Cameron, 2008). Herdina and Jessner (2002) have proposed a dynamic model of multilingualism based on Dynamic Systems Theory, which posits that there are no separate language systems and that bi/multilingualism produces a change in the systems involved, as well as in the degree of metalinguistic and metacognitive awareness of the speaker (Jessner, 2006). English learners add new features (not A *new language*) to their unitary repertoire, as they then assemble, select and enact the features that are most meaningful for the interaction at hand.

Of course, TESOL teachers have to be mindful of the sociopolitical dimension connected to the power hierarchy of *English and the other language. But it is important to understand that the inventory of signs and meanings that bilingual students develop is not compartmentalized into items belonging to *English and items belonging to the other language. The language repertoire of bilingual students is unitary (Otheguy et al., 2015; Otheguy, García, & Reid, 2018), as is that of those students considered monolingual. In learning *English, emergent bilinguals extend their repertoire with additional features that they appropriate and use differently depending on the listeners. Bilingual speakers engage overtly in translanguaging when interacting with bilingual listeners in unmonitored situations such as the home and community. But if interacting with those who are said to speak *English only or "the other language" only, bilinguals are forced to select only from those linguistic features of their repertoire with which there is overlap with the listeners. In most cases, this means that bilinguals are forced to speak with less than half of the resources in their repertoire. This last point is important to consider when thinking about language education, for it turns out that the gap observed between those students labeled "English Language Learners" and others is *produced* when they are taught and assessed with less than half of their repertoire. A translanguaged TESOL profession could change this.

In 2014, García outlined five principles of what it would mean for TESOL to understand *English and English education through translanguaging (García & Li Wei, 2014). We repeat them here:

1. The English language is not a system of structures, rather languaging through what is called English is practicing a new way of being in the world,
2. "Native" *English speakers are neither the norm nor the objective fact, and yet positioning them as such creates an order of indexicality (Blommaert, 2010) that favors the language practices of white prestigious monolingual speakers,
3. Learning *English is not linear, and does not result in *English monolingualism. Rather, students are emergent bilinguals with full capacities who add new features and foreground some features, and not others, as they interact with different interlocutors and tasks.
4. Bilinguals are not simply speakers of a first and a second language, but use their unitary repertoire dynamically to interact in the world,
5. The teaching of *English cannot be enacted in total isolation of other language practices because speakers' translanguaging is always with them. Instead, teachers must leverage the students' existing repertoire and encourage the appropriation of new features into the learner's unitary repertoire.

Many TESOL teachers think of translanguaging only as scaffold, that is, they understand it only as temporarily using the students' home language to learn *English. They understand the *trans-* as simply going across two named languages and they claim to use it to support emergent bilingual students' meaning-making. But the translanguaging theory that we espouse in this chapter goes *beyond* named languages, and thus beyond simple scaffolds.

We posit that translanguaging has the potential to be *transformative* for all students whose language practices have been minoritized because it wipes out the psycholinguistic reality of the English language as a simple structure of forms that are objectively the norm. Instead, translanguaging acknowledges the invention of the English language norm and makes evident the political and economic reasons for upholding it in schools, which render those whose language practices are different as inferior and unqualified. In its transgression, translanguaging pedagogy has the capacity to transform *English classrooms and the subjectivities of those language-minoritized students within them. Translanguaging takes us *beyond* what we have learned to call "language," as the teacher acts on the students' translanguaging with political intent. As we will see, translanguaging in Ms. Winter's classroom is what Flores (2014) has called "a political act."

3 The Classroom and the Research Project

The classroom at the center of this chapter is that of Ms. Winter, a teacher in a borough of New York City. Though Ms. Winter is an ELA teacher – her New York State teaching certification is for secondary English education, and not English as a New Language education (ENL) – her classroom includes many emergent bilingual students. Learning alongside them are bilingual students not labeled English Language Learners as well as African American students whose English practices are marginalized by both the school and society at large. As we will see, though an ENL teacher only pushed into one of her four classroom blocks, she enacted with *all* students a critical translingual pedagogy that encouraged them to view *English as a complex set of linguistic features and social practices that could be integrated into their rich existing linguistic repertoires and fostered their criticality around *English itself, setting up opportunities for students to interrogate the ideologies that elevate one form of English (and one group of English speakers) and devalue others.

3.1 The Project

The classroom examples we feature in this chapter emerge out of a larger research project that took place over 9 months in 2015–2016. The project, an ethnographic case study of Ms. Winter's ELA classroom carried out by Seltzer (2017), involved co-designing a yearlong ELA curriculum that aimed to challenge the ideologies that lie beneath the traditional *English classroom. Together, Seltzer and Ms. Winter designed a series of units around such topics as exploring linguistic diversity, understanding links between language and power, and grappling with the role of language in our identities. To engage students in this inquiry, Seltzer and Ms. Winter drew on a variety of multilingual, multidialectical, and multimodal texts ranging from spoken word poetry to sketch comedy to political speeches to blog posts. They also designed a number of literacy activities that engaged students in an interrogation of language ideologies through the use of translanguaging in their own writing across different written genres like poetry, reflective journals and, ultimately, a college essay.

Seltzer and Ms. Winter began their collaboration by reading theoretical work across fields like bilingual and TESOL education, English education, and sociolinguistics. They engaged in rich discussions about this theory, talking through how these ideas might be applied to Ms. Winter's practice. Once the school year began, Seltzer observed Ms. Winter's classroom approximately three times per week. Taking on the role of a participant-observer, she looked for the ways in which Ms. Winter translated her new learning and thinking into her lesson planning and delivery as well as her interactions with students. Seltzer sat with students at their tables, listening and at times participating in their conversations about the class content. She had informal conversations with students during lunch, after class, and in the hallways. In this way, Seltzer maintained twin lenses on how the teacher and the students were shaped by and themselves shaped understandings of *English in the classroom.

Seltzer's weekly observations of Ms. Winter's classroom resulted in a large body of data, including field notes, reflective memos, audio recordings and transcriptions of classroom sessions, student and teacher work, and informal interviews with Ms. Winter and select students. Analysis of this data included multiple rounds of both inductive and deductive coding and elements of discourse analysis (Allan, 2008; Gee, 2011). Data analysis was also subject to member checks and peer debriefing to increase its credibility and build trust with participants (Lincoln & Guba, 1985). In addition, the triangulation of multiple data points enabled Seltzer to create thick descriptions that took multiple perspectives into account and painted a fuller picture of the teaching and learning that occurred.

3.2   Research Site and Participants

The project took place at South Bronx High School[5] (SBHS), a small school that served approximately 440 students in 2015–2016. SBHS, which had been part of the 2014–2015 cohort of schools participating in the City University of New York – New York State Initiative on Emergent Bilinguals (CUNY-NYSIEB) Project, was made up of students whose demographics reflected that of its neighborhood. According to the school's demographic information from 2015–2016, 71% of students were identified as "Hispanic" and 26% were labeled "Black", and nearly 90% qualified for free and reduced lunch. Students whom the state identified as "English

---

[5] The name of the school is a pseudonym.

Language Learners" made up 19% of the overall population, most of whom spoke Spanish.

As a participant in the CUNY-NYSIEB project, SBHS committed to improving the experiences of emergent bilinguals in the school community (for more on the CUNY-NYSIEB project, see García & Kleyn, 2016). When Seltzer was assigned to the school as a research assistant in 2014, she provided professional development and worked with a small group of teachers to integrate translanguaging strategies into their teaching. It was in this capacity that she worked closely with Ms. Winter, who not only demonstrated an avid interest in translanguaging but also expressed her desire to continue working with the approach outside of her participation in CUNY-NYSIEB. Because of this, and the fact that Seltzer and Ms. Winter had known one another for more than 10 years (they had been colleagues when Seltzer herself was an ELA teacher at SBHS), Seltzer approached Ms. Winter about partnering for this larger research study and Ms. Winter enthusiastically accepted.

The students in Ms. Winter's four blocks of 11th grade ELA mirrored the larger demographics of the school. Most of her students were Latinx and African American, though she also taught several students whose families had recently immigrated from Yemen and several countries in West Africa and one white student who had moved to New York the previous year from the South. Students were introduced to the project in the first week of classes, had the opportunity to ask questions about their potential participation, and were provided with a letter of consent that both they and their parents/guardians could sign. All but three of Ms. Winter's students agreed to participate in the project and, over the course of the year, several became interested in talking to Seltzer about what she was seeing and hearing, providing her with important insights into the research.

As will be shown in the next section, Ms. Winter and her students shaped a critical translingual approach to *English instruction. To understand how such an approach can result in meaningful critique of the kinds of myths that reify monoglossic understandings of *English, we organize the finding from this classroom study around the three strands that make up what García, et al. (2017) have termed a translanguaging pedagogy. First, we describe how Ms. Winter's *translanguaging stance* regarding the "acquisition" of *English enabled her to broaden and redefine the language and vocabulary of the classroom and make space for students' diverse language practices. Next, we explore Ms. Winter's *translanguaging design*. By organizing her curriculum around multilingual, multidialectal, and multimodal texts that were metalinguistic in nature, Ms. Winter invited students' sophisticated understandings of those ideologies that elevate certain language practices above others. The use of these different texts also provided students with models for engaging in their own translingual writing. Lastly, we explore Ms. Winter's *translanguaging shifts* that revealed her own critical stance towards *English and fostered this criticality in students. Though Seltzer and Ms. Winter were the initial architects of the curriculum, it was the students' translanguaging and their complex metacommentary (Rymes, 2014) that shape this discussion of teaching *English.

4 Translanguaging *Stance*: Broadening and Redefining Classroom Language

Early in their planning work, Seltzer and Ms. Winter spoke at length about subtle shifts in language that revealed new ways of thinking about *English in the classroom. As noted in the vignette that opens this chapter, instead of using the word "language," Ms. Winter took up the terms "languaging" and "language practices." Rather than uphold the myth that the teaching of *English can be enacted separately from other language practices (García, 2014), Ms. Winter's use of the term "language practices," as well as "Englishes" and "linguistic repertoire," point to her critical stance. Though these choices about language may seem small, taken together they created a sense of flexibility around traditional concepts in the *English classroom. For example, early in the year, Ms. Winter introduced an on-going reflective journaling project. As students engaged with new ideas about language in the classroom, Ms. Winter asked them to connect those ideas to things they read outside of class, came across on social media, heard from friends and family, etc. Students shared their journal entries with one another, and several became the basis for whole-class discussions throughout the year. When introducing the language journal, Ms. Winter explicitly opened up the assignment to linguistic flexibility:

> So, your language journal is yours, right? It's about your language use, your language practices, and your identity. So you can write in whatever style of language or language practices you see fit. You want to be paying attention to how you use language and how that connects to who you are. (Classroom transcript, 11/5/15)

Ms. Winter's redefinition of *English was integral to broadening the scope of the class overall. During one class discussion, one African American student and one Latinx student, Jania and Steven, were engaged in a debate about the difference between "standard" English and "proper" English, which they argued were separate concepts. The debate had emerged after students were asked to answer the question, "Do you have to use 'proper' English to sound smart?" The provocative question engaged the whole class in lively discussion, and after Jania and Steven had talked for a few minutes, Ms. Winter stepped in:

> The two of you are bringing up an important point, which is why I used quotation marks. There's no standard definition of "proper" English. If there were a "proper" then there'd be an "improper." We've talked all year about the idea of language practices, not right or wrong, or good or bad, or proper or improper. So the question I'm asking with "proper" in quotation marks is, if we use any other of our language practices, are people going to misjudge us as unintelligent? Do people only judge you as smart if you use only what's considered "standard" or "proper" English? (Classroom transcript, 3/14/16)

In her reframing of Jania and Steven's debate over the difference between "proper" and "standard" English, Ms. Winter is, in effect, asking students not to lose sight of the forest for the trees. This broader take on language practices and the ideologies that deem certain Englishes "proper" (or "standard") and others "improper" made way for students to see *past* such terms. Through this reframing – and through her choice to surround the word "proper" in quotation marks in her question – Ms.

Winter modeled a contestation of the term's authority and of the larger language ideologies that render certain practices "proper" and others not. In short, Ms. Winter's stance emerged through her redefinition of certain terms that are ideologically naturalized in the *English classroom. This broadening of the shared language of the classroom, as we will see in the next section on *translanguaging design*, made room for students to openly contest such terms and concepts themselves.

5 Translanguaging *Design*: Multilingual, Multimodal Texts as Mentors

Throughout the academic year, Ms. Winter created lessons, literacy activities, small projects, group activities, and other instructional designs that aimed to bring to the surface students' translanguaging and their metacommentary (Rymes, 2014), or their talk about language itself. At the center of many of these designs were texts that served as translingual mentors (Seltzer, 2020) for students' own translanguaging and articulations of linguistic understandings. Sketch comedy by the duo Key and Peele provided insights into how African American people are not only master linguistic style shifters (Alim & Smitherman, 2012) but also experts on how different English practices are viewed in our society. Spoken word poets Jamila Lysicott and Melissa Lozada-Oliva served as mentors for how an artists' linguistic medium – their translanguaging and language play – can elucidate powerful messages about language and power. And, of course, authors like Gloria Anzaldúa, Amy Tan, and Alice Walker, among others, demonstrated the role that language – and Englishes in particular – plays in the lives and identities of minoritized people. It was through engagement with these mentors – reading excerpts of their work, analyzing both the content of what they read as well as the linguistic choices they made, and making connections between these texts and their own understandings of language – that students were privy to examples of translanguaging in action by established writers and artists and voiced their own criticality about *English.

After reading a blog post by a bilingual writer about his experiences in school, Ms. Winter facilitated a whole-class discussion around the question of whether teachers at the school "tend to have a bias for or against the language practices you use." Students voiced that indeed teachers did have a bias against their language practices, in particular their use of Spanish in school. Students Juan, Natasha, and Jacqui shared the following experiences:

> Juan: I see it sometimes when I start speaking Spanish, the teachers that don't speak Spanish be like, "speak only in English."
> Natasha: I remember that happened to me. The teacher told me that it was rude but I didn't find it rude because it was like eight kids in the classroom and we all spoke Spanish.
> Jacqui: That's like the passage we read… I want to be comfortable to use my languages when I want to. Like I shouldn't be criticized for the way I speak. If I want to speak this language I want to speak it. Maybe it's helping me more than English. (Classroom transcript, 2/28/16)

Juan and Natasha, both emergent bilinguals from the Dominican Republic, shared similar experiences about Spanish being explicitly devalued and penalized by teachers at their school. Both students point out how their teachers voiced a common ideology: that *English is the only language appropriate for school and that is "rude" to speak anything else, even if, like in Natasha's class, all the students speak Spanish. These "discourses of appropriateness" (Flores & Rosa, 2015) are commonplace in schools and beneath them are raciolinguistic ideologies that render people of color "linguistically deviant even when engaging in linguistic practices positioned as normative or innovative when produced by privileged white subjects" (p.150). In other words, the appeals for emergent bilinguals to speak "English only" because it is the only "appropriate" language ring hollow: even if students like Juan and Natasha speak *English, they will still be *heard* by their teachers as "rude," not to mention less intelligent, less professional, and less competent.

When Jacqui, a bilingual Latinx student of Puerto Rican descent who was not labeled an "English Language Learner," jumped into the conversation, we see her resistance to this silencing of Spanish. Citing the class reading explicitly, Jacqui resists such criticism of speakers like her for "using my languages when I want to." Going against one of García's (2014) "myths" around *English and *English learning, that "switching" languages is detrimental and that speaking only *English is most helpful to emergent bilinguals, Jacqui asserts that perhaps it is her other languages that are helping her *more* than *English.

In addition to providing them the opportunity to voice their critical metacommentary about *English, Ms. Winter's translanguaging design featured models of how students could use their own translanguaging in their writing. The final unit of the academic year was an author study of translingual authors, or those that integrate different language practices in ways that transgress monoglossic language ideologies (for more on this author study see Seltzer, 2020). Students were grouped and assigned an author whose work they would study over the course of 5 weeks. Each week, Ms. Winter organized students' engagement with that author's work around one of five themes: the authors' influences, voice, linguistic choices, engagement with audience, and censorship and critique. To engage in discussions around these topics, students read excerpts of the writers' published work as well as short biographical readings, articles and criticism, and interviews with the authors. The articles and interviews chosen were those that dealt specifically with how language was used in the authors' work. The combination of the authors' writing and writing *about* their writing provided models of both translingual text production and critical metacommentary about language. For example, in addition to reading excerpts from *The Color Purple,* students studying Alice Walker also read an interview in which Walker talked about her linguistic choices for the character of Celie, watched a video clip of her reading and discussing her poetry, and read think-pieces on the use of African American Vernacular English[6] in writing.

---

[6] Though there are many terms to describe this language practice, we have chosen to use African American Vernacular English, or AAVE, because it is the term that Ms. Winter elected to use with students.

As students read about how their assigned authors thought about audience or made choices about how to integrate different language practices in writing, they were also posed questions about their own writing. How (if at all) might they "mesh" different language practices in their writing? In what ways (if any) would they accommodate their audience, who might not understand their languages practices? What would they do if faced with critique or push-back about their translingual writing? Some students expressed ambivalence about translanguaging in their writing, citing reasons such as fear of being misunderstood or getting penalized by a reader for not using "standard English" only. Others, however, took up the invitation to integrate languages other than *English into their "academic" writing, which took the form of a mock college essay in which students were tasked with articulating their thoughts on the role of language and language ideologies in their lives. This translanguaging design, inspired by the authors studies, aimed to bring forth not only students' learning over the course of the year but also their experimentation with translingual writing. One student, Andrew, who was of African American and Dominican descent but often expressed insecurity about his ability to speak Spanish, demonstrated his own grappling with language ideologies in his essay.

Andrew began his essay by retelling an event that made him aware of his own language practices and how those practices related to (mis)perceptions of him by those in authority. During an interview for an internship, Andrew "slipped" in his response to the interviewer's question of why he would be a good candidate, saying, "I think because of my determined mentality and how fast and good I work, I will be good for this job and also I ain't no slacker. I get the job done by any means." Andrew realized later that this response, which made his interviewer's "eyebrows raise," may have been the reason he did not get the internship. In a draft of his college essay, he reflects on that realization:

> I have seen those who speak my language practices succeed and yet our language is still considered inferior. We grow up in a society where the way white people speak is considered the "correct" way of speaking. What makes the way they speak so different than ours? Throughout our country's history the white population has been dominant and we, Hispanics and African Americans, have been struggling, struggling to make us all feel equal but things aren't. Our country is run by rich white men and women so people view the way they speak as the "correct" way of speaking and we get judged because we do not speak "proper" English like them. We get put in a category of unintelligent speakers.
> My mother always told me just because yo hablo un poquito de Español does not make me dumb! Just because I curse does not mean I am a criminal! (College Essay, Andrew)

Here we see Andrew's articulation of his understanding of raciolinguistic ideologies and their impact on speakers like him. Writing with a sense of history and using the rhetorical device of repetition, Andrew writes that because of forces of white supremacy, people like him have been "struggling, struggling to make us all feel equal but things aren't." He makes the explicit connection that because of the dominance of "white men and women" in the U.S., their ways of speaking English have been deemed "correct" and "proper" (terms Andrew puts in quotation marks) and that "Hispanics and African Americans" like him are heard as "unintelligent." After this section, Andrew sets two lines of his essay apart from the others, letting them stand alone on the page. Here he includes translanguaging, meshing linguistic features that are said to be from English and Spanish to make the point that his use of language in ways that do not merely reflect what is deemed to be "appropriate English" or "appropriate Spanish" do not make him "dumb" or a "criminal."

These two lines show Andrew's critical metalinguistic awareness. Andrew demonstrates his understanding that, as a bilingual writer, he has access to linguistic features which are said to be from Spanish, as well as those that are said to be from English. In *English classrooms, features that are regarded as being from Spanish are often forbidden, just the same way as profanity is. But Andrew makes the point that when he uses features from Spanish in an *English essay, he is engaging in feature selection of the same type that he does when he includes, or not, "curses." That is, he is not restricting his language repertoire in writing to features that are authorized in the *English classroom. Instead, he is writing using the full critical and creative power of his extended repertoire. This in no way makes him "dumb" or a "criminal." This powerful two-line paragraph seems to serve as an emotional appeal to his reader, driving home his point through the use of translanguaging as well as other rhetorical devices like repetition and the use of exclamation points. This explicit critique of "proper" English and the ideologies that reify it – as well as the translanguaging used to express that critique – came to the surface because Ms. Winter's pedagogical design actively invited it. By providing students with translingual mentors that integrated their language practices in ways that destabilized oppressive language ideologies, Ms. Winter made space in the *English classroom for students like Andrew to demonstrate their own creativity and criticality (Li Wei, 2011).

6   Translanguaging *Shifts*: Invoking a Language of Solidarity

Translanguaging shifts are the "moves" that teachers make that respond to students' languaging, questions, and critique, none of which can be predicted. A teacher's translanguaging design must be flexible enough to accommodate these shifts; in fact, these shifts often signal places in the design that could be changed or adapted to better meet the needs and interests of the students. In Ms. Winter's case, her shifts demonstrate her commitment to destabilizing such "myths" as the existence of "native English speakers" or "standard English." A close analysis of one such classroom shift, which occurred in response to a student's question, reveals Ms. Winter's use of a *language of solidarity* (Seltzer, 2017), which not only allies her with her students, but also upends her role as the "linguistic expert" in the *English classroom and instead foregrounds her status as a co-learner (García & Li Wei, 2014). During one class, Ms. Winter paused a conversation when she noticed students struggling to answer her questions about a particular text. After she reassured students that the work they were engaged in was "really sophisticated stuff," Oscar, an emergent bilingual student who had moved from the Dominican Republic only

2 years prior, asked a question that pushed Ms. Winter to expand upon her role as a co-learner:

> Ms. Winter: We're doing really sophisticated stuff in our class because you guys are extremely intelligent and can handle it. But the outside world isn't quite ready for us. So if you're feeling like, "I'm not sure how to answer this, I don't really get this question," that's ok. These are really big questions and I think a lot of the teachers at this school don't quite have the – they don't think about language the way we do in here.
> Oscar: Including yourself?
> Ms. Winter: Well … I certainly have evolved a lot in my thinking about language over the course of this year. Because I've learned a lot with you guys about the history of different language practices and how people who have power determine what language is considered good or valid and people who don't have power, their languages – or language practices – are considered inferior. But that's not actually the case. There's not good or bad, there's just different. (Classroom transcript, 3/14/16)

By first acknowledging the complexity of the task and then characterizing the class as engaged in a kind of radical learning, Ms. Winter set the classroom apart from "the outside world." Though Ms. Winter, a white, elite-educated, monolingual English-speaking woman, did not find herself marginalized by those ideologies that devalue certain language practices, she aligned herself with her students over "society" and even over some of her fellow educators at the school. This, in particular, seemed to prompt Oscar to question Ms. Winter's affiliation with students ("we") rather than other teachers ("they"). By asking Ms. Winter if she, herself, thought like those teachers, Oscar was understandably attempting to figure out where Ms. Winter stood. In her response, Ms. Winter takes up a co-learning stance (García & Li Wei, 2014), which "moves the teacher and the learner toward a more 'dynamic and participatory engagement' in knowledge construction" (p.112). She credits her "evolution" to the learning she has done "with" students. Interestingly, a few minutes after this exchange, Oscar offered his thoughts on whether, as the class was discussing, writers should change their language practices to be compatible with what has been legitimated as the "standard." The following exchange ensued:

> Oscar: I think no, Miss, we shouldn't change our language practices because then it's never gonna change. If we keep changing our language practices, everybody's gonna keep thinking that we're not educated – that the way we speak is not educated. So if we start, maybe, incorporating our language practices, they gonna get, like, a different perspective.
> Ms. Winter: Well, that's right up there as one of the most intelligent things I've heard today. Really, really profound. If we always adjust our language practices, then we perpetuate, we keep up, the idea that there are certain ways of speaking that are good and certain ways that are bad. So let's not change, let's use our language practices and resist the ideas of what's good and what's bad that society has. (Classroom transcript, 3/14/16)

In his response, Oscar seemed to take up the language of solidarity set forth by Ms. Winter in her initial classroom shift. His use of "we" and "our" could be seen as referring to a classroom of writers (or, perhaps more broadly, a larger community of writers whose language practices do not align with expectations of a "standard"), and that by "incorporating our language practices," perhaps "they" will gain a different perspective. Oscar's comment, which earned high praise from Ms. Winter, prompted her to express an even stronger language of solidarity, aligning herself with students and encouraging the class as a whole to "use our language practices and resist" society's marginalization of those practices. Though it is important to restate that Ms. Winter had not experienced this kind of linguistic marginalization – in fact she would quite easily fit the ideological mold of the "native English speaker" tasked with teaching *English in "standard," "academic" ways – her shifts in the classroom reveal her desire to serve, instead, as an ally and co-learner with her students.

7   Discussion & Implications

In their discussion of what they term a translingual orientation in TESOL teacher education, Flores and Aneja (2017) ask a series of important questions:

> How would TESOL teacher education look if we provided spaces for students to develop projects that explore this linguistic diversity through a translingual lens? How might this help these programs more effectively prepare students—regardless of their language backgrounds—to become agents of change in challenging monoglossic language ideologies? (p.460)

We believe the examples from Ms. Winter's 11th grade ELA classroom presented in this chapter provide a window into how we might begin to answer such questions. We also draw on Ms. Winter's classroom to push these questions even further: what might it look like for *all* teachers of *English – across *all* program types – to take up a translingual orientation and challenge the monoglossic ideologies that inform the teaching of *English?

Through the examples of Ms. Winter's translanguaging pedagogy – her stance, design, and shifts – in action, as well as students' metacommentary and writing that was brought to the surface through this pedagogy, we can see several implications and possibilities for the field of *English teaching, particularly the TESOL field. First, teachers of *English must become well-versed in recent translanguaging scholarship which actively resists the very myths and misconceptions about English and English speakers articulated by García in 2014. Rather than tacitly uphold such naturalized ideas as the existence of a native speaker or an objectively standard form of the English language, *all* educators – but particularly those tasked with teaching *English to language-minoritized speakers – must engage with post-structural theories of languaging that can contribute to their translanguaging stances. Like Ms. Winter's small linguistic turn from using the term "language" to "language practices," teachers of *English can model their own shifting and evolving stance in ways that ally them with their language-minoritized students.

Second, educators must do more than teach English as though it is an isolated, bounded system devoid of history and socio-political significance. Ignoring the myriad ways that speakers of English around the world appropriate and shape English not only ignores a global reality; it ignores the very languaging students are engaged in on a daily basis. Instead, teachers of *English must explicitly design classroom activities, choose texts, and pose questions that foster students' criticality of English as a named language and turn their attention to the ways in which minoritized speakers – including them! – have *always* appropriated *English in creative and critical ways. In doing so, teachers invite *all* language-minoritized students to take up linguistic solidarity (Martínez, 2017) with one another, collectively critique oppressive language ideologies, and integrate features of different Englishes into their repertoires on their own terms. As we saw in Andrew's college essay, when given the opportunity, students can voice sophisticated critical metalinguistic awareness in ways that are linguistically inventive and rhetorically powerful – writing skills that will find students much success outside the classroom.

Lastly, teachers of *English – especially those whose language practices, backgrounds, and lived experiences are different from their students – must be open to the kinds of shifts that position them as co-learners. Given Ms. Winter's positionality as a white, monolingual English-speaking woman, she fit the ideological model of who "should" teach *English to language-minoritized students. Instead, Ms. Winter attempted to subvert this positioning by designing a flexible curriculum that enabled her to shift with the questions and interests of her students. No lesson was too rigid for the kinds of conversations about language that emerged authentically from students' metacommentary. No project was closed off to negotiations about changes and extensions of the proposed task. In this way, Ms. Winter communicated the message that she was receptive to students' inquiries and interests and that her own thinking evolved by learning alongside them. These kinds of small shifts are integral for teachers of *English who wish to take up translanguaging pedagogy.

8 Conclusion

In this chapter we have questioned conceptions of *English that have resulted in the separation of *English language education into programs for different language-minoritized students. For some, such as African American students, the thinking has been that their English has "non-standard" features. Their language education thus focuses on silencing a dialect that some call "African American Vernacular." For others, such as Latinx bilingual students, the thinking has been that their language evidences "language mixing," that they "code-switch" between English and Spanish. In providing these Latinx bilingual students with an English-only education, the focus is on encouraging a total shift to *English, stigmatizing and silencing their bilingualism. It is important to note that the bilingualism of Latinx students is recognized in schools only when it falls along the beginning points of *English language development, that is, when they are labeled "English Language Learners." Then schools buckle down, making visible a "problem" that has to be remediated. Schools focus on intensive ESL or TESOL instruction, as if learners did not already have a language repertoire. That repertoire then becomes invisible and schools fail to acknowledge what students know how to do with language, their languaging,

unless it consists only of features that are socially associated with what is named
∗English.

We argued in this chapter that translanguaging theory can transform the teaching
of ∗English to *all* language-minoritized learners. It can do so first and foremost
because translanguaging does not reify named languages that one *has*, but takes a
feature-based approach to what speakers *do* with their linguistic and multimodal
repertoire. Furthermore, translanguaging also takes a speaker/listener-based
approach to communication and language learning. If listening subjects and audiences are most important to developing speakers, then it behooves us to familiarize
all students with translanguaging. Translanguaging theory provides a conceptual
platform to work against the naturalization of ∗English that often accompanies
∗English education of all types. For example, translanguaging pedagogical practice
develops listeners and interlocutors who are attuned to the bilingual performances
of Latinx students, especially those who are labeled "English language learners." At
the same time, translanguaging pedagogy develops Latinx listeners who acknowledge and legitimate the linguistic practices of their African American friends. In
centering the linguistic and multimodal feature selection practices of African
American and bilingual students, and not an object named ∗English, translanguaging theory transforms our understanding of the process of performing, teaching and
learning ∗English.

Lest we are misunderstood, we emphasize here that TESOL and bilingual spe-
cialists are needed to teach bilingual students, and especially those who are emergent bilinguals. But ELA and general education teachers, with understandings of
translanguaging and dynamic bilingualism, are also needed. We advocate for a
translanguaging approach that engages *all* language-minoritized students. By making students aware of how ∗English operates in education and society to create differences and inequalities, translanguaging theory can do much more than
simply develop the ∗English language performances of emergent bilinguals.
Translanguaging theory can transform the way we have naturalized an object called
∗English as the language of U.S. schools for purposes of exclusion and stigmatiza-
tion, instead of recognizing the diverse language practices that students bring with
them and with which they perform outside of classrooms. As Ms. Winter has done,
translanguaging can transform ELA/TESOL instruction, focusing with intent on
how bilingual and multidialectal students perform language with their existing
semiotic repertoire, and revealing the invention of school ∗English in ways that
continue to produce unequal opportunities in U.S. society.

References

Alim, H. S., & Smitherman, G. (2012). *Articulate while Black: Barack Obama, language, and race in the US*. Oxford, UK: Oxford University Press.
Allan, E. J. (2008). *Policy discourses, gender, and education: Constructing women's status* (Vol. 11). New York, NY: Routledge.

Blommaert, J. (2010). *The sociolinguistics of globalization*. Cambridge, UK: Cambridge University Press.

De Bot, K., Lowie, W., & Verspoor, M. (2005). *Second language acquisition: An advanced resource book*. London, UK/New York, NY: Routledge.

Flores, N. (2014). *Let's not forget that translanguaging is a political act*. https://educationallinguist.wordpress.com/2014/07/19/lets-not-forget-that-translanguaging-is-a-political-act/

Flores, N., & Aneja, G. (2017). "Why needs hiding?" Translingual (re)orientations in TESOL teacher education. *Research in the Teaching of English, 51*(4), 441–463.

Flores, N., & Rosa, J. (2015). Undoing appropriateness: Raciolinguistic ideologies and language diversity in education. *Harvard Educational Review, 85*(2), 149–171.

García, O. (2009). *Bilingual education in the 21st century: A global perspective*. Malden, MA/Oxford, UK: Wiley/Blackwell.

García, O. (2014). TESOL translanguaged in NYS: Alternative perspectives. In L. Baecher & R. Johnson (Eds.). *NYS TESOL Journal, 1*(1), 2–10.

García, O., Flores, N., & Spotti, M. (Eds.). (2017). *Handbook of language and society*. New York, NY/Oxford, UK: Oxford University Press.

García, O., Johnson, S., & Seltzer, K. (2017). *The translanguaging classroom. Leveraging student bilingualism for learning*. Philadelphia, PA: Caslon.

García, O., & Kleyn, T. (Eds.). (2016). *Translanguaging with multilingual students: Learning from classroom moments*. New York, NY/London, UK: Routledge.

García, O., & Li Wei. (2014). *Translanguaging: Language, bilingualism and education*. London, UK/New York, NY: Palgrave Macmillan.

Gee, J. P. (2011). *How to do discourse analysis: A toolkit*. New York, NY: Routledge.

Gutiérrez, K. D. (2001). What's new in the English language arts: Challenging policies and practices, ¿ y qué? *Language Arts, 78*(6), 564–569.

Herdina, P., & Jessner, U. (2002). *A dynamic model of multilingualism*. Clevedon, UK: Multilingual Matters.

Hornberger, N. H. (2003). Continua of biliteracy. In N. H. Hornberger (Ed.), *Continua of biliteracy: An ecological framework for educational policy, research, and practice in multilingual settings* (pp. 3–34). Clevedon, UK: Multilingual Matters.

Jessner, U. (2006). *Linguistic awareness in multilinguals: English as a third language*. Edinburgh, UK: Edinburgh University Press.

Lambert, W. E. (1974). Culture and language as factors in learning and education. In F. E. Aboud & R. D. Meade (Eds.), *Cultural factors in learning and education* (pp. 91–122). Bellingham, Washington: 5th Western Washington symposium on learning.

Larsen-Freeman, D., & Cameron, L. (2008). *Complex systems and applied linguistics*. Cambridge, UK: Cambridge University Press.

Li Wei. (2011). Moment analysis and translanguaging space: Discursive construction of identities by multilingual Chinese youth in Britain. *Journal of Pragmatics, 43*, 1222–1235.

Lincoln, Y. S., & Guba, E. G. (1985). *Naturalistic inquiry* (Vol. 75). London, UK: Sage.

Lippi-Green, R. (2012). *English with an accent: Language, ideology, and discrimination in the United States* (2nd ed.). London, UK/New York, NY: Routledge.

Makoni, S., & Pennycook, A. (Eds.). (2007). *Disinventing and reconstituting language*. Clevedon, UK: Multilingual Matters.

Martínez, D. C. (2012). *Expanding linguistic repertoires: An ethnography of Black and Latina/o youth transcultural communication in urban English language arts classrooms* (Unpublished Doctoral Dissertation). University of California, Los Angeles, CA.

Martínez, D. C. (2017). Imagining a language of solidarity for Black and Latinx youth in English language arts classrooms. *English Education, 49*(2), 179.

Otheguy, R., García, O., & Reid, W. (2015). Clarifying translanguaging and deconstructing named languages: A perspective from linguistics. *Applied Linguistics Review, 6*(3), 281–307.

Otheguy, R., García, O., & Reid, W. (2018). A translanguaging view of the linguistic system of bilinguals. *Applied Linguistics Review*. https://doi.org/10.1515/applirev-2018-0020

Pennycook, A. (2017). Translanguaging and semiotic assemblages. *International Journal of Multilingualism, 14*(3), 269–282. https://doi.org/10.1080/14790718.2017.1315810

Rymes, B. (2014). *Communicating beyond language: Everyday encounters with diversity.* New York, NY: Routledge.

Seltzer, K. (2017). *Resisting from within: (Re)Imagining a critical translingual english classroom* (Unpublished doctoral dissertation), The Graduate Center, CUNY, New York, NY.

Seltzer, K. (2019). Performing ideologies: Fostering Raciolinguistic literacies through role-play in a high school English classroom. *Journal of Adolescent & Adult Literacy, 63*(2), 147–155.

Seltzer, K. (2020). Translingual writers as mentors in a high school "English" classroom. In S.M.C. Lau and S. Van Viegen (Eds.). *Plurilingual pedagogies: Critical and creative endeavors for equitable language (in) education* (pp. 185–204). Springer.

Chapter 3
The Need for Translanguaging in TESOL

Sabrina F. Sembiante and Zhongfeng Tian

Abstract In response to the multilingual turn, the field of TESOL has not yet pro-pelled itself away from monolingual orientations despite fleeting attention to the concepts of plurilingualism and translingual pedagogy. In this chapter, we argue in favor of the merits of translanguaging for the field of TESOL, both as distinct from other popular language orientations flooding the language fields and necessary given its unique social justice-oriented practice and theoretical stance. We describe the challenges that scholars have experienced in finding traction for multilingualism in general, and translanguaging specifically, in the TESOL field and argue that these stem from ideological misrepresentations and/or from fear of disrupting the power inherent in valuing English above other languages. Our purposes are to question, uncover, and discuss resistance to the holistic support of emergent bilingual stu-dents' and teachers' rich language repertoires, with a particular eye towards the role of the TESOL International Association, the largest organization for English lan-guage educators, in promoting or hindering these efforts. Addressing several cri-tiques that have surfaced in response to translanguaging, we contend that a translanguaging lens represents a paradigm shift away from prioritizing English as a second or foreign language towards recognition of emergent bilinguals' multilin-gual repertoires and their fluid language practices.

Keywords Translanguaging · TESOL · Neoliberalism · Multilingualism · English · Bilingual · Multilingual

S. F. Sembiante (✉)
College of Education, Department of Curriculum, Culture, and Educational Inquiry,
Florida Atlantic University, Boca Raton, FL, USA
e-mail: ssembiante@fau.edu

Z. Tian
College of Education and Human Development, Department of Bicultural-Bilingual Studies,
The University of Texas at San Antonio, San Antonio, TX, USA
e-mail: zhongfeng.tian@utsa.edu

© Springer Nature Switzerland AG 2020   43
Z. Tian et al. (eds.), *Envisioning TESOL through a Translanguaging Lens*,
Educational Linguistics 45, https://doi.org/10.1007/978-3-030-47031-9_3

1 Introduction

Since the "multilingual turn" (May, 2014) that ensued across the fields of bilingual education, second language acquisition, and applied linguistics, where monolingual language norms were called into question, a plethora of terms and orientations have emerged to characterize and distinguish the various perspectives and positions on language/s (e.g., flexible bilingualism, metrolingualism, plurilingualism, hybrid language practices, codemeshing, codeswitching, translingual practice). As a theory and a pedagogy, translanguaging (García & Li, 2014) distinguishes itself from these and other language orientations through its "explicit concern with social justice and linguistic inequality" (Poza, 2017, p. 108) and in its advocacy against "the oppression and marginalization of national and colonial subjects that accompanied the rise of earlier language ideologies" (Poza, 2017, p. 108).

In response to the multilingual turn, the field of TESOL has not yet propelled itself away from monolingual orientations despite fleeting attention to the concepts of plurilingualism (e.g., Taylor & Snoddon, 2013) and translingual pedagogy (Canagarajah, 2013). In this chapter, we argue in favor of the merits of translanguaging for the field of TESOL, both as distinct from other popular language orientations flooding language fields and necessary given its unique social justice-oriented practice and theoretical stance. We describe the challenges that scholars have experienced in finding traction for multilingualism in general, and translanguaging specifically, in the TESOL field and argue that these stem from ideological misrepresentations and/or from fear of disrupting the power inherent in valuing English above other languages. Addressing several critiques that have surfaced in response to translanguaging, we contend that a translanguaging lens represents a paradigm shift away from prioritizing English as a second or foreign language (ESL/EFL respectively) towards recognition of emergent bilinguals' multilingual repertoires and their fluid language practices. Thus, translanguaging pedagogy is advantageous in its potential to imbue agency and transformation into the language learning and teaching process for the TESOL field. We conclude with research and practical implications of translanguaging as a necessary, divergent path for TESOL.

We write this chapter as two multilingual scholars who emerge from and identify with the bilingual education field.[1] While our training in the U.S. has imbued our stance with U.S.-centric views, as immigrants to the U.S., we also carry the language and cultural experiences from our heritage countries, South Africa and China, which also inform and shape our positionality. Our academic orientations are sociological in nature, comprising of the intersections of bi/multilingualism, social justice, and education. Beyond our own individual research interests within bilingual

---

[1] While we use the terms bilingual and multilingual to reflect the use of two or more languages, we are cognizant of the limitations of these terms in light of translanguaging and linguistic fluidity that we argue for in this chapter. We use these labels as a way of positioning our identities with reference to mainstream understandings of language, but still recognize the problematic nature of such terms when advocating for linguistic diversity, in particular with respect to power/hierarchies and marginalized/minoritized ways of languaging.

education, we are forthright in our shared agenda to promote and advocate for multilingualism as a human right in education and to seek justice for multilingual and multidialectal teacher and student populations in the U.S. and beyond. At the time of writing this manuscript, we proposed a special issue in a journal affiliated with the TESOL organization on the topic of "Translanguaging in TESOL". In the proposal, we highlighted the difference between plurilingualism and translanguaging, argued for the unique necessity of translanguaging to inform language practices in English-medium educational contexts, and encouraged further critical examination of translanguaging and its potential for the TESOL community. We received several responses from TESOL-affiliated reviewers stating that a translanguaging-focused issue would be redundant with TESOL Quarterly's previous special issue on plurilingualism (Taylor & Snoddon, 2013), and thus, this issue was not certain to add to the knowledge base of the field. These comments revealed several assumptions that were both surprising and erroneous in our eyes: that plurilingualism was synonymous with translanguaging; that the topic of multilingualism was finite and had been wholly explored in TESOL; that the topic was peripheral rather than central to the needs of the TESOL field; and that the ideas presented in the special issue on plurilingualism had had a meaningful-enough impact on TESOL to shift the organization and render further discussion redundant. Our anecdotal experience is not enough to imply outright that TESOL Quarterly is resistant to translanguaging and we do not include it as evidence of this necessarily. However, the response we received brings to our attention the underlying issues and paradigmatic schism across language fields, and provides a starting point for the discussion and analysis of these trends.

Our shared agenda and the above experience prompted our further research and inquiry into this issue and the writing of this chapter. In it, our purposes are to question, uncover, and discuss resistance to the holistic support of emergent bilingual students' and teachers' rich language repertoires, with a particular eye towards the role of the TESOL International Association (TESOL IA), the largest organization for English language educators, in promoting or hindering these efforts. TESOL IA[2] is an organization designed for and managed by professionals who are interested in the teaching of English as a second or foreign language. The organization provides materials and resources regarding professional development, research, standards, and advocacy on English language teaching. We focus expressly on TESOL IA because, as the largest organization for English language educators, it reaches over 11,000 researchers, educators, and professionals in the field (as of 2018 membership) and as a result, is highly influential in shaping ideas and policies related to English language teaching. A concurrent objective is to highlight the potential of translanguaging to help reorient TESOL-aligned practices and research and address current shortcomings in the positioning of its flagship organization. We would like to be clear that our focus is not aimed at critiquing or denying the importance or

---

[2] We use the acronym "TESOL IA" to distinguish when we are talking about the TESOL organization in contrast to our use of the acronym "TESOL" which denotes the field of research and practice.

relevance of the current perspectives exhibited in TESOL, but to participate in macro-level discourse to address the lack of representation of significant multilingual topics in this important organization and its influential publications and programs. We hope our chapter encourages critical reflection of these issues that will galvanize further attention, action, and reorientation towards emergent bilingual students' and teachers' "other languages" in TESOL.

2　The Contentious History of Bi/Multilingualism in TESOL

An ongoing critique and concern of the TESOL organization is the call for TESOL to embrace a more multilingual identity. The earliest accusation took place in the mid-1960s, with an altercation between Rudy Troike, future director of the National Association of Bilingual Education (NABE), and James Alatis, founding member and first executive director of TESOL, in which Troike accused Alatis of leading a TESOL organization that was "bad for bilingual education both organizationally and professionally" (Fishman, 2009, p. 316). In response, Alatis created the Bilingual Education Interest Section (BEIS) and a few spaces for bilingual education-related presentations as part of TESOL's annual conference (Fishman, 2009). As director of the Center for Applied Linguistics (CAL), Troike continued his opposition by writing several editorials against the use of traditional ESL approaches (e.g., the Direct Method, Grammar Translation, Audiolingual Method; Troike, 1976b), labeling these as hazardous to children (Troike, 1976a), and calling attention to the 1974 ruling of the Lau Remedies stating that "a bilingual program is required at the elementary and intermediate levels, and an ESL program is declared to be not appropriate" (OCR sets guidelines, 1975).

2.1　TESOL and NABE Collaboration and Divergence

In its early years, during the civil rights movement, TESOL had worked closely with NABE as two bodies with the similar concern of advocating for the education of students whose home languages were not English. The kinship between NABE and TESOL emerged in part because the founding members of TESOL had acknowledged "speakers of other languages" in its acronym and in its vision rather than just a focus on teaching English as a second or foreign language (García, 2014). However, the two organizations diverged when NABE focused its activism towards supporting the reauthorization of the Bilingual Education Act (García, 2014). Meanwhile, TESOL expanded its membership and international presence with the help of substantial government and private funding made available between 1950 and 1970 for the explicit purpose of expanding the teaching of English (Alatis & Straehle, 1997; Phillipson, 2009a). These funds were made available by the U.S. government and other prosperous organizations (e.g., Rockefeller Foundation), interested in the expansion of U.S. interests after World War II and recognizing the commercial and political opportunities that would proliferate through instruction of English nationally and abroad (Alatis, 1980; Alatis & Straehle, 1997).

Instead, NABE developed its identity around advocating for "educational equity and excellence for bilingual/multilingual students", becoming the "only national professional organization devoted to representing bilingual/multilingual students and bilingual education professionals" (NABE, 2018). This stood in contrast to TESOL IA's positioning as "the trusted global authority for knowledge and expertise in English language teaching" and their vision of advancing "the expertise of professionals who teach English to speakers of other languages in multilingual contexts worldwide" (Mission and Values, 2019). The significant difference in the organizations' mission and vision resulted in Fishman's (2009) apt observation: "seldom have [there existed]…two more different organizations: TESOL and NABE" (p. 314). That is not to say that NABE has never wavered in its advocacy towards bi/multilingualism. Although optimistic and supportive of the promise of Title VII and its reauthorization in 1974 for bilingual education ("NABE history", 2019), NABE also gradually experienced a shift towards more assimilationist English trends as an organization (García, 2019a). For example, most presentations at the NABE conference in the mid-2000s were centered on teaching English ("Past NABE conferences", 2019). While NABE has recovered some interest in multilingualism since, the organization has not yet wholeheartedly welcomed the exploration of translanguaging theory and practice.

2.2 Subsequent Critiques of the TESOL Organization

Since then, TESOL has voiced its support of bilingual education, issuing a position (but not policy) statement encouraging multilingualism (i.e., TESOL, 2004), and refuting notions of conflict between ESL and bilingual education (Cummins, 2009). This has not hindered other dissenters from voicing their independent critiques of TESOL's focus on second and foreign language learning of English rather than multilingualism (e.g., Auerbach, 1993; Lucas & Katz, 1994; Phillipson, 1992). A second assembled appeal for a more multilingually-focused TESOL emerged in the form of a BEIS symposium in TESOL's 2008 conference entitled "Imagining Multilingual TESOL", later published in TESOL Quarterly's June 2009 volume. The focal purpose of the symposium was to highlight the multilingual repertoires of the students and teachers represented by TESOL and encourage the organization to reflect that multilingual reality more inclusively in its vision, mission, and focus (Taylor, 2009). Acknowledging this as a contentious topic (Taylor, 2009), authors highlighted TESOL's need to: (a) identify the diverse languages spoken by students learning English (Taylor, 2009), (b) articulate a position encouraging the use of bilingual instructional strategies while discouraging the exclusion of students' home language in that instruction (Cummins, 2009), (c) recognize students' home languages by labeling students as emergent bilinguals[3] rather than English language learners (García, 2009a), (d) maintain relevancy as an international organization designed to meet the local and global needs of a multilingual world (Silver, 2009), (e) ensure sustainable English teaching that protects and ensures national language maintenance (Phillipson, 2009a), and (f) actively promote multilingualism by supporting mother-tongue medium instruction in international contexts (Skutnabb-Kangas, 2009).

A third summons emerged in 2013 with a TESOL Quarterly special issue on plurilingualism, challenging TESOL to actively recognize and incorporate learners' multilingualism at the individual level (Council of Europe, 2001). Riding on the wave of a palpable zeitgeist around linguistic fluidity and hierarchy that had developed in the fields of language education (Taylor & Snoddon, 2013) and featuring some of the same contributors from the 2009 published symposium, authors argued for the organization's embrace of more multi/pluri/translingual views and approaches in the teaching of English. In defining plurilingualism, authors described it as the focus on "unique aspects of individual repertoires and agency" (Marshall & Moore, 2013, p. 474) rather than the "broader social language context/contact(s) and the existence of several languages in a particular situation" connoted by multilingualism (Marshall & Moore, 2013, p. 474). Contributors argued for (a) recognition and value of teachers' plurilingualism as an instructional resource (Ellis, 2013; Maandebo Abiria, Early, & Kendrick, 2013), (b) encouraging students' to engage their plurilingual competencies in support of their production of academic English texts (Maandebo Abiria et al., 2013; Marshall & Moore, 2013; Willans, 2013), (c) adopting a critical stance towards plurilingual approaches that guards against neoliberal pressures (Flores, 2013a), and (d) departing from contemporary TESOL methodologies founded upon language compartmentalization (Lin, 2013). In the symposium section, authors presented examples of plurilingual pedagogical approaches across international settings, showcasing their application in a variety of English teaching contexts.

To mark the inception of a new journal in the NYS TESOL affiliate, García (2014) echoed parallel sentiments in her invited article, calling for the decentralization of English in TESOL by focusing on the power of translanguaging to support the entire repertoire of emergent bilingual students. Despite her encouragement for ESL and bilingual educators to join forces around translanguaging, there has been little action or change to merge the goals and foci of TESOL and bilingual education organizations (e.g., Sembiante, 2016). Instead, after García's usage of translanguaging (Williams, 1994) gained traction in bilingual education (i.e., García, 2009b), other socio- and applied linguistics scholars (mostly outside of TESOL) revived existing theories or conceived new theories to represent the different facets, constructs, and meanings of multilingualism, resulting in a current "panoply of

---

[3] García's term "emergent bilingual" generally refers to the K-12 context in U.S. schools. A term that may be more inclusive of adult education or which more broadly captures the languaging of a range of students and teachers may be "emergent-to-advanced".

lingualisms" (e.g., polylingualism, metrolingualism, multilingualism, plurilingualism, codemeshing; Marshall & Moore, 2018).

2.3   The Primacy of English in TESOL

Despite the presence of rich debate in academic journals around the nuanced similarities and differences across the lingualisms and the dynamic research documenting practical application of these theories, the majority of this work continues to be published outside of TESOL journals. In their place, TESOL persists in publishing research with a primary focus on English as a lingua franca (e.g., Matsumoto, 2018), as a foreign language (e.g., Lee & Lee, 2018; Teng, Sun, & Xu, 2018), as a second language (e.g., Bernstein, 2018; Lee & Mak, 2018), and as a native language (Levis, Sonsaat, Link, & Barriuso, 2016; Winke et al., 2018). For example, the latest special issue of TESOL Quarterly, as of the writing of this manuscript, concerned the connection between TESOL and English-medium instruction (2018, volume 52, issue 3). The danger in providing so much publication space and attention towards English in these different formats is the legitimization of concepts of language (i.e., first language, second language, native speaker, standard English) that have long been critiqued as a theoretical impossibility and as damaging deficit approaches (e.g., Kachru, 1994; Ortega, 2013; Phillipson & Skutnabb-Kangas, 1986; Sledd, 1969). A more serious allegation is the harmful social, psychological, economic, and political consequences that often result when English-medium education remains lauded and unquestioned even in a subtractive dominant-language form (Skutnabb-Kangas, 2009). In turn, such situations have the potential to reinforce social inequality under a neoliberal world order and to generate deficit orientations towards varieties of English that differ from the variety positioned as standardized.

Without contextualizing the sociopolitical role of English and its hegemonic potential, sole attention towards the teaching and learning of English in international contexts remains dangerous, and has even been equated to "crimes against humanity" (Skutnabb-Kangas, 2009). In maintaining its power in the linguistic hierarchy, English and a continued focus on its teaching, testing, and publishing implicitly (a) stigmatizes the languages and language varieties that English has dominated, (b) glorifies English as better (i.e., more superior, useful, beneficial), and (c) rationalizes and monopolizes interlinguistic relationships for access to the benefits of the cultures associated with English (Phillipson & Skutnabb-Kangas, 2013). Moreover, a continued focus on English within the pages of TESOL journals nullifies the issues and critiques of previous advocates for multilingualism present throughout TESOL's history. The question remains: Why, after successive calls for reorientation towards multilingual perspectives, does TESOL continue to resist acknowledging and empowering the role of emergent bilingual students' and teachers' other languages?

3   Why Translanguaging?

As previously mentioned, a "panoply of lingualisms" (Marshall & Moore, 2018) have emerged in the aftermath of the multilingual turn (May, 2014) that capture and contrast different perceptions and paradigms of multilingualism. What differentiates translanguaging from other post-structural terms (e.g., polylingualism, metrolingualism, multilingualism, plurilingualism, codemeshing, code-switching) is its validating and humanistic stance, breaking static conceptions of language as a sealed entity or a system of prescriptive rules/structures. A translanguaging approach is further distinguished by its social justice agenda, and its intent to position the fluid language practices of language-minoritized students as a political act (García & Li, 2014). Unique from other fluid languaging conceptualizations such as multilingualism (Canagarajah, 2011), translanguaging is designed to be transformative, eliminating hierarchies and prejudice towards languaging practices as it is studied and applied (García, 2014). For example, in contrast to the history and origin of plurilingualism, translanguaging was borne out of a need to empower language- minoritized students, to protect their language rights, and to affirm their complex discursive practices (García, 2009b; García & Kleifgen, 2010). Thus, a translanguaging lens affords an examination of students' fluid language practices in service of their purposes, identities, and meaning-making (Otheguy, García, & Reid, 2015), instead of at their expense (e.g., to bolster English linguistic imperialism or its commodification to fuel globalizing economies; Phillipson, 2009a; Flores, 2013a).

Such promises are crucially needed in TESOL to stand in fierce opposition to top-down, modernist, or neoliberal forces and to challenge the monolingual orthodoxy which dominates the TESOL field (Flores & Aneja, 2017; Valdés, 2020). Translanguaging's potential for TESOL is described poignantly by García when she states "Translanguaging could be a mechanism for social justice, debunking misconstructions about English, its speakers, learning English, bilingualism, and teaching English in a way that we as TESOL educators have long held dear" (2014, p. 4). We echo this advocacy and in the subsequent sections, further illustrate our reimagining of TESOL within the potential of translanguaging through repositioning English (E), Speakers of Other Languages (SOL), and Teaching (T).

4   Translanguaging and TESOL

In this section we address how we take up translanguaging and what promises translanguaging could bring to the TESOL field. We argue that a translanguaging lens could catalyze TESOL to embrace a multilingual identity by repositioning "English (E)" and "Speakers of Other Languages (SOL)." More importantly, a translanguaging lens could *transform* TESOL to contribute to a social justice agenda by rethinking what "Teaching (T)" means and how to better educate all emergent bilinguals deeply and justly.

4.1   Translanguaging

Translanguaging scholarship emerged in response to the post-structural paradigm shift in the "multilingual turn" (May, 2014; Ortega, 2013) or "post-multilingualism" era (Li, 2016) in which entrenched ideologies that frame monolingualism as the norm have been rejected and "language has begun to be conceptualized as a *series of social practices and actions* by speakers that are embedded in a web of *social and cognitive relations*" (García & Li, 2014, p. 9, original emphasis). Within these conversations, translanguaging has been theorized as a practice and a process – a practice to describe how bi/multilinguals organically engage in everyday language performances to make sense of their bilingual worlds (García, 2009b) and a process of multilingual speakers/writers making meaning with their single semio-linguistic repertoire (rather than separate linguistic systems), from which they dynamically, strategically, and functionally select and inhibit (or not) language and semiotic features to suit the sociolinguistic purposes of the context (García, 2009b; García & Li, 2014). A translanguaging lens defines bilinguals' language practices and languaging processes on their own terms – multilingual language users perform complex, fluid discursive practices that go beyond (or transcend) the conventions of socially/politically/geographically constructed named languages and encompass multisensory and multimodal forms of communication (Li Wei, 2017b; Otheguy et al., 2015). Such theorization disrupts conceptualizing language(s) as separate compartments in a hierarchical relationship and empowers language-minoritized individuals (García & Kleifgen, 2010; Vogel & García, 2017) by emphasizing their agency – their criticality and creativity (Li, 2011) – to mediate social and cognitive activities in different contact zones.

With the critical theoretical framing of translanguaging, it has also been advocated as a pedagogy in support of bilingual students' text and content comprehension, academic language development, and socioemotional and political stances (Creese & Blackledge, 2015; García, Johnson, & Seltzer, 2017). A translanguaging pedagogy calls upon both teachers and students to draw upon their entire semio-linguistic repertoires strategically in academic learning by recognizing bilingualism as a resource and validating hybrid language practices in English-dominated, monolingual classrooms (Canagarajah, 2011; García, 2009b). Rather than positioning multilingual learners as non-natives based upon their home language(s) and limited English, teachers in a translanguaging classroom treat students as "legitimate users of fluid language forms that reflect the dynamic nature of the communities they come from" (Flores, 2013b, p. 283) and provide heteroglossic, meaningful educational contexts that leverage all the language practices that they bring to school (Flores & Schissel, 2014; Khote & Tian, 2019). Therefore, as García and Kleifgen (2018) argue, "a translanguaging pedagogy is not simply a series of strategies and scaffolds, but also a philosophy of language and education that is centered on a bilingual minoritized community" (p. 80). It ultimately aims to liberate learner agency to the fullest and to transform schooling in ways that advance a social justice agenda (Tian & Link, 2019).

4.2   Translanguaging and E

"English (E)" in TESOL has been traditionally conceptualized under a structuralist notion as an objective fact possessed by native speakers or a prescriptive system of syntactic, semantic, morphological, and phonetic rules (Holliday, 2006; Phillipson, 1992). Such static conception privileges the acquisition of standardized American or British English as the norm while establishing a native/non-native speaker dichotomy, a hierarchy between inner circle Englishes, and the racialization of English as connected to Whiteness in which only those speaking a White-affiliated standardized American English are conceived as legitimate users/teachers of English. However, a translanguaging lens introduces a marked shift in repositioning "English" and aims to free languages and language varieties from linguistically structured hierarchies/inequalities.

With its post-structural focus on how to *language* (as a verb), a translanguaging or a translingual orientation (Canagarajah, 2013; García, 2009b) posits that "language resources are borrowed, mixed, and reconstructed as people use them for their needs in everyday life" (Canagarajah, 2014, p. 770). In other words, languages are variable, mobile, mixed, and are always in a fluid state of *becoming* within social, cultural, political and historical contexts (Blommaert, 2010). "English" in this sense is not a static/fixed noun but a progressive verb with an emergent status: there is no pure entity called standard English with a system of preconstructed grammatical rules; instead English is a social practice being (re)negotiated and (re) configured by multilingual speakers over time according to their values, interests, and language repertoires in various communicative situations. Different English-ing and English varieties along with "multiple grammars, vocabulary, accents, and pragmatic discourse conventions" (Marlina, 2014, p. 7) emerge from this process (see more work about World Englishes and English as a lingua franca in e.g., Canagarajah, 2006; Jenkins, 2006; Kachru, 1990; Kachru & Smith, 2008; Seargeant, 2012). A translanguaging lens therefore celebrates the dynamic, fluid, heterogeneous nature of "English" (English itself transcends the historical/political/geographical boundaries) and legitimizes all English varieties emerging from creative and critical language users under different situational and cultural contexts (see more in Canagarajah, 2014; García & Lin, 2018).

Moreover, with its critical theoretical underpinning on liberating minoritized languages, a translanguaging lens recognizes and critiques the hegemonic power of standardized English. As Seltzer and de los Ríos (2018) argue, a translanguaging orientation views "English" as "an ideological 'named language' (Makoni & Pennycook, 2006; Otheguy, García, & Reid, 2005) that leaves out the language practices of many language minoritized [speakers]" (p. 50). The mythical "standard English" is an idealized socially/politically established construct which centralizes White, prestigious monolingual speakers as the standard for linguistic mastery, keeping the power in the hands of a few. Translanguaging thus tends to destabilize the hegemonic discourses about minoritized languages/language varieties and to counteract monolingual bias which perpetuates ideologies of linguistic separation, purity, and English supremacy in language education.

4.3 Translanguaging and SOL

"Speakers of Other Languages (SOL)" in TESOL has been traditionally referred to as English as a Second Language (ESL) learners or English as a Foreign Language (EFL) learners. The distinction between these two primarily lies in the context of learning; that is, whether the target language, English, is widely used by the outside community beyond the classroom. For example, if students learn English in the U.S. where English is the dominant, societal language, they are conventionally categorized as ESL learners. However, such nomenclature is problematic as it is implicitly linked to "processes of (self-)otherization" (Prada & Turnbull, 2018, p. 10):

> Otherization refers to the "binary of us versus them" (Jamal, 2008, p. 116) and assumes (racial, religious, cultural) teachable/learnable differences between the learner's world and the world of the target language natives. When languages are presented as foreign or second, learners are socialized into the notion that the target language is less pertinent to their everyday realities. Perhaps more importantly, this presentation bolsters the notion that L2/FL learners are second to native speakers, as they are epistemologically construed as ever-learners whose communicative potential is summarized by their status as L2/FL speakers. Similarly, this nomenclature also ignores the realities of those learners who have "multiple native languages" (Rothman & Treffers-Daller, 2014, p. 1), perpetuating misconceptions that do not coincide with today's societies, and continuing to promote the one-fits-all view of learner profiles in the FL/L2 language classroom.

As Prada and Turnbull (2018) sharply point out, the terminologies referring to language learners commonly used in TESOL (e.g., SOL, EFL/ESL learners, English language learners) reflect entrenched monolingual ideologies which artificially create false dichotomies (e.g. native/non-native, standard/non-standard) to normalize English as a monolithic entity and view multilingual speakers as deficient or needing remediation for not acquiring native-like proficiency (Bonfiglio, 2010). These framings also ignore the complexity of students' linguistic profiles, the language varieties they have developed and yield for different purposes in the different areas of their lives, and only focus on what they lack, rather than what they have already achieved in their ever-expanding linguistic repertoire (García & Kleifgen, 2018).

A translanguaging lens rejects "linguistic Othering" (Flores, 2013b) and the imagined/idealized native-speaker as the target model. In a translanguaged TESOL classroom, language learners are encouraged to bring their diverse funds of knowledge (Moll, Amanti, Neff, & Gonzalez, 1992) and full range of cultural and linguistic repertoires as strategic resources; they are empowered to develop their criticality, creativity (Li, 2011), and agency in academic tasks. Therefore, to liberate language learners from the othering notion of ESL/EFL and protect minoritized speakers' language rights, we, adhering to García's (2009a) advocacy (also see García,

Kleifgen, & Falchi, 2008), propose to refer to SOL as emergent bilinguals in TESOL. This terminological change emphasizes students' potential in developing their bilingualism on their bilingual continua, seeing their home language and bilingual practices as resources in contributing to their English language development. More importantly, "emergent bilinguals are seen as having an *advantage* over those who speak English only and for whom becoming bilingual will be more difficult" (García, 2009a, p. 322, emphasis added). They are positioned as "knowers, thinkers, and imaginative meaning-makers" (García, 2014, p. 8) with multilingual repertoires and abilities to navigate successful communication in different contact zones (Pennycook, 2012) rather than "ever-learning, underperforming individuals who seek to meet a standard that is external to their experience" (Prada & Turnbull, 2018, p. 12). For us, the term "emergent bilinguals" decentralizes the hegemonic power of English and reclaims the bi/multilingual purpose of TESOL: learning English is to expand students' linguistic repertoire to include new, additional features to develop multilingual skills and competences. As Li Wei (2017a) said at a TESOL Summit in Greece, "Every lesson in TESOL should be about *English-in-multilingualism*, not just English" (p. 2, emphasis added).

4.4   Translanguaging and T

With "E" and "SOL" being repositioned through a translanguaging lens, we finally turn to illustrate how translanguaging could transform "Teaching (T)" in this section. Influenced by second language acquisition theories, traditional English teaching has been dominated by monolingual ideologies, enforcing students to ignore the metalinguistic affordances of their other languages and navigate English as a monolingual speaker according to valued, standardized notions of a national language while holding the native speaker as the idealized target model and positioning the teaching/learning goal as acquiring native-like proficiency. However, such goals not only seem impossible and unnecessary, but also deviate from the real purpose of learning English. As Li Wei (2017b) states,

> The actual purpose of learning new languages – to become bilingual and multilingual, rather than to replace the learner's L1 to become another monolingual – often gets forgotten or neglected, and the bilingual, rather than monolingual, speaker is rarely used as the model for teaching and learning. (p. 8)

Through a translanguaging lens which takes a holistic, dynamic view of learner's language development, the true, ultimate goal of teaching/learning English is to organically expand an individual's holistic, complex semio-linguistic repertoire to appropriate and incorporate new cultural and linguistic features, experiences, and values with old ones for strategic, flexible, and functional use under different contact zones (Khote & Tian, 2019; Prada & Turnbull, 2018). Therefore, such orientation disrupts the traditional view of seeing English teaching/learning as a linear, expectation-riddled addition of developing double monolingualism and rejuvenates the bilingual purpose of learning English.

Translanguaging in this sense affords counter-narratives to conventional approaches (such as the Direct Method and Communicative Language Teaching) to English language education. It places students' emergent bilingualism at the center and strategically creates heteroglossic educational spaces for all learners to draw upon their entire cultural and linguistic repertoires as resources in meaning making and performing academic tasks (García, 2009b; García & Li, 2014). Some extant studies have demonstrated the potential of utilizing translanguaging pedagogies in different specific ways to contribute to English reading and writing (e.g., García & Li, 2014; García & Kleyn, 2016). For instance, by grouping students according to their home language but heterogeneously by English language ability, teachers allowed students to use their full linguistic repertoires to share opinions and co-construct understandings of English texts in group discussions. Students in this case could serve as linguistic resources to one another, helping to build off their ideas and language (García & Li, 2014). Furthermore, by intentionally choosing culturally relevant texts (which resonated with students' backgrounds/communities) or texts incorporating translanguaging as a literary device, teachers created an inclusive environment where students felt safe/comfortable and their identity affirmed. This strategy not only enhanced students' active participation and comprehension, but also enabled students to bring their whole selves/voices into the classroom (Ebe, 2016). In English writing activities, by opening up the drafting space without mandating their language use, teachers created more opportunities for students to express their thoughts and then gauged students' language use and needs more specifically (Fu, 2003).

We see that translanguaging holds the promise of being a scaffold to understand English lessons and produce English texts, and more importantly, it could *transform* TESOL classrooms into a hybrid space which recognize the value and importance of local English and other language varieties and affiliated cultures. What can become fostered in these spaces is cross-cultural/linguistic awareness among learners (Canagarajah, 2014; Sifakis, 2004) in English teaching. Overall, a translanguaging lens represents a paradigm shift from the teaching of English language to employing emergent bilinguals' fluid language practices in support of their English learning, thereby giving them more agency and transforming the role of English teachers and students (García, 2014). It further challenges the monolingual model which centers on native-speakerism and English supremacy and teaches emergent bilinguals in more socially just and meaningful ways.

5   Translanguaging's Lack of Traction in TESOL

Thus far, translanguaging has experienced very little traction in TESOL. Although the organization has published several articles and pieces featuring translanguaging (e.g., approximately 23 or 6% of articles in *TESOL Quarterly* since 2013 and 14 or

4% of articles in *TESOL Journal* since 2014), these only represent a small portion of the number of articles published in the pages of these journals each year and since 2013/2014. Moreover, fewer translanguaging-related topics and approaches are discussed in TESOL's other, more ubiquitous avenues of publication and outreach (i.e., TESOL Connections, The English Language Bulletin, The TESOL blog, Interest Section Newsletters, White Papers, News Briefs, Policy Briefs). In Canagarajah's (2016) review of TESOL's half a century of pedagogy, research, and theory, he mentions the field's "growing realization that English cannot be separated from other languages" (p. 19) but spends a sole, brief paragraph describing the attention provided to plurilingualism and other multilingual approaches, admitting to room for further exploration. Bilingual education remains an auxiliary interest section in TESOL's annual conference rather than a foundational throughline undergirding all activities. In this section, we discuss TESOL's current status and our views on the potential factors that limit TESOL's ability or willingness to embrace a more multilingual positioning in its purview and advocacy.

TESOL IA is a non-profit professional organization that has grown to have immense power, presence, and influence as the "largest organization for English language educators" (TESOL, 2016). It currently positions itself as a "leader in the field of English language teaching" (TESOL 2018a, p. 2), and reports its purpose to be "the teaching and learning of English as an additional language" (TESOL, 2018b). Having experienced a "great desire to be all things to all people" (Alatis, 1987, p. 18), TESOL IA currently employs 23 staff members to manage its numerous subdivisions comprising conference services, finance and administration, membership and strategic communications, professional learning and research, and publishing and product development. The organization has been led by an executive director and governed by a 12-member board of directors since its inception, and includes staff members that preside over marketing, data analysis, and press inquiry matters (TESOL, 2018a). In its first twenty years, TESOL IA established and maintained a substantial number of publications (e.g., TESOL newsletter, TESOL Quarterly, training program and membership directories, bibliographies, professional preparation materials, textbooks), the majority of which were purchasable and which directly funded the TESOL organization. These materials reached more than 1800 libraries and educational institutions in 1987 (Alatis, 1987) and have certainly expanded in their reach since.

Along with an increasing availability of publications each year and the emergence of the TESOL Press as its publication hub, TESOL IA's net worth has grown from $24,000 in 1966 (or $182, 213 in 2017 when accounting for inflation; Alatis, 1987) to $5,898,345 in 2017 (TESOL Annual Report, 2016–2017). Its impressive revenue is aided in part by the other services it offers (i.e., online courses, certificate programs, academies) and the membership dues it collects annually from its 11,690 members. TESOL IA has also garnered authority and impact from its alliances with governmental bodies (e.g., United States Department of State), professional unions (e.g., American Federation of Teachers), publishing houses (e.g., Oxford University Press; Houghton Mifflin Harcourt; Cambridge University Press), and educational organizations (e.g. VIPABC, National Geographic Learning, VIPkid) who commit their (financial and other) support of the organization's mission. Notably, several of the supporting or allied organizations are exclusively focused on promoting the learning of English (i.e., the British Council, the Center for English Language Learning, China Daily twenty-first Century, and VIPkid; TESOL Annual Report, 2016–2017). In a 2018 press release describing the alliance formed between TESOL IA and China Daily twenty-first Century (an English education media company that is a subsidiary of China's sole national English-language newspaper), TESOL IA will provide professional learning events, teacher workshops, language teaching events such as speech competitions, and English language publications to China. In exchange, TESOL IA will receive access to 2000 new Chinese members who will form "a new generation of Chinese TESOL professionals" and "help increase TESOL's global presence and connectivity" (Cutler, 2019).

This picture may be the very situation that researchers in language education, informed and vigilant of the dangers of neoliberalism, have warned against. At a systemic level, neoliberalism results when the market and state merge to exert control in the form of corporate governance (Klein, 2007), such as when institutional forces encourage the flow of capitalism that benefits transnational corporations and economically-privileged individuals and groups (Flores, 2013a). In the age of new capitalism, the education field has increasingly become colonized by the economic field (Flores, 2013a), with language playing a more central role in the economic and media success of people, companies, products, and nations (Fairclough, 2002). The linguistic capital endowed to the holder of a privileged language (in this case, English) and these individuals' belief in the power and legitimacy of English translates into a market price that sustains the continued promotion of English and the social, political, and financial growth of organizations who participate in its enterprise (Bourdieu, 1992). What has resulted is a "global explosion of commercial English language teaching" (Gray, 2010a, p. 714), the branding and commodification of English and of the organizations providing English as service or product (Gray, 2010b), and the rise of a financially lucrative publishing industry (Gray, 2010a). Propelling this trend is the interest of publishing houses to keep publishing their books in monolingual English in order to attract a larger, more international market. When these activities are pursued without a critical lens towards the threat of hegemony, the potential for English linguistic neoimperialism intensifies, transforming English into colonizing tender in global linguistic market (Block, 2008; Phillipson, 2008). These associations between neoliberalism and TESOL are not new: TESOL has previously been critiqued as an export item for the British and Americans that perpetuates the colonial domination of other languages and cultures, positioning Western life and language as progressive, indispensable, and superior (e.g., Bunce, Phillipson, Rapatahana, & Tupas, 2016; Flores & Anjea, 2017; García, 2014; Lin & Luke, 2006; Motha, 2006; Phillipson, 1992, 2008, 2009b).

Returning to our original question, the lack of traction that translanguaging (among other multilingual approaches) has experienced in TESOL may emerge, in part, from TESOL IA's current status and identity, and the neoliberal forces that it adheres to, which in turn, strengthen its persistent and predominant alignment towards English. In contrast, hybridity in language practices, such as those engendered by translanguaging, have been taken up and popularized in other fields of language education. Scholars in foreign language (FL) have begun to acknowledge the affordances of translanguaging and the importance of a holistic perspective of bilingualism if they are "to effectively prepare FL learners to engage in the multiple discursive practices of bilinguals outside the classroom in the real world" (Turnbull, 2016, p. 6). Although Turnbull's ideas have received critique from García (2019b) for not sufficiently challenging modernist language ideologies, the dialogue that Turnbull and others' work have promulgated around entertaining translanguaging as a new avenue for FL education is productive in and of itself, promoting future inquiry into this area. Studies in FL shed light on how translanguaging provides creative and agentive avenues of scaffolding, meaning making, and negotiation in FL classrooms that have previously been restricted by dominant monolingual language pedagogies (e.g., Leung & Scarino, 2016; Stathopoulou, 2016; Wang, 2016; Li Wei, 2017a, 2017b).

Scholars in second language acquisition have also begun to spurn monolingualism and nativeness in favor of bi/multilingual approaches and perspectives (Lynch, 2017; May, 2014; Ortega, 2013). Researchers are deconstructing core SLA concepts of language proficiency, age of language acquisition, and cross-linguistic influences through a bilingual lens and through the tenets of translanguaging (e.g., Canagarajah, 2011; Butler, 2012). Stemming from concepts of dynamic bilingualism (García, 2009a, 2009b) in bilingual education, translanguaging emerged and was quickly engaged and extended within the bilingual education field (e.g., García & Lin, 2016; Blackledge & Creese, 2010; Creese & Blackledge, 2010; Hornberger & Link, 2012). Since 2009, researchers in bilingual education have further conceptualized, extended, and applied translanguaging theory and practice with emergent bilingual students and teachers in a range of dual language and English medium contexts (e.g., Gort, 2015; Gort & Sembiante, 2015; Palmer, Martínez, Mateus, & Henderson, 2014; Martínez, Hikida, & Durán, 2014; Sayer, 2013; Li & García, 2017). As demonstrated in these examples, bi/multilingual approaches and perspectives have been leveraged in other language education fields previously aligned with monolingual orientations. Not only does this uptake evidentiate the relevance and validity of multilingual approaches to language education, but also the achievability of such a shift for TESOL and its central organization.

The multilingual turn in the fields of language education have also created a productive space for the discussion and critique of translanguaging as researchers and practitioners consider and apply the theories and practices in their different language fields. Several examinations of its meaning and implications have elicited suggestions for expansion, disagreement over conceptualizations, and concerns for further thought. In proposing new avenues for translanguaging research, Poza (2017) suggests forging more ties to critical pedagogy while Turner and Lin (2017) recommend acknowledging named languages to enhance the theory's potential. In voicing their concerns, MacSwan (2017) argues for the necessity of recognizing discrete languages and their linguistic evidence (e.g., codeswitching) while Jaspers (2018) warns of translanguaging's unrealistic claims as a socially transformational and critical force. While some scholars have already considered some of the implications for translanguaging in TESOL (e.g., García, 2014; Canagarajah, 2014; Li Wei, 2017a, 2017b), there are many more areas for generative discussion available to TESOL-affiliated scholars who might carve a new, nuanced path for the meaning and use of translanguaging in TESOL.

In the same vein, multilingual approaches are not immune to neoliberal concerns, with connections between neoliberalism and the rise of bi/multi/plurilingualism having been identified by several scholars. While some name translanguaging explicitly (Block, 2018; Flores & Bale, 2016; Kubota, 2014), others discuss plurilingualism and alternative multilingual approaches in general (Block, Gray, & Holborow, 2012; Flores, 2013a), cautioning against the promotion of multilingualism as the latest desirable characteristic of the ideal, enterprising neoliberal subject who adapts themselves to meet the needs and desires of larger economic forces (Foucault, 2008). Scholars suspicious of this trend suggest several avenues for future inquiry: (a) acknowledge that fluid language practices are not a European development, but have existed and continue to exist in all parts of the world (Flores, 2013a), (b) consider critically whose interests are served by popularity of different bi/multi/pluri-lingualisms to guard against the commodification of multilingualism in similar ways to that of English (Flores, 2013a; Kubota, 2014), (c) problematize and deconstruct the limits of linguistic and societal norms so as to break down the current capitalistic order (Flores, 2013a; Kubota, 2014), (d) expand multilingual approaches to encompass and attend practically to redistribution issues in a political economy (Block, 2018), (e) reflect critically on monoglossic language constraints in academic publishing (Flores & Bale, 2016; Kubota, 2014), and the privileged English and bi/multi/plurilingual statuses of scholars within academic institutions who "accrue cultural, economic, and symbolic capital from presenting and publishing [in this system] while moving further away from real-world problems" (Kubota, 2014, p. 17). These neoliberal concerns and the aforementioned critiques of translanguaging are ripe for examination by TESOL members who can pioneer and conceive of responses and implications in ways that are specific to the interest of other TESOL members and the organization-at-large.

6   Conclusion and Implications

In his invited article to celebrate the 20 years of TESOL organization's existence, Alatis (1987) advised members to keep an eye on the future expansion of TESOL and how international its members wanted the organization to become. As TESOL IA nears its 53rd anniversary, we call on its members to consider critically the organization's identity and positioning and the necessity and potential of its role in advocating for all the languages of its emergent bilingual students and teachers. The design and vision of the TESOL organization before the postmodern turn (e.g., Susen, 2015), the social turn (e.g., Block, 2003), and the multilingual turn (e.g., May, 2014) cannot be the same as existed after these paradigm shifts have brought past errors to light. That is, many advances in research and understanding of the benefits and necessity of multilingualism as opposed to a separate, monoglossic focus on English have emerged since the organization's founding in 1966. As the current professional and industry giant that it is now, TESOL IA has a responsibility to move away from being "everything to everyone", and instead, use its power and its market presence to take a meaningful stand for students' other languages, regardless of the profit, power, and influence it may lose temporarily in doing so. The concessions made in the past (e.g., the addition of a bilingual interest section, the publication of a position statement on multilingualism, and a special issue on plurilingualism), are no longer adequate and cannot exist concurrently while publishing, sponsoring, and promoting articles, teaching materials, and professional development programs that negate or ignore the language fields' new understanding of multilingualism and multilingual approaches.

To take its multilingual turn, TESOL can consider the affordances of translanguaging as a (a) theoretical paradigm that shifts foundational assumptions and perspectives in the field, (b) pedagogy informing TESOL teacher education and professional development, and (c) organic languaging practices occurring naturally and authentically in TESOL classrooms. These three areas of inquiry present multidimensional avenues into the exploration of translanguaging by the diverse stakeholders and members represented by TESOL. The theoretical potential of translanguaging might be examined by scholars, while both researchers and practitioners can investigate the pedagogical possibilities of incorporating translanguaging into instruction, and students and teachers can consider how their organic translanguaging practices are supportive of their English learning and use. Translanguaging can provide the crossroads for Bilingual Education and TESOL to work together, with both organizations and fields communally pursuing a focus away from English towards language heterogeneity and towards transforming limiting structures and conceptions of language. Our hope is that TESOL will heed the incessant call throughout its history to shift its macro-discourse and embrace an identity that advocates for English language learning and teaching through support of bi/multilingualism. Translanguaging can be the vehicle in support of those efforts to help reposition English in the eyes of TESOL as only one of the languages in teachers and students' rich language repertoires.

Acknowledgements We would like to express our appreciation to Dr. Ofelia García for her support and encouragement of this piece. Her valuable and constructive suggestions enhanced the arguments and conceptualization, while echoing the importance of this work. We would also like to extend our thanks to Dr. Alain Bengochea and Dr. Jamie L. Schissel for their tireless manuscript review and constructive feedback which helped us to further refine and improve the ideas in this piece.

References

Alatis, J. E. (1980). National language policy: Making the implicit explicit. In J. F. Povey (Ed.), *Language policy and language teaching: Essays in honor of Clifford H. Prator* (pp. 11–24). Culver City, CA: English Language Services.

Alatis, J. E. (1987). The growth of professionalism in TESOL: Challenges and prospects for the future. *TESOL Quarterly, 21*(1), 9–19.

Alatis, J. E., & Straehle, C. A. (1997). The universe of English: Imperialism, chauvinism, and paranoia. In L. E. Smith & M. L. Forman (Eds.), *World Englishes 2000* (pp. 1–20). Honolulu, Hawaii: University of Hawaii.

Auerbach, E. (1993). Reexamining ESL only in the ESL classroom. *TESOL Quarterly, 27*, 9–32.

Bernstein, K. A. (2018). The perks of being peripheral: English learning and participation in a preschool classroom network of practice. *TESOL Quarterly, 52*(4), 798–844.

Blackledge, A., & Creese, A. (2010). *Multilingualism: A critical perspective*. London, UK: Continuum.

Block, D. (2003). *The social turn in second language acquisition*. Edinburgh, Scotland: Edinburgh University Press.

Block, D. (2008). Language education and globalization. In S. May & N. H. Hornberger (Eds.), *Encyclopedia of Language and Education* (Vol. 1, pp. 1–13). Berlin, Germany: Springer.

Block, D. (2018). The political economy of language education research (or the lack thereof): Nancy Fraser and the case of translanguaging. *Critical Inquiry in Language Studies, 15*(4), 237–257.

Block, D., Gray, J., & Holborow, M. (2012). *Neoliberalism and applied linguistics*. London, UK: Routledge.

Blommaert, J. (2010). *The sociolinguistics of globalization* (Cambridge approaches to language contact). Cambridge, UK/New York, NY: Cambridge University Press.

Bonfiglio, T. P. (2010). *Mother tongues and nations: The invention of the native speakers*. Berlin, Germany: Walter de Gruyter.

Bourdieu, P. (1992). *Language and symbolic power*. Cambridge, UK: Polity.

Bunce, P., Phillipson, R., Rapatahana, V., & Tupas, R. (Eds.) (2016). *Why English? Confronting the hydra*. Bristol, UK: Multilingual Matters.

Butler, Y. G. (2012). Bilingualism/multilingualism and second-language acquisition. In T. K. Bhatia & W. C. Ritchie (Eds.), *The handbook of bilingualism and multilingualism* (2nd ed., pp. 109–136). Oxford, UK: Wiley-Blackwell.

Canagarajah, A. S. (2006). The place of world Englishes in composition: Pluralization continued. *College Composition and Communication, 57*, 586–619.

Canagarajah, A. S. (2011). Translanguaging in the classroom: Emerging issues for research and pedagogy. In W. Li (Ed.), *Applied linguistics review* (Vol. 2, pp. 1–27). Berlin, Germany: De Gruyter Mouton.

Canagarajah, A. S. (2013). *Translingual practice: Global Englishes and cosmopolitan relations*. Abingdon, UK: Routledge.

Canagarajah, A. S. (2014). In search of a new paradigm for teaching English as an international language. *TESOL Journal, 5*(4), 767–785.

Canagarajah, A. S. (2016). TESOL as a professional community: A half-century of pedagogy, research, and theory. *TESOL Quarterly, 50*(1), 7–41.

Council of Europe. (2001). *A common European framework of reference for languages: Learning, teaching, assessment*. Cambridge, UK: Cambridge University Press.

Creese, A., & Blackledge, A. (2010). Translanguaging in the bilingual classroom: A pedagogy for learning and teaching? *Modern Language Journal, 94*(1), 103–115.

Creese, A., & Blackledge, A. (2015). Translanguaging and identity in educational settings. *Annual Review of Applied Linguistics, 35*, 20–35.

Cummins, J. (2009). Literacy and English language learners: A shifting landscape for students, teachers, researchers, and policymakers makers. *Educational Researcher, 38*(5), 382–83.

Cutler, D. (2019, March 8). *TESOL announces continued partnership with 21st century education* [Press Release]. Retrieved from https://www.tesol.org/about-tesol/press-room/2019/03/08/tesol-announces-continued-partnership-with-21st-century-education

Ebe, A. E. (2016). Student voices shining through: Exploring translanguaging as a literary device. In O. García & T. Kleyn (Eds.), *Translanguaging with multilingual students: Learning from classroom moments* (pp. 57–82). New York, NY: Routledge.

Ellis, E. (2013). The ESL teacher as plurilingual: An Australian perspective. *TESOL Quarterly, 47*(3), 446–471.

Fairclough, N. (2002). Language in new capitalism. *Discourse and Society, 13*(2), 163–166.

Fishman, J. A. (2009). Is a fuller relinguification of TESOL desirable? *TESOL Quarterly, 43*(2), 313–317.

Flores, N. (2013a). The unexamined relationship between neoliberalism and plurilingualism: A cautionary tale. *TESOL Quarterly, 47*(3), 500–520.

Flores, N. (2013b). Silencing the subaltern: Nation-state/colonial Governmentality and bilingual education in the United States. *Critical Inquiry in Language Studies, 10*(4), 263–287.

Flores, N., & Aneja, G. (2017). "Why needs hiding?" Translingual (re)orientations in TESOL teacher education. *Research in the Teaching of English, 51*(4), 441–463.

Flores, N., & Bale, J. (2016). Socio-political issues in bilingual education. In O. Garciá & A. Lin (Eds.), *Encyclopedia of Language and Education* (3rd ed., Vol. 5, Bilingual Education, pp.1–13). Dordrecht, The Netherlands: Springer.

Flores, N., & Schissel, J. L. (2014). Dynamic bilingualism as the norm: Envisioning a Heteroglossic approach to standards-based reform. *TESOL Quarterly, 48*(3), 454–479.

Foucault, M. (2008). *The birth of biopolitics: Lectures at the college de France, 1978–1979.* New York, NY: Picador.

Fu, D. (2003). *An island of English.* Portsmouth, NH: Heinemann.

García, O. (2009a). Emergent bilinguals and TESOL: What's in a name? *TESOL Quarterly, 43*(2), 322–326.

García, O. (2009b). *Bilingual education in the 21st century: A global perspective.* Oxford, UK: Wiley/Blackwell.

García, O. (2014). TESOL translanguaged in NYS: Alternative perspectives. *NYS TESOL Journal, 1*(1), 2–10.

García, O. (2019a, April 28). Personal interview.

García, O. (2019b). Reflections on Turnbull's reframing of foreign language education: Bilingual epistemologies. *International Journal of Bilingual Education and Bilingualism, 22*(5), 628–638.

García, O., Johnson, J., & Seltzer, K. (2017). *The translanguaging classroom: Leveraging student bilingualism for learning.* Philadelphia, PA: Caslon.

García, O., & Kleifgen, J. A. (2010). *Educating emergent bilinguals: Policies, programs, and practices for English language learners* (1st ed.). New York, NY: Teachers College Press.

García, O., & Kleifgen, J. A. (2018). *Educating emergent bilinguals: Policies, programs and practices for English language learners* (2nd ed.). New York, NY: Teachers College Press.

García, O., Kleifgen, J. A., & Falchi, L. (2008). *Equity in the education of emergent bilinguals: The case of English language learners* (Equity Matters Research Review No. 1). New York, NY: Teachers College. Retrieved from https://eric.ed.gov/?id=ED524002

García, O., & Kleyn, T. (2016). *Translanguaging with multilingual students: Learning from classroom moments.* New York, NY: Routledge.

García, O., & Li, W. (2014). *Translanguaging: Language, bilingualism and education.* New York, NY: Palgrave Macmillan.

García, O., & Lin, A. (2016). Translanguaging and bilingual education. In O. García, A. Lin, & S. May (Eds.), *Bilingual Education (Vol. 5). Encyclopedia of Language and Education* (pp. 117–130). New York, NY: Springer.

García, O., & Lin, A. (2018). English and multilingualism. In P. Seargeant, A. Hewings, & S. Pihlaja (Eds.), *Routledge handbook of English language studies* (pp. 77–92). New York, NY: Routledge.

Gort, M. (2015). Transforming literacy learning and teaching through translanguaging and other typical practices associated with "doing being bilingual". *International Multilingual Research Journal, 9*(1), 1–6.

Gort, M., & Sembiante, S. F. (2015). Navigating hybridized language learning spaces through translanguaging pedagogy: Dual language preschool teachers' languaging practices in support of emergent bilingual children's performance of academic discourse. *International Multilingual Research Journal, 9*(1), 7–25.

Gray, J. (2010a). The branding of English and the culture of the new capitalism: Representations of the world of work in English language textbooks. *Applied Linguistics, 31*(5), 714–733.

Gray, J. (2010b). *The construction of English: Culture, consumerism and promotion in the ELT Global Coursebook*. Basingstoke, UK: Palgrave Macmillan.

Holliday, A. (2006). Native-speakerism. *ELT Journal, 60*, 385–387.

Hornberger, N. H., & Link, H. (2012). Translanguaging and transnational literacies in multilingual classrooms: A bilingual lens. *International Journal of Bilingual Education and Bilingualism, 15*(3), 261–278.

Jamal, A. (2008). Civil liberties and the otherization of Arab and Muslim Americans. In A. Jamal & N. Naber (Eds.), *Race and Arab Americans before and after 9/11: From invisible citizens to visible subjects* (pp. 114–130). Syracuse, NY: Syracuse University Press.

Jaspers, J. (2018). The transformative limits of translanguaging. *Language & Communication, 58*, 1–10.

Jenkins, J. (2006). Current perspectives on teaching world Englishes and English as a lingua franca. *TESOL Quarterly, 40*, 157–181.

Kachru, B. (1990). World Englishes and applied linguistics. *World Englishes, 9*, 3–20.

Kachru, B. (1994). Monolingual bias in SLA research. *TESOL Quarterly, 28*(4), 795–800.

Kachru, B., & Smith, L. E. (2008). *Cultures, contexts, and world Englishes*. New York, NY: Routledge.

Khote, N., & Tian, Z. (2019). Translanguaging in culturally sustaining systemic functional linguistics: Developing a Heteroglossic space with multilingual learners. *Translation and Translanguaging in Multilingual Contexts, 5*(1), 5–28.

Klein, C. (2007). The valuation of plurilingual competences in an open European labour market. *International Journal of Multilingualism, 4*, 262–282.

Kubota, R. (2014). The multi/plural turn, postcolonial theory, and neoliberal multiculturalism: Complicities and implications for applied linguistics. *Applied Linguistics, 37*(4), 1–22.

Lee, I., & Mak, P. (2018). Metacognition and metacognitive instruction in second language writing classrooms. *TESOL Quarterly, 52*(4), 721–1122.

Lee, K., & Lee, H. (2018). An EAP professional development program for graduate students in an English-medium instruction context. *TESOL Quarterly, 52*(4), 1097–1107.

Leung, C., & Scarino, A. (2016). Reconceptualizing the nature of goals and outcomes in language/s education. *The Modern Language Journal, 100*(S1), 81–95.

Levis, J. M., Sonsaat, S., Link, S., & Barriuso, T. A. (2016). Native and nonnative teachers of L2 pronunciation: Effects on learner performance. *TESOL Quarterly, 50*(4), 894–931.

Li, W. (2011). Moment analysis and translanguaging space: Discursive construction of identities by multilingual Chinese youth in Britain. *Journal of Pragmatics, 43*, 1222–1235.

Li, W. (2016). New Chinglish and the post-multilingualism challenge: Translanguaging ELF in China. *Journal of English as a Lingua Franca, 5*(1), 1–25.

Li Wei. (2017a). *Translanguaging and the Goal of TESOL*. Summit on the Future of the TESOL Profession. Retrieved from https://www.tesol.org/docs/default-source/ppt/li-wei.pdf?sfvrsn=0&sfvrsn=0

Li Wei. (2017b). Translanguaging as a practical theory of language. *Applied Linguistics, 39*, 1–23. https://doi.org/10.1093/applin/amx039

Li, W., & García, O. (2017). From researching translanguaging to translanguaging research. In K. King, Y.-J. Lai, & S. May (Eds.), *Research Methods (Vol. 10). Encyclopedia of Language and Education*. New York, NY: Springer. https://doi.org/10.1007/978-3-319-02329-8_16-1

Lin, A. (2013). Toward paradigmatic change in TESOL methodologies: Building plurilingual pedagogies from the ground up. *TESOL Quarterly, 47*(3), 521–545.

Lin, A., & Luke, A. (2006). Special issue introduction: Coloniality, postcoloniality, and TESOL: Can a spider weave its way out of the web that it is being woven into just as it weaves? *Critical Inquiry in Language Studies, 3*(2&3), 65–73.

Lucas, T., & Katz, A. (1994). Reframing the debate: The roles of native languages in English-only programs for language minority students. *TESOL Quarterly, 28*, 537–562.

Lynch, A. (2017). Bilingualism and second language acquisition. In N. Van Deusen-Scholl & S. May (Eds.), *Second and Foreign Language Education, Encyclopedia of Language and Education (Vol. 4)* (pp. 43–55). Dordrecht, The Netherlands: Springer.

Maandebo Abiria, D., Early, M., & Kendrick, M. (2013). Plurilingual pedagogical practices in a policy-constrained context: A northern Ugandan case study. *TESOL Quarterly, 47*(3), 567–590.

MacSwan, J. (2017). A multilingual perspective on translanguaging. *American Educational Research Journal, 54*, 167–201.

Makoni, S., & Pennycook, A. (Eds.). (2006). *Disinventing and reconstituting languages*. Clevedon, UK: Multilingual Matters.

Marlina, R. (2014). The pedagogy of English as an international language (EIL): More reflections and dialogues. In R. Marlina & R. A. Giri (Eds.), *Pedagogy of English as an international language: Perspectives from scholars, teachers and students* (pp. 1–19). New York, NY: Springer.

Marshall, S., & Moore, D. (2013). 2B or not 2B plurilingual? Navigating languages literacies, and plurilingual competence in postsecondary education in Canada. *TESOL Quarterly, 47*(3), 472–499.

Marshall, S., & Moore, D. (2018). Plurilingualism amid the panoply of lingualisms: Addressing critiques and misconceptions in education. *International Journal of Multilingualism, 15*(1), 19–34.

Martínez, R., Hikida, M., & Durán, L. (2014). Unpacking ideologies of linguistic purism: How dual language teachers make sense of everyday translanguaging. *International Multilingual Research Journal, 9*(1), 26–42.

Matsumoto, Y. (2018). "Because we are peers, we actually understand": Third-party participant assistance in English as a lingua franca classroom. *TESOL Quarterly, 52*(4), 845–876.

May, S. (Ed.). (2014). *The multilingual turn: Implications for SLA, TESOL and bilingual education*. New York, NY: Routledge.

Mission and Values. (2019). In *TESOL International Association*. Retrieved from https://www.tesol.org/about-tesol/association-governance/mission-and-values

Moll, L., Amanti, C., Neff, D., & Gonzalez, N. (1992). Funds of knowledge for teaching: Using a qualitative approach to connect homes and classrooms. *Theory Into Practice, 31*(2), 132–141.

Motha, S. (2006). Decolonizing ESOL: Negotiating linguistic power in U.S. public school classrooms. *Critical Inquiry in Language Studies, 3*(2&3), 75–100.

NABE. (2018). *NABE's mission*. Retrieved December 20th, 2018 from http://nabe.org/nabes-mission

NABE history. (2019, June 8). Retrieved from http://nabe.org/nabehistory

OCR sets guidelines for fulfilling Lau decisions. (1975). Linguistic. *Reporter, 18*(1), 5–7.

Ortega, L. (2013). Ways forward for a bi/multilingual turn in SLA. In S. May (Ed.), *The multilingual turn: Implications for SLA, TESOL and bilingual education*. New York, NY: Routledge.

Otheguy, R., García, O., & Reid, W. (2015). Clarifying translanguaging and deconstructing named languages: A perspective from linguistics. *Applied Linguistics Review, 6*(3), 281–307.

Palmer, D. K., Martínez, R. A., Mateus, S. G., & Henderson, K. (2014). Reframing the debate on language separation: Toward a vision for translanguaging pedagogies in the dual language classroom. *The Modern Language Journal, 98*(3), 757–772.

Past NABE conferences. (2019, June 8). Retrieved from http://www.nabe-conference.com/past-nabe-conferences.html

Pennycook, A. (2012). *Language and mobility: Unexpected places*. Bristol, UK: Multilingual Matters.

Phillipson, R. (1992). *Linguistic imperialism*. Oxford, UK: Oxford University Press.

Phillipson, R. (2008). The linguistic imperialism of neoliberal empire. *Critical Inquiry in Language Studies, 5*(1), 1–43.

Phillipson, R. (2009a). English in globalisation, a lingua franca or a lingua frankensteinia? *TESOL Quarterly, 43*(2), 340–344.

Phillipson, R. (2009b). *Linguistic imperialism continued*. New York, NY: Routledge.

Phillipson, R., & Skutnabb-Kangas, T. (1986). *Linguicism rules in education*. Roskilde, Denmark: Roskilde University Centre, Institute VI.

Phillipson, R., & Skutnabb-Kangas, T. (2013). Linguistic imperialism and endangered languages. In T. K. Bhatia & W. C. Ritchie (Eds.), *The handbook of bilingualism and multilingualism* (2nd ed.). Malden, MA: Wiley-Blackwell.

Poza, L. (2017). Translanguaging: Definitions, implications, and further needs in burgeoning Inquiry. *Berkeley Review of Education, 6*(2), 101–128.

Prada, J., & Turnbull, B. (2018). The role of translanguaging in the multilingual turn: Driving philosophical and conceptual renewal in language education. *EuroAmerican Journal of Applied Linguistics and Languages, 5*(2), 8–23.

Rothman, J., & Treffers-Daller, J. (2014). A prolegomenon to the construct of the native speaker: Heritage speaker bilinguals are natives too! *Applied Linguistics, 35*(1), 93–98.

Sayer, P. (2013). Translanguaging, texmex, and bilingual pedagogy: Emergent bilinguals learning through the vernacular. *TESOL Quarterly, 47*(1), 63–88.

Seargeant, P. (2012). *Exploring world Englishes: Language in a global context*. New York, NY: Routledge.

Seltzer, K., & de los Ríos, C. V. (2018). Translating theory to practice: Exploring teachers' raciolinguistic literacies in secondary English classrooms. *English Education, 51*(1), 49–79.

Sembiante, S. (2016). Translanguaging and the multilingual turn: Epistemological reconceptualization in the fields of language and implications for reframing language in curriculum studies. *Curriculum Inquiry, 46*(1), 45–61.

Sifakis, N. C. (2004). Teaching "EIL" – Teaching "international" or "intercultural" English? What teachers should know. *System, 32*(2), 237–250.

Silver, R. (2009). Professional relevance in a multilingual world. *TESOL Quarterly, 43*(2), 332–335.

Skutnabb-Kangas, T. (2009). What can TESOL do in order not to participate in crimes against humanity? *TESOL Quarterly, 43*(2), 335–339.

Sledd, J. (1969). Bi-dialectalism: The linguistics of white supremacy. *The English Journal, 58*(9), 1307–1329.

Stathopoulou, M. (2016). From 'languaging' to 'translanguaging': Reconsidering foreign language teaching and testing through a multilingual lens. In *Selected Papers of the 21st International Symposium on Theoretical and Applied Linguistics* (ISTAL 21), pp. 759–774.

Susen, S. (2015). *The 'postmodern turn' in the social sciences*. London, UK: Palgrave Macmillan.

Taylor, S. K. (2009). Paving the way to a more multilingual TESOL. *TESOL Quarterly, 43*(2), 309–313.

Taylor, S. K., & Snoddon, K. (2013). Plurilingualism in TESOL: Promising controversies. *TESOL Quarterly, 47*(3), 439–445.

Teachers of English to Speakers of Other Languages. (2004). *Position statement on multilingualism* [Position Statement]. Retrieved from https://www.tesol.org/docs/pdf/2933.pdf?sfvrsn=2&sfvrsn=2

Teng, L. S., Sun, P. P., & Xu, L. (2018). Conceptualizing writing self-efficacy in English as a foreign language contexts: Scale validation through structural equation modeling. *TESOL Quarterly, 52*(4), 911–942.

TESOL. (2016). TESOL International Organization: Your partner for successful English language teaching [Online Brochure]. Retrieved from https://www.tesol.org/docs/default-source/pdf/abouttesol_final.pdf?sfvrsn=27f6eadc_0

TESOL. (2018a). 2018 annual report of the TESOL International Organization. Retrieved from https://www.tesol.org/docs/default-source/annual-reports/12-16-tesolar_2018_web.pdf?sfvrsn=3cdef8dc_2

TESOL. (2018b). Second amended and restated bylaws of the TESOL International Organization. Retrieved from https://www.tesol.org/docs/defaultsource/governance/tesol-bylaws.pdf?sfvrsn=6d4aefdc_6

Tian, Z., & Link, H. (Eds.) (2019). Positive synergies: Translanguaging and critical theories in education. *Translation and Translanguaging in Multilingual Contexts 5*(1), 1–93.

Troike, R. C. (1976a). Warning – ESL (traditional) may be hazardous to children. *Linguistic Reporter, 19*(1), 2–7.

Troike, R. C. (1976b). Toward a better way to teach English. *Linguistic Reporter, 19*(3), 2.

Turnbull, B. (2016). Reframing foreign language learning as bilingual education: Epistemological changes towards the emergent bilingual. *International Journal of Bilingual Education and Bilingualism.* https://doi.org/10.1080/13670050.2016.1238866

Turner, M., & Lin, A. M. Y. (2017). Translanguaging and named languages: Productive tension and desire. *International Journal of Bilingual Education and Bilingualism, 23*(4), 423-433.

Valdés, G. (2020). Sandwiching, Polylanguaging, Translanguaging, and Codeswitching: Challenging monolingual dogma in institutionalized language teaching. In J. MacSwan & C. J. Faltis (Eds.), *Codeswitching in the classroom: Critical perspectives on teaching, learning, policy, and ideology* (pp. 114–147). New York, NY: Routledge.

Vogel, S., & García, O. (2017). Translanguaging. In G. Noblit (Ed.), *Oxford research encyclopedia of education.* Oxford, UK: Oxford University Press.

Wang, D. (2016). Translanguaging in Chinese foreign language classrooms: Students and teachers' attitudes and practices. *International Journal of Bilingual Education and Bilingualism.* https://doi.org/10.1080/13670050.2016.1231773

Willans, F. (2013). The engineering of plurilingualism following a blueprint for multilingualism: The case of Vanuatu's education language policy. *TESOL Quarterly, 47*(3), 546–566.

Williams, C. (1994). *Arfarniad o Ddulliau Dysgu ac Addysgu yng Nghyd-destun Adysg Uwchradd Ddwyieithog,* [An evaluation of teaching and learning methods in the context of bilingual secondary education]. Unpublished doctoral thesis, University of Wales, Bangor, Maine.

Winke, P., Lee, S., Ahn, J. I., Choi, I., Cui, Y., & Yoon, H. (2018). The cognitive validity of child English language tests: What young language learners and their native-speaking peers can reveal. *TESOL Quarterly, 52*(2), 274–303.

Chapter 4
Framing the Realities of TESOL Practice Through a Translanguaging Lens

Graham Hall

Abstract While the professional and methodological literature surrounding TESOL has, until recently, promoted monolingual, English-only approaches in the classroom, the deployment of multilingual resources and repertoires has long been a reality in many TESOL classrooms around the world. Although many teachers perceive a value in drawing on all the learners' own linguistic resources to support learning, the multilingual classroom has, until now, been an 'elephant in the room' in the professional discourse of the field.

This chapter will therefore explore the realities of TESOL practice through the 'lens' of 'translanguaging'. Having established an understanding of translanguaging which underpins the subsequent discussion, the chapter traces the emergence of monolingual ideologies and approaches within the methodological literature of TESOL in the early twentieth century. It notes how the literature overlooked localized bi- and multilingual pedagogies, and the consequent gap between TESOL 'theory' and 'practice'. It then offers evidence of widespread contemporary multilingual classroom practices, drawing on both secondary sources and primary survey data documenting the practices and attitudes of teachers around the world towards monolingual teaching and translanguaging in the classroom. The chapter concludes with a call for further professional discussion of translanguaging, particularly in teacher training and education programmes, to facilitate teachers' professional development and support classroom practice.

Keywords Monolingual assumption · Monolingual methods · Postmethod bi- and multilingual teaching · TESOL (Teaching English to Speakers of Other Languages) · Translanguaging

G. Hall (✉)
English Language and Linguistics, Department of Humanities, Lipman Building, Northumbria University, Newcastle upon Tyne, UK
e-mail: g.hall@northumbria.ac.uk

© Springer Nature Switzerland AG 2020
Z. Tian et al. (eds.), *Envisioning TESOL through a Translanguaging Lens*,
Educational Linguistics 45, https://doi.org/10.1007/978-3-030-47031-9_4

1 Introduction

As with all pedagogy, the teaching of English to speakers of other languages (TESOL) is an ideologically informed social practice (Creese, 2017). Consequently, most academic and methodological accounts of the field suggest that, until recently, TESOL has been underpinned by a 'monolingual assumption', that is, the belief that all activity in a language classroom should take place in English (Hall & Cook, 2012). Yet across the profession, belief in the monolingual assumption has been less universal than is often claimed; what is fashionable amongst academics and methodologists does not necessarily reflect the beliefs and practices of English teachers working in varied contexts around the world. Thus, whilst the deployment of multilingual resources and repertoires has long been a reality in many TESOL classrooms, it has been, until recently, an 'elephant in the room' in the professional discourse of English language teaching.

Since the 1990s, however, there has undoubtedly been a shift in the academic and socio-political climate surrounding TESOL that has challenged discourses that promote 'English-only' teaching. The emergence of a 'social turn' within applied linguistics (Block, 2003), which draws on sociolinguistic and socio-historical perspectives to recognise difference, diversity and uncertainty in language teaching and learning, and of 'ecological' and 'complexity' approaches to language, language learning and the language classroom (e.g., van Lier, 2004, on 'ecological' understandings; Larsen-Freeman & Cameron, 2008, and Mercer, 2016, on 'complexity' approaches), have led to new understandings of the dynamic interrelationships between TESOL classrooms and their wider social context, and of what is possible, effective and appropriate in class. Meanwhile, there is increasing acknowledgement that so-called 'non-native speakers' of English now outnumber 'native speakers' globally (Crystal, 2012; Seargeant, 2016), that is, that English is not the primary or home language of most of its speakers around the world, the vast majority thus speaking at least one other language and drawing on English as part of their wider linguistic repertoire (see Sect. 2 for further discussion of terminology). Alongside the effects of globalization and contemporary migration, this has contributed to an increased acknowledgement and re-evaluation of bi- and multilingualism in individual and societal language use (e.g., Blackledge & Creese, 2010), and the recognition and increasing de-stigmatization of translanguaging, both beyond and, consequently, within TESOL classrooms (e.g., Anderson, 2018; Li, 2018).

The chapter will therefore use the 'lens' of translanguaging to frame the realities of TESOL practice. It will initially trace the emergence of monolingual ideologies and approaches within the methodological literature of TESOL in the early twentieth century. It will also note the ways in which the literature focused (and, to a large extent, still focuses) on theoretical and methodological *change*, rather than taking account of localized continuities of practice, leading to a disjunct between translanguaging 'in theory' and 'in practice' in TESOL. The chapter will then offer evidence of widespread contemporary multilingual and translanguaging practices in

TESOL classrooms. It concludes with a call for further professional discussion of translanguaging, particularly in teacher education programmes, in order to facilitate teachers' professional development, and to recognise and support its place in classroom practice. First, however, the chapter briefly outlines the terminological challenges that exploring translanguaging in TESOL poses, and the conceptualization of translanguaging which underpins the subsequent discussion.

2   Translanguaging: Establishing an Understanding

Translanguaging is described in a variety of ways within its rapidly developing literature. It is, for example: 'a concept' but also 'a practice' (Creese, 2017); 'a process' and 'a form of interaction', but also 'a pedagogy' (Conteh, 2018); and 'a continuum' (Anderson, 2018; Williams, Lewis, & Baker, 1996) but also 'a lens' (this volume!). Additionally, while some descriptions implicitly recognise a place for named or defined languages, referring, for example, to speakers who 'codeswitch' and 'shuttle between languages' (e.g., Canagarajah, 2011), others overtly challenge the notion or relevance of defined languages in translanguaging, seeing it more as 'the deployment of a speaker's full linguistic repertoire without regard for watchful adherence to the socially and politically defined boundaries of named languages' (Otheguy, García, & Reid, 2015, p.281). Clearly, this range of understandings can be challenging for practitioners and theorists alike. However, central to the conception of translanguaging underpinning this chapter is the focus on how individuals may 'use all their language resources to achieve their purposes' (Conteh, 2018, p.446); in this discussion, that purpose is to learn the new language – English. Translanguaging pedagogies also present opportunities for learners to make links between their linguistic experiences within the classroom to those beyond (ibid.; also Blackledge & Creese, 2010).

This understanding of translanguaging is therefore broad and inclusive. Yet in uncovering the ways in which 'all language resources' may be used within TESOL practice, the discussion has to draw upon terminology which derives from different conceptual frameworks – as Canagarajah (2013a, p.8) notes, it is often challenging to discuss a new paradigm (i.e., 'translanguaging') when the available terms belong to a previous paradigm. Thus, whilst 'monolingualism', 'monolingual classrooms', and 'English-only teaching' are relatively unproblematic from a terminological perspective and will be treated as broadly synonymous throughout the chapter, this discussion also includes bi- and multilingual teaching – here seen as classroom practice(s) through which learners can access their full linguistic repertoire in support of learning – within its understanding of translanguaging. The chapter's translanguaging lens emphasises these linguistic repertoires as fluid and dynamic resources rather than as reified, named languages (Canagarajah, ibid.).

Furthermore, it is important to note that the terms 'native' and 'non-native speaker', also occasionally used in the chapter, are essentially problematic, particularly when viewed through a bi- or multilingualism or a translanguaging lens, as they mix notions of birthplace, expertise, identity and language ownership in ways which do not reflect either language practices or attitudes to language(s) (Canagarajah, 2013b; Rampton, 1990). Still widely used within the field, however, the terms are deployed in this chapter, albeit with reservation, when they are part of the specific discourse being discussed (for example, when discussing the promotional materials of some private language schools, see Sect. 3).

3   The Emergence of Monolingual Language Teaching

While histories of methods and approaches in TESOL often characterise the field as being 'in ferment' (Richards and Rodgers, 2014, p.254) and subject to 'fashions and trends' (Adamson, 2004), support for monolingual teaching within the methodological literature remained remarkably constant for most of the twentieth century. This was, as Allwright and Hanks (2009, p.38) note, an era in which 'a profusion' of 'competing' language teaching methods emerged (e.g., the Direct Method, Audiolingualism, Communicative Language Teaching, Task-based Language Teaching; see, for example, Larsen-Freeman & Anderson, 2011, or Thornbury, 2017, for fuller accounts of these and other methods), each underpinned by differing theories of language and of language learning. Yet the idea that all classroom activity should take place in English remained for the most part unchallenged. Monolingual teaching was not unknown before this period, however. Kelly (1969, p.10), for example, finds evidence of the Direct Method in the fifth century writings of St Augustine, Butzkamm and Caldwell (2009:27) describe monolingual edicts and subsequent punishments for those who spoke their own languages in medieval monastery schools, and Phillipson notes instances of monolingual teaching in secondary school language education (1992, pp.186–7). Nonetheless, what differed from the late nineteenth century onwards was the extensive promotion of monolingualism in the language-teaching literature, soon gaining the status of an unchallenged assumption held by theorists and methodologists (Hall & Cook, 2012), and, as we shall see, within certain sectors of the English language teaching profession (if not necessarily, as noted above, by all language teachers around the world).

The emergence of the monolingual assumption and English-only teaching at this time is often ascribed to the largely European and US-based academics of the Reform Movement. Reformers vigorously opposed the Grammar-translation Method – characterized, and arguably caricatured, as simply the written translation of individual exemplificatory sentences (Howatt with Widdowson, 2004, pp.151–165) – which dominated foreign language teaching in secondary schools. As an alternative, Reformers advocated the primacy of speech in language learning (especially a focus on the teaching of pronunciation), the use of connected texts rather than isolated sentences, and a speaking-oriented classroom methodology (ibid., pp.187–209). While these ideas inevitably led to a reduction in the use of learners' own languages in the classroom and an increase in the use of English (or other languages being learned), it is significant that not all Reform academics were dogmatically opposed to any use of other languages in the classroom. Henry Sweet, for example, a leader of the Reform Movement in Britain, supported the use of translation when teaching vocabulary (1899/1964, p.194), while some Reformers saw value in activities whereby learners converted connected texts in their own language into texts in the language being learned (Howatt with Widdowson, 2004, p.191). Thus while the Reform Movement's rejection of grammar-translation is often seen as being synonymous with the case for monolingual teaching, this is a logical, and arguably ideological, 'sleight of hand' used to exclude the use of any and all other languages in language teaching and learning (Cook, 2010, p.15).

Rather than academic Reformers and their focus on language teaching in state-sponsored secondary schools, therefore, the belief in monolingual, English-only classrooms was in fact most significantly championed by private language schools. Over the course of the twentieth century, private sector TESOL subsequently developed into a global industry (Kerr, 2016), and became particularly influential within the field (Holliday (1994, 2005), for example, conceives of a predatory and professionally over-zealous private-sector or commercial British, Australia, North America (BANA) culture within TESOL which assumes and promotes its method- ological superiority, including the monolingual assumption, over 'mainstream' English language teaching). The well-known *Berlitz* chain of language schools was founded on the principle of monolingual classrooms, in which the use of other languages in class was seen as 'necessarily defective and incomplete' (Berlitz, 1916, p.4, in Kerr, 2016, p.518), and it is still marketed in this way today:

> With the Berlitz Method, all communication during class takes place in the target language. Instructors are native speakers and use a conversational approach based on listening and speaking … Our method was designed to allow learners to speak without translation … Learners take on the new language the same way they did their first – with natural ease. (Berlitz.co.uk; n.d.)

Where Berlitz led, other language schools followed. The monolingual principle was widely adopted in private sector language schools, and as with Berlitz schools, has similarly been carried forward to the present day. For example, *Inlingua*'s 300 private language schools in 35 countries employ 'only the target language' in classes taught by native-speaker teachers (Inlingua.com; see also Kerr, 2016).

The private sector's acceptance of English-only teaching was driven by a number of context-related factors. Classes in which learners speak a variety of differing languages and/or where native-speaker teachers do not know the language(s) of their students appeared, to many, to make bilingual teaching impossible (Hall and Cook, 2012). Meanwhile, the interests of both publishers and private language schools coincided in their promotion of monolingual products (e.g., courses and textbooks) which could be marketed worldwide without variation, and consequently deployed by native-speaker teachers, without (so the logic ran) the need to refer to and draw upon knowledge of other languages, or the expertise of speakers of those languages (Hall & Cook, 2012; Phillipson, 1992). From this perspective, any form of multilingualism or translanguaging in the classroom was undesirable.

Also significant in the development of English-only Direct Method teaching in the early twentieth century, which the Berlitz approach exemplifies, was a shift in the purposes for which languages were learned. What had been seen, prior to this period, as an academic or intellectual pursuit to develop the mind and read literature in its original language became a more instrumental activity for learners who were preparing to travel, do business and otherwise engage with English speakers (Hall & Cook, 2012; Howatt with Widdowson, 2004). Implicit in this new goal was the assumption that students were being readied to communicate in monolingual environments in ways which emulated native speakers. There was little or no acknowledgement that many learners would need to operate in bi- or multilingual environments or engage in code-switching or translanguaging (Hall & Cook, 2012; Sridhar & Sridhar, 1986).

Furthermore, while the Direct Method made little headway in secondary school contexts, for reasons of class sizes, the lack of native-speaker teachers and other often resource-based practicalities, the underlying assumption, that languages are learned for instrumental or utilitarian purposes, did take hold (Kerr, 2016). This carried with it the associated implications for secondary institutions of increased spoken English and less use of other languages, and was realised through the Oral Method and, subsequently, situational language teaching, based around the work of Harold Palmer and A.S. Hornby in the 1920s and 1930s (Howatt with Widdowson, 2004). The Oral Method emphasised the primacy of spoken language but also reintroduced to language classes the selection of carefully graded material to be presented to students, whilst situational teaching presented, then practised new language through 'situations'. While neither approach explicitly excluded the use of other languages in the classroom, situational language teaching can be regarded as a forerunner of the still widely deployed PPP (presentation-practice-production) lesson (Richards & Rodgers, 2014) which, drawing on an essentially behaviourist conception of learning to encourage pattern practice and drilling of prescribed language, remains a fundamentally monolingual approach to language teaching.

In the United States, meanwhile, the emergence in the 1940s of audiolingualism also drew on behaviourist notions of learning via 'good habit formation' (e.g., the drilling of sentences and memorization). As potential sources of 'bad habits', errors were to be avoided, the primary cause of error being seen as 'interference' from the learners' L1. Consequently, learners' own languages and bi- and multilingual language use was to be avoided in class, the monolingual assumption by now being deeply embedded in theorists' and methodologists' conceptions of what constituted effective language teaching.

By the 1970s, therefore, TESOL had reached a point where the monolingual assumption was ubiquitous within the academic and methodological literature surrounding the profession. Indeed, so deep-seated was this perspective that the role of other languages in the classroom, and the possibility of allowing learners to draw on and deploy their multilingual resources in support of learning (or as a goal for communicating more generally) rarely needed to be ruled out explicitly. With very few exceptions (for example, Dodson, 1967; Butzkamm, 1989), the possibilities of bilingual teaching and multilingual classrooms were simply overlooked and remained undiscussed. For instance, the emergence of Communicative Language Teaching (CLT) in the late 1960s and 1970s has generally been characterized as a paradigmatic break with the past, indeed as a 'revolution' (Bolitho, Gower, Johnson, Murison-Bowie, & White, 1983). This perspective, however, overlooks key continuities between CLT (and related approaches such as Task-based Language Teaching (TBLT), Content-based Instruction (CBI), and Content and Integrated Language Learning (CLIL) which are, as Richards and Rodgers (2014) note, logical developments in the application of CLT principles) and the previously promoted language methods briefly reviewed in this chapter. That is, the perceived purpose of English language teaching, preparing learners to speak to native speakers, remained fundamentally unchanged, with the central tenet of CLT, 'communicative competence', which learners need to develop in order to become successful communicators in English, 'treated as a monolingual capability, that is, as communication within a single language' (Leung & Scarino, 2016, p.85). Furthermore, as SLA research became the dominant body of theoretical knowledge informing TESOL from the 1970s onwards, its emphasis on a natural and universal order of second language acquisition (e.g., Krashen, 1982) and the need for meaning-focused input, output, activities and tasks during learning meant that any possible roles for other languages in the classroom (e.g., paying conscious attention to similarities and differences between English and learners' own languages) remained unexplored. Consequently, the monolingual assumption and promotion of English-only teaching went largely unchallenged in the theoretical and methodological literature surrounding TESOL until the late twentieth century.

4 The Changing Context and the Changing Classroom

Both the social and academic context of TESOL have changed in recent years, however, as 'communication within the contemporary context of globalization increasingly takes place across languages and cultures' (Leung & Scarino, 2016, p.85; see also this chapter's Introduction). There is increasing recognition that many learners will engage in bi- or multilingual communication, which will involve, but will not take place exclusively within, English. Many will speak English not to so-called 'native-speakers' but to other 'non-native speakers', as a *lingua franca* (Jenkins, 2007; Seidlhofer, 2011). And in so doing, many will wish to maintain their cultural and linguistic identity when communicating across cultures, realized through the related practices of speaking a non-native variety or *lingua franca* form of English, or by switching between languages, or through translanguaging.

Consequently, the goals of language learning and teaching are being significantly re-oriented. While a strong instrumental rationale still exists (i.e., now learners should learn to communicate multilingually, as this is their contemporary 'real-world' communicative context), broader, non-utilitarian perspectives are now much more widely recognised. Kerr (2016, p.521) notes the US-based MLA Ad Hoc Committee on Foreign Languages' (2007) suggestion that the desired outcomes of language teaching in universities should be 'educated speakers who have deep translingual and transcultural competence', whereby the acquisition of functional language abilities supports the development of 'critical language awareness, interpretation and translation, historical and political consciousness, social sensibility, and aesthetic perception'. Meanwhile, in Europe, the Common European Framework of Reference for Languages (i.e., CEFR; Council of Europe, 2001) promotes plurilingualism, pluriculturalism and the development of 'plurilingual competence' (p.4) as the desired goals of language teaching and learning, whereby a language(s) user:

> does not keep … languages and cultures in strictly separated mental compartments, but rather builds up a communicative competence to which all knowledge and experience of language contributes and in which languages interrelate and interact. In different situations, a person can call flexibly upon different parts of this competence to achieve effective communication with a particular interlocutor. For instance, partners may switch from one language or dialect to another, exploiting the ability of each to express themselves in one language and to understand the other. (ibid.)

This represents a clear break with the monolingual and native-speaker oriented approach of the past, which, although the terminology of both the MLA and CEFR publications is not explicit, conceives of the goals of language learning through a translanguaging lens.

Such viewpoints are supported by developments in theory and research. From a psycholinguistic perspective, Cook (2001) critiques perspectives of language learning which maintain that languages are separated and compartmentalised within learners' (or, as Cook importantly reconceptualises them, 'bilingual language users') minds. Cook suggests that languages are instead 'interwoven' and integrated in users' minds in a state of compound bilingualism (which Cook (2002) terms Multicompetence), meaning that they have a different knowledge of both (or all) their languages compared to monolingual speakers' knowledge of a language. Likewise, Cummins (2007) suggests that such interdependence across languages means that, for multilingual speakers, the development of a skill or proficiency in one language assists the development of similar abilities in the other(s) (i.e., a 'Common Underlying Proficiency' exists). From this, Cummins (2008) calls for an end to 'the two solitudes assumption', that is, the belief that languages should be kept strictly separate and be taught in a monolingual classroom.

Meanwhile, the emergence of socio-cultural perspectives on language learning (e.g., Lantolf, 2000) suggest that language is a tool through which learning is mediated, via mental processes such as planning, noticing or reasoning. Taking this perspective forward through a translanguaging lens, learners' linguistic repertoires provide a tool through which learning is scaffolded, whilst also helping them develop and maintain interpersonal collaboration and interaction, processes which are also seen as central to language development (Vygotsky, 1978). Furthermore, this conception of language learning, as a socially-mediated activity in which meaning is constructed through interaction with others, has much in common with ecological perspectives on education which emphasise the specific historical, cultural and social contexts of learning, both within and beyond the classroom (Conteh & Meier, 2014; see also Sect. 1: Introduction). Language, languages, and the linguistic repertoires and knowledge that learners and teachers bring to the classroom are central to this understanding of the context for learning.

Thus, the merits of bilingual teaching, multilingual classrooms, and translanguaging are being re-evaluated within the field of TESOL. As the multilingual character of contemporary communication is affirmed, language teaching, it is posited, should aim to develop learners' multilingual capabilities, in order that they can 'move between linguistic systems' as multilingual language users, rather than as 'developing native speakers' of English (Leung & Scarino, 2016, p.91). Such thinking fundamentally challenges the monolingual assumption within language teaching, as learners, now seen as 'multiple language users' (Belz, 2002), draw on their linguistic repertoires within the 'multilingual speech community' of the language classroom (Edstrom, 2006). From this translanguaging perspective, the linguistic experiences of learners in class are therefore linked to their experiences beyond the classroom (see Sect. 2), whereby teachers might ask not what they can offer to linguistically 'deficient or novice' students, but how they can 'let students bring into the classroom the dispositions and competencies which they have richly developed outside the classroom', lessons thereby becoming sites for 'translingual socialization' (Canagarajah, 2013a, p.184).

The chapter will shortly examine the extent and ways in which such multilingual practices are now realised within contemporary English language teaching. First, however, the chapter will examine how the theoretical literature and the monolingual assumption of the twentieth century, outlined in previous sections, conveyed only a narrow view of TESOL practice during that era, and how the apparent dominance of English-only teaching during the twentieth century may in fact have been challenged by many teachers around the world. In keeping with an ecological perspective on TESOL, the importance of context becomes evident.

5 Challenging the Discourse: 'Method', Monolingual Teaching and 'Myths'

The chapter has already hinted on a number of occasions that all is perhaps not what it seems when discussing the dominance of the monolingual assumption and English-only teaching in TESOL during the twentieth century. It is clear that a monolingual perspective permeated the academic and professional literature surrounding English language teaching, was widely adopted within the private sector of the profession, and was also extremely influential in many other types of English language classrooms. And it is also clear that the case for English-only teaching was predominantly conceptualised (either explicitly or implicitly) through the promotion of individual language teaching methods, that is, 'a single set of precepts for teacher and learner classroom behaviour' that 'if faithfully followed … will result in learning for all' (Nunan, 1991, p.3). Writing from a critical perspective, Pennycook (1989) notes how the concept of method and of individual methods maintain a specific set of interests that favoured 'Western' approaches to language teaching over non-Western practices, and enable academic experts, methodologists, and indeed commercial publishers to exert 'control' over teachers (see also Holliday's (2005) reference to 'BANA' culture earlier in this chapter). In effect, therefore, the long-standing focus on methods within the field served to create and sustain the professional discourse surrounding monolingual, English-only teaching.

Beyond issues of power and 'control' within TESOL, the notion of method and methods has been critiqued in other ways which are significant for our understanding of the extent to which the monolingual assumption, so strongly promoted within the methodological literature, really permeated throughout the profession in practice. As Pennycook (ibid., p.602) notes, 'there is little evidence that methods ever reflected classroom reality', Hunter and Smith (2012, pp.430–431) consequently suggesting that a 'mythology' has developed around methods which has 'packaged up', simplified and stereotyped complex and contested past and present practices. In other words, although the methodological literature until recently presented English-only teaching as paradigmatic across the profession and therefore around the world, this overlooks the locally constituted nature of ELT practices (Smith, 2003). It also prioritises the understandings of largely Anglo-American methodologists over the varied experiences and teaching traditions of English language teachers working in a vast array of contexts around the world (Hunter and Smith, 2012). In many settings, therefore, bi- and multilingual language teaching, and translanguaging within classrooms, continued – and still continues, as we shall see in Sects. 6 and 8.

Criticisms of method (as a concept) and of methods emerged in and subsequently took hold from the 1990s onwards, and it is no coincidence that as faith in methods within TESOL has faded, the monolingual assumption and the promotion of English-only teaching has been increasingly questioned. As TESOL arguably moves 'beyond methods' (Kumaravadivelu, 2003, 2006, 2012) into an era of 'postmethod discourse' (Akbari, 2008), classroom practice is conceptualised as emerging from 'bottom-up' rather than 'top-down' processes, that is, from teachers' own 'sense of plausibility' (Prabhu, 1990, p.172) based on their experiences in context. Thus, Kumaravadivelu (2012, pp.12–16) suggests three principles for postmethod pedagogy, each of which seems to provide opportunities for recognising and facilitating multilingual teaching and classroom translanguaging where appropriate:

- *Particularity,* whereby pedagogy must be sensitive to the local institutional, social and cultural contexts of language teaching, teachers and learners.
- *Practicality*, whereby teachers are encouraged to theorize from their own practice and practice their own theories, thereby breaking the hierarchical relationship between theorists and practitioners as, respectively, producers and consumers of knowledge.
- *Possibility*, whereby the socio-political consciousness of teachers and learners is fostered so they can 'form and transform their personal social identity'.

Thus, in the early twenty-first century, the particularities, practicalities, and possibilities of translanguaging offer a way for TESOL professionals to engage more fully, both in theory and in practice, with the changing ways in which learners around the world use English as part of their wider linguistic repertoire and construct and/or maintain their identities through language. Kerr (2016, p.523) suggests that although popular beliefs about the desirability of monolingual teaching and native-speaker teachers will remain, supported and catered to by private sector organisations, 'most teachers will need little persuading' that bi- and multilingual teaching and translanguaging are desirable, as 'this confirms their own practice-driven understanding of language classrooms'.

6 Acknowledging Translanguaging in Practice

As academic and theoretical perspectives on TESOL have 'caught up' with TESOL practice, an increasing number of studies have documented bi-lingual teaching, code-switching and 'code choice' (emphasising learner choice during classroom interaction and teachers' pedagogic decisions before and during lessons), and translanguaging in the classroom. It is notable that the studies' theoretical frameworks have changed over time, with 'translanguaging' emphasised much more frequently in recent years (post *circa*-2010), whilst 'bi-lingual teaching', 'L1 use', 'code-switching' and even 'translation' tend to underpin publications prior to this period. (In this section, these various frameworks will be regarded as analogous within our wider translanguaging lens. Pennycook, (2013, p.30.5) for example, clearly conceptualises translation in ELT as a form of translanguaging through his suggestion that translation is a means through which diverse and meanings 'can start to flow in and out of languages' as teachers and learners search for new ways to represent society through language. Similarly, García, Ibarra Johnson, and Seltzer (2017, p.15) and Mertin (2018, p.95) also explore the value of translation activities as part of their understanding of translanguaging in the classroom).

Thus, the continuation of translation in English language teaching (e.g., Benson, 2000) and, indeed, grammar-translation (e.g., Nasrin, 2005, writing about Bangladesh) is evident, especially in contexts where the teacher and learners' share a language. Furthermore, bilingual teaching and code-switching have been documented in TESOL classrooms from, for example, Botswana to Brazil, Hong Kong to Hungary, and Spain to Sri Lanka (Arthur, 1996; Canagarajah, 1999; Carless, 2008; Fabrício and Santos, 2006; Nagy and Robertson, 2009; Unamuno, 2008, respectively; these and many other contexts are documented in Hall and Cook's wider review, 2012, pp.277–278). Furthermore, 'code choice classrooms' have also been documented in the particular bilingual setting of Canada (e.g., Dailey-O'Cain & Liebscher, 2009), and in the US, Australia and New Zealand (e.g., Levine, 2011; Edstrom, 2006; Kim & Elder, 2008, respectively). The use of translation in reading and writing activities (Kern, 1994), in the teaching of English for Specific Purposes (Tudor, 1987), and as the norm in university-level language teaching (Malmkjær, 1998) has also been recorded. Meanwhile, more recent studies which draw more explicitly on translanguaging perspectives include, for example, those focusing on

South Korean (Li & Luo, 2017), Swedish (Rosén, 2017), UK (Anderson, 2018), US-based (García & Kano, 2014) TESOL classrooms.

It is evident, therefore, that many, and arguably most, English language classrooms around the world have remained to some extent multilingual over the last 100 years, despite the promotion of monolingual teaching and the assumption within the language teaching literature that English-only classes were the norm across the field. Despite its absence, until recently, from the public discourses of TESOL, teaching which draws on learners' full linguistic repertoires and uses multiple languages within the classroom has in many contexts never ceased or been 'stamped out' (Butzkamm, 2003, p.29).

7 Translanguaging in the Classroom: Continuing Key Questions and Debates

The continuation of bi- and multilingual teaching throughout the twentieth century and the current support for translanguaging in the theoretical and methodological literature surrounding TESOL raises a number of key questions for academics, teachers and teacher educators alike, however. The earliest conceptions of translanguaging saw it as 'a *purposeful* cross-curricular strategy for the *planned and systematic* use of two languages for teaching and learning inside the same lesson' (Conteh, 2018, p.445, citing Lewis, Jones, & Baker, 2012, p.3; emphasis added). Williams et al. (1996, p.9) also discuss the need for 'purposeful' translanguaging, arguing that 'there is a need to build on and extend good practice' (p.13), which includes recognizing the differing linguistic abilities of learners, their differing ages and so forth (p.41). Echoing this, there have been a number of more recent calls for research into 'judicious' or 'optimal' use of the learners' other language(s) in the classroom (e.g., Macaro, 2009), use which is 'principled' (Edstrom, 2006) and which provides insights into 'when and why' learners' own language(s) might be used in support of learning (Hall & Cook, 2013). Although such calls are generally located in literature which focuses on 'L2' or 'own language' use in the classroom, they can all be accommodated within a translanguaging lens which focuses on how learners 'use all their language resources' to learn English (Conteh, 2018, p.446; see also Sect. 2).

This search for key principles and good practice in classroom translanguaging *is* necessary – language learners clearly require input and output opportunities in English, and too much use of other linguistic resources may deprive them of this. In the absence of clear guidance as to how multilingual teaching and translanguaging in the classroom may be successfully developed, there is also concern that some teachers may be developing arbitrary and undiscriminating practices. And yet given ideas surrounding postmethod pedagogy (see Sect. 5) and teachers' own contextual knowledge, they are also best placed to decide what is most appropriate for their own classrooms (Hall & Cook, 2013; Macmillan & Rivers, 2011).

A number of studies of bi- and multilingual classrooms have therefore started to identify when and how principled translanguaging takes place in TESOL class-rooms, for example, by: fulfilling pedagogical goals such as scaffolding the devel-opment of new language; facilitating empathy, rapport, collaboration and interaction between learners; and supporting learners in making connections between the class-room and their wider context, including the maintenance and development of their identities. Bringing together the ideas of Rolin-Ianziti and Varshney (2008) and Kim and Elder (2008), translanguaging in the classroom might fulfil 'medium-oriented' functions (e.g., teaching or explaining grammar or vocabulary), 'frame-work' functions (e.g., organising and managing the classroom through giving instructions, setting tasks etc.), and 'social' functions (e.g., building rapport and social relationships).

Furthermore, the extent to which and how translanguaging and multilingual teaching takes place is likely to depend on teachers' and learners' perceptions of its legitimacy and value (Hall & Cook, 2013). On the one hand, some studies report that, despite its widespread occurrence within TESOL, many teachers feel 'guilty' when translanguaging takes place (e.g., Macaro, 2009; Butzkamm & Caldwell, 2009). Others suggest that teachers who are able to draw on a bi- or multilingual repertoires themselves regard drawing upon multiple languages as 'regrettable but necessary' (e.g., Macaro, 2006, p.68). Clearly, 'teacher guilt' about translanguaging practices in the classroom is widespread, and is almost certainly in part a result of the English-only discourses which have until recently dominated TESOL (see Sect. 3); teacher guilt is not, though, 'a healthy outcome of pedagogical debate' (Macaro, 2006, p.69). And of course, in keeping with discussions earlier in the chapter, teach-ers' (and learners') attitudes towards translanguaging may vary according to their cultural environment or other contextual influences such as their own language background, perceptions of the learners' abilities and attitudes, and local educa-tional traditions.

Thus, whilst the reality and value of translanguaging and multilingual teaching is now more widely recognised within the field of TESOL, its acceptance and realiza-tion in the classroom is inevitably more uneven across the profession. Alongside some teachers' feelings of guilt on the one hand, it is also important to note con-cerns around the 'lure' of translanguaging (as a new theoretical concept within the field, if not a new practice) for others (Matsuda, 2014, p.480). Matsuda detects 'a complex mix of reactions' amongst teachers to translanguaging – 'the desire to use the new and exciting notion, the frustration of not fully understanding what it looks like or how it works, and even the fear that the new ideas are going to push them out of their comfort zone' (ibid.). Canagarajah (2013b) also remarks on teachers' calls for more help in the face of 'unsettling questions for pedagogy', and suggests that the theorization of translanguaging might have 'far outpaced' principled pedagogi-cal practices for its advancement in the classroom (p.41).

Consequently, the next section of this chapter will bring together relevant insights from a global survey of classroom translanguaging practices, undertaken in order to develop further the empirical base for discussing these key questions and debates, for example: how and why are all linguistic resources in the classroom used by teachers and learners to facilitate learning?; are such practices principled and purposeful?; what are teachers' attitudes towards translanguaging in class?; and how might these vary according to contextual factors and learners' differing needs? The discussion will therefore focus on the ways in which translanguaging is enacted as an essential part of TESOL classrooms in order to redress the concern that theorization has outpaced principled pedagogical practice.

8 The Realities of Translanguaging Practice: A Global Overview

The data presented here are drawn from a recent survey of the ways in which bi- and multilingual practices are deployed in English language classrooms around the world (as reported by teachers themselves), teachers' attitudes towards such translanguaging practices, and teachers' perceptions of their institutional culture and the culture and discourse of TESOL more generally in relation to the use of linguistic resources other than English in the classroom. The survey also sought to establish whether practice and perceptions are associated with contextual variables such as the type of institution, learners' English language level, and teachers' experience. The survey drew on the views of 2785 primary, secondary and tertiary teachers working in 111 countries around the world, and was supported by 17 semi-structured interviews undertaken with a representative sample of participants. A number of themes emerged which are relevant to this chapter (for a full description of the project, see Hall & Cook, 2013).

8.1 Widespread Translanguaging Practices

One of the survey's primary findings, which by this point in the chapter will come as little surprise, is that the use of languages other than English is extremely common in TESOL classrooms around the world. For teachers, medium-oriented functions in particular draw on a range of language resources; for example, 62% and 58% of teachers reported explaining vocabulary and explaining grammar respectively through the learners' own languages *always*, *often* or *sometimes*, whilst 72% reported that they similarly explained meanings in other languages when they were unclear in English. There were slightly fewer reports of translanguaging to carry out framework and social functions within the classroom, but with 43% of teachers giving instructions in languages other than English, and 53% reported drawing on the learners' own languages to develop rapport and a good classroom atmosphere, teachers' engagement with translanguaging pedagogy is evidently widespread.

Teachers also reported significant learner use of languages other than English during classes. Whilst this was sometimes through deliberate and structured activities (e.g., the use of bilingual dictionaries and word lists or the explicit comparison of English grammar to the grammar of their own languages, reported as taking place *always*, *often* or *sometimes* by 71.8% and 70.6% of teachers respectively), 45.4% of teachers similarly noted learners' less formal preparation for tasks and activities in their own languages before switching to English.

Within this broad picture, variations can be found within the data. In keeping with this chapter's earlier discussion (see Sect. 3), both teachers' and learners' translanguaging in the classroom is reported as being substantially higher in the state sector than in private institutions. For example, 80.6% of teachers working in state schools report engaging in translanguaging in order to explain when meanings in English are unclear (i.e., a medium-oriented function), compared to a (still significant) 60.2% of private school teachers (likewise, for developing rapport and a good classroom atmosphere (i.e., a social function), the figures are 59% and 45.1% respectively). Meanwhile, teachers with lower proficiency classes (defined here as beginner to pre-intermediate learners) draw on a wider range of linguistic resources than those teaching higher level students (i.e., intermediate to advanced proficiency). For example, 54.3% of the former give instructions in languages other than English compared to 28.9% of the latter (i.e., a 'framework' function), while 67.6% of teachers' explain vocabulary (i.e., a medium-oriented function) through other languages to lower proficiency learners compared to 54% to higher level students. Both of these trends are perhaps not unexpected.

Furthermore, it is also worth noting that although these statistics for teacher and learner translanguaging are significant, is seems likely that, as self-report accounts of classroom practice, the data actually under-represents the extent to which languages other than English are used in class. Other self-report accounts of teachers' use of other languages, for example, identify substantial differences between stated and actual practice (e.g., from a stated 10% to an actual 23% for Edstrom, 2006), while Levine (2014, p.337) suggests that use of the learners' own language is unmarked, yet significant, in many 'arguably crucial moments' in the classroom.

8.2 Teachers' Attitudes towards Translanguaging in the Classroom

The survey reveals that teachers' attitudes towards the use of languages other than English in the classroom are complex and nuanced. While 61.4% of teachers believed or strongly believed that they should try to 'exclude' the learners' own languages from the classroom, a greater number, 73.5%, reported allowing other languages to be used 'only at certain points of the lesson' – Sect. 8.1 (above) identified what uses, and thus what points of lessons, these are. Implicit in these responses – i.e., 'certain points of the lesson' – is a sense that teachers are considering when translanguaging practices are most appropriate in classes. In other words, teachers *are* taking a principled approach to the use of languages in the classroom, albeit one which, in the absence of a clear professional discourse and discussion of the issue, they are most likely developing by themselves (see discussion in Sect. 7). From this, it is perhaps unsurprising that a sense of 'guilt' about translanguaging in the classroom was somewhat less prevalent amongst teachers who participated in this survey than is suggested by several other studies (e.g., Macaro, 2009; Littlewood & Yu, 2011, and also noted in Sect. 7 of this chapter). While 36% of participating teachers said they felt guilty if translanguaging took place, 37.9% said they did not.

To summarise, while the vast majority of teachers (90.1%) either *agreed* or *strongly agreed* that English should be the *main* language used in the TESOL class-room, there is clear evidence that most teachers do *not* pursue monolingual, English-only teaching, with a substantial majority (76.4%) suggesting that they can decide for themselves the balance between English and other languages in their classes. There is also an implicit sense that such decisions are based around an understanding of when translanguaging might be more and less appropriate during lessons for pedagogic reasons, but also because, as the survey uncovered, many teachers (56.7%) feel that learners can express their cultural and linguistic identity more easily if the can draw upon their wider linguistic repertoires.

As with teachers' reported translanguaging classroom practices (see previous Sect. 8.1), attitudes towards multilingual teaching also varied according to both sector and level of the learners' being taught. Private sector teachers conveyed a stronger sense of support for English-only teaching, 63.4% trying to exclude use of the learners own languages from the classroom compared to 50.8% of state school teachers. Meanwhile, although just 57.6% of private sector survey participants allowed multilingual activity in class at certain points of the lesson, this figure rose to 78.4% in state schools. Beyond these attitudes, which to a large extent reflect (and support) the trends exemplified in the teachers' reports of their day-to-day classroom practice, the proportion of teachers who believed that English should be the main language of TESOL classrooms, and the number who felt guilty if language(s) other than English were used in the classroom, were reported as being similar across both private and public institutions. Meanwhile, there was a slight and arguably unsurprising tendency for teachers of learners with lower English language proficiencies to allow translanguaging at certain parts of the lesson (75.7% compared to higher proficiency students' teachers' 70.2%), and to be slightly less focused on excluding languages other than English more generally (48.3% compared to 55.6% for those teaching higher level learners).

8.3 Translanguaging and the Cultures of TESOL: Perceptions and Paradoxes

When reflecting upon the ways in which monolingual and bi- and multilingual teaching may be encouraged or discouraged within their wider professional contexts, teachers who participated in the survey indicated that a strong preference for

English-only teaching – and thus against learners drawing upon all of their linguistic resources in support of learning – still exists amongst a range of other stakeholders within the field. This is in spite of the realities of teachers' own multilingual classroom practices, the changing context of English learning and use, and the changing theoretical and methodological attitudes towards translanguaging, documented in Sect. 4 of this chapter.

Although, as we have seen (Sect. 8.2), most teachers agreed that they can decide the balance of English and bi- and multilingual approaches in their own classroom for themselves, many also reported that their 'institution expects classes to be taught in English' (63% of survey participants *agreed* or *strongly agreed* with this statement); likewise when reporting whether their learners expect English-only classes (49.6% of teachers *agreed/strongly agreed*); where appropriate, their learners' parents expectations (52.3% *agreed/strongly agreed*); ministries of education (46% *agreed/strongly agreed*), and, indeed, whether other 'teachers in my institution feel that classes should be taught only in English' (59% of surveyed teachers *agreed/ strongly agreed* with this statement).

These perspectives convey a clear sense that, whilst support for the monolingual assumption and English-only teaching is far from universal across the field (e.g., over one third of teacher did *not* feel their institution expected an English-only approach), many TESOL stakeholders continue to prioritise monolingual teaching and, as a corollary, discourage (or seek to prohibit) translanguaging in the classroom. For many teachers, there remains a clear tension between the realities of their own classroom practices in which translanguaging plays a regular, often systematic and necessary role and the beliefs and expectations of their institutional managers and, indeed, their learners (although it is notable that parents of younger learners are more widely reported as favouring English-only teaching than the learners themselves!). For Copland and Neokleous (2011, p.271), this leaves many teachers 'damned if they [do]… and damned if they do not' allow for, or facilitate use of, the learners' own languages and translanguaging more generally in class.

That so many participants felt that their fellow teachers appeared to support English-only classes, a higher proportion than, for example, their learners, parents and ministries of education, also seems particularly noteworthy and, indeed, somewhat paradoxical; why might many teachers engage in and facilitate principled translanguaging practices in their own classrooms, yet assume that their colleagues would support monolingual teaching? The survey data reveals one possible explanation.

8.4   Teacher Training, Teacher Experience
and Translanguaging

A large majority of teachers reported that the pre-service and in-service training they had experienced discouraged the use of other languages in class (confirmed by 67.4% of survey participants for their pre-service training and 68.8% of teachers for their in-service teacher training, while just 19.2% of and 18.4% of respondents respectively disagreed with this perspective). Yet in qualitative survey data, many also identified a gap between their experiences on teacher-training programmes and their subsequent classroom experiences. Furthermore, in related interview data with the sample of 17 teachers who had participated in the survey and which included teachers from a range of national contexts and type of institutions, speakers of English as their main or as an additional language, and teachers with differing lengths of teaching service, it became apparent that teacher experience appeared to be a more significant determiner of views about monolingual or bi- and multilingual teaching than other criteria. The most experienced teachers appeared to be more open to translanguaging in the classroom than their less-experienced counterparts, to an extent that cut across national boundaries and institutional contexts. For the more experienced teachers, drawing upon languages other than English in class was a pragmatic response to the learners' immediate pedagogic and social needs, and it was evident that their own personal theorizing and practice had developed over time, as they challenged the monolingual discourses promoted on their teacher training programmes (as a teacher working in Japan noted about the evolution of her views, 'I thought wait a second, it's not working. It doesn't work').

It seems, therefore, that many English language teachers develop translanguaging approaches in the classroom over the course of their teaching careers, as they progress further away from their training programmes, and in light of the realities of their professional experiences. In the absence, until recently, of any real engagement with the issue within the theoretical and methodological literature, and with few opportunities to reflect on and develop their perspectives within an accommodating professional discourse (for example, there remains, at present, relatively little discussion of bi- and multilingual teaching at major TESOL-oriented conferences, although as Kerr (2016) notes, this is starting to change), this has largely taken place on an individual basis. While teachers are developing their own principles and insights as to when translanguaging is appropriate in the classroom – all survey and interview participants could explain when and why languages other than English were used in their classrooms, for example – the suspicion lingers that most teachers are operating in isolation, sometimes with a sense of guilt, without the support they may need in order to discuss and share good practice or analyse the limitations of their approach to translanguaging in the classroom. In effect, there is not only a disjunct between 'theory' and 'practice' in TESOL (albeit one which is now gradually closing), but also significant gap between what teachers need to explore and reflect upon during their teacher training and education programmes, and what actually happens and/or needs to happen in the classroom. Without addressing the 'elephant in the room' of translanguaging, in its many and varied forms and with all its potential to facilitate learning and teaching, to prepare learners for the ways in which they are likely to use language beyond the classroom, and to recognize, maintain and develop learners' linguistic and cultural identities, teacher training and education programmes are failing to prepare and support teachers in this vital element of classroom life. As the 'long silence' around bi- and multilingual teaching (Cook, 2010, pp.20–36) in TESOL comes to an end, teacher trainers and educators need to take forward professional discussion of translanguaging with teachers to facilitate their professional development and support classroom practice.

9 Conclusion

The deployment of learners' full linguistic repertoires in the TESOL classroom is not a new phenomenon. In many contexts, the use of learners' own languages in class has been commonplace for as long as English has been taught. What *has* changed over time is the ways in which this has been either ignored and shunned, or accepted and (re)conceptualised within the field or, more accurately, by differing sectors and stakeholders in the field. As Canagarajah notes (2006, p.6), we should be suspicious of unifying narratives and overarching explanations of intellectual and social developments. TESOL is a diverse and complex activity, characterised by differing viewpoints, interests and biases (ibid.), a perspective which this chapter has aimed to reflect when tracing the rise of monolingual discourses in TESOL in the twentieth century, the development of a 'theory-practice' divide in which the existence of and possibilities surrounding bi- and multilingual teaching were not recognised in the methodological literature, the changing social context for TESOL which has facilitated increased recognition of translanguaging as a social and classroom practice, and the current range of global practices and perspectives on translanguaging within the field.

However, it is evident that despite increased recognition and support for the use of all learners' linguistic resources within the classroom, teachers still face substantial challenges in developing, sharing and reflecting on what is and is not appropriate and effective practice. Whilst the theoretical and methodological literature may have started to catch up with, document and reconceptualise longstanding classroom practices, this does not seem to have thus far fully permeated the professional discourse TESOL. Although an increasing and welcome number of practical publications outline key debates and activities for teachers (e.g., González Davies, 2004; Kerr, 2014), teacher training and education programmes, teacher conferences, and indeed the informal teacher-to-teacher conversations that are part of everyday school life do not yet appear to engage with or provide a forum for discussion of the practicalities of bi- and multilingual teaching and translanguaging within the classroom.

Yet as Postmethod discourses (Kumaravadivelu, 2003, 2006, 2012) become more influential within TESOL, opportunities exist to recognize and value more fully teachers' own theorizing about, and insights into, the affordances that translanguaging offers in the classroom. Acknowledging more clearly the bottom-up understandings around translanguaging of experienced and expert practitioners, many of whom readily embed translanguaging practices into their teaching, can serve to challenge the often top-down continuing promotion of monolingual teaching by other stakeholders in the field, such as institutional managers. It can also challenge the monolingualism inherent in many popular language teaching methods, narrowing the gap between theory and practice in TESOL as the case for and realities of translanguaging in TESOL are recognised rather than ignored or dismissed. Understanding both the complexity and diversity of TESOL's past and present, and recognising the experiences and practices of teachers working in a multitude of contexts around the world, can help end the problematic silence around translanguaging within the profession as we frame the realities of TESOL practice through a translanguaging lens.

Acknowledgements   The author acknowledges the work of co-researcher Professor Guy Cook in the research project on which the latter stages of this chapter are based. The project was supported by the British Council's ELT Research Awards scheme.

References

Adamson, B. (2004). Fashions in language teaching methodology. In A. Davies & C. Elder (Eds.), *The handbook of applied linguistics* (pp. 604–622). London, UK: Blackwell.

Akbari, R. (2008). Postmethod discourse and practice. *TESOL Quarterly, 42*(4), 641–652.

Allwright, D., & Hanks, J. (2009). *The developing language learner: An introduction to exploratory practice.* Basingstoke, UK: Palgrave Macmillan.

Anderson, J. (2018). Reimagining English language learners from a translingual perspective. *ELT Journal, 72*(1), 26–37.

Arthur, J. (1996). Code switching and collusion: Classroom interaction in Botswana primary schools. *Linguistics and Education, 8*, 17–33.

Belz, J. (2002). The myth of the deficient communicator. *Language Teaching Research, 6*(1), 59–82.

Benson, M. (2000). The secret life of grammar translation – Part 2. *Studies in Humanities and Sciences, XXXX*(1), 97–128.

Berlitz, L. (n.d.). *About us: Method.* Retrieved from https://www.berlitz.co.uk/berlitz-method

Blackledge, A., & Creese, A. (2010). *Multilingualism: Critical perspectives.* London, UK: Continuum.

Block, D. (2003). *The social turn in second language acquisition.* Edinburgh, Scotland: Edinburgh University Press.

Bolitho, R., Gower, R., Johnson, K., Murison-Bowie, S., & White, R. (1983). Talking shop: The communicative teaching of English in Non-English speaking countries. *ELT Journal, 37*(3), 235–242.

Butzkamm, W. (1989/2002). *Psycholinguistik des Fremdsprachenunterrichts. Natürliche Künstlichkeit: Von der Muttersprache zur Fremdsprache.* Tübingen: Francke. (Nature and artifice. From mother tongue to foreign language: a psycholinguistic approach) English summary in Weinstock, H. (Ed.), (1991). *English and American Studies in German.* A supplement to Anglia (pp. 171–175). Tübingen, Germany: Neimeyer.

Butzkamm, W. (2003). We only learn language once. The role of the mother tongue in FL classrooms: Death of dogma. *Language Learning Journal, 28*, 29–39.

Butzkamm, W., & Caldwell, J. (2009). *The bilingual reform: A paradigm shift in foreign language teaching*. Tübingen, Germany: Narr studienbücher.

Canagarajah, A. S. (1999). *Resisting linguistic imperialism*. Oxford, UK: Oxford University Press.

Canagarajah, A. S. (2006). TESOL at forty: What are the issues? *TESOL Quarterly, 40*(1), 9–34.

Canagarajah, A. S. (2011). Codemeshing in academic writing: Identifying teachable strategies of translanguaging. *Modern Language Journal, 95*(3), 401–417.

Canagarajah, A. S. (2013a). *Translingual practice: Global Englishes and cosmopolitan relations*. Abingdon, UK: Routledge.

Canagarajah, A. S. (2013b). Negotiating Translingual literacy: An enactment. *Research in the Teaching of English, 48*(1), 40–67.

Carless, D. (2008). Student use of the mother tongue in the task-based classroom. *ELT Journal, 62*(4), 331–338.

Conteh, J. (2018). Key concept: Translanguaging. *ELT Journal, 72*(4), 445–446.

Conteh, J., & Meier, G. (Eds.). (2014). *The multilingual turn in languages education: Opportunities and challenges*. Bristol, UK: Multilingual Matters.

Cook, G. (2010). *Translation in language teaching*. Oxford, UK: Oxford University Press.

Cook, V. (2001). Using the first language in the classroom. *Canadian Modern Language Review, 57*(3), 402–423.

Cook, V. (2002). Language teaching methodology and the L2 user perspective. In V. Cook (Ed.), *Portraits of the L2 user* (pp. 325–344). Clevedon, UK: Multilingual Matters.

Copland, F., & Neokleous, G. (2011). L1 to teach L2: Complexities and contradictions. *ELT Journal, 65*(3), 270–280.

Council of Europe. (2001). *Common European framework of reference for languages: Learning, teaching, assessment*. Cambridge, UK: Cambridge University Press.

Creese, A. (2017). Translanguaging as an everyday practice. In B. Paulsrud, J. Rosén, B. Straszer, & Å. Wedin (Eds.), *New perspectives on Translanguaging and education* (pp. 1–9). Bristol, UK: Multilingual Matters.

Crystal, D. (2012). A Global Language. In P. Seargeant & J. Swann (Eds.), *English in the world: History, diversity and change* (pp. 151–177). Abingdon, UK: Routledge.

Cummins, J. (2007). Rethinking monolingual instructional strategies in multilingual classrooms. *Canadian Journal of Applied Linguistics (CJAL)/Revue Canadienne de Linguistique Appliquee (RCLA), 10*(2), 221–240.

Cummins, J. (2008). Teaching for transfer: Challenging the two solitudes assumption in bilingual education. In J. Cummins & N. Hornberger (Eds.), *Bilingual education: Encyclopedia of language and education* (Vol. 5, 2nd ed., pp. 65–75).

Dailey-O'Cain, J., & Liebscher, G. (2009). Teacher and student use of the first language in foreign language classroom interaction: Functions and applications. In M. Turnbull & J. Dailey-O'Cain (Eds.), *First language use in second and foreign language learning* (pp. 131–144). Bristol, UK: Multilingual Matters.

Dodson, C. (1967/1972). *Language teaching and the bilingual method*. Bath, UK: Pitman.

Edstrom, A. (2006). L1 use in the L2 classroom: One teacher's self-evaluation. *Canadian Modern Language Review, 63*(2), 275–292.

Fabrício, B., & Santos, D. (2006). The (Re-)framing process as a collaborative locus for change. In J. Edge (Ed.), *(Re)locating TESOL in an age of empire* (pp. 65–83). Basingstoke, UK: Palgrave Macmillan.

García, O., Ibarra Johnson, S., & Seltzer, K. (2017). *The Translanguaging classroom: Leveraging student bilingualism for learning*. Philadelphia, Pennsylvania: Caslon.

García, O., & Kano, N. (2014). Translanguaging as process and pedagogy: Developing the English writing of Japanese students in the US. In J. Conteh & G. Meier (Eds.), *The multilingual turn in languages education: Opportunities and challenges* (pp. 292–299). Bristol, UK: Multilingual Matters.

González Davies, M. (2004). *Multiple voices in the translation classroom*. Amsterdam, The Netherlands: John Benjamins.

Hall, G., & Cook, G. (2012). State-of-the-art: Own-language use in language teaching and learning. *Language Teaching, 45*(3), 271–308.

Hall, G., & Cook, G. (2013). Own-language use in ELT: Exploring global practices and *attitudes*. In *ELT Research Paper 13/01*. London, UK: British Council.

Holliday. (1994). *Appropriate methodology and social context*. Cambridge, UK: Cambridge University Press.

Holliday, A. (2005). *The struggle to teach English as an international language*. Oxford, UK: Oxford University Press.

Howatt, A. with Widdowson, H. (2004). *A history of English language teaching*. Oxford, UK: Oxford University Press.

Hunter, D., & Smith, R. (2012). Unpackaging the past: 'CLT' through ELTJ keywords. *ELT Journal, 66*(4), 430–439.

Inlingua. (n.d.). Retrieved from: https://www.inlingua.com/inlingua-method/

Jenkins, J. (2007). *English as a lingua franca: Attitude and identity*. Oxford, UK: Oxford University Press.

Kelly, L. (1969). *25 centuries of language teaching*. Rowley, MA: Newbury House.

Kern, R. (1994). The role of mental translation in second language reading. *Studies in Second Language Acquisition, 16*, 441–461.

Kerr, P. (2014). *Translation and own-language activities*. Cambridge, UK: Cambridge University Press.

Kerr, P. (2016). Questioning English-only classrooms. In G. Hall (Ed.), *The Routledge handbook of English language teaching* (pp. 513–526). Abingdon, UK: Routledge.

Kim, S.-H., & Elder, C. (2008). Target language use in foreign language classrooms: Practices and perceptions of two native speaker teachers in New Zealand. *Language Culture and Communication, 21*(2), 167–185.

Krashen, S. (1982). *Principles and practice in second language acquisition*. Oxford, UK: Pergamon.

Kumaravadivelu, B. (2003). *Beyond methods: Macrostrategies for language teaching*. New Haven, CT: Yale University Press.

Kumaravadivelu, B. (2006). *Understanding language teaching: From method to Postmethod*. Mahwah, NJ: Routledge.

Kumaravadivelu, B. (2012). *Language teacher education for a global society*. London, UK: Routledge.

Lantolf, J. (Ed.). (2000). *Socio-cultural theory and second language learning*. Oxford, UK: Oxford University Press.

Larsen-Freeman, D., & Anderson, M. (2011). *Techniques and principles in language teaching* (3rd ed.). Oxford, UK: Oxford University Press.

Larsen-Freeman, D., & Cameron, L. (2008). *Complex systems and applied linguistics*. Oxford, UK: Oxford University Press.

Leung, C., & Scarino, A. (2016). Reconceptualizing the nature of goals and outcomes in language/s education. *Modern Language Journal, 100*(Supplement), 81–95.

Levine, G. (2011). *Code choice in the language classroom*. Bristol, UK: Multilingual Matters.

Levine, G. (2014). Principles for code-choice in the foreign language classroom: A focus on grammaring. *Language Teaching, 47*(3), 332–348.

Lewis, G., Jones, B., & Baker, C. (2012). Translanguaging: Origins and development from school to street and beyond. *Educational Research and Evaluation: An International Journal on Theory and Practice, 18*(7), 641–654.

Li, S., & Luo, W. (2017). Creating a Translanguaging space for high school emergent bilinguals. *The CATESOL Journal, 29*(2), 139–162.

Li, W. (2018). Translanguaging and co-learning: Beyond empowering the learner. *EAL Journal, 5*, 32–33.

Littlewood, W., & Yu, B. (2011). First language and target language in the foreign language class-room. *Language Teaching, 44*(1), 64–77.

Macaro, E. (2006). Codeswitching in the L2 classroom: A communication and learning strategy. In E. Llurda (Ed.), *Non-native language teachers: Perceptions, challenges and contributions to the profession* (pp. 63–84). Amsterdam, The Netherlands: Springer.

Macaro, E. (2009). Teacher Codeswitching in L2 classrooms: Exploring 'optimal use. In T. Yoshida, H. Imai, Y. Nakata, A. Tajino, O. Takeuchi, & K. Tamai (Eds.), *Researching language teaching and learning: An integration of practice and theory* (pp. 293–304). Oxford, UK: Peter Lang.

Macmillan, B., & Rivers, D. (2011). The practice of policy: Teacher attitudes toward 'English only'. *System, 39*(2), 251–263.

Malmkjær, K. (Ed.). (1998). *Translation & language teaching: Language teaching & translation.* Manchester, UK: St. Jerome Pub.

Matsuda, P. (2014). The Lure of Translingual writing. *PMLA, 129*(3), 478–483.

Mercer, S. (2016). Complexity and language teaching. In G. Hall (Ed.), *The Routledge handbook of English language teaching* (pp. 473–485). Abingdon, UK: Routledge.

Mertin, P. (2018). *Translanguaging in the secondary school.* Woodbridge, VA: John Catt Educational Ltd.

MLA Ad Hoc Committee on Foreign Languages. (2007). *Foreign languages and Higher Education: New structures for a changed world.* Retrieved from: https://www.mla.org/Resources/Research/Surveys-Reports-and-Other-Documents/

Nagy, K., & Robertson, D. (2009). Target language use in English classes in Hungarian language schools. In M. Turnbull & J. Dailey-O'Cain (Eds.), *First language use in second and foreign language learning* (pp. 66–86). Bristol, UK: Multilingual Matters.

Nasrin, M. (2005). *A justification for using a grammar-translation method in ELT classrooms in Bangladesh.* 39th annual IATEFL Cardiff conference selections (pp. 29–30). Canterbury, UK: IATEFL.

Nunan, D. (1991). *Language teaching methodology.* New York, NY: Prentice Hall.

Otheguy, R., García, O., & Reid, W. (2015). Clarifying translanguaing and deconstructing named languages: A perspective from linguistics. *Applied Linguistics Review, 6*(3), 281–307.

Pennycook, A. (1989). The concept of method, interested knowledge, and the politics of language teaching. *TESOL Quarterly, 23*(4), 589–618.

Pennycook, A. (2013). Translingual English. *Australian Review of Applied Linguistics, 31*(3), 30.1–30.9.

Phillipson, R. (1992). *Linguistic imperialism.* Oxford, UK: Oxford University Press.

Prabhu, N. S. (1990). There is no best method – Why? *TESOL Quarterly, 24*(2), 161–714.

Rampton, B. (1990). Displacing the 'native speaker': Expertise, affiliation and inheritance. *ELT Journal, 44*(2), 97–101.

Richards, J., & Rodgers, T. (2014). *Approaches and methods in language teaching* (3rd ed.). Cambridge, UK: Cambridge University Press.

Rolin-Ianziti, J., & Varshney, R. (2008). Students' views regarding the use of the first language: An exploratory study in a tertiary context maximizing target language use. *Canadian Modern Language Review, 65*(2), 249–273.

Rosén, J. (2017). Spaces for Translanguaging in Swedish education policy. In B. Paulsrud, J. Rosén, B. Straszer, & Å. Wedin (Eds.), *New perspectives on Translanguaging and education* (pp. 38–55). Bristol, UK: Multilingual Matters.

Seargeant, P. (2016). World Englishes and English as a lingua Franca. In G. Hall (Ed.), *The Routledge handbook of English language teaching* (pp. 13–25). Abingdon, UK: Routledge.

Seidlhofer, B. (2011). *Understanding English as a lingua franca.* Oxford, UK: Oxford University Press.

Smith, R. (Ed.). (2003). *Teaching English as a foreign language 1912–36: Volume 1 Wren and Wyatt.* London, UK: Routledge.

Sridhar, K., & Sridhar, S. (1986). Bridging the Paradigm Gap: Second language acquisition theory and indigenized varieties of English. *World Englishes, 5*(1), 3–14.

Sweet, H. (1899/1964). *The practical study of languages: A guide for teachers and learners.* London, UK: Dent. Republished by Oxford University Press in 1964, Makin R. (ed.).

Thornbury, T. (2017). *Scott Thornbury's 30 language teaching methods.* Cambridge, UK: Cambridge University Press.

Tudor, I. (1987). Using translation in ESP. *ELT Journal, 41*(4), 268–273.

Unamuno, V. (2008). Multilingual switch in peer classroom interaction. *Linguistics and Education, 19,* 1–19.

van Lier, L. (2004). *The ecology and semiotics of language learning: A sociocultural perspective.* Dordrecht, The Netherlands: Kluwer.

Vygotsky, L. (1978). *Mind in society: The development of higher psychological processes.* Cambridge, MA: Harvard University Press.

Williams, C., Lewis, G., & Baker, C. (1996). *The language policy: Taking stock. Pwyso A Mesur: Y Polisi Iaith.* Caernarfon, Wales: CAI Language Studies Centre.

Part II
Translanguaging in TESOL Teacher Education

Chapter 5
"No, Professor, That Is Not True": First Attempts at Introducing Translanguaging to Pre-service Teachers

Elena Andrei, Amanda K. Kibler, and April S. Salerno

Abstract This chapter considers the complexities of conceptualizing and introducing translanguaging to pre-service teachers by analyzing the first author's experiences as a teacher educator in her initial effort at discussing translanguaging and its pedagogical implications in a second language learning course. Discussions about translanguaging were marked by respectful but contentious debate, in which students differed strongly from their teacher in their responses and opinions related to translanguaging and its relationship to code-switching. This study's purpose, conducted in the spirit of teacher inquiry, is to examine the reflections of both the instructor and her students in seeking to understand and interpret the literature on translanguaging. We found that this process can pose significant challenges for teacher educators and their students and raises important questions about the relationship between scholarly and practitioner communities in the language education field.

Keywords Translanguaging · Code-switching · Teacher education · Teacher inquiry · TESOL · Narrative analysis

E. Andrei (✉)
College of Education and Human Services, Cleveland State University, Cleveland, OH, USA
e-mail: e.andrei@csuohio.edu

A. K. Kibler
College of Education, Oregon State University, Corvallis, OR, USA
e-mail: amanda.kibler@oregonstate.edu

A. S. Salerno
School of Education and Human Development, University of Virginia,
Charlottesville, VA, USA
e-mail: aprilsalerno@virginia.edu

© Springer Nature Switzerland AG 2020
Z. Tian et al. (eds.), *Envisioning TESOL through a Translanguaging Lens*,
Educational Linguistics 45, https://doi.org/10.1007/978-3-030-47031-9_5

1   Introduction

The importance of preparing teachers to support the language and literacy development of their minoritized bilingual students cannot be overstated, and the growth of
scholarship in this area in the last 50 years is nothing short of phenomenal. Part of
this growth, as many would expect, has been a series of debates among researchers
in the field, addressing, among other issues, which instructional programs or practices are most effective, how languages are learned in (and outside) of school settings, how we should describe patterns of language development, and how we can
best define learners themselves. The latest contribution to these ongoing conversations is the question of what theoretical lenses best describe bilinguals' cognitive
structures and languaging practices, with the notion of translanguaging (García,
2009a) making a recent, dramatic, and sustained entrance as a possible response.
Debates such as these among researchers – oftentimes collegial but at other times
less so – are part and parcel of academia, and in many circumstances, can signal the
infusion of new voices and perspectives, the examination of taken-for-granted
assumptions, and in turn, the eventual development and maturation of a field,
regardless of the specific outcome.

Where does teacher education fit into this picture? Teacher education standards
for TESOL teacher education in the US, for example, state that those who prepare
future teachers of minoritized bilinguals are obliged to equip teacher candidates
with "knowledge of second language acquisition theory and developmental process
of language to set expectations for and facilitate language learning" (TESOL, 2019,
p. 6). A previous draft iteration of the standards, under which the current study was
conducted, specifically addresses translanguaging:

> 1c. Candidates demonstrate knowledge of language processes (e.g., interlanguage, *trans-
> languaging*, language progressions, social and academic language, and individual vari-
> ables) to facilitate and monitor ELs' language learning in English." (TESOL, 2017, p. 3,
> emphasis added).

This knowledge, it is thought, informs teachers' practice and helps guide their
instructional decision-making, but the standard itself underscores this complexity,
in that some of the language processes cited above – interlanguage and translanguaging, for example – are derived from very different perspectives on language
and language development.[1] At the forefront of our concerns is the introduction of
new theories, such as translanguaging, in this conversation. Some previous theoretical developments, like the introduction of more socially oriented theory and research
in applied linguistics, are slightly easier to summarize and share with teachers
because of multiple decades of hindsight, although such debates are far from
"resolved." How to teach translanguaging theory is less clear for teacher educators,
however,   because   ideas   are   still   being   developed,   and   translational

---

[1] The final version of the standards does not include this list. However, the draft standards are relevant because they were in circulation at the time of our study, and they raise the question of how
a profession addresses new theoretical developments.

publications – aimed at situating new ideas in a broader context for classroom teachers – are just being written (see García, Johnson, & Seltzer, 2017, or Fu, Hadjioannou, & Zhou, 2019, which were not available when the event we recount here occurred). It is natural that, as new ideas are proposed, emphasis has been placed on how they *differ* from ideas before them, but what can be done to help future (and current) teachers understand and critically evaluate how these innovations fit into what they already know about language use and development? As teacher educators frame ideas for students as new and developing, what challenges might arise?

In this chapter, we use narrative inquiry (Connelly & Clandinin, 2006) to explore the complexities of conceptualizing and introducing translanguaging to pre-service teachers by analyzing the first author's experiences as a TESOL teacher educator in her initial effort at discussing translanguaging and its instructional implications in a second language learning course. This study's purpose, conducted in the spirit of teacher inquiry (Cochran-Smith & Lytle, 2009), is to examine the reflections of both the instructor and her students in seeking to understand and interpret the literature on translanguaging, which was a challenging endeavor for all involved. Research questions we explore are: (1) How does a teacher educator introduce translanguaging in a second language learning course? (2) What happens when pre-service teachers are introduced to the concept of translanguaging?

1.1 Relevant Literature

Data was collected at a time (2017) when researchers were in the process of grappling with translanguaging theories and pedagogies as they related to minoritized bilingual students. In 2013, Palmer and Martínez had already published an extensive review of scholarship that convincingly argued for the importance of "helping teachers come to these more robust understandings of bilingual language practices and the interactional dynamics of bilingual contexts" (p. 269). In line with this argument, they later wrote a practitioner-oriented article in *Language Arts* (2016) that did just this, explaining how and why linguistic hybridity matters for teachers. This piece was published, however, just before the emergence of a highly contentious debate regarding the differences between code-switching and translanguaging theories. The debate focuses on whether multilinguals switch between languages or have one large linguistic repertoire (e.g., MacSwan, 2017; Otheguy, García, & Reid, 2018). Amid this debate, little pedagogical or practitioner-oriented guidance written by those outside the theoretical discussions existed at the time of this study to help teachers (and teacher educators) sift through this most recent set of disagreements among scholars. However, in their roles, language teacher educators must navigate these debates as they help students make sense of our evolving understanding of language.

Further, we were surprised to discover how little empirical work has delved into the ways in which future (or current) teachers come to understand these new ideas through courses or professional development. Although it is recognized that teachers' identities and ideologies mediate their understandings of translanguaging and other hybrid language practices (Martínez, Hikida, & Durán, 2015), research in teacher education settings has tended to explore educators' own uses of translanguaging (e.g., Musanti & Rodríguez, 2017) or have applied a translanguaging lens to teachers' multilingual instructional approaches without teachers' use of the term themselves (e.g., Van Viegen Stille, Bethke, Bradley-Brown, Giberson, & Hall, 2016).

The situation we explored was somewhat different, however, in that Elena, the first author, introduced the term "translanguaging" directly as part of an effort to integrate current theory and research into her course. To do this, Elena drew upon translanguaging publications from García (García, 2017; García & Kleyn, 2017), which focused on an asset-based orientation toward bilinguals; that languages are organized as a single integrated repertoire; and that students should be able to use all their language resources to make meaning.

Her pre-service teachers were not a *tabula rasa*, however; they came with existing understandings of language hybridity developed through previous university coursework and/or life experiences, and what were initially somewhat distant scholarly debates in applied linguistics suddenly became immediate tensions in the classroom. Just as teacher education students bring their own personal beliefs about other language questions to classrooms (Faltis & Valdés, 2016), we found that the students had their own preconceptions about hybrid-language theory.

2   Methods

In designing this study, we drew heavily from narrative analysis (Riessman, 2008), specifically narrative inquiry involving teachers as inquirers and "curriculum planners" (Ciuffetelli Parker, Pushor, & Kitchen, 2011; Connelly & Clandinin, 1988). In this tradition, teachers' stories are valued as important intellectual contributions to the development of classroom practices, curriculum, instruction, and educational theory. Connelly and Clandinin (1988) remind us of the nature of these narratives, in that, "each of us, not only teachers, keeps telling and retelling stories about our past. And in the telling of our stories we work out new ways of acting in the future" (p. xvi). We discovered the importance of this vibrancy when we first set out to analyze data using a more traditional coding process, parsing data into inductive codes, based on themes (Marshall & Rossman, 2015). These methods had served us well for other projects, but we found that with this project, the chunking of data came at the expense of losing meaning. Here, there was something inherently important about the narrative structure that helped us understand and describe what was actually happening in the classroom as the teacher and students considered the complexities of translanguaging theory. The importance of the inter-connected nature of data is a theme prevalent within narrative analysis. Mishler (1999), for example, discussed narratives as "socially situated actions" in which data – in his case, interview data – reveal an "unfolding scene" (p. 19). The importance of maintaining the connectedness of Elena's story drew us to inquire into – and present in this chapter – her narrative as a whole, rather than in individual coded chunks.

In Connelly and Clandinin's tradition, we turned first to the construction of the narrative. We believed that the way the story was constructed matters (Riessman, 2008), and we believed that story must originate with Elena herself. Connelly and Clandinin (1990) wrote:

> In narrative inquiry, it is important that the researcher listen first to the practitioner's story, and that it is the practitioner who first tells his or her story. This does not mean that the researcher is silenced in the process of narrative inquiry. It does mean that the practitioner, who has long been silenced in the research relationship, is given the time and space to tell her or his story so that it too gains the authority and validity that the research story has long had. (p. 4)

In this sense, Amanda and April became partners with Elena as she told her story by asking clarifying questions; probing for additional information about the sequence of events, the context, and the students' responses; and offering interpretations. After our discussions, Elena created a complete draft of the narrative itself, which we felt was important because we wanted the initial version to be in her words. As it was revised, however, we incorporated additional data, a process Connelly and Clandinin (1990) described as typical of narrative inquiry that involves researcher-practitioner collaborative relationships. We found that Amanda's and April's questioning helped flesh out the narrative. Responses to this questioning came from Elena's fieldnotes and reflections, students' written responses to questions about translanguaging, and audio-recordings and transcriptions of classroom discussion of translanguaging. These multiple data sources helped us feel confident in the triangulation of our findings (Erickson, 1986) and in the narrative itself.

We took several additional steps to improve our study's credibility. Connelly and Clandinin (1990) cautioned that: "At the completion of a narrative study, it is often not clear when the writing of the study began" (p. 7). This rang true for us; however, Amanda and April helped bound the narrative (Riessman, 2008): that it would begin with Elena's introduction of translanguaging theory to the course and would end with the students' final course meeting and discussion of translanguaging. This bounding we believe captured the beginning and end of Elena's consideration of translanguaging with this group of students. Amanda and April also helped identify the moment of disagreement that occurred when she introduced the concept of translanguaging as what Webster and Mertova (2007) called a critical event, a moment that reveals "a change of understanding or worldview by the storyteller" (p. 73). A critical event, they wrote, is for the storyteller "a change experience" that cannot be predicted (p. 74).

To ensure our analysis of the narrative was systematic, we used Connelly and Clandinin's (2006) three "commonplaces of narrative inquiry" – place, temporality, and sociality – as "checkpoints for a novice inquirer" (p. 479). We include Table 5.1 to demonstrate how we accounted for each of Connelly and Clandinin's three commonplaces within the narrative.

We now present Elena's uninterrupted narrative of her experience introducing translanguaging in her course. We then turn to an analysis of this critical event,

Table 5.1 Application of Connelly and Clandinin's commonplaces of narrative inquiry

	Connelly & Clandinin's (2006) definition	Process of inquiry in our study
Place	"By place we mean the specific concrete, physical, and topological boundaries of place where the inquiry and events take place" (p. 480–481).	Analyzing the physical classroom space, as nested within the university setting, and how it influenced teaching and learning.
Temporality	"Narrative inquirers do not describe an event, person, or object as such, but rather describe them with a past, a present, and a future" (p. 479).	Analyzing how the educational, disciplinary, and professional backgrounds of the instructor and students played a role in how the events unfolded. Recognizing that we would not be able to fully represent students in all of their multiple identities.
Sociality	"By social conditions, we mean the existential, the environment, surrounding factors and forces, people and otherwise, that form the individual's context" (p. 480).	Analyzing events in the context of ongoing professional discussions, as well as the immediate context of this course and other courses that students might enter in the future.

followed by an analysis of the roles played by place, temporality, and sociality in both building and resolving tensions that arose in the classroom around the introduction of translanguaging.

3 Elena's Narrative

I am currently an assistant professor of TESOL and a TESOL program coordinator at a U.S. public urban university in the Upper-Midwest. I was an English as a second language (ESL) teacher and school coordinator at a public middle school in the Southern US and a secondary English as a foreign language (EFL) teacher in my native Romania. I primarily see myself as an ESL professional, even though I have taught both ESL and EFL. My research and my teacher education experience have focused mostly on elementary and secondary (grades K-12) ESL in the United States. I see myself as sequentially bilingual and bicultural, transnational, and also a non-native English-speaking professional.

In 2017, I had been at my institution for one academic year. I started thinking it would be important for my students not to leave the program without knowing what translanguaging is or at least having heard about it. It seemed the concept was becoming increasingly popular at professional conferences. Although I first heard about translanguaging in a course I took as a doctoral student, I also vividly remember attending the TESOL conference in 2017 in Seattle, where David and Yvonne Freeman and others (Freeman et al., 2017) talked about translanguaging. The following summer I read García and Kleyn's (2017) edited book, *Translanguaging with Multicultural Students*, that included contributions on translanguaging in classrooms, related activities and lessons, classroom practices, and students' language use. After reading it, I decided to include the concept of translanguaging in one of the TESOL courses I would teach the next semester, specifically, the course focused on second language learning. I decided to introduce the term as a theoretical concept with possible applications for the language learning classroom. I thought this course might be a useful place for a primarily theoretical introduction, given that students would take an additional methods course the next term in which they would explore pedagogy in more detail.

Through my work as a teacher and teacher educator, I have met and worked with students classified as English learners (ELs) and other teachers who have taught them. As part of this work, I have personally heard negative and deficit-oriented discourse about these students from my peers in schools and sometimes in higher education, too. These experiences increased my desire to introduce the term of translanguaging. Above and beyond the course objectives and the TESOL standards for teacher education the TESOL program is required to address, I wanted to introduce students to a new theoretical orientation and provide them with tools and language to see minoritized bilinguals from an assets-oriented perspective and think about the use of their language resources as a whole in the classroom. I thought that translanguaging, among other concepts, might help me achieve that goal.

Before the semester, I prepared the syllabus and besides deciding to introduce the concept, I also added a new assignment, a conversation partner activity in collaboration with the campus's ESL center for international students. The assignment provided an opportunity to apply some of the concepts we would discuss in class: second language acquisition (SLA) stages; culture; funds of knowledge (Moll, Amanti, Neff, & Gonzalez, 1992) and funds of identity (Esteban-Guitart & Moll, 2014), and, important in this narrative, translanguaging. The conversation partner assignment included meeting and conversing weekly with an international student on campus.

As mentioned earlier, I consider myself a K-12 ESL professional. In general, students in the TESOL courses I have taught were mostly K-12 ESL professionals working (or preparing to work) in U.S. schools. Although the course I was teaching fulfilled the requirements for individuals who wanted to pursue TESOL careers in both international and domestic settings, public and private, in my first semester at my current institution, all but one student were K-12 ESL professionals interested in U.S. schools. So, that was the population I expected to have in my course that semester. The class had 20 undergraduate and graduate students. Of the 20 students, I was surprised that seven were undergraduate students studying linguistics rather than education, and one was a linguistics graduate student.

The class met once weekly for 3 h in the evenings. I introduced the term translanguaging during Week 4, at which time I think we had already developed a nice learning community. I fostered meaningful relationships with students by listening to their experiences in classrooms, and validating their ideas/opinions. Additionally, I used ice-breaker activities in which students interacted with each other. I had also made sure that I greeted each student before class, much like we ask teachers to do. The physical space of our classroom was small, and we made it welcoming. The room had single chairs with tables set in rows, a projector, computer hook-ups, and a blackboard with chalk. As a class, the students and I always re-arranged the chairs in groups or circles, depending on the activity, and put them back in rows after class.

3.1   Week 4

The first time I introduced the term translanguaging was through a KWL chart (where K stands for what students already know, W for want they want to learn and L for what they learned; Ogle, 1986). I asked students to fill in the "know" and the "want to learn" sections of the chart. Most said that they had not heard about translanguaging at all and that they were curious about it. I then shared a video from García (2017) presenting key ideas about translanguaging.

After the video, I got a lot of pushback on the term translanguaging, especially from the students studying linguistics. Several of them asked me, "How it is different from code-switching?" I drew upon what I learned at the conference mentioned above, explaining that translanguaging assumes a bilingual person is not two monolingual persons in one while code-switching regards a bilingual person as drawing upon two separate codes. I made a drawing on the board that looks like this (see Fig. 5.1).

At that time, I was not yet aware that authors writing from a code-switching theoretical perspective would contest this description (e.g., MacSwan, 2017). I went on to explain that translanguaging helps us see how bilingual people, or emergent bilinguals, are able to access all their language resources while communicating (García, 2009b).

Fig. 5.1 Graphic from class

The students who studied linguistics shook their heads in disagreement. One of them looked at me and said, "No, Professor, that is not true. That is code-switching."

Although they were disagreeing with me, they said this in a really friendly way: I could tell that by the smiles on their faces and the light in their eyes. When I saw their reaction, though, I thought, *Maybe they have a deeper perspective on language, as students of linguistics, than I do.* At this point, I also wished I had met with the students' linguistics program coordinator and asked her what they had learned about code-switching, or when I planned the KWL chart that I had included code-switching, in addition to translanguaging.

I know disagreement in the classroom is not a bad thing, and I position and view myself as a teacher learner (MacDonald & Weller, 2017) and a researcher of my teaching practices. By that time, when I introduced the term translanguaging for the first time, I knew my students well; as noted earlier, we had already established a good classroom community and built strong relationships. In addition, I position myself as an instructor who appreciates what students bring to the table, and I strive to practice what I teach and use *their* funds of knowledge (Moll et al., 1992) and funds of identity (Esteban-Guitart & Moll, 2014). I strive to listen to students' opinions in a way that validates them, even when they are sharing misconceptions, and go from there.

As the classroom conversation continued that day, I tried to mediate this disagreement by explaining that as "linguistics people," they might have a different and more detailed perspective on language and the brain. I also explained my understanding of what epistemology means: it is how we view and learn about the world. For example, one can think there is the capital-letter "T" Truth, but someone else might believe there are many lowercase-letter "t" truths (to paraphrase critical and constructivist paradigms explained by Guba & Lincoln, 1994).

With this explanation, students were still unclear and unconvinced that translanguaging was different from code-switching. Thus, they pressed me, asking, "So how do translanguaging and code-switching differ?" We had a short discussion about how both terms assume the use of all language resources available to one person, and we agreed that from the outside, translanguaging and code-switching look and sound the same; it is just how we think of the world and how we think of people who know two or multiple languages. However, they continued to press me for a concrete example of this difference, and I was at a loss. In efforts to respond to their concerns, I gave an explanation that started like this: From the outside, they look the same. Context, though, might make the difference. You do code-switching when you are forced to use one language over another. For example, you are bilingual in English and Arabic, but you have to use English with your teacher, as that is the common code between you and her; you have to use Arabic with your mom, as she does not speak English. But when you talk with your friend, who speaks like you, both Arabic and English, you pick the language that fits the purpose, which is more like translanguaging.

These examples came to me on the spot based on the discussion we had just had, but as I discovered later, they weren't consistent with these theories. My examples implied that the participants in an interaction defined code-switching or translanguaging, when in fact it is the theoretical stances and interpretations that differ, rather than the observable phenomena or the individuals involved. At the time, however, I was most concerned with making sure students were following me and not disregarding the concept of translanguaging. I wanted to lead and guide the discussion in a way that accommodated and validated their knowledge about code-switching gained from their linguistics training while opening the opportunity to consider a new concept, translanguaging. In other words, it was important to show concrete examples for both theories rather than stating one wasn't "correct," and the difficulty arose because differences between translanguaging and code-switching are conceptual and interpretive rather than concrete or observable.

By the look in their eyes, students did not seem convinced, and I said: "OK, this is the first time we are talking about this term, and it is normal to have questions and be confused. So let's give it some time and read more and talk more and see where we are, where we get to. I think for now, let's just agree to use the term translanguaging for what you also may think of as code-switching." With this said, I moved to the next item on our agenda. In hindsight, students might not have been as much "confused" as they were disagreeing with the concept of translanguaging or simply maintaining their understanding of code-switching, or perhaps even seeing me as the one whose explanations were confused. It was not until Week 11 that we returned to the concept of translanguaging.

3.2   Week 11

All students had to read about translanguaging before class. The objective was to provide additional exposure to the concept (which I planned from the beginning of the semester) and have a whole-class discussion about translanguaging in light of our Week 4 discussion, these additional readings, and the conversation partner assignment. The readings consisted of (1) a "short and sweet" blog article from *EAL Journal* (2016) on translanguaging and its definition; (2) a chapter by García (2009b) on bilingualism/multilingualism, bilingual/multilingual programs and practices, and translanguaging in the classroom, and (3) a quick Q&A on what translanguaging is and its benefits (Celic & Seltzer, 2011, pp. 1–6). As their entry slips for the class, students had to write definitions of translanguaging.

At the start of class, students shared in small groups how conversations with their international student partners were going. I also specifically reminded them to discuss what they would write in their reports about funds of knowledge/identity, culture, SLA stages, and translanguaging, all concepts covered prior to class. While students were talking, I moved around the room to listen. I spent a lot of time with one group, who asked me what translanguaging looks like and how they might see it with their partners. Before I responded, I reminded the students of our Week 4 class and how we decided that we would revisit the concept of translanguaging later in the semester for further clarification. I returned to my earlier example, saying that they might not necessarily see translanguaging in their interactions with their conversation partners because translanguaging (as I had defined it in Week 4) could only be seen in conversations between two bilingual people who share common languages. Because none of the students shared non-English langauges with their partners, I suggested that they could ask their international partners about how they use their first languages (L1s) and second languages (L2s) at home, for example, to find out about their translanguaging practices. I then provided an example of translanguaging I might experience at home with my husband. At the time there was talk in the news about tax reform, specifically changing the number of tax brackets. My example used those current events as content: My husband and I would talk in Romanian and say something like: "*Nu ştiu exact cum o să ne afecteze pe noi efectiv* tax brackets-*urile astea, plus că diferă de la un* bill *la altul. Va trebui să mai citim.*" ("I don't know exactly how these tax brackets will affect us; in addition, they differ from one bill to the other. We have to read more about it.").

I went on to explain that if you know the context of this being about Romanians in the US who are both bilingual in the same languages, then you know it is translanguaging. As I had explained in Week 4, if you think of code-switching as something you are forced to do in a context because that is the language/code you need to use to communicate, then this is not code-switching. In this example, my husband and I chose the words that seemed most precise from either language to talk about the taxes and tax reforms, which I considered to be translanguaging.

An education student pressed me, "Can you give me more examples of translanguaging?" She is a student who always asks me specific questions, and I appreciate the challenge. As mentioned earlier, I appreciate "difficult moments" in the classroom. Telling them they were wrong related to translanguaging and code-switching might risk shutting them off and losing them. It was more important to me to keep them engaged and get them thinking even about half-truths – through the example I provided – until we could reach total agreement.

In response, I returned to my original example from Week 4 about two students in a class who share the same L1 and how they might try to figure out what the teacher just said in their shared language, in hopes of relating the idea to her current field placement. "OK," said the student, "so translanguaging is just the use of two languages?" I was concerned that this late in the semester, she still did not understand that translanguaging emphasized an assets-based orientation and the pedagogical usefulness of encouraging students to use language resources from their full repertoires. I worried that our conversations about differences between code-switching and translanguaging had distracted her. So I answered, "Yes." She said, "Well, I thought it was more complicated than that." I replied, "No, do not try to complicate things." As always, I appreciated questions from the students and tried to connect the concept of translanguaging to their experience. I must admit I was surprised how difficult this concept was both for students who know about code-switching and those who did not. I also noticed the need of students to link and apply this immediately to their classroom practice.

After the group discussion, we moved to a whole-class discussion on the day's readings, led by one of the graduate students. She started by asking, "What is translanguaging?" Several students replied and the common theme of their responses was the use of two languages whenever needed. This common understanding seemed to be aligned with the examples and discussions we had had so far, though it did not directly address students' understanding of its relationship with code-switching. However, I noticed that a linguistics student described it as, "translanguaging/code-switching, however you want to call it."

Although her description did not align with my original intention of introducing translanguaging, and it probably would not satisfy theorists ascribing to either translanguaging or code-switching theories, it really made me think how we as a classroom community had reached an important point in our academic discussion. The student had shown willingness to include multiple ideas for the sake of our learning community and to promote cooperative, inclusive conversation. This phrasing – "translanguaging/code-switching, however you want to call it" – became something students and I repeated as a sort of symbol of our good classroom community.

3.3   Week 13

As a course wrap-up, I wanted to hear what students thought about translanguaging in general and in relation to code-switching and funds of knowledge and funds of identity, by way of a short writing time followed by a short whole-class discussion. I specifically framed the writing and the discussion as a way to gauge their thinking at the semester's end rather than looking for one particular right or wrong answer. Students' written answers and contributions to the discussion were varied, and they echoed our class discussions by mentioning translanguaging and code-switching being similar but different and as supports and tools for bilingual learners. The students did not seem to leave the course with "correct" definitions and conceptualizations of translanguaging or code-switching, as scholars define them, although they did show knowledge of the existence of both ideas. Several students still acknowledged confusion between the two terms. I could also read loud and clear students' needs to learn more about how to apply the ideas in their teaching. In our short discussion, I specifically did not express any judgments as I really wanted to hear from them.

The whole semester's experience on teaching translanguaging, for me, highlighted how difficult it is to teach new and complex concepts to students of varying backgrounds. As a teacher learner, I reached out to my close peers and collaborators and shared my experience and my learning, and through these conversations, we decided to initiate this narrative inquiry project. This narrative exploration allowed me as a practitioner scholar: (1) to reinforce my good teaching principles of creating a good classroom community and valuing my students' voices and ideas, (2) to examine what happened more closely and with a reflective stance, and (3) to reach out to my fellow language educators as part of our own community of scholars. Thus, I had the opportunity to pause, reflect, interpret, and think about how I would approach this differently the next time in a way that both shares ongoing scholarly debates with students and emphasizes how theoretical perspectives can be used to interpret the same phenomena differently.

4 Interpretation and Discussion

4.1 Understanding the Critical Event

As we created and re-created this narrative together, through Elena's recounting and Amanda's and April's questions to help her explore this experience, we were struck by the profound challenges facing teacher educators who are committed to valuing students' varied background knowledge and classroom community within the context of dynamic, complex, and at times divisive scholarly debates that can stretch teacher educators' expertise in new ways. The critical event in this narrative – a student's polite but pointed "No, Professor, that is not true" – made visible tensions that we argue are understudied in relation to translanguaging in particular and ongoing theoretical debates more generally. Leading up to this event, Elena had been exposed to translanguaging through professional conferences and readings aimed at teacher educators and teachers. Her commitment to keep her students "current" led her to introduce the concept in her courses, even if just to make them familiar with the term. Through exploration of sources that sought to distance the new concept of translanguaging from existing ones like code-switching, Elena introduced the topic in ways that provoked the narrative's critical event.

The critical event (Webster & Mertova, 2007) led to a situation in which Elena needed *connection* – rather than distance or difference – between the theories in order to maintain relationships with and among her students. Without readily available materials to do this for her, Elena created examples in attempting to honor students' insistence on code-switching's validity while also working to help them understand the new concept, translanguaging. As she explained, she was unprepared for this moment; although her examples were at times "half truths" that reflected her own nascent understandings of these theories and not those that scholars in these debates would endorse, she used them to keep the dialogue going with her students as they all sought to deepen their knowledge. In the end, students left the course with a range of translanguaging definitions, not what the instructor intended but what she felt was an important step in having students develop new understandings of language and bi/multilingualism and complicate their previous understandings. This variation, in many ways, reflects the current field of applied linguistics, in which discussions about translanguaging are characterized by debate and difference of opinion, rather than consensus or unproblematic agreement. With all due respect to the complexity of these issues, the one student's final assessment of the issue, "translanguaging/code-switching, however you want to call it" perhaps represents the reality of the practitioner field better than he could have known.

5   Conclusion and Implications

This narrative highlights several complexities and tensions that face teacher educators on a regular basis: the epistemological and disciplinary differences found between instructors and their students and among students themselves, the desire to share with students new and developing ideas that you might not yet have mastered yourself, and the need to navigate disagreements in the classroom in ways that keep students engaged and feeling that their knowledge and contributions are valued. The fact that these were enacted around translanguaging is perhaps not surprising but nonetheless is highly instructive for scholars and educators engaged in the study and teaching of language. No teaching event is perfect, and we acknowledge that had Elena been able to study issues of translanguaging and code-switching further before teaching about them, the contours of this narrative would likely have been different. However, it offers a valuable potential moment of reflection for the field as it grapples with translanguaging and its implication for scholarship and pedagogy.

First, we feel that it highlights the need for ongoing translational pieces from multiple scholarly perspectives that help teacher educators and their students understand relationships between theories and their relative contributions, emphasizing what they share, how they differ, and what scholars' informed opinions are regarding their pedagogical implications. In an analysis of other teacher-education data (Salerno, Andrei, & Kibler, 2019), we argue that what might be lost in discussions focused on current advances in theory is that teachers might still hold fundamental misconceptions about language and language development, contradicting ideas that current scholars might actually agree upon but which remain unaddressed in many contemporary conversations. As a result, we call for ongoing explorations like that of Palmer and Martínez (2016) to support the work of teacher educators and their students in understanding evolving theories of language in the context of ever-changing debates. We believe the translation of theory into practice can be a dynamic, complex, non-linear, and much-contested pursuit. Little research has explored how theories of bilingualism affect preservice teachers' language-teaching knowledge and practices (Faltis & Valdés, 2016). In the spirit of collaborative teacher inquiry that we embraced (Cochran-Smith & Lytle, 2009), we encourage other language teacher educators and classroom teachers to join us in considering how theories of bilingualism affect teacher education and language-teaching practices.

Second, teacher educators who are embarking on teaching new concepts, such as translanguaging or any other developments that are just being written about, can: present students with multiple theoretical perspectives, provide a variety of examples in which students can work together to apply varied theories to classroom practice, and encourage students to apply and explore the implications of these theories in their own practice. Related to translanguaging theory specifically, we recommend that teacher educators not get bogged down in distinguishing classroom examples of code-switching from translanguaging. We believe that the reason that Elena had trouble providing examples of contrasts between the two is because the differences are largely theoretical rather than observable. In this sense, the theories provide differing explanations for practices in a classroom that might look identical to a teacher watching them. We recommend that teacher educators instead focus on helping teachers understand the benefits of exploring various theoretical lenses, which places significant knowledge demands on teacher educators, particularly given the dynamic nature of current theoretical discussions about language. For all theories of multiple/hybrid language use, teachers must understand how the theories align with pedagogies that support equitable and socially just classroom instruction; students' multilingual resources are precious assets, to be leveraged for helping students reach instructional goals, and to be nurtured for the great value with which they enrich students' lives.

Finally, we make a humble call for community in scholarly conversations, in hopes that our work as researchers can seek to embody some of the same generosity and patience that Elena and her students achieved in their conversations together. Such efforts can help us balance a knowledge that academic debate is vital to the development of a field with the understanding that we must also attend carefully to how we discuss these ideas, and how we enact them through our work with future and current teachers.

References

Celic, C. & Seltzer, K. (2011). *Translanguaging – A CUNY-NYSIEB guide for educators.* CUNY-NYSIEB. Retrieved from http://www.nysieb.ws.gc.cuny.edu/files/2012/06/FINAL-Translanguaging-Guide-With-Cover-1.pdf. https://doi.org/10.15427/or048-02/2019sp

Ciuffetelli Parker, D., Pushor, D., & Kitchen, J. (2011). Narrative inquiry, curriculum making, and teacher education. In J. Kitchen, D. Ciuffetelli Parker, & D. Pushor (Eds.), *Narrative inquiries into curriculum making in teacher education* (pp. 3–18). Bingley, UK: Emerald. https://doi.org/10.1108/S1479-3687(2011)00000130004

Cochran-Smith, M., & Lytle, S. L. (2009). *Inquiry as stance.* New York, NY: Teachers College Press.

Connelly, F. M., & Clandinin, D. J. (1988). *Teachers as curriculum planners: Narratives of experience.* New York, NY: Teachers College Press. https://doi.org/10.1177/019263658907351318

Connelly, F. M., & Clandinin, D. J. (1990). Stories of experience and narrative inquiry. *Educational Researcher, 19*(5), 2–14. https://doi.org/10.3102/0013189X019005002

Connelly, F. M., & Clandinin, D. J. (2006). Narrative inquiry. In J. L. Green, G. Camilli, & P. B. Elmore (Eds.), *Handbook of complementary methods in education research* (pp. 477–489). Mahwah, NJ: Lawrence Erlbaum.

EAL Journal. (2016). *What is translanguaging?* Retrieved from https://ealjournal.org/2016/07/26/what-is-translanguaging/

Erickson, F. (1986). Qualitative methods in research on teaching. In M. C. Wittrock (Ed.), *Handbook of research on teaching* (3rd ed., pp. 119–161). New York, NY: Macmillan.

Esteban-Guitart, M., & Moll, L. (2014). Funds of identity: A new concept based on the funds of knowledge approach. *Culture & Psychology, 20*(1), 31–48. https://doi.org/10.1177/1354067X13515934

Faltis, C. J., & Valdés, G. (2016). Preparing teachers for teaching in and advocating for linguistically diverse classrooms: A vade mecum for teacher educators. In D. H. Gitomer & C. A. Bell (Eds.), *Handbook of research on teaching* (pp. 549–592). Washington, DC: AERA. https://doi.org/10.3102/978-0-935302-48-6_8

Freeman, D., Freeman, Y., Schwarzer, D., Ramirez, A., Gilmetdinova, A., & Soto, M. (2017, March 21–24). *Exploring translanguaging as a phenomenon, ideology, and pedagogy content area: Bilingual education*. Seattle, WA: TESOL Convention.

Fu, D., Hadjioannou, X., & Zhou, X. (2019). *Translanguaging for emergent bilinguals: Inclusive teaching in the linguistically diverse classroom*. New York, NY: Teachers College Press.

García, O. (2009a). *Bilingual education in the 21st century*. West Sussex, UK: Wiley-Blackwell.

García, O. (2009b). Education, multilingualism and translanguaging in the 21st century. In T. Skutnabb-Kangas, R. Phillipson, A. K. Mohanty, & M. Panda (Eds.), *Social justice through multilingual education* (pp. 140–158). Bristol, UK: Multilingual Matters. https://doi.org/10.21832/9781847691910-011

García, O. (2017). *What is translanguaging?* (YouTube video). Retrieved from https://www.youtube.com/watch?v=veylQoGrySg

García, O., & Kleyn, T. (Eds.). (2017). *Translanguaging with multilingual students: Learning from classroom moments*. New York, NY: Routledge. https://doi.org/10.3138/cmlr.72.4.578

García, O., Johnson, S. I., & Seltzer. (2017). *The translanguaging classroom: Leveraging student bilingualism for learning*. Philadelphia, PA: Caslon Publishing. https://doi.org/10.2128 3/2376905x.9.165

Guba, E. G., & Lincoln, Y. S. (1994). Competing paradigms in qualitative research. In N. K. Denzin & Y. S. Lincoln (Eds.), *Handbook of qualitative research* (pp. 105–117). Thousand Oaks, CA: Sage. https://doi.org/10.1177/1094428109332198

MacDonald, M., & Weller, K. (2017). Redefining our roles as teachers, learners, and leaders through continuous cycles of practitioner inquiry. *New Educator, 13*(2), 137–147. https://doi.org/10.1080/1547688X.2016.1144121

MacSwan, J. (2017). A multilingual perspective on translanguaging. *American Educational Research Journal, 54*(1), 167–201. https://doi.org/10.3102/0002831216683935

Martínez, R. A., Hikida, M., & Durán, L. (2015). Unpacking ideologies of linguistic purism: How dual language teachers make sense of everyday translanguaging. *International Multilingual Research Journal, 9*, 26–42. https://doi.org/10.1080/19313152.2014.977712

Marshall, C., & Rossman, G. B. (2015). *Designing qualitative research*. London, UK: Sage.

Mishler, E. G. (1999). *Storylines: Craft artists' narratives of identity*. Cambridge, MA: Harvard University Press.

Moll, L. C., Amanti, C., Neff, D., & Gonzalez, N. (1992). Funds of knowledge for teaching: Using a qualitative approach to connect homes and classrooms. *Theory Into Practice, 31*(2), 132–141. https://doi.org/10.1080/00405849209543534

Musanti, S. I., & Rodríguez, A. D. (2017). Translanguaging in bilingual teacher preparation: Exploring pre-service bilingual teachers' academic writing. *Bilingual Research Journal, 40*, 38–54. https://doi.org/10.1080/15235882.2016.1276028

Ogle, D. M. (1986). K-W-L: A teaching model that develops active reading of expository text. *Reading Teacher, 39*, 564–570. https://doi.org/10.1598/rt.39.6.11

Otheguy, R., García, O., & Reid, W. (2018). A translanguaging view of the linguistic system of bilinguals. *Applied Linguistics Review*. https://doi.org/10.1515/applirev-2018-0020

Palmer, D. K., & Martínez, R. A. (2013). Teacher agency in bilingual spaces: A fresh look at preparing teachers to educate Latina/o bilingual children. *Review of Research in Education, 37*(1), 269–297. https://doi.org/10.3102/0091732X12463556

Palmer, D. K., & Martínez, R. A. (2016). Developing biliteracy: What do teachers really need to know about language? *Language Arts, 93*, 379–384.

Riessman, C. K. (2008). *Narrative methods for the human sciences*. Los Angeles, CA: Sage.

Salerno, A. S., Andrei, E., & Kibler, A. K. (2019). Teachers' misunderstandings about hybrid language use: Insights into teacher education. *TESOL Journal*. https://doi.org/10.1002/tesj.455

TESOL International Association (TESOL). (2017). *Draft 2017 TESOL standards for P-12 teacher education programs*. TESOL. Retrieved from https://www.tesol.org/docs/default-source/advocacy/tesol_standards-p12-teacheredprograms-public-draft.pdf?sfvrsn=0. https://doi.org/10.2307/3588053.

TESOL International Association (TESOL). (2019). *Standards for initial TESOL pre-K-12 teacher preparation programs*. TESOL. Retrieved from https://www.tesol.org/docs/default-source/books/2018-tesol-teacher-prep-standards-final.pdf?sfvrsn=4. https://doi.org/10.2307/3588053.

Van Viegen Stille, S., Bethke, R., Bradley-Brown, J., Giberson, J., & Hall, G. (2016). Broadening educational practice to include translanguaging: An outcome of educator inquiry into multilingual students' learning needs. *The Canadian Modern Language Review, 72*(4), 480–503. https://doi.org/10.3138/cmlr.3432

Webster, L., & Mertova, P. (2007). *Using narrative inquiry as a research method*. London, UK: Routledge. https://doi.org/10.4324/9780203946268

Chapter 6
Reenvisioning Second Language Teacher Education Through Translanguaging Praxis

Matthew R. Deroo, Christina M. Ponzio, and Peter I. De Costa

Abstract In this chapter, we present two case studies of a pre-service and in-service teacher as they make sense of translanguaging as theory and pedagogy with particular attention to their adoption of a translanguaging stance. Specifically, we asked: What course and field experiences support PST and ISTs' adoption of a translanguaging stance as a part of their knowledge and dispositions as TESOL educators? Our data, comprised of multimodal discussion posts, teaching artifacts, and reflective journals, reveal that through the interplay of coursework and field experiences, Elle and Katie problematize their personal language ideologies, confront resistance to translanguaging at the school, district, and state levels, and recognize the interplay between their individual convictions and the systemic barriers in schooling. At the close of our chapter, we outline the implications of this work for teacher education programs that are committed to having their students engage in translanguaging praxis. We conclude with examples and recommendations for structuring course and fieldwork to support teacher preparation and education through a translanguaging lens.

Keywords Teacher education · Translanguaging stance · Teacher knowledge · Teacher dispositions · Praxis

M. R. Deroo (✉)
Department of Teaching and Learning, School of Education and Human Development, University of Miami, Coral Gables, FL, USA
e-mail: deroomat@miami.edu

C. M. Ponzio
Curriculum, Instruction and Teacher Education, Michigan State University, East Lansing, MI, USA
e-mail: cponzio@msu.edu

P. I. De Costa
Department of Linguistics and Languages, Michigan State University, East Lansing, MI, USA

Department of Teacher Education, Michigan State University, East Lansing, MI, USA
e-mail: pdecosta@msu.edu

© Springer Nature Switzerland AG 2020
Z. Tian et al. (eds.), *Envisioning TESOL through a Translanguaging Lens*, Educational Linguistics 45, https://doi.org/10.1007/978-3-030-47031-9_6

U.S. education has increasingly been confronted with a mismatch between the linguistic identities and practices of its teaching force and the students it serves. Where most U.S. teachers are typically monolingual (Bunch, 2013; Goodwin, 2017), the school-aged population has shifted to become much more linguistically diverse (Wiley, 2014). Given this mismatch, it is unsurprising that White middle and upper class linguistic norms have historically dictated the criteria for success in U.S. classrooms, marginalizing students' whose linguistic practices do not align with these norms (Paris & Alim, 2017; Valdés, 2016). Consequently, the language practices of children and families of color in the U.S. are deemed "'inferior' to a supposed gold standard–the norms of white, middle-class, monolingual monocultural America" (Alim & Paris, 2015, p. 79). In other words, the so-called "language gap" often used to explain away academic disparities among bi/multilingual and immigrant-origin learners is a reflection the hegemonic presence of the "white listening subject" in U.S. classrooms (Flores & Rosa, 2015, 2019).

This mismatch between the linguistic, cultural and racialized backgrounds of teachers and students needs to be investigated against an evolving TESOL professional development backdrop, one which Hall (2016) observes is characterized by and subject to fashions and trends in accordance with evolving approaches (e.g., a shift towards student-centered learning) that occur in broader education. Working from a critical language education perspective, scholars have long advocated for teachers to adopt pedagogies that embrace learners' diverse linguistic practices as resources for academic learning–and more importantly, as inextricable facets of their identities (Cenoz & Gorter, 2011; Cummins, 2008; Hawkins & Norton, 2009; Moll, Amanti, Neff, & Gonzalez, 1992). However, teacher preparation and development programs in general and teaching practica in particular have yet to catch up (Fillmore & Snow, 2018). As Goodwin (2017) contends, the predominately White U.S. teaching force tends to be "uncomfortable with or unprepared" to support emergent bi/multilingual and immigrant-origin learners who tend to be lumped together under the undifferentiated umbrella term of "diversity" (p. 440).

Mainstream teacher preparation programs must not only equip teachers with knowledge related to additional language development, but also challenge them to develop *nuanced* perspectives of students' cultural and linguistic backgrounds and resources that can be leveraged for learning (Fillmore & Snow, 2018)–thus decentering White monolingual English ways of knowing and being (Flores & Aneja, 2017). Furthermore, while issues such as teacher-fronted classes (Balasubramanian, & Shunnaq, 2018), project-based learning (Beckett & Slater, 2018) and blended learning (Hinkelman, 2018) continue to warrant attention, it is vitally important that the TESOL Practicum (Richards & Farrell, 2011), a cornerstone of teacher preparation that requires teacher candidates to engage in practice teaching under the supervision of a mentor teacher, not be overlooked as an opportunity for pre-service (PSTs) and in-service teachers (ISTs) to problematize how learners' diverse linguistic identities may be marginalized in U.S. classrooms and claim agency to enact linguistically-sustaining pedagogies despite the monolingual English bias (Blommaert, 2010, 2013; De Costa et al., 2017).

In our work as teacher educators, linguists, and educational researchers, we draw upon existing scholarship and our previous work to envision how translanguaging pedagogy might enable beginning and practicing educators to problematize monolingual English language beliefs, embrace ever-growing linguistic diversity, and adopt pedagogies that can truly sustain emergent and experienced bilingual[1] learners' dynamic meaning-making practices (Canagarajah, 2011; Pennycook, 2008; Poza, 2017). In light of and given recent calls for teacher reflexivity (De Costa, 2015) and critical praxis (Waller et al., 2017) in order to bridge the gap between identity, theory and practice, we echo Goodwin's (2017) assertion that teachers of linguistically-diverse learners need space to critically examine their own linguistic identities, beliefs, and practices alongside those of their students. Specifically, we look to translanguaging's potential to disrupt the hegemonic influence of both the standardization and politics of named languages associated with particular nations or social groups. As García and Otheguy (2019) acknowledge, "from a social perspective, multilinguals may be correctly said to use many different named languages," while translanguaging describes their "unitary linguistic repertoire" (p. 9). By challenging the social construction of named languages, translanguaging as a pedagogy of language centers the "creativity" and "criticality" of emergent bi/multilingual learners, who fluidly and agentively negotiate communication by leveraging their dynamic meaning-making system (García & Li Wei, 2014). Likewise, educators who enact translanguaging pedagogy reject hegemonic notions of "correctness" or "native-likeness" as the objective for students' language development (Poza, 2017). We concur with García et al.'s (2017) assertion that educators must engage in translanguaging praxis and subsequently develop a translanguaging stance (i.e., a set of philosophies, beliefs, and ideologies) that reflects an asset-based orientation (Lucas & Villegas, 2013) toward learners' cultural and linguistic resources.

Building on our previous work (Deroo & Ponzio, 2019; Deroo, 2020), this chapter grew from our collaborative inquiry in the field of teacher education and our ongoing instruction of the 124 PSTs and ISTs we have learned with and from at a large Midwest university in the U.S. over the past seven semesters. Across semesters, the intersection of our PSTs and ISTs' course and field work provides space for them to interrogate old dispositions and form new ones that reflect a translanguaging stance and apply their emerging understandings as translanguaging educators. We share two case studies to illuminate what patterns emerge for PSTs and ISTs as they develop (1) the theoretical and practical understandings of translanguaging, and (2) the necessary dispositions underlying translanguaging stance–including the need for PSTs and ISTs to confront pre-existing beliefs and dispositions about languaging. Specifically, we asked: What course and field experiences support PST and

---

[1] Consistent with García, Johnson, and Seltzer (2017), we employ the terms "emergent bi/multilinguals" to refer to those students whose bilingualism in two or more languages is emerging, or developing. We use this term to center on bi/multilingual learners' rich linguistic resources rather than using the term "English learner," which centers English and reflects the pervasive monolingual English ideology in the U.S. and elsewhere that we seek to problematize in our work.

ISTs' adoption of a translanguaging stance as a part of their knowledge and dispositions as TESOL educators? We conclude with examples and recommendations for structuring course and fieldwork to support educators' exploration, adoption, and negotiation of a translanguaging stance.

1 Theorizing Translanguaging Praxis

We integrate Howard and Levine's (2018) conceptual framework for language teacher learning with García et al.'s (2017) translanguaging pedagogy to analyze how our PSTs and ISTs adopt the knowledge, dispositions, and beliefs of translanguaging TESOL educators. Howard and Levine's framework integrates perspectives of teacher learning (Darling-Hammond & Bransford, 2005) with the characteristics, knowledge and practices of linguistically-responsive educators (Fillmore & Snow, 2018; Lucas & Villegas, 2013). Therefore, Howard and Levine's (2018) framework helps us to distinguish between three facets of language teachers' learning identified in the first column of Table 6.1.

Of particular importance to our work is Howard and Levine's (2018) contention that, "[underlying] the knowledge, practices, and dispositions of preservice teachers are the visions of what is possible, which can motivate teachers to question status

Table 6.1 Theoretical framework

Language teacher learning (Howard & Levine, 2018)	Translanguaging pedagogy (García et al., 2017, p. 28)
Developing particular *knowledge*, or understandings, required to support bilingual learners	Translanguaging educator's *stance*, or underlying philosophical or ideological system, reflects three core beliefs:
	1. Recognize that students' language and cultural practices "work *juntos* and enrich each other."
	2. View students' families and communities as resources to be leveraged for learning.
	3. Perceive classrooms as "a democratic space where teachers and students *juntos* co-create knowledge, challenge traditional hierarchies, and work toward a more just society."
Employing asset-based *orientations*, or dispositions, to students' diverse linguistic and cultural resources.	
Adopting pedagogical practices to support emergent bi/multilinguals' language and literacy development alongside academic learning	A translanguaging educator *designs* units, lessons, instruction, and assessments that purposefully integrate learners' home and school language and cultural practices.
	A translanguaging educator *shifts* his or her curriculum, instruction, and assessment according to "el movimiento de la corriente," referring to the flow of learners' dynamic bilingualism (p. 28).

quo classroom practices (Cochran-Smith, 1991) and continue to reinvent themselves and improve their teaching" (p. 144) In other words, expanding what possibilities PSTs and ISTs imagine for teaching and learning among emergent bi/multilinguals can disrupt the presence of monolingual ideology in their understandings and dispositions in favor of translanguaging pedagogy.

As reflected in the second column of Table 6.1, we map the three strands of García et al.'s (2017) translanguaging pedagogy–stance, design, and shifts–onto Howard and Levine's framework to help us consider *what* knowledge, practices and dispositions PST and ISTs need to develop as educators in order to enact translanguaging pedagogy. We focus on PSTs and ISTs' adoption of a translanguaging stance, which García et al. (2017) define as "the philosophical, ideological, or belief system that teachers can draw from to develop their pedagogical framework" (p. 27). In fact, García et al. (2017) contend that without this stance, teachers cannot leverage learners' full linguistic repertoire as a part of translanguaging pedagogy. Adopting a translanguaging stance also requires teachers to question the monolingual bias inherent in school-based language practices and position students' language practices as fundamental resources, rather than deficits, that work together, or "*juntos*." García et al. (2017, p. 50) outline the following three beliefs that underpin a translanguaging stance (see Table 6.1, column two at top). These beliefs emphasize students' and their families' identities and practices as fundamental for learning, where teachers and learners democratically co-construct learning. In the context of our study, we analyzed the emergence of these three beliefs throughout Elle and Katie's learning as evidence of their developing translanguaging stances. Furthermore, we traced the occurrence of these learning outcomes to identify what particular course and field learning experiences fostered the development of our case teacher participants' knowledge and dispositions as translanguaging TESOL educators.

2 Methods

2.1 Context

Matt and Christina both taught the TESOL Practicum, a 16-week course (condensed into 7 weeks during the summer) offered to undergraduates and graduates enrolled in a Teaching English to Speakers of Other Languages (TESOL) certification program. The undergraduate-level course is a part of PSTs' TESOL minor, which leads to their TESOL certification from the State's department of education for either elementary or secondary education according to their majors. In this university context, undergraduate students choose a major, which refers to the field of focus during the course of their study, and a minor, which refers to the secondary concentration of courses that often complement their major. The graduate-level course leads to ISTs' TESOL certification across grades Kindergarten through grade 12 (K-12). Students in our classes are predominately White, female, and monolingual, though

Table 6.2 Teacher demographics

Teacher	Level	Race	Teaching experience	Grade/subject	Language(s)
Elle	Undergraduate	White	Pre-service	Elementary language arts	English
Katie	Graduate	White	4 years	High school, social studies	English

a small subset identify as bilingual. This aligns with national demographic trends for the wider U.S. teaching force (U.S. Department of Education, 2016). In this present chapter, we focus on the teacher-learning of two students (see Table 6.2), who serve as common cases (Yin, 2018). Elle (PST) took Christina's course in Summer 2017, and Katie (IST) took Matt's course in Spring 2017.

2.2 Course

Both courses were taught online and used García and Li Wei's (2014) *Translanguaging* text as a primary means for introducing students to translanguaging.[2] The undergraduate course is one of only two online courses offered to PSTs in their teacher preparation program, while the course offered to ISTs is a part of a graduate program implemented entirely online. PSTs enrolled in the undergraduate course used Google Classroom as a course management system to make asynchronous weekly posts in reflection to course readings, concepts, theories, and ideas; at the graduate level, ISTs used Desire2Learn (D2L), an online learning platform. As a part of their discussion posts, students completed a variety of assignments (Deroo & Ponzio, 2019) to reinforce course readings which we outline in Table 6.3. Online exchanges between students and course instructors in response to the readings often result in numerous exchange as students' initial posts are elaborated upon, questioned, and responded to by classmates. We also met with students twice a semester via the web application Zoom to process course learning in real time.

Additionally, coursework was complemented by experiences in the field. To meet State certification requirements, the undergraduate-level course requires 20 h in a field placement with a TESOL educator. The graduate-level course requires 60 h, split between a K-6 and 7-12 classroom setting. PSTs and ISTs reflected on their field placements each week, which provided us with insight into their classroom experiences. At the end of the semester, students were tasked with enacting a culminating project within the field, either in their mentor teachers' classrooms or their places of employment. PSTs designed and taught a lesson, which they reflected on when they wrote letters to their future selves at the end of the semester. ISTs

---

[2] Beginning in Fall 2017, we started using García et al.'s (2017) *The translanguaging classroom: Leveraging student bilingualism for learning.*

Table 6.3 Course assignments in support of students' meaning-making about translanguaging

Dynamic bilingualism and the affordances of translanguaging	Create a slide with two images to contribute to the "Visualizing Translanguaging" document on Google Slides
	one to represent the previous notions of language
	another to represent languaging/translanguaging.
	For this task you will seek to solidify in your mind--through non-linguistic means--how translanguaging is a different lens with which to view language systems.
Recasting the narrative to focus on students' linguistic repertoires and respond to naysayers	Pull out a Tweet-able quote from the chapter that you would share with other educators to shift their language lenses and instructional practices. How would you advise the hypothetical teachers the scenarios provided to modify their instruction, remove the underlying other-ing, and support students' translanguaging practices? What are practical, actionable steps could they take? Post as a script for what you would say, incorporating what you have learned from García and Li Wei as well as from personal experiences to support your advice. You may find it helpful to refer to the Tweet-able quotes you and your classmates have compiled to support your explanation.
Making sense of translanguaging through semiotic mapping	Create a graphic organizer to represent three categories in relationship to translanguaging:
	1. Its theoretical underpinnings
	2. Its affordances
	3. Its strategies for enactment
	Accompanying your visual representation, write one paragraph (approximately 200–300 words) in which you explain your graphic organizer to your classmates. Explain the main concepts in your graphic organizer and the relationships among those concepts.

created a professional development session for their colleagues where they introduced the theory of translanguaging, raised awareness for the influence of language ideologies in teaching and learning, and promoted adoption of translanguaging pedagogy.

2.3 Data Collection and Analysis

Following their completion of our course, Elle and Katie signed consent forms, allowing us to use their TESOL Practicum coursework in our ongoing research. For this chapter, our data is comprised of Elle and Katie's multimodal discussion posts, field-based reflective journals, and follow-up interviews. These interviews lasted approximately 45 min each, followed a semi-structured protocol, and were transcribed verbatim. We frame this chapter as qualitative case study research (Yin, 2018), and call upon multiple forms of data to allow for crystallization (Richardson, 1994). That is, we analyzed the different data sources to make sense of the complex interactions underlying Elle and Katie's learning about translanguaging. For purposes of this chapter, we enact a comparative case study approach, which is suitable for analyzing commonalities and differences across sites (Miles, Huberman, & Saldaña, 2014). In focusing on Elle and Katie, we do not seek to generalize their experiences. Rather, we demonstrate how their participation in the TESOL Practicum course allows teacher-educators to consider the ways in which course design can support PST and IST to adopt the knowledge, dispositions, and beliefs of translanguaging TESOL educators.

For analysis, we organized data from discussion posts, reflective journals, and our interviews into a two-column chart for Elle and Katie (see Table 6.4). We used our theoretical frame (Table 6.1) to code instances where Elle and Kate demonstrated knowledge, disposition, or imagined practice, either in favor or opposition, of the three beliefs of a translanguaging stance (García et al., 2017). In instances where more than one appeared in the same segment, we allowed for cross-coding. As we

Table 6.4 Example of two-column data analysis

Framework	Elle	Katie
Beliefs about students' language use [Course]	I think that the use of their home language is extremely important. [Discussion Post Week #1]	When I first began teaching, those ahead of me reminded me the importance of enforcing an English-only speaking policy in my classroom, which I never took to. It was unnatural to not allow my students to speak in a language that represented so much of their individual and cultural identity. [Discussion Post Week #1]
Employing asset-based *orientations*, or dispositions, to students' diverse linguistic and cultural resources.		
Beliefs about students' language use [Practicum]	The teacher gave me a new book to read with them, we started reading new books from their bags.	While Ashley and I were talking, another student, who I will call Josie, came over to us and asked if I would help her with her paragraphs, too. Josie and Ashley began discussing Ashley's evidence and quote, and Josie gave her own take on the meaning of the evidence Ashley chose to include. [Field Placement Week #5]
Recognize that students' language and cultural practices "work *juntos* and enrich each other."	I then wondered why a teacher would ever want to ban students from using their native language. [Field Placement Week #1]	
Perceive classrooms as "a democratic space where teachers and students *juntos* co-create knowledge, challenge traditional hierarchies, and work toward a more just society."		

analyzed these instances, we also sought to identify whether these beliefs emerged within course or field work, and when in the sequence of the course they emerged.

Across our data analysis, we asked analytical questions of the data (i.e., what experiences or tools supported learning, how did they build upon already-present understandings of bilingual teaching, how did they apply translanguaging theory to praxis?). We looked across our coding for both Elle and Kate to explore similarities and differences in their learning and the emergence of their translanguaging stances. In what follows, we first share our findings from Elle and Katie's separate learning experiences in the TESOL Practicum before bringing our comparative analysis together in the discussion section.

3 Findings

3.1 Elle: A Pre-service Teacher's Trajectory to Adopting a Translanguaging Stance

Elle, an elementary language arts education PST, enrolled in the 7-week online undergraduate-level practicum course for TESOL minors in summer 2017. While the course was accelerated, it was the only course she took at the time. Therefore, Elle was able to fully dedicate her time and attention to the TESOL practicum without need to focus on other classes.

During a retrospective interview in spring 2018, Elle described herself as: "Female. White. I…um…I guess, with culture, I don't know, just like you're basic American. Not afraid to experience other cultures, but not completely submerged in other cultures." Like many undergraduate TESOL minors enrolled in our university's teacher preparation program, Elle identified as a monolingual English speaker. While she studied Spanish for 4 years in high school, she had not yet been been abroad and did not consider her experience adequate to call herself bilingual. Elle was advised to choose a TESOL minor to support her future job viability. Beyond this, she cited her desire to be prepared to teach the "growing Hispanic population" in Southeast Michigan and address the "struggle" they experience in schools. Her initial view of her students reflected a deficit-based view of her potential future students, their racialized identities, and their linguistic repertoires (Flores & Rosa, 2015).

3.1.1 Elle's Starting Place

Elle was introduced to translanguaging during the first week of the course while reading García and Li Wei (2014). In her first discussion post, she provided a directive to teachers to try "to relate to their ESL students" and understand "struggle[s] of the ESL student to comprehend in order to learn." Of importance, is that in describing learners as "ESL students," Elle delineated them separately from a hypothetical and presumably native English speaking teacher who is unfamiliar with the challenge of learning additional languages. She noted ESL students "tend to have a harder time making friends because other students who speak English fluently judge the student for not having the proper tools to communicate…students may try once or twice to converse with the ESL student, but typically stop because the ESL student doesn't have much to say in return." This anecdote reveals how Elle, through her monolingual lens, perceived "ESL students" as dependent on the willingness of others to negotiate the perceived language barrier.

Elle's lack of familiarity with translanguaging is unsurprising, given her limited exposure to the theory and its pedagogical implementation in her previous teaching or learning experiences. In a follow-up interview about her own language practices, Elle explained that while she had studied Spanish in high school, she considered herself monolingual: "I couldn't, like, go to a Spanish-speaking country and get by by myself with no resources or other people." She also shared her experience with her intermediate Spanish teacher who "was very set in her ways" and did not permit students to use English, "to ask questions to kind of problem solve more." As she recalled, "I would whisper to my friends in English to ask questions to clear up confusion, and a lot of times that got me in trouble for talking while the teacher was talking. I can hardly remember anything that I learned in those last two years of Spanish because I was never able to solidify that information in my native language." While Elle criticized this practice in her interview, she acknowledged in an initial discussion post her belief that "only using the second language [was] vital" to fostering learners' language development. Like her former Spanish teacher, Elle's initial stance excluded students' language and cultural practices as resources for learning. In fact, Elle's own experience learning Spanish reflects the traditional hierarchies that García et al. (2017) criticize in favor of creating "a democratic space where teachers and students *juntos* co-create knowledge (p. 50).

3.1.2 Coursework

Looking across Elle's discussion posts demonstrated how she used this online space to make sense of theoretical concepts from course readings and connected them to general hypothetical examples. For instance, in a revised iteration of her first discussion post, she paraphrased the course text, explaining that "languaging 'shapes our experiences' and that language is not just a code system, but a way in which our experiences are stored and drawn upon." She then extended her understanding of languaging to classroom practice, noting: "[It] seems that the experiences of an ESL student are what is going to make it easier for them to language with the second language being learned. Therefore, trying to teach the rules and specifics of the second language is not what is going to benefit the ESL student the most."

More specifically, Elle contended that teachers should create experiences for students to contextualize their language learning. For example, "instead of looking at a book that is in English," she suggested that an ESL teacher could take students to a butterfly house to support students writing descriptive sentences about butterflies, providing keywords and pictures to focus their language learning. Elle's recommendation exemplified a practice-based orientation toward language learning, moving from paraphrasing the course text to make her own claim. However, without hands-on classroom experience, Elle was limited to describing the possibilities of translanguaging pedagogy in hypothetical terms.

In the same post, Elle acknowledged that though learners' language practices are inextricably part of their identities, they may be marginalized by traditional language hierarchies that privilege some language practices over others. Elle explained, "The forces of society, and some schools in particular, sort of block bilinguals into one group…This causes the bilingual student to try and force themselves into being monolingual learners causing them to only rarely practice fluid language speaking of both languages." Elle also empathized with bilingual learners stating, "the consequence of that is that when they are put into that society that wants them to be able to speak the second language like a monolingual student, their advantage becomes a disadvantage to them because this is a difficult task for someone who understands two languages." In Elle's later discussion posts and field placement reflections, she returned to the idea that excluding learners' home languages from the classroom marginalizes their linguistic and cultural resources.

3.1.3 Fieldwork

Elle's field placement provided an opportunity for her to apply conceptual knowledge from coursework and confront the tensions of adopting translanguaging pedagogy for her own teaching, an experience she would not have had in the online course alone. Elle was placed in an elementary ESL classroom at a public school in Southeast Michigan, which she described as being "a lot like my community except for one difference. These people wear burkas, hijabs, and speak Arabic with each other … I felt a little out of place with nothing covering my hair, my bright red hair. I felt like I stuck out like a sore thumb, but I didn't let this discourage me from how I would feel in the classroom." First, her use of the phase "these people" along with her description of the cultural and linguistic practices reflected in the field placement community denotes an essentialized perspective of individuals within the community. Second, Elle shared the tension she experienced, perceiving herself as a cultural and linguistic outsider in her field placement context.

Recognizing Ecological Resources

Elle focused her attention on facilitating a small group reading activity in the field with three boys "new to the country in the last month." In her reflection, Elle narrated their shared reading task as an opportunity for them to co-construct meaning. She observed that all students in the classroom had "book bags," which acted as semiotic resources. Elle described how she and the three boys took turns reading;

when she asked questions, the boys would translanguage to support each other in answering. Connecting this experience back to the course readings, Elle observed:

> This was cool and really made me think of our text because this is like one of those extra cognitive abilities that these bilinguals have. I then wondered why a teacher would ever want to ban students from using their native language. This benefitted the students and myself because the kids were able to collectively answer my questions using both [English and Arabic].

Here, she used first-hand experience to question monolingual English-only class-room policies and highlight how she and the students negotiated their shared pur-pose for communication.

Application and Reflection

Though Elle's field placement reflection provided evidence of an emerging translan-guaging stance, she also found that translanguaging pedagogy conflicted with school-based practices that center standard monolingual English and a teacher-centered "locus of control" (García & Sylvan, 2011). Elle and her classmates were asked to explain how a translanguaging approach shifted their lens for viewing lan-guage teaching and learning, identify the affordances of adopting such an approach, and explicate the challenges it presents to educational stakeholders. Elle asked, "How in the world are you supposed to have a translanguage based approach being done in the classrooms of your district if you have 140 different languages coming to the table? Isn't it just easier to have your teachers make their students only speak English? Then the question for assessment offices becomes, how do we score this?" While Elle problematized this, suggesting that "the challenge lies in helping the district's students keep this part of their identity alive, while also trying to keep test scores up [and] dropout rates low," she struggled to perceive how a translanguaging stance could be adopted within monolingual English paradigms. Likewise, her field placement led Elle to acknowledge the discomfort teachers feel when they relin-quish control to support their learners' translanguaging practices:

> My students speak some great English, but a lot of times if they want to have a small con-versation with a friend, or they don't understand the direction in English, they revert back to Arabic…I didn't want to tell them to stop using Arabic while sitting there with me, but I also had no clue what they were talking about and that stressed me out a lot…especially since I don't know Arabic.

The conflict Elle experienced in managing her small reading group reemerged in the same discussion post, where she connected Proposition 227 (for a review of U.S. language-in-education policy, see De Costa & Qin, 2016), which required all public schools in California to enforce an English-only policy for classroom instruc-tion, to the relationship between language and power for a teacher and students. "From a teaching standpoint, I feel as if [an English-only policy] gives the teacher power or makes them feel like an authority figure, especially if they do not know a second language, because then students can't communicate amongst each other in a language that they know and the teacher does not know." Here Elle alluded to her placement experience to describe how language separation positions the teacher as having power to limit students' language use in order to manage behavior.

Missing from Elle's emerging translanguaging stance, however, were instances where she viewed students' families and communities as resources to be leveraged for learning (Belief #2, García et al., 2017). Furthermore, there were instances that suggested that her emerging translanguaging beliefs continued to conflict with the "two solitudes" perspective of languaging (Cummins, 1979, 2008). Within her lesson plan for her field placement, Elle was prompted to set a translanguaging objective and make note of particular instances where she would strategically employ translanguaging pedagogy. However, in her reflection, Elle explained that she did not explicitly plan for translanguaging "aside from letting students discuss in whichever language made the most sense to them." Likewise, in reflection, Elle shared that her cooperating teacher "sort of had to give [her boys] the lesson again in the first language, and with that information and her help to translate to English what they wanted to say, they were able to fill out the intro and conclusion part of the outline." She then asked, "[H]ow can I get the message across to my students when I don't speak the same first language as them, and they need portions or the whole lesson translated in order to be able to compile some type of work, and not just sit there doing nothing because they don't have a clue what is going on?" Despite the earlier successes she shared, where she negotiated meaning with students using their linguistic resources, this reflection suggests that Elle had returned to translation as the major means for conveying information from teacher to students.

Elle began the semester with a deficit-oriented view of hypothetical ESL students' cultural and linguistic resources, in contrast to the dispositions underlying a translanguaging stance (García et al., 2017). As she developed a theoretical understanding of translanguaging through coursework, she was able to extend her learning to field placement classroom, which prompted Elle to problematize how classroom practices and school policies could marginalize learners' cultural and linguistic resources in order to maintain traditional hierarchies. In that respect, Elle appeared to embody what Howard and Levine (2018) describe as the ability by "preservice teachers … to question status quo classroom practices … and continue to reinvent themselves and improve their teaching" (p. 144). Additionally, while Elle struggled to move away from English-only teacher-centered practices, there were also moments where she demonstrated evidence of an emerging translanguaging stance, namely, an asset-based orientation toward students' linguistic and cultural resources and movement toward a more democratic, co-constructed perspective of classroom learning.

3.2 Katie: An In-Service Teacher's Trajectory to Adopting a Translanguaging Stance

Katie, a high-school social studies teacher with 4 years of teaching experience, enrolled in the graduate-level TESOL practicum course in spring 2017. She completed 30 h of her field placement in a sixth grade language arts classroom in the same district where she taught. In contrast to Elle, Katie demonstrated an asset-based orientation (Lucas & Villegas, 2013) to supporting her students' language and cultural practices at the start of our course. That is, Katie refused to sanction the monolingual stance advocated by her colleagues, believing "it was unnatural to not allow my students to speak in a language that represented so much of their individual and cultural identity." However, across the course, it took Katie time to make sense of translanguaging which she initially viewed as "a completely new way to learn, think, and produce [language]." Katie's learning across the course demonstrates how course readings, discussions, and practical experiences scaffolded over time supported her emerging translanguaging stance.

3.2.1 Coursework

Katie, in a follow-up interview, reflected on her learning trajectory across the course and noted her greatest connection from classroom learning to actual practice "probably came out in my posts." After reading the introductory chapter in *Translanguaging* (García & Li, 2014), Katie stated the theory was "something I have never heard of in my study of language and instruction in the public setting." Katie, in her initial post shared she tried "to think of examples when my students [engage] their own translanguaging," but had difficulty coming up with instances. She stated, "it is hard to identify those examples when I am out of the classroom" Despite this, Katie demonstrated a willingness to "be more mindful to using them and listening for them."

As evidence of her commitment to this orientation, Katie revealed an emerging awareness for translanguaging across social contexts. She recounted to her classmates 2 weeks later about a National Public Radio (NPR) broadcast (Greene, 2016) she encountered featuring, "a Punjabi hockey announcer in Canada who uses his own translanguage to relate hockey terms to a Punjabi audience who are not as familiar with the sport as other Canadians." Appropriately, Katie connected the fluidity of language practices afforded by translanguaging to her teaching context, noting such an approach provided ways for students to "find ways to use language to advocate for themselves and their cultural identities." Katie told her classmates she would share such perspectives with her students by having them listen to the NPR recording and "discuss other examples of diversity, inclusion, translanguaging, and globalization." In this instance, Katie revealed her desire to apply her growing understanding of translanguaging from course learning to her teaching in support of students' learning. This approach reinforced Katie's claim "it is important to allow ALL student voices to be heard in the classroom, and to value and listen to the perspective behind those voices, so the audience can connect the cultural, historical context to the words that are used." Using the NPR broadcast, Katie shared how she imagined co-construction of languaging in new ways with youth to ratify their identities. Katie's post also revealed her emerging understanding of how to leverage community resources, such as hockey in a localized context, to support her students' learning (García et al., 2017).

3.2.2 Fieldwork

Similar to Elle, the practicum experience reinforced Katie's learning about translanguaging beyond course readings. Katie compared teaching in support of emergent bi/multilingual students in her field placement with her own pedagogy. Additionally, the practicum afforded her the opportunity to work with students in a small group setting in contrast to experiences in her own classroom, where as the teacher of record, her attention would have been divided among the whole class. Therefore, the practicum experience allowed Katie space to draw theory and practice together, which could have implications for her emerging translanguaging stance within her own classroom.

Observation

For example, in her placement Katie observed bilingual students' engagement with the novel *Tuck Everlasting* (Babbitt, 2015). Katie reflected in her field experience journal how two bilingual students, Ashley and Josie (pseudonyms), engaged in co-construction of knowledge as they composed a written analysis about Winnie, the novel's protagonist. Ashley was struggling to express what she viewed as the protagonist's curiosity in her writing, so Katie helped Ashley to process her ideas verbally. This support then allowed Ashley to express her ideas in writing. When another student, Josie, joined them to ask for assistance, the locus of control shifted (García & Sylvan, 2011). As Katie explained, "Josie and Ashley began discussing Ashley's evidence and quote, and Josie gave her own take on the meaning of the evidence Ashley chose to include. Together, the girls were deepening learning [and] their own learning by giving their own perspectives."

Katie connected this interaction to the description of "pupil-directed translanguaging" from her course reading, where "the physical environment strongly influences how individuals interact, form, and share their perspectives," where "students [can] get to know each other on a more personal level, which can help meaning-making occur more naturally … When bilinguals have to find new information they can language and use meaning-making resources by reading or speaking to others." Katie further reflected on how both the physical environment and interaction support students' "metacognition and extend one's zone of proximal development to acquire new knowledge." This example demonstrates how Katie's interactions with

Ashley and Josie created a democratic space in which traditional hierarchies of schooling were challenged (Belief #3, García et al., 2017). In a small group setting, Katie relinquished her original position as expert to allow Ashley and Josie to support one another as agentive meaning-makers. What is also interesting is that similar to Elle's experience in facilitating a small group reading experiences, Katie observed how students' language and cultural practices "work *juntos* and enrich each other" through Ashley and Josie's peer interaction. Specifically, Katie's reflection reveals her recognition that students' will leverage their translanguaging practices as well as the ecological resources in the classroom to co-construct knowledge when the teacher centers the "locus of control" within students' own language practices (García & Sylvan, 2011).

Application

Based on observing her mentor teacher's use of *Tuck Everlasting* in her field placement, Katie noted her desire to use literature in her own classroom. She posted about using the novel *Number the Stars* (Lowry, 1989). Katie reported, "I want to synthesize how the story of Jews escaping persecution amid World War II is very similar to refugees seeking shelter from the war in Syria and other places affected by ISIS in the Middle East." She suggested pairing the text with "a documentary on Frontline produced by the Public Broadcasting System that covered individual stories from people who have experienced this life today." Kate noted this approach would further support her students' abilities "to engage and discuss other current events, while also relating to what is going on in the text." We see how Katie's proposed plan for future instruction sought to affirm the lived experiences and identities of her students, reflecting an understanding of *juntos* (Belief #1, García et al., 2017). However, this plan might also unintentionally reify strong emotions for students who have experienced trauma.

Later in the semester, Katie shared a different example for how she was able to synthesize course learning across reading, discussion posts, and her practicum. Katie reported having her students read biographical excerpts "of an individual from the Scientific Revolution and Enlightenment through their textbook, a novel, and articles from newsela [website]." Next, she allowed students to engage in subject area meaning-making. She reported as students worked in small groups "some of them used Google Translate, others translated individual words in their L1 ... to make up summaries about what they've read." In the activity, Katie noted "students used both English and their L1 to debate meaning, develop a common understanding, and put together ideas." In her reflection, Katie recounted: "The greatest benefit from translanguaging is increased diversity and reinvention and evolution of culture, which is very cool to observe happening in real time, being around so many bilingual speakers in the classroom." Despite Katie's growing understanding of translanguaging, some of her assumptions revealed a need for further development. Katie shared in a post, "From my own experience, I believe translanguaging instructional strategies work best when students share a common L1, in addition to being literate in their L1." Katie then recounted using a current events article in her students' home language as well as in English, "to allow students to connect protests in their home country to the protest that starts the French Revolution." Katie assumed that using texts written in students' native language "would allow them to comprehend the article written in English at a higher lexile than they are used to reading in class." Yet, she discovered that a number of students had difficulty comprehending the article in their home language. She recounted, "students chose to read the article in English and translate unknown words into their L1, instead of reading the article in their native language and translating it into English." While attending to the cultural aspects of students' learning, Katie's comments about translation, similar to Elle's, reflect a belief that negotiation of meaning was limited to translating between two distinct languages.

4   Discussion

Tracing Elle and Katie's emerging translanguaging stance through course and field work reveals similarities and differences in their starting and ending points within the course. While not generalizable, these two cases provide teacher educators with meaningful insights into how they might design their courses in support their PSTs and ISTs growth in taking up translanguaging stances. In this section, we discuss the significance of our findings and then provide implications for how these cases might shape the field to teacher education, especially as we recommend sustained work in supporting a translanguaging stance beyond a single course and field placement.

First, the integration of Elle and Katie's course and field experiences proved to be essential for (1) connecting their theoretical understandings of translanguaging to practice, and (2) facilitating the development of their translanguaging stance. While Elle acknowledged how traditional language hierarchies marginalize learners' diverse linguistic and cultural identities in U.S. classrooms in course discussions, it was not until she began her field placement that she problematized these hierarchies within her own ideology and practice. Elle's discussion posts and field placement reflections provided her space to confront her own discomfort as a linguistic and cultural outsider in her placement as well as the challenge of managing a small group of students. Furthermore, her field placement in a bilingual context provided Elle with an opportunity to see translanguaging in practice. Likewise, Katie's learning was directly connected to her role as a social studies educator, which she referred to across her coursework. Since the disciplines of the social studies are culturally bounded, Katie's ongoing learning about translanguaging revealed her continual interrogation of the cultural aspects of languaging. We see this exemplified in her desire to share the NPR broadcast with her students, her use of *Number the Stars* (Lowry, 1989) as a classroom text to draw connections to the current persecution of refugees, and her inclusion of L1 news articles to highlight the role of protests in revolutionary movements. However, in her attempt to support students' lived experiences by applying tenets of translanguaging, we recognize that Katie's approach might be problematic. That is, in discussing aspects of terrorism and geno-cide with students, the conversation may bring forth strong emotions or feelings of trauma for those who lived through such events. A translanguaging stance might therefore present an overly idealized view of what leveraging resources can accomplish.

Just as Elle and Katie's field experiences provided an opportunity to connect theory to practice, so too did their experiences in the field inform their coursework, particularly in instances where they explicitly the confronted monolingual bias. This was evident in Katie's pushback against her colleagues' English-only stance, which she saw as unequally positioning students by prohibiting the use of their home languages as resources. By extension, Elle leveraged her field placement experience within her coursework through imagined conversations with colleagues, administrators, and policy makers where she advocated for translanguaging. In other words, the dialectical intersection of Elle and Katie's course and field experi-ences allowed them to extend translanguaging theory to practice. Second, Elle and Katie began and ended the semester from different places with respect to their emerging translanguaging stances. Early in the course, Elle seemed to perceive teachers as the "purveyors" of English to students in an ESL setting. In contrast, Katie exhibited an asset-based orientation (Lucas & Villegas, 2013) toward her stu-dents' linguistic and cultural resources, viewing deprivation of students' home lan-guages as the loss of a vital resource for cultural understanding.

By the end of the course, Elle demonstrated some evidence of the knowledge and dispositions of a translanguaging TESOL educator, namely recognition of students' language and cultural practices as resources that "work *juntos* and enrich each other," (Belief #2, García et al., 2017) though she struggled to relinquish the locus of control in favor of situating the classroom as "a democratic space" for co-construction of meaning between teacher and students (Belief #1, García et al., 2017). What is also missing from Elle's emerging translanguaging stance is evi-dence that she viewed students' families and communities as resources to be lever-aged for learning, which is the third belief underlying a translanguaging stance. In looking across her learning opportunities in course and field work, the TESOL practicum curriculum did not afford her space to explicitly explore and engage with this belief, demonstrating additional learning experiences beyond course and field-work may be needed.

In contrast, Katie's emerging translanguaging stance revealed a greater willing-ness to situate the "locus of control" within students' linguistic resources as well as those of their families and communities (García & Sylvan, 2011). Though we saw evidence of Katie's growing translanguaging stance, we also acknowledge her pes-simism: "I do not think that adopting a curriculum that supports translanguaging education would have space in the language learning model adopted in schools. Since many states and measures have an "English only" approach to language learn-ing, I do not see translanguaging gaining enough momentum to take the place of the language learning department in priorities in education." While we are greatly encouraged by how Elle and Katie grew through our courses, we realize more work is needed to foster a translanguaging shift in schools, particularly as we consider how to best support new and practicing teachers in confronting pervasive English-only policies and standardized tests in favor of translanguaging (Palmer, 2018).

5 Implications

5.1 Course Design and Curricula

Considering Elle and Katie's learning as comparative case studies helped us identify what outcomes emerge from particular learning opportunities within our course. Through course readings and discussions, Elle and Katie began articulating their understanding of translanguaging as a theory and pedagogy; within their practicum field contexts, they connected their theoretical understanding to practice as they began noticing translanguaging within how their students were already learning. Additionally, as our work with Elle and Katie demonstrates, in field placements, teachers need specific opportunities beyond direct observation of mentor teachers to engage with students and their language practices. In looking across these experiences, we argue that TESOL teacher preparation and education programs can go further to leverage the dialectical relationship between course learning and field experiences and provide opportunities for PSTs and ISTs to connect the two in their application of translanguaging theory to praxis. For instance, they could explore English-only policies that have marginalized linguistic diversity (see García et al., 2008) as well as initiatives that have countered the influence of these policies, such as the Lau v. Nichols U.S. Supreme Court case. To humanize the reality of such policies, they could read narrative-based texts, such as *Rethinking Bilingual Education* (Barbian, Gonzales, & Mejia, 2017), to expand their awareness of the pervasiveness of language ideologies in U.S. schools and their implications for individual learners. These narratives could also provide text-based examples of translanguaging in practice.

Elle and Katie have also reminded us that beginning and practicing teachers need opportunities to explicitly engage their existing monolingual language ideologies (Deroo & Ponzio, 2019) based on their experiences as language learners and teachers, as well as the broader structures and policies enacted across the U.S. educational system in order to develop a translanguaging stance. What we found to be particularly generative for their learning were assignments where they had authentic purposes and audiences to confront the monolingual bias, such as advocating for translanguaging among colleagues, administrators, and policy makers. As Elle and Katie entered these conversations, they explicitly problematized monolingual ideology within their own teaching practice as well as within the broader educational system.

5.2   Field Based-Learning and Practicum Experiences

In our context, PSTs' placements are coordinated by the teacher preparation program while ISTs are asked to find their own placements within their districts. We acknowledge that teacher preparation programs approach practicums in a variety of ways, but hope the findings from this study provide additional insights into the affordances and challenges of field-based practicum. Elle's field placement experience with a bilingual mentor teacher in a bilingual Arabic-English speaking community was atypical of the experiences of the majority of PSTs in our program. For example, most of our PSTs are placed in multilingual classrooms with mentor teachers who are monolingual English speakers and where unofficial English-only policies are reflected in the school culture. Overwhelmingly, many PSTs over the past seven semesters have expressed concern about enacting translanguaging pedagogy in their required lesson plans when their mentor teachers enforce an English-only policy. In contrast, Elle not only observed translanguaging in action, but felt a sense of agency to explore her own developing translanguaging stance. When compared with her peers, Elle's experience reinforces the importance of purposefully selecting mentor teachers whose teaching practices align with pedagogical perspectives put forth within coursework (De Costa, 2015; Richards & Farrell, 2011). However, we acknowledge the challenge this presents for teacher preparation programs, particularly those with a large number of teacher candidates.

Katie's practicum experience in a sixth grade English language arts classroom allowed her to build upon her already-present assets-based view of bilingualism as she observed another teacher's practice. That is, she was less concerned with the implications of her course- and field-based learning in the context of another teacher's classroom and more concerned about applying practicum learning to her own class. Katie's experience suggests that the quality of placement might be less of a concern for ISTs required to participate in field experiences as part of their certification process than with PSTs, though assignments should still support application of course learning to teaching practice.

The resistance to translanguaging in placement experiences, as reported by the PSTs and ISTs we work with is not unique; if anything, such resistance reflects the challenges that teachers often encounter when disrupting "traditional hierarchies" in order to "work toward a more just society" as a part of adopting translanguaging pedagogy (García et al., 2017, p. 58). As our previous work illustrates (Deroo & Ponzio, 2019), prejudices against translanguaging pedagogies within school and society undermine teachers' sense of agency to enact translanguaging in their classrooms. Therefore, we continue to revise our course to support teachers as they encounter such resistance. For example, we present teachers with scenarios where they must address a fellow teachers' push-back to translanguaging by reflecting on these possible interactions in writing. Recently, we have also added an assignment where teachers compose an email asking for administrative report from an imagined administrator. PSTs and ISTs articulate the challenges experienced by emergent bi/multilingual students and their teachers when they are tasked with high-stakes testing–specifically, testing that contradicts translanguaging paradigms. Collectively, we maintain that beginning and experienced teachers need opportunities to not only make sense of translanguaging within their personal experiences and pedagogies, but to also develop a sense of agency to resist existing societal pressures that reinforce English dominant language ideologies (Deroo & Ponzio, 2019).

Our experience as teacher-educators shows that teachers need more than one class and one field experience to adopt a translanguaging stance. We recognize a need for increased synergy across departments of teacher education in alignment with translanguaging pedagogy, especially for teacher educators outside TESOL teacher preparation. In keeping with efforts to adopt a language-based approach to content instruction for English language learners (de Oliveira, 2016), we wonder what it would look like to infuse this work into content-specific methods courses in English, social studies, mathematics, arts education, and so forth. Likewise, in schools and districts, translanguaging pedagogy needs to be woven into the opportunities teachers have for continued professional learning. Like Katie, we acknowledge the challenges of translanguaging stance being taken up more broadly in school, district, state, and federal educational policies. Therefore, we argue that the work of uprooting monolingual paradigms in favor of pedagogies that sustain students' diverse linguistic and cultural practices must continue with teachers who can resist subtractive English-only policies from the classroom level (De Costa & Qin, 2016).

As a part of this work, teachers must recognize that even additive perspectives of bilingualism perpetuate the monolingual bias. This work goes beyond viewing emergent bi/multilingual students' diverse language and cultural practices as resources for classroom learning–learning that is seen as being in service of developing, "the linguistic practices of the white listening subject when appropriate (Flores & Rosa, 2015, p. 152). Instead, as white listening subjects, teachers must develop the capacity to critique how their "ears"ill continue to hear deficiency if they continue seeing their emergent bi/multilingual students' development of the practices of the "white speaking subject" as the objective for learning. Consistent with Flores and Rosa's (2015) call for focused "scrutiny of the white listening subject," we view translanguaging as an avenue to disrupt White monolingual English educators' views of language, starting with how they understand language practices to reside in bi/multilingual learners' minds not as separate systems, but fluid and integrated repertoires–which can then lead to questions as to why notions of language separation and correctness emerged in the first place. We invite other teacher educators to join us in considering the following questions:

- How do we support beginning and practicing teachers to interrogate their own language ideologies as a part of a translanguaging shift?
- How can reflection and collaboration support teachers in developing and enacting a translanguaging stance as they engage in translanguaging praxis?
- How can we support teachers' enactment of translanguaging pedagogies?
- What additional support do teachers need to confront monolingual paradigms with their students, in their schools and districts, and in school policies more broadly?

Moreover, our work suggests implications for additional research, including studies that follow teachers over time in order to document their learning trajectories in adopting and enacting a translanguaging stance, which is vitally important to facilitating translanguaging praxis, beyond a single semester and reinforced by observation of teaching practices in classroom spaces.

We have found from our work as teacher-educators that shifts in supporting PST and ISTs to take up a translanguaging stance is possible. Our hope is that this chapter provides insight into how beginning and practicing teachers' might adopt a translanguaging stance where they not only view their students as "resourceful" agents (Pennycook, 2012, p. 99) of their own languaging, but also perceive their agency to resist monolingual English ideologies from the ground up. We echo our colleagues in this edited volume in calling for increased resistance to conventional monolingual bias and English hegemony within TESOL education in favor of the critical and liberating turn that translanguaging represents.

References

Alim, H. S., & Paris, D. (2015). Whose language gap? Critical and culturally sustaining pedagogies as necessary challenges to racializing hegemony. *Journal of Linguistic Anthropology, 25*(1), 66–86.

Babbitt, N. (2015). *Tuck everlasting* (40th anniversary edition). New York, NY: Square Fish/Farrar Straus Giroux.

Balasubramanian, C., & Shunnaq, S. R. (2018). Teacher-fronted classes. In J. I. Liontas & M. DelliCarpini (Eds.), *The TESOL Encyclopedia of English language teaching*. https://doi.org/10.1002/9781118784235.eelt0821

Barbian, E., Gonzales, G., & Mejia, P. (Eds.). (2017). *Rethinking bilingual education: Welcoming home languages in our classrooms*. Milwaukee, Wisconsin: Rethinking schools.

Beckett, G. H., & Slater, T. (2018). Project-based learning and technology. In J. I. Liontas & M. DelliCarpini (Eds.), *The TESOL Encyclopedia of English language teaching*. https://doi.org/10.1002/9781118784235.eelt0427

Blommaert, J. (2010). *The sociolinguistics of globalization*. Cambridge, UK/New York, NY: Cambridge University Press.

Blommaert, J. (2013). Citizenship, language, and superdiversity: Towards complexity. *Journal of Language, Identity & Education, 12*(3), 193–196. https://doi.org/10.1080/15348458.2013.797276

Bunch, G. C. (2013). Pedagogical language knowledge: Preparing mainstream teachers for English learners in the new standards era. *Review of Research in Education, 37*(1), 298–341. https://doi.org/10.3102/0091732X12461772

Canagarajah, S. (2011). Translanguaging in the classroom: Emerging issues for research and pedagogy. *Applied Linguistics Review, 3*(2), 21–26.

Cenoz, J., & Gorter, D. (2011). Focus on multilingualism: A study of trilingual writing. *The Modern Language Journal, 95*(3), 356–369.

Cochran-Smith, M. (1991). Learning to teach against the grain. *Harvard Educational Review, 61*(3), 279–311.

Cummins, J. (1979). Linguistic interdependence and the educational development of bilingual children. *Review of Educational Research, 49*(2), 222–251. https://doi.org/10.3102/00346543049002222

Cummins, J. (2008). Teaching for transfer: Challenging the two solitudes assumption in bilingual education. In J. Cummins & N. H. Hornberger (Eds.), *Bilingual education* (2nd ed., pp. 65–75). New York, NY: Springer.

Darling-Hammond, L., & Bransford, J. (2005). *Preparing teachers for a changing world: What teachers should learn and be able to do*. San Francisco, CA: Jossey-Bass.

De Costa, P. I. (2015). Tracing reflexivity through a narrative and identity lens. In Y. L. Cheung, S. B. Said, & K. Park (Eds.), *Advances and current trends in language teacher identity research* (pp. 135–147). New York, NY: Routledge.

De Costa, P. I., & Qin, K. (2016). English language education in the United States: Past, present and future issues. In L. T. Wong & A. Dubey-Jhaveri (Eds.), *English language education in a global world: Practices, issues and challenges* (pp. 229–238). Hauppauge, NY: Nova Science Publishers.

De Costa, P. I., Singh, J., Milu, E., Wang, X., Fraiberg, S., & Canagarajah, S. (2017). Pedagogizing translingual practice: Prospects and possibilities. *Research in the Teaching of English, 51*(4), 464–472.

De Oliveira, L. (2016). A language-based approach to content instruction (LACI) for English language learners: Examples from two elementary teachers. *International Multilingual Research Journal, 10*(3), 217–231.

Deroo, M. R. (2020). Translanguaging pedagogy to support bi/multilingual students' language learning in social studies: "How we communicate everything". In A. Slapac & S. Coppersmith (Eds.), *Beyond language learning instruction: Transformative supports for emergent bilinguals and educators* (pp. 231–266). Hershey, PA: IGI Global.

Deroo, M. R., & Ponzio, C. (2019). Confronting ideologies: A discourse analysis of in-service teachers' translanguaging stance through an ecological lens. *Bilingual Research Journal, 42*, 1–18.

Fillmore, L. W., & Snow, C. E. (2018). What teachers need to know about language. In C. T. Adger, C. E. Snow, & D. Christian (Eds.), *What teachers need to know about language* (pp. 8–51). Bristol, UK: Multilingual Matters.

Flores, N., & Aneja, G. (2017). Why needs hiding? *Translingual (re)orientations in TESOL Teacher Education, 51*, 23.

Flores, N., & Rosa, J. (2015). Undoing appropriateness: Raciolinguistic ideologies and language diversity in education. *Harvard Educational Review, 85*(2), 149–171.

Flores, N., & Rosa, J. (2019). Bringing race into second language acquisition. *The Modern Language Journal, 103*(S1), 145–151. https://doi.org/10.1111/modl.12523

García, O., Johnson, S. I., & Seltzer, K. (2017). *The translanguaging classroom: Leveraging student bilingualism for learning*. Philadelphia, PA: Caslon.

Garcia, O., Kleifgen, J. A., & Falchi, L. (2008). *From English language learners to emergent bilinguals. equity matters. Research review no. 1*. Retrieved from Campaign for Educational Equity, Teachers College, Columbia University website: HYPERLINK https://eric.ed.gov/?id=ED524002

García, O., & Li Wei. (2014). *Translanguaging: Language, bilingualism and education*. Basingstoke, Hampshire/New York, NY: Palgrave Macmillan.

García, O., & Otheguy, R. (2019). Plurilingualism and translanguaging: Commonalities and divergences. *International Journal of Bilingual Education and Bilingualism, 23*(1), 1–19. https://doi.org/10.1080/13670050.2019.1598932

García, O., & Sylvan, C. E. (2011). Pedagogies and practices in multilingual classrooms: Singularities in pluralities. *The Modern Language Journal, 95*(3), 385–400. https://doi.org/10.1111/j.1540-4781.2011.01208.x

Goodwin, A. L. (2017). Who is in the classroom now? Teacher preparation and the education of immigrant children. *Educational Studies, 53*(5), 433–449. https://doi.org/10.1080/00131946.2016.1261028

Greene, D. (2016, May 26). *Sports*. Hockey night in Canada Punjabi edition. Retrieved from: https://www.npr.org/2016/05/27/479696652/hockey-night-in-canadapunjabi-edition

Hall, G. (2016). Method, methods and methodology. Historical trends and current debates. In G. Hall (Ed.), *The Routledge handbook of English language teaching* (pp. 209–223). New York, NY: Routledge.

Hawkins, M., & Norton, B. (2009). Critical language teacher education. In A. Burns & J. Richards (Eds.), *The Cambridge guide to second language teacher education* (pp. 30–39). Cambridge, MA: Cambridge University Press.

Hinkelman, D. (2018). Blended learning. In J. I. Liontas & M. DelliCarpini (Eds.), *The TESOL encyclopedia of English language teaching*. https://doi.org/10.1002/9781118784235.eelt0400

Howard, E. R., & Levine, T. H. (2018). What teacher educators need to know about language and language learners: The power of a faculty learning community. In C. T. Adger, C. E. Snow, & D. Christian (Eds.), *What teachers need to know about language* (pp. 143–176). Bristol, UK: Multilingual Matters.

Lowry, L. (1989). *Number the stars*. Boston, MA: Houghton Mifflin.

Lucas, T., & Villegas, A. M. (2013). Preparing linguistically responsive teachers: Laying the foundation in preservice teacher education. *Theory Into Practice, 52*(2), 98–109. https://doi.org/1 0.1080/00405841.2013.770327

Miles, M. B., Huberman, A. M., & Saldaña, J. (2014). *Qualitative data analysis: A methods sourcebook* (3rd ed.). Thousand Oaks, CA: SAGE.

Moll, L. C., Amanti, C., Neff, D., & Gonzalez, N. (1992). Funds of knowledge for teaching: Using a qualitative approach to connect homes and classrooms. *Theory Into Practice, 31*(2), 132–141. https://doi.org/10.1080/00405849209543534

Palmer, D. K. (2018). *Teacher leadership for social change in bilingual and bicultural education*. Bristol, UK: Multilingual Matters.

Paris, D., & Alim, H. S. (Eds.). (2017). *Culturally sustaining pedagogies: Teaching and learning for justice in a changing world*. New York, NY: Teachers College Press.

Pennycook, A. (2008). Critical applied linguistics and language education. In N. H. Hornberger (Ed.), *Encyclopedia of language and education* (pp. 169–181). Boston, MA: Springer.

Pennycook, A. (2012). *Unexpected places: Language and mobility* Multilingual Matters.

Poza, L. (2017). Translanguaging: Definitions, implications, and further needs in burgeoning inquiry. *Berkeley Review of Education, 6*. https://doi.org/10.5070/B86110060

Richardson, L. (1994). Writing: A method of inquiry. In N. K. Denzin & Y. S. Lincoln (Eds.), *Handbook of qualitative research* (pp. 516–529). Thousand Oaks, CA: Sage.

Richards, J. C., & Farrell, T. S. C. (2011). *Practice teaching: A reflective approach*. Cambridge University Press.

U.S. Department of Education. (2016). *The state of racial diversity in the educator workforce*. Washington, DC: U.S. Department of Education, Office of Planning, Evaluation and Policy Development, Policy and Program Studies Service.

Valdés, J. (2016). Entry visa denied: The construction of symbolic language borders in educational settings. In O. García, N. Flores, & M. Spotti (Eds.), *The Oxford handbook of language and society* (pp. 321–348). Oxford, UK: Oxford University Press.

Waller, L., Wethers, K., & De Costa, P. I. (2017). A critical praxis: Narrowing the gap between identity, theory, and practice. *TESOL Journal, 8*(1), 4–27.

Wiley, T. G. (2014). Diversity, super-diversity, and monolingual language ideology in the United States: Tolerance or intolerance? *Review of Research in Education, 38*(1), 1–32. https://doi.org/10.3102/0091732X13511047

Yin, R. K. (2018). *Case study research and applications: Design and methods* (6th ed.). Los Angeles, CA: SAGE.

Chapter 7
Learning to Teach English for Justice from a Translanguaging Orientation

Elizabeth Robinson, Zhongfeng Tian ⓘ, Elie Crief, and Maíra Lins Prado

Abstract This research study investigated how undergraduate students understood translanguaging in relationship to language, culture, and power; and how they embodied translanguaging in a TESOL Certificate course to see if translanguaging as pedagogy affords students the elements necessary to teach for justice. Through collaborative qualitative methods utilizing teacher research we analyzed the course work of 19 student participants in the course to see their learning and application of translanguaging. We found the student participants, in response to learning about translanguaging, demonstrated understandings of the connection between language, culture, and power, and its importance in teaching emergent bilinguals. However, we also found that participants struggled with translanguaging in their teaching practice and mostly resorted to using TESOL strategies rather than embodying translanguaging. This research sheds light on the process, program and evaluation of teacher preparation and illuminates the ways in which program design and instructional strategies can best prepare teachers to teach for justice.

Keywords Translanguaging · Justice · Teacher education · TESOL · Undergraduate students · Pedagogy

E. Robinson (✉)
Suffolk University, Boston, MA, USA
e-mail: erobinson@suffolk.edu

Z. Tian
The University of Texas at San Antonio, San Antonio, TX, USA
e-mail: zhongfeng.tian@utsa.edu

E. Crief
University of Pennsylvania, Philadelphia, PA, USA
e-mail: ecrief@gse.upenn.edu

M. L. Prado
Faculdade de Direito de São Bernardo do Campo, São Bernardo do Campo, SP, Brazil
e-mail: contact@mairalp.com

© Springer Nature Switzerland AG 2020
Z. Tian et al. (eds.), *Envisioning TESOL through a Translanguaging Lens*,
Educational Linguistics 45, https://doi.org/10.1007/978-3-030-47031-9_7

This study takes place in unprecedented times in the United States. Intolerance and hatred are exacerbated under the current administration. The reactionary political atmosphere, largely created by the current government, is promoting divisiveness both nationally and internationally. In the current volatile political environment nativist sentiments are driving policies that overtly discriminate against immigrants and refugees. Civil rights and laws protecting women, people of color, and LGBTQ (Lesbian, Gay, Bisexual, Transgender, Queer) people are being dismantled. Political rhetoric has normalized racist discourse and hate speech.

Language can be used as a tool to reinforce prejudice and discrimination. The language a person speaks is often seen to indicate one's nationality or belonging to a country, culture, environment, class, race or ethnicity. In the U.S., while English is not the official language, its hegemonic features tend to mask the country's plurality of languages. Sixty-six million people (21.8% of the population) speak a language other than English at home. In particular, Spanish is spoken at home by forty-one million U.S. residents (U.S. Census Bureau, 2017). Spanish is the most spoken non-English language in the U.S. and the fastest growing student population in the U.S. is Spanish-speaking (Flores, 2017). However, language policies do not support this reality. Many states and school districts employ English-only policies. The ideology that drives these policies erases the heterogeneity of students. These policies are based on a deficit point of view that sees students' language diversity as a problem to rectify rather than a resource. Being discriminated against based on the language one speaks or being forbidden to use one's language has devastating effects on students.

It is crucial to build inclusivity and understanding through education to counter the growing intolerance and discrimination. As academics, teachers, and students, we believe that translanguaging, a teaching theory and approach that uses all students' cultural and linguistic repertoires in learning, provides the theoretical and pedagogical tools to create compassionate and transformative classrooms. Working in the TESOL field, we understand the power of language. We believe it is our responsibility to use language in transformative ways. Translanguaging offers hope for building transformative classrooms (García, 2009a; García & Li, 2014). We have specifically chosen to explore translanguaging, as we believe that it represents an important shift from English-only policies and the traditionally monolingual teaching of English to teaching language for justice (Ladson-Billings, 2015). Translanguaging values students' bi/multilingualism as a resource and strategically incorporates their cultures, languages, experiences, and stories into classrooms (García & Kleyn, 2016). We believe that translanguaging holds the promise of challenging the hegemonic power of English and leveraging language-minoritized student practices to create more equitable classrooms. In other words, we see translanguaging as a potential way to teach English for justice.

This research stemmed from the collaboration between two of the authors, Zhongfeng and Elizabeth and Elizabeth's desire to bring together her goal of teaching for justice and her work in TESOL teacher preparation. Translanguaging as theory and pedagogy shares these same goals. For Elizabeth learning and teaching about translanguaging was revolutionary having come from years of preparing teachers using principles and practices of Sheltered English Instruction (SEI). With the purpose of preparing students to teach for justice, this research studies how the explicit teaching of translanguaging theory and pedagogy in a TESOL certificate course, open to all undergraduate students, was taken up by students. Previous work (Robinson, Tian, Martínez, & Qarqeen, 2018) introduced translanguaging in the same TESOL course a semester earlier (Spring 2017) and showed promising results among student participants in terms of an epistemic shift in their understanding of language theory and language education. To go beyond just introducing translanguaging, we built on the previous findings to better integrate translanguaging into the course. This research study was conducted in the fall of 2017. We asked three questions in our research:

1. How do undergraduate student participants understand translanguaging in relationship to language, culture and power?
2. How do participants enact translanguaging in their microteaching?
3. Does translanguaging as pedagogy in a TESOL course afford participants the elements necessary to teach for justice?

In the writing of our study, we are influenced by the work of García, Kleifgen, and Falchi (2008) in viewing all languages as resources for teaching; and we use the term "emergent bilinguals" for people in the process of learning another language. This term recognizes their emergent status of becoming bilinguals, highlighting the advantages these students have rather than focusing on their need to learn English (García, 2009b). In this chapter, we also use the term ELLs (English Language Learners) as it was the term used in the course when it was taught and it is also a commonly used term in the field of TESOL.

Within the political and social context of the United States we see translanguaging as a powerful tool for teacher education. Our intent is to prepare our undergraduate students, who aspire to teach English, to counter deficit monolingual ideologies through a translanguaging approach to language, culture and power. Next, we further explain our understandings of justice and what it means to us to teach English for justice. Our methodology section will introduce each of the authors of this collaborative study, explore the classroom context of the study, and share our processes of data collection and analysis. We will then elaborate on how participants understood translanguaging and how we saw evidence of important critical understandings of language, culture, and power. In our discussion section we draw on our conceptual framework to make sense of our findings and where we are in terms of preparing our participants to teach English for justice. We end with conclusions on our own teaching and implications for future work in TESOL teacher preparation in order for all teachers to teach English for justice.

1   Conceptual Framework

1.1   *Justice*

At the core of our research team is our collective commitment to work for justice through language and through our teaching. Language shapes our understandings, our learning, our knowledge and thus our power. Teaching, and the teaching of language, hold the promise of opening up new and more just ways of understanding and being in our world. In our research team, we have spent hours discussing justice. We believe that we need to broaden our focus from just examining social and human interactions to consider the ways that human injustices impact all aspects of our world. We are influenced by Gloria Ladson-Billings' call for a focus on "Just Justice" (2015). She explains that what is needed is a "fundamental rethinking of our work and our task as human beings" (Ladson-Billings, 2015) to confront the tremendous injustices that keep our society and our world so far away from what we know is just, fair and equitable. Ladson-Billings urges educational researchers to take up the term justice instead of focusing on a specific definition of justice such as social justice. She explains, that for educational researchers, this rethinking to address justice, "just justice", entails making two shifts in the work we do.

The first shift is critiquing Western approaches to justice and looking broadly around the world for more comprehensive theories of justice. While some of our research team members are socialized in Western academic traditions and very much informed by the fields of social justice education (Adams, Bell, & Griffin, 2007), and multicultural education and culturally responsive education (Banks, 1996; Gay, 2000; Ladson-Billings, 1994; Nieto, 1992), we recognize and invite broader understandings. We collectively work to expand on these Western understandings of justice by seeking out other perspectives and conceptions of justice such as those belonging to colonized and/or indigenous peoples. We do this by exploring various academic literature on colonization (Battiste, 2000) for non-Western approaches to justice and indigenous practices (Smith, 2012; Tuck, 2009) and for broader understandings of interactions between humans and the natural world. Simultaneously, we work to ensure that the makeup of our team is culturally, linguistically and ethnically diverse. In our research, we continuously work to broaden our own understandings of justice by learning from as many perspectives as possible. One small shift we have made due to our belief in the transformative power of language and terminology, is explicitly adopting a focus on justice rather than social justice. The term justice encompasses discussion about all components of Earth rather than limiting the discussion to only societal factors that are considered when using the term social justice.

The second shift, in order to rethink the work of educational researchers and confront injustices, entails moving from viewing justice as a theory to enacting justice as praxis. We understand praxis to be the simultaneous engagement in theory, research, and action to bring about change that is grounded in respect for our world and all things inhabiting our world. Justice as praxis in teaching then requires teachers to engage theory, conduct classroom research and enact changes in their own practices that respect and support all students for the purpose of bettering our world. Our overarching goal is to explore ways to implement our ever-shifting theories of justice into our own practice of researching and teaching as well as into future teachers' practices. We strive to challenge and ultimately to change existing unjust language and literacy educational practices (García & Kleifgen, 2018).

1.2 Teaching English for Justice through Translanguaging

Our constantly evolving understandings of justice feed our immediate research goal of investigating ways to teach English for justice. On our journey of striving toward justice in our TESOL certificate courses, we are guided by the theory of translanguaging (García, 2009a; García & Li, 2014) in seeking to provide access to English in culturally and linguistically sustaining ways. Translanguaging theory critiques structures of dominance and prioritizes non-dominant ways of knowing and speaking. By openly critiquing the dominance of English, translanguaging "helps to disrupt the socially constructed language hierarchies that are responsible for the suppression of the language of many minoritized peoples" (Otheguy, García, & Reid, 2015, p. 283). We view this critiquing of English dominance as akin to the challenging of Western ideas of justice in Ladson-Billings' (2015) call for "just justice".

As well as a theory, translanguaging is also a pedagogy. Translanguaging pedagogy is made up of three framing concepts: stance, design, and shifts (García, Johnson, & Seltzer, 2017). Stance is a commitment by teachers to value bilingual students' full language repertoires as a human right and a learning resource. Translanguaging lesson design establishes connections across home, school, and community languages and cultures through curricula. Translanguaging shifts are required when unforeseen and unplanned classroom interactions demand variations. When teachers engage in translanguaging pedagogy they leverage students' bilingualism for learning, which levels the playing field and advances justice (García, Johnson, & Seltzer, 2017). We believe that translanguaging as a theory and as pedagogy is an equitable tool teachers can employ to teach for justice.

The other theoretical tool that guides our journey toward teaching English for justice is our *Teachers for Justice* model in Fig. 7.1 below. Our objectives as teacher educators are for critical teachers to be able to: (1) recognize practices and structures that sustain inequalities (2) critique status quo practices and structures that sustain inequalities and (3) engage in practices that support all learners. Figure 7.1 shows how recognizing, critiquing and practicing are all connected practices, yet practicing is the largest component of teacher's work. Each of these objectives can be further understood and assessed by looking for specific critical goals and objectives that have been taken from the literature on preparing teachers for diverse students and on preparing teachers to work with ELLs. We use this model to assess how we are doing in preparing future teachers to teach for justice.

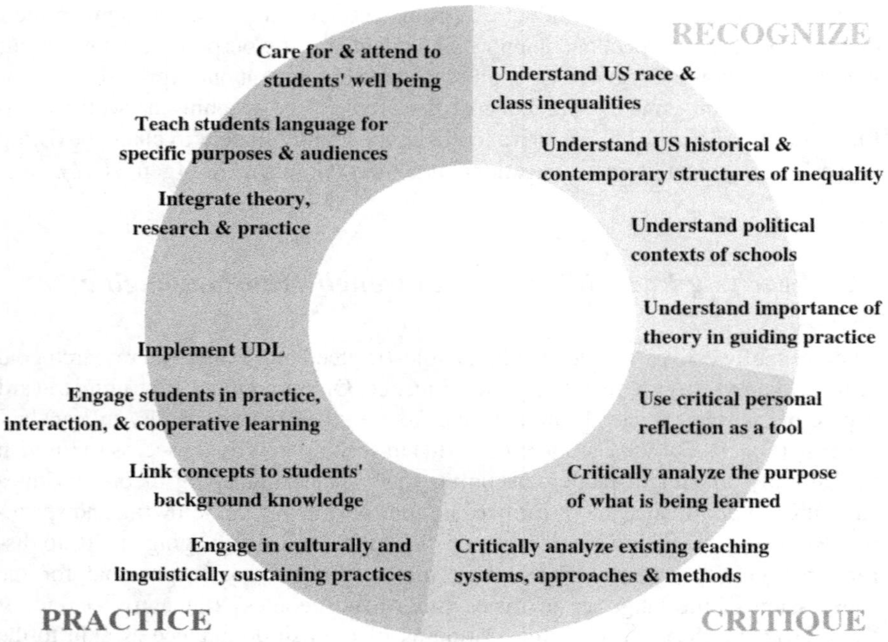

Care for & attend to
students' well being

RECOGNIZE

Understand US race &
class inequalities

Teach students language for
specific purposes & audiences

Understand US historical &
contemporary structures of inequality

Integrate theory,
research & practice

Understand political
contexts of schools

Understand importance of
theory in guiding practice

Implement UDL

Engage students in practice,
interaction, & cooperative learning

Use critical personal
reflection as a tool

Link concepts to students'
background knowledge

Critically analyze the purpose
of what is being learned

Engage in culturally and
linguistically sustaining practices

Critically analyze existing teaching
systems, approaches & methods

PRACTICE   CRITIQUE

Fig. 7.1 Teachers for justice model

2 Methodology

This qualitative study drew on methods of teacher research (Cochran-Smith & Lytle, 1993) to explore how student participants learn and apply translanguaging in an undergraduate TESOL course entitled *Strategies for Working with English Learners*, offered in Fall 2017. This study was conducted by a team of researchers, rather than just the course teacher, in order to explore translanguaging from different perspectives. Thereby, we designed the study to recognize and value the unique experiences (both etic and emic) and critical roles of each of the researchers. We acted as knowledge brokers to mutually inform and reinforce one another's understanding of translanguaging during our research process. We drew on models of teacher action research to take a flexible, context-specific approach to problem-solving and implementing necessary changes in the *Strategies for Working with English Learners* course that was being simultaneously taught and researched (Blumenreich & Falk, 2006; Chandler-Olcott, 2002).

2.1 The Researchers

Our research team consisted of four members. Elizabeth was the professor who developed the TESOL Certificate courses and who was the instructor of the *Strategies for Working with English Learners* course. Zhongfeng, was a doctoral student from another institution who was knowledgeable about translanguaging. He assisted with micro teaching and videotaping in the course. Elie was an undergraduate student working with Elizabeth as a Research Assistant. He was also enrolled as a student in the course. Maíra, was an ESL (English as a Second Language) teacher interested in pursuing a TESOL Certificate. She audited *Strategies for Working with English Learners* the following year in Fall 2018.

Elizabeth Robinson was born and raised in Boston, U.S. She speaks English and studied French throughout her schooling. She taught English in South Korea for 2 years and in Spain for 3 years. Her Spanish is much stronger than her Korean but her love for both of these cultures and for working translingually and transculturally has infused her professional work. After receiving a masters' degree in applied linguistics she taught ESL in public schools for 3 years. In 2004, Elizabeth went back to school for a doctoral degree in Language, Literacy and Culture from UMass Amherst. Her focus in all her work is on preparing teachers to work in linguistically and culturally sustaining ways. She has been a professor at Suffolk University in Boston since 2008 and at the time of the study she served as the Director of the Undergraduate Education Studies Program and the TESOL Certificate Program.

Zhongfeng Tian is originally from China, and a multilingual speaker of Mandarin and English with conversational fluency in Cantonese. He holds a Master of Education degree in TESOL from Boston University and at the time of the study was a doctoral candidate majoring in Curriculum and Instruction with a specialization in Language, Literacy, and Culture at Boston College. As a former ESL/EFL teacher, he worked with students of different age groups and cultural and linguistic backgrounds in China, Cambodia, and U.S. His research is theoretically grounded in translanguaging and critical pedagogies, and he strives to transform emergent bilinguals' learning experiences through creating heteroglossic, meaningful educational contexts.

Elie Crief grew up in a small town 1 h away from Paris, France. He speaks French and English. He also studied Spanish during his secondary and postsecondary education. He graduated from Suffolk University with a Bachelor of Science in Sociology and a concentration in Education Studies. He has been a research assistant working with this group on translanguaging projects since September 2017. His interest in education is to make classrooms become inclusive spaces and his bilingual status gives him firsthand experience to understand how language plays a role in educational settings.

Maíra Lins Prado was born and raised in São Paulo region, Brazil, and speaks Portuguese and English. She went to a language school for both Italian and French, and learned Spanish on her own. She started teaching English to students of different learning levels at 17 years old. She has a degree in Law from Faculdade de

Direito de São Bernardo do Campo in Brazil and worked as a lawyer for a few years, providing multilingual legal services in Brazil. In 2017 she decided to redirect her career back to the teaching of English and translation. She then moved to New Hampshire, U.S., and joined our research group at Suffolk University.

2.2 Context

Shifting from SEI to Translanguaging This study took place at a city university located in Massachusetts, U.S. The previous education policies in the state required all teacher candidates, regardless of their content area, to be certified in Sheltered English Immersion (SEI) to work with English learners. SEI requires teachers to use clear, direct, simple English and a wide range of scaffolding strategies (Short & Echevarria, 1999) to make content area instruction more accessible to learners while developing their academic language proficiency.

Within this language policy context, Elizabeth, as the director of the Education Studies Program of this university, developed a TESOL Certification program in 2017 to equip teacher candidates with SEI theory and practice. While preparing the TESOL program, Elizabeth met one of the authors, Zhongfeng, who shared with her his knowledge of translanguaging. Elizabeth felt that translanguaging deeply connected with her goal of teaching language for justice, particularly its mobilization of students' full linguistic repertoires. This was a welcome contrast to the state's SEI model which utilizes English only and excludes the rich sociocultural and linguistic experiences that all students can bring to learning tasks. During their initial meetings in January 2017, Zhongfeng and Elizabeth decided to explore what would happen as they worked to change the TESOL Certificate that had been designed from an SEI approach to a translanguaging-informed TESOL Certificate.

Implementing Translanguaging Figure 7.2 below demonstrates the components that were included in implementing translanguaging in this study. With a strong belief in the educational promise of translanguaging and an ultimate goal of preparing teachers to teach English for justice, Elizabeth collaborated with Zhongfeng to integrate a translanguaging pedagogical orientation across the two required courses of the TESOL Certificate program: *Strategies for Working with English Learners* and *TESOL Practice*. The course under examination in this chapter was, *Strategies for Working with English Learners* offered in Fall 2017. Guided by our *Teachers for Justice* model, the course focused on recognizing and critiquing educational inequalities and practicing just ways to teach all learners. As the instructor Elizabeth grounded her teaching in a sociocultural approach. She implemented translanguaging as a new component to transform the course from an SEI-based approach into a translanguaging-informed approach through three tactics: teaching about translanguaging, creating translanguaging spaces, and asking students to apply translanguaging strategies. She regularly consulted with Zhongfeng and Elie for feedback and their perspectives on each of these tactics.

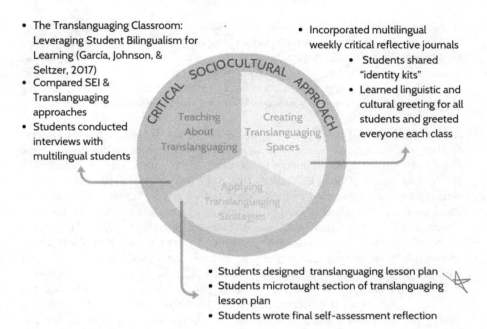

- The Translanguaging Classroom: Leveraging Student Bilingualism for Learning (García, Johnson, & Seltzer, 2017)
- Compared SEI & Translanguaging approaches
- Students conducted interviews with multilingual students

- Incorporated multilingual weekly critical reflective journals
  - Students shared "identity kits"
  - Learned linguistic and cultural greeting for all students and greeted everyone each class

CRITICAL SOCIOCULTURAL APPROACH

Teaching About Translanguaging

Creating Translanguaging Spaces

Applying Translanguaging Strategies

- Students designed translanguaging lesson plan
- Students microtaught section of translanguaging lesson plan
- Students wrote final self-assessment reflection

Fig. 7.2 Implementing translanguaging

Teaching About Translanguaging Elizabeth selected the book *The Translanguaging Classroom: Leveraging Student Bilingualism for Learning* (García, Johnson, & Seltzer, 2017) as the core text for this course and introduced topics including translanguaging theory, stance, design and assessment throughout the whole semester. She asked students to conduct interviews with multilingual students who are traditionally considered "English learners/non-native English speakers". The purpose of having students conduct this research was for them to learn about "ELLs'" educational and living experiences in the U.S., and to engage students in regular conversations about the connections among language, culture, and power to develop a political understanding of TESOL. In addition, Elizabeth encouraged students to compare and contrast SEI and translanguaging as theoretical and pedagogical approaches. She explicitly shared her belief in translanguaging as a more just approach to teaching emergent bilinguals.

Creating Translanguaging Spaces Elizabeth intentionally created educational spaces to engage students in drawing upon their full cultural and linguistic repertoires when participating in class activities. Specifically, students were asked to write weekly critical reflection journals to document their thoughts and learning trajectories. Students were encouraged to clarify, think, and write in any language they felt comfortable. Moreover, students learned the linguistic and cultural rituals for greetings in all the languages present in the class, and greeted every member of the class in their own language at the beginning of each class session. Additionally,

Elizabeth asked each student to share their "identity kits" (who they are in terms of cultural and linguistic backgrounds, personal interests, and any other things that are significant to them) at the beginning of the semester (Elizabeth also shared hers as a modeling practice). This served as a good opportunity to get to know each other for the purpose of establishing an inclusive learning community and developing students' multilingual and multicultural awareness/appreciation.

Asking Students to Apply Translanguaging Strategies Elizabeth designed opportunities in the course for students to apply what they learned in designing lesson plans and microteaching. Students were introduced to Universal Design for Learning (Rose & Meyer, 2000) and Backwards Design (Wiggins & McTighe, 2005) as two principles for designing curriculum to support all learners. Students were asked to draw on these principles to design a translanguaging lesson planning template (adapted from the core textbook García, Johnson, & Seltzer, 2017). They could choose any teaching topics related to their own interests but needed to consider how to use different translanguaging strategies and approaches to address the needs of emergent bilinguals. Each student was asked to microteach a section of their lesson in 7–10 min while the class acted as "students". Students were required to show the rationale, goals, content objectives, language objectives and the translanguaging strategies they would use during their microteaching. A short debrief session followed each microteaching in which students received feedback from Elizabeth and their classmates. A final step was for students to watch the videos of their own microteaching and then engage in a written reflection and assessment of themselves and how the lesson went, what worked and what might be done differently.

In summary, in this course, Elizabeth engaged students holistically in understanding, experiencing, and reflecting upon translanguaging as theory and pedagogy to develop a critical perspective of issues related to emergent bilinguals. The goal was for students to engage with translanguaging to foster necessary skills to teach English for justice.

2.3 Participants

Twenty-six undergraduate students enrolled in the course *Strategies for Working with English Learners* and nineteen of them, fourteen female and five male (aged 19–22), agreed to participate in the study. None of these students had any previous teaching experience. Notably, these courses are open to any undergraduate students interested in working with English learners or obtaining a TESOL certification. Thus the participating students held diverse cultural and linguistic backgrounds. This was very different from traditional demographics in the state's teacher preparation programs (which were predominantly White, monolingual speakers). Among the nineteen participating students, there were seven self-identified monolingual English speakers and twelve bilingual students who spoke English in addition to

Cambodian, Spanish, Russian, Portuguese, Italian, Haitian Creole, Pashtu, and Polish. Moreover, students also studied different subject areas including business, history, fine arts, biology, sociology, Spanish, and Asian studies. Table 7.1 below provides information on all the participants.

2.4 Data Sources

To gain a rich, in-depth understanding of how students learned and applied translanguaging, we collected five sets of artifacts generated from students' participation in class activities and student assignments. They are: (1) students' reading responses to multiple assigned texts including the book *The Translanguaging Classroom: Leveraging Student Bilingualism for Learning* (García, Johnson, & Seltzer, 2017); (2) students' weekly reflective journals in which they were asked to respond to a journal prompt at the beginning of most classes; (3) students' ethnographic interviews with multilingual speakers; (4) students' final portfolios including a philosophy of teaching statement, a translanguaging lesson plan, a reflection on their microteaching, an SEI/ESL classroom observation and reflection, and a resume; and (5) fifteen videotapes of students' microteaching sessions.

Table 7.1 Students participant information

Number	Pseudonym	Gender	Language background	Major
1	Arthur	M	English /Portuguese	History
2	Chris	F	English	Fine arts
3	Ivan	M	Russian/English	Business
4	Hannah	F	English	Psychology
5	Carmen	F	English/Spanish	Business
6	Isabella	F	English/Cambodian	Sociology
7	Grace	F	English	Biology
8	Martina	F	English/Italian/Spanish	Business
9	Emily	F	English	History
10	Alex	F	English	English
11	William	M	English/Polish	Government
12	Riley	F	English	English
13	Chloe	F	English	Psychology
14	Sofia	F	English/Haitian	Psychology
15	Tina	F	English/Haitian	Sociology
16	Laila	F	English/Pashtu	Psychology
17	Bruno	M	English/Spanish	Physics
18	Richard	M	English (Spanish major)	Spanish
19	Kim	F	English/?	Asian studies

2.5   Data Analysis

Using principles of systematic data analysis (Halsall et al., 1998; Hubbard & Power, 1999), we first organized students' artifacts by creating individual profiles for each of our participants. Therefore, we ended up with nineteen profiles consisting of all five data sources mentioned above. In our first round of data analysis we divided 8 profiles up among our research team to see what would emerge from the data. Elie, Zhongfeng and Elizabeth conducted this first round of reading our assigned student profiles and documenting our thoughts on them, bearing in mind our research questions. As a team we next engaged in iterative collective analysis of each profile. As one of us presented our reflections/notes on individual profiles, the rest of the team members memoed. We subsequently engaged in member checks to compare thoughts about each profile and inductively code (Maxwell, 2013) for common themes across the profiles. We also coded for students' understandings of translanguaging in relation to language, culture, and power, and for how they enacted translanguaging in lesson designs and microteaching scenarios.

Our second round of analysis beginning in the fall of 2018 included Maíra. At this time Maíra was auditing the *Strategies for Working with English Learners* course that was being taught for a third time. This experience provided her with knowledge of translanguaging. Both Maíra and Zhongfeng held an outside perspective on the data being analyzed, as they did not attend the course under examination. On the other hand, Elizabeth as the instructor and Elie as a student in the Fall 2017 course held insider perspectives. The combining of these two perspectives contributed to the findings' trustworthiness (Lincoln & Guba, 1985). Our entire data analysis process valued and intentionally drew upon our own linguistic and cultural backgrounds, experiences, and identities. Table 7.2 below demonstrates the different roles of each member of our research team across the duration of this research project.

3   Findings

This section of the chapter responds to our first two research questions by elaborating on the findings from our analysis. First, we show how data reflect the ways that participants understood translanguaging in relationship to language, culture and power by highlighting individual quotes from class assignments. Next, we share the ways that participants enacted translanguaging based on our analysis of the translanguaging lesson plans they designed and their microteaching.

Table 7.2 Researchers' roles

Timeline	Fall 2017	March–July 2018	September–December 2018	November 2018–January 2019
Study process	Strategies for working with English learners course	Data analysis First round (8 student profiles)	Data analysis Second round (19 student profiles)	Manuscript writing
Elizabeth	Designed course Taught course	Created profiles Shared reflection on each profile Memoed Discussed findings Inductively coded	Completed analysis process from round 1 for all 19 cases Created themes Deductively coded Created color coded chart with themes and student excerpts	Co-wrote
Zhongfeng	Designed course Assisted with microteaching			
Elie	Enrolled as student in the course			
Maíra				

3.1 Participants' Understandings of Translanguaging in Relationship to Language, Culture and Power

As authors and researchers we believe in the interconnectedness of language, culture and power. Our hope for this study was that by teaching about translanguaging in the TESOL Certificate program the students would understand this important relationship as well. Our analysis of participants' understandings of translanguaging showed these concepts were clearly highlighted in their work and writing. We came up with four major themes in response to the question of how the participants understood translanguaging in relationship to language, culture and power. First, we recognized that most participants viewed translanguaging as a method or a group of strategies. Second, we identified the ways the participants made sense of language related to translanguaging. Third, we saw that participants recognized and valued cultures. Finally, we saw that some of the participants also demonstrated an awareness of power relationships. We recognize that in separating out each of these components we lose the focus on their connection. We explore the implications of our findings in the discussion section.

Translanguaging as Strategies While analyzing the participants' assignments, it became evident that their understanding of translanguaging was directly connected to teaching strategies. This is not surprising considering translanguaging was introduced to them in the class *Strategies for Working with English Learners*, which focused on teaching methods seen through a translanguaging perspective.

We found in both Riley's[1] reflection paper about her microteaching exercise, as well as her reflection paper produced from observing an ESL classroom, she referenced translanguaging as different teaching strategies.

I attempted to use as many translanguaging strategies that I could by allowing the students to draw pictures, as well as put their half of the story in any language that they felt comfortable with as long as they could summarize what they meant. … [The teacher] used a few translanguaging methods such as bringing up visuals on a PowerPoint as she went over key vocab that they should have used in their project, and reviewed everything to make sure that they had made the right ideas connected to their vocab words. By working with each other the students could also use the translanguaging method of using everyone's knowledge as tools to their project. … The methods of translanguaging seemed to do very well in this classroom, and it was clear that the students had been learning a lot because of these methods. (Riley)

Every mention Riley made of translanguaging in these excerpts was as methods or strategies. They were listed as allowing students to express themselves through drawings, through languages they were comfortable with, group activities using all of the students' funds of knowledge as tools, and teacher presentation that included visuals. Translanguaging was not mentioned as a theory or teaching approach more than practical activities to support learning in the classroom.

Hannah also wrote about translanguaging as techniques in her lesson plan, as well as in her later reflection paper on her microteaching exercise.

Using visuals are a useful translanguaging technique, as it allows me to communicate with my students in multiple ways. … I definitely still could have included some translanguaging techniques. Letting students discuss the grammar in their own language or ponder how the rules apply and can be different could be included in my lesson. (Hannah)

Hannah planned her microteaching activity around the use of visuals, which she saw as a translanguaging technique that allowed multiple forms of communication among her students. Multimodality, the use of visuals or combining audio and visual texts, was a commonly cited strategy participants attributed to being translanguaging. Hannah later criticized her own microteaching for lacking enough translanguaging techniques, such as allowing discussions among the students in their own language. The use of students' various languages as resources in the classroom would have been more in line with our understandings of translanguaging. Hannah recognized she could have gone further than only using multimodality to support her students.

Translanguaging and Language We found that all of the participants recognized that allowing the strategic use of emergent bilinguals' language repertoire was beneficial to students' learning. The vast majority of participants clearly included activities in their lesson plans that required or allowed the use of multiple languages. Although Martina's micro teaching activity itself was not about language, her lesson plan about business incorporated the use of multiple languages by students and the teacher.

---

[1] Student names are pseudonyms.

Translanguaging Objectives:

- *In small groups, students discuss their own perceptions of culture in their home languages and English,* then discuss it with the rest of the class in both languages;
- *Individual self-writing: students translate a vocabulary word bank and use their skills to compare and contrast mission and vision statements of companies in English and in their home languages;*
- *Teacher-student: Teachers gives class overview in home language and English. Teacher shows content in slides with important vocabulary words in both languages.*
- *Materials: Slides with content in both languages. Small case text for students to identify role of readers in corporate culture, available in both languages.* (Martina)

Martina organized the translanguaging objectives within the lesson plan to provide an environment that supported both English and students' home language. She encouraged students to have discussions about the class theme in small groups in both home languages and English. Attention was given to allowing students to translate the necessary vocabulary for the lesson. Martina also planned for herself as a teacher to give a class overview and provide class materials such as slides both in English and in students' home language. This demonstrates her understanding of translanguaging as embracing the students' linguistic backgrounds. Her planning implies the teacher should already be bilingual or make an effort in the direction of incorporating languages other than English in class.

In her teaching philosophy, Emily supported the importance of allowing the strategic use of students' language repertoire in the classroom as learning support.

I feel as though it is always important to take in account the students' bank of knowledge and to let them use whatever language they are comfortable in, while also helping them learn English and more skills. (Emily)

Emily acknowledged the importance of recognizing and allowing students to use their own knowledge and linguistic backgrounds while helping them learn English and other skills. All of the participants at some point observed the value of language support in the learning of emergent bilinguals, even though not all of them deliberately included it in their lesson plan. We see this as a clear awareness of the value of home languages and language diversity as resources in classrooms, instead of a problem to hinder learning that should be avoided. There is no evidence the participants believe in or value an English-only method and mentality. This worth assigned to language diversity can be seen in statements such as in Bruno's class observation assignment, and in Hannah's teaching philosophy.

Another great strategy that the teacher used was speaking Spanish. … The teacher also made it evident to the students to think in both languages, their home language and English to try and think of their response as it would make it easier for them in the long run. (Bruno)
   It is also important to recognize how these different experiences can add to the class as a whole, since everyone has their own set of abilities and knowledge to share. This especially includes looking at the cultural and linguistic backgrounds of students and setting up the classroom in a way that gives them resources. ELL students specifically need certain resources and techniques in order to properly communicate their knowledge. (Hannah)

Bruno considered the use of language to be a valuable strategy in class, both speaking Spanish, as well as encouraging the emergent bilinguals to think in both their home language and English. Hannah considered each students' linguistic background as ability and knowledge they were able to share. Hannah also acknowledged bilingual students' need for specific communication resources.

Translanguaging and Culture We also found that participants made deep connections with culture in their understandings of translanguaging. Nearly all the participants developed pedagogical stances that viewed diverse cultural backgrounds as resources that contributed to emergent bilinguals' learning and identity affirmation. Here we selected two quotes from the philosophy of teaching statement in participants' final portfolios to demonstrate their beliefs in the value of culture when working with emergent bilinguals.

> *I encourage diversity in culture and students to share and express parts of themselves to the classroom; that will make them feel like they are in a strong community rather than just a classroom.* (Riley)
> *I welcome diversity and acknowledge that each student brings their own culture, identity, and experiences, that impact the ways in which they learn. I will strive to see cultures intermingling and shaping our classroom through collaborative group work and assignments.* (Chris)

Both Riley and Chris recognized the importance of bringing in and valuing different cultures in a classroom (they "encourage" and "welcome" "diversity in culture"). They pointed out that by engaging students in "intermingling" diverse cultures, identities, and experiences collaboratively, teachers could potentially develop "a strong community" more than "just a classroom": a heterogeneous, inclusive educational space where every student develops a sense of belonging and feels safe and affirmed to express themselves. This in turn could positively impact students' learning. From these two quotes, we saw that by the end of the course the participants demonstrated multicultural awareness and appreciation and developed their disposition toward leveraging cultural diversity and building community for all learners through teaching practices.

While some participants recognized culture individually as a valuable resource to be incorporated in teaching practices, there were other participants who demonstrated a holistic understanding of culture, language, and power in translanguaging pedagogy. As Erin pointed out in her teaching philosophy statement in the final portfolio:

> *We need to incorporate culture and language into our lessons as well. When teaching to a diverse group of students each and every culture should be acknowledged and taken in to account. Most textbooks are set up to only include White culture and that also needs to change.* (Erin)

Evidently, Erin firstly emphasized that every student's culture and language should be both acknowledged and incorporated in lesson designs and teaching practices. She further problematized U.S. textbooks being White culture-centered and the need for them to reflect more cultural diversity. We saw that she also developed a critical cultural awareness which acknowledged the hegemonic nature of White culture in U.S. education that leaves out many other minoritized cultures. When

Erin explained her teaching philosophy informed by translanguaging pedagogy she demonstrated an inseparable relationship between language, culture, and power.

Translanguaging and Power In addition to making connections to language and culture, we also saw that participants understood translanguaging in relation to power. Below we have selected several representative quotes from participants' different assignments to illustrate how they recognized and critiqued the unequal power structures embedded in U.S. society, the education system, and classrooms.

In an interview with a multilingual speaker who was categorized as an "English learner" Chris, a self-identified monolingual English speaker, sincerely expressed what she learned:

> *I learned how incredibly fortunate I am to have been born in the U.S. as an English speaker. Unlike my interviewee, I was privileged to have a great education where I would understand everything easily because it was taught in my language… (my interviewee) came over to the US at age 16 and had to work instead of going to school.* (Chris)

Undoubtedly, Chris recognized her privilege and power as a native English speaker in an English-dominated society who was educated under an English-only policy. She also showed an emergent empathetic understanding of language-minoritized speakers in the U.S. Her quote generally demonstrated her critical understanding of the hegemonic power of English within U.S. society and the different roles ascribed to speakers of different languages.

Similarly, Carmen, a bilingual speaker of Spanish and English, also acknowledged the "mythical" superior power of English when she was asked to write about her own language experiences in her journal:

> *Sometimes I cannot find the proper way to express myself in English and I try to do it in Spanish, but people look down on that. There have been numerous times when my parents have questioned why I talk to my sister in both languages. They always wanted us to speak just one type of language b/c to them someone that speaks both at a time means someone with disorganized thoughts.* (Carmen)

She felt denigrated for her use of home language because Spanish is a minoritized language and viewed in American society as inferior to English. Besides this, even her parents were opposed to her language mixing or translanguaging practices. From Carmen's words, it is clear to see that people still hold misconceptions of linguistic purism (to avoid "cross-contamination" of languages), which reflects a monolingual understanding of languages as separate, fixed entities (García, 2009a). Carmen realized the linguistic hierarchies in U.S. society (the hegemony of English) and problematized the social stigma associated with translanguaging practices of language-minoritized speakers.

In addition to developing a critical awareness of the dominance of English in U.S. society and the education system, participants also critiqued the unequal power dynamics between teacher and student in traditional U.S. classrooms. After learning about translanguaging pedagogy and other related sociocultural theories of language teaching, several participants demonstrated a new imagination of the classroom environment in their philosophy of teaching statement:

To foster the best education through my teaching practices, I feel it is critical to be a student under the knowledge of my own students, therefore showing the respect and value that I have for those I am teaching. Cultivating an environment where the learning and teaching is mutual for everyone is key for utilizing all knowledge present. (Hannah)

I believe in the students becoming the teachers in the classroom. I believe that we are all students and can learn from each other. (Chris)

I believe that the teacher role is to guide providing access to information rather than acting as the primary source of it. (Martina)

All these quotes share one common theme: they aim to disrupt the traditional power held by teachers. The participants' words demonstrate an understanding of teachers' and students' roles as dynamic and of the shifting and reciprocal knowledge or expertise in classrooms. This educational philosophy echoes translanguaging pedagogy which positions all students as competent knowledge contributors/producers along with teachers and encourages them to bring in their diverse funds of knowledge and full cultural and linguistic repertoires. Students in this sense are empowered to develop their agency, creativity, and criticality (Li, 2011) in different learning tasks.

To summarize, we found that participants fostered critical understandings of power structures in both macro- (U.S. society and education system) and micro- (U.S. classroom) levels. They recognized the dominant power of English and how it devalues minoritized language practices and produces harmful effects in society and in education systems. Further, they challenged the traditional power dynamics in classrooms by reimagining an equal relationships between teachers and students. We believe that the formation of these critical awareness could contribute to developing their pedagogical stance in teaching English for justice.

3.2 Students' Enactment of Translanguaging

Our goal of preparing students to teach for justice requires that as teacher educators we go beyond the teaching of translanguaging as both theory and pedagogy. We wanted the participants to be able to embody translanguaging in their teaching practices. Elizabeth designed the course so that participants would recognize the inequalities created by English supremacy, and be able to critique English-only practices. However, the praxis that informs our work of preparing teachers for justice requires engaging in practice. Theories and understandings alone will not achieve teaching for justice. We need to understand how the participants embodied what they were taught.

There are two required courses for the TESOL Certificate. *Strategies for Working with English Learners* provides a theoretical preparation and *TESOL Practice* provides opportunities to put theories into practice. Because we conducted our research in the theoretical course, there were not as many opportunities for participants to demonstrate how they would implement translanguaging in their teaching practice as they have in the *TESOL Practice* course. However, our data included lessons that the participants designed and videos of the participants' microteaching, both of which highlighted participants' teaching practices. Our analysis showed that the participants enacted translanguaging in two ways. First, the majority of them designed translanguaging lesson plans that valued and used the linguistic repertoires of emergent bilinguals. Second, participants employed various strategies to support emergent bilinguals in their microteaching.

Translanguaging in Design Translanguaging lesson design is one of the three framing concepts that make up translanguaging pedagogy (García, Johnson, & Seltzer, 2017). We analyzed the lessons participants designed in order to see how they planned to enact translanguaging. Our analysis of 19 lesson plans revealed that 17 of those lesson plans had language objectives that recognized the linguistic diversity of emergent bilinguals. The other two lessons made reference to drawing on students' cultural backgrounds, but did not include any consideration or use of students' diverse linguistic repertoires.

Almost all of the lesson plans that included translanguaging allowed students to use both their home language and English to complete some of the class objectives such as writing assignments or participating in group work. An example of creating these multilingual spaces in lesson plan designs can be seen in the lesson objectives for Ivan's biology lesson:

Students will be able to:

- *Recognize and track biology vocabulary cognates*
- *Work in groups to complete the quiz using both English and their home languages*
- *Use both English and their home languages to write notes relative to the class topic*
- *Read their notes to each other and ask for opinions and comments in both languages* (Ivan)

Ivan's lesson objectives demonstrated his willingness to allow languages other than English into his lesson to facilitate students' participation and learning. This allowance was mirrored in almost all the participants' lesson plans. While consideration of languages and making spaces for languages other than English is helpful for emergent bilinguals, their home languages are not being valued for the contribution they can make to lessons.

There were very few lesson plan designs that drew on the linguistic repertoires of emergent bilingual students as a source of knowledge for the lesson. Two stand out as moving beyond using multilingual resources as a scaffold for students' learning. One was Riley's lesson about the structure of fictional stories. Her goal was for groups of students to create a story using a variety of languages. Here is her translanguaging objective:

Create a story that has a diverse amount of languages, each section of the story written by a new member of the group. These stories will be fiction based, and in the short story category. (Riley)

Martina's lesson on business ethics was the other lesson plan that incorporated the linguistic resources of students. Below are her translanguaging lesson plan objectives which were also shared above:

- *In small groups, students discuss their own perceptions of culture in their home languages and English, then discuss it with the rest of the class in both languages*
- *Individual self-writing: students translate a vocabulary word bank and use their skills to compare and contrast mission and vision statements of companies in English and in their home languages* (Martina)

Both of these participants designed lessons that incorporated linguistic diversity in the leaning objectives of the lessons. They went further than just allowing spaces for multiple languages within the lesson. Riley wanted students to create a multilingual text and Martina wanted students to use their home languages and cultures to make comparisons and contrasts. They both used languages other than English as resources in their lesson plans to raise their metalinguistic and cross-cultural awareness.

Microteaching Strategies We recognized in analyzing participants' assignments to answer our first research question that participants understood translanguaging primarily as a method or a group of strategies for working with emergent bilinguals. This finding was corroborated in our analysis of microteaching videos. In answering our second question about the ways that participants embodied translanguaging, the data demonstrated participants enacting specific strategies to carry out translanguaging.

Arthur microtaught a lesson on Chinese Dynasties. He worked hard to master the correct pronunciation of key vocabulary words in Mandarin. Arthur viewed the strategy of defining key concepts and terms in a language other than English as translanguaging. His written reflection on his microteaching identified his use of Mandarin words as a translanguaging strategy:

> *I thought that the translanguaging techniques that I used throughout my lesson were effective, especially my use of Mandarin Chinese throughout the lesson.* (Arthur)

Another common strategy participants attributed to translanguaging pedagogy was multimodality, utilizing multiple means of representing the materials and information they were introducing in their microteaching. An example of the embodiment of multimodality was Chris's art lesson. Chris asked students to work in pairs to guide each other through a blind recreation of an image. Students were encouraged to use any signs, languages or means of communication necessary to complete the task. As an artist, Chris embodied a strategy that she knew well and believed in. She explained in the debriefing following her microteaching that the way she incorporated translanguaging into her lesson was through multimodality. Chris's philosophy of teaching statement further demonstrated her beliefs in multimodality and hands-on work as valuable learning strategies:

> *I believe in the use of multi-modality as a learning tool for each type of learner. Visuals and hands-on experience with materials will help my students succeed in my classroom.* (Chris)

In summary, participants demonstrated their enactment of translanguaging primarily in their lesson designs. The majority of lesson plan designs included translanguaging as a scaffolding tool by allowing students to use texts in their home languages and providing translations for students. However, there were fewer instances of participants who used multiple languages during their microteaching. For example, in her Spanish lesson, Carmen taught Spanish verbs through the medium of English. As another example, Arthur's lesson on Chinese Dynasties, explored briefly above, used a language other than English by introducing Mandarin words. Richard's lesson on a Spanish poet also incorporated both Spanish and English in the microteaching. Richard read the poem in Spanish, and he provided a translation in English and analyzed the poem with the class using English and Spanish.

Overall, everyone, except for two participants, incorporated multiple languages in some way into their lesson plans to enact translanguaging as a scaffolding tool in their pedagogical design. There were three participants who used translanguaging to legitimize languages other than English in their microteaching and build metalinguistic and cross-cultural awareness.

4 Discussion

In this section, we explore what we learned from our findings section regarding participants' understandings and enactments of translanguaging to answer our third research question about whether translanguaging as pedagogy in the *Strategies for Working with English Learners* course afforded participants the elements necessary to teach for justice. Drawing on our theoretical understandings we next visualize what teaching for justice might entail. As the prefix *trans-* suggests crossing between, we cross between our theoretical tools: justice as praxis (Ladson-Billings, 2015), our teaching for justice model, and translanguaging pedagogy (García, Johnson, & Seltzer 2017) to show in Fig. 7.3 below our understandings of translanguaging pedagogy for justice.

Each of these theoretical tools is supported by three simultaneous and dialectic components. In Fig. 7.3, justice as praxis is the larger context of our work and requires the simultaneous engagement in theory, research and practice. Teaching for justice entails recognizing inequalities, critiquing existing inequalities and enacting culturally and linguistically sustaining practices. The inner circle demonstrates translanguaging pedagogy and its three components: (1) a teacher's stance in valuing bilingual students' full language repertoires as a human right and a learning resource, (2) a teacher's lesson designs to support and connect home, school and community languages and cultures, and (3) a teacher's spontaneous shifts in classroom interactions to support meaning making and learning. We use Fig. 7.3 to evaluate our practice and whether or not it has afforded our participants the elements necessary to engage in translanguaging pedagogy for justice.

We initially experienced disappointment upon recognizing that participants viewed translanguaging not as a powerful new approach in the field of teaching emergent bilinguals, but rather as a method consisting of employing different strategies, such as scaffolding and multimodality in order to support emergent bilinguals. However, we reminded ourselves of our goal and of our theoretical framework of

Fig. 7.3 Translanguaging
pedagogy for justice

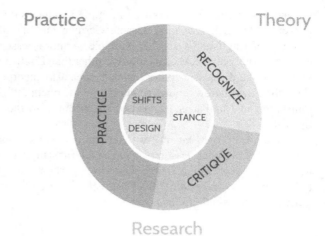

teaching for justice. We recognized the injustice of our assigning the responsibility of realizing the potential of translanguaging to our participants. We needed to include ourselves, and most notably the course professor in our analysis. We concur with Jaspers' (2018) work on the limits of translanguaging to be transformative. This study, the course under investigation, and our writing of this project all promote the dominance of English. Any disappointments then, should be aimed at ourselves, not our participants.

An important component of teaching for justice, as well as developing a translanguaging stance, is learning to recognize inequalities. As researchers we recognize the inequalities we are involved in perpetuating through our own insistence on using English. For our participants, at a macro-level, they recognized the linguistic hierarchies (the hegemony of English) in the U.S. society and in the education system. At a micro-level they recognized the inequalities that exist in traditional classroom power dynamics and they reimagined more equal relationships between teachers and students. Once injustices are recognized we must have tools to critique and counter these unjust practices. Theories and research, two of the components of praxis, are these tools. While our analysis does not show participants' recognition of translanguaging as theory, participants clearly theorized the importance of language and culture in teaching. Participants also engaged in critiquing power in their criticism of dominant White culture and also monolingual practices. Participants' research, which entailed interviewing multilingual students, also provided deeper awareness of the relationship between dominance and privilege and power through non-monolingual perspectives.

Teaching practice is the third component of each of the theoretical frameworks we have woven together in Fig. 7.3. Lacking more opportunities in this class for participants to engage in teaching practices, we looked at their lesson plans as evidence of what they would do in a classroom. We saw definitive signs of participants' translanguaging design in their lesson plans. Almost all participants included space or allowances for multiple languages in their lesson plans. However, in the one opportunity participants had to teach, we saw many enact practices such as lecturing through PowerPoints that upheld the dominant role of the teacher. Few participants provided the space for languages other than English. The most common translanguaging strategy was the use of multimodality where participants used imagery, text and/or oral language in their lessons. While implementing a strategy such as the use of multimodality in a lesson does not constitute teaching for justice, it must be noted that participants took up a great deal of the elements in Fig. 7.3 necessary to teach for justice. We have all made important progress but, we cannot claim to prepare students to teach for justice without first being honest about the dominant practices we as researchers, and teacher educators are engaged in, and second, providing them many more opportunities to engage in teaching practices that not only acknowledge minoritized languages and cultures but insist on sustaining them and drawing on them as teaching resources.

5   Conclusions

This collaborative qualitative study explored how students understood and enacted translanguaging in a TESOL certificate course *Strategies for Working with English Learners*. We analyzed students' coursework and microteaching through thematic analysis combined with the multiperspectivity of the researchers. We found that by engaging with translanguaging as theory and pedagogy in multiple ways throughout the whole semester, students developed a pedagogical stance which valued cultural and linguistic diversity and recognized the hegemony of English and unequal power dynamics between teachers and students in classrooms. Generally speaking, all the students embraced translanguaging as a better way (compared to strict English-only instruction in SEI) to work with emergent bilinguals.

Students employed a set of strategies in their lesson designs and microteaching practices to accommodate emergent bilinguals' needs. Some of these strategies were providing translations, allowing the use of home languages, and adopting multimodality. However, we were concerned that these teaching strategies only represented a symbolic feature of "linguistic tourism" (Matsuda, 2014, p. 482), i.e., a touristic representation of linguistic diversity in a classroom. Students at this stage mainly understood translanguaging as a group of mechanic strategies. We argue that translanguaging pedagogies need to go beyond this level and foster students' critical language awareness in teaching. As García and Kleifgen (2018) point out, "a translanguaging pedagogy is not simply a series of strategies and scaffolds, but also a philosophy of language and education that is centered on a bilingual minoritized community" (p. 80). We echo this interpretation.

Implications for TESOL teacher preparation and for us moving forward are to recognize translanguaging as a philosophy, a process and a perspective. We must be explicit in all our course materials and in our teaching about our goals of learning to teach English for justice from a translanguaging orientation. We must also recognize this goal as a long term project. We believe one of the first inequalities that must be recognized is monolingualism. We recommend this be done by inter-rogating perceptions of language and by teaching about translanguaging as it theo-rizes language. An understanding of the fluidity and non-bound nature of our linguistic repertoires would help future teachers tap into what García, Johnson, and Seltzer (2017) refer to as the *translanguaging corriente*, the flow of bilingualism in classrooms for the purpose of meaning-making. They could see that the best way to promote justice in classrooms is by leveraging the cultural and linguistic knowledge of all students as teaching and learning resources.

We believe it is unrealistic for us to expect participants to implement translan-guaging in transformative ways when it has not been modeled for them. As teacher educators we have to move beyond simply teaching about translanguaging theory and pedagogy. Perhaps it is more fruitful to show students sample lesson plans with concrete translanguaging practices infused in the planning in order that they can come to see concretely how theoretical concepts are applied in the classroom con-text. We must ourselves model what it means to teach for justice. We believe we need to recognize the injustices we perpetuate by teaching in English-only. Through critiquing our own practice we have come to see that we must teach differently by drawing on all the linguistic and cultural resources of our TESOL students. Translanguaging can only be transformative if it occurs at all levels of teaching. Along with preparing our TESOL students, we must prepare ourselves to teach English for justice.

References

Adams, M., Bell, L. A., & Griffin, P. (Eds.). (2007). *Teaching for diversity and social justice* (2nd ed.). New York, NY: Routledge.

Banks, J. A. (Ed.). (1996). *Multicultural education, transformative knowledge, and action: Historical and contemporary perspectives*. New York, NY: Teachers College Press.

Battiste, M. (Ed.). (2000). *Reclaiming indigenous voice and vision*. Vancouver, BC: UBC Press.

Blumenreich, M., & Falk, B. (2006). Trying on a new pair of shoes: Urban teacher–learners conduct research and construct knowledge in their own classrooms. *Teaching and Teacher Education, 22*(7), 864-873.

Chandler-Olcott, K. (2002). Teacher researcher as a self-extending system for practitioners. *Teacher Education Quarterly, 29*(1), 23–38.

Cochran-Smith, M., & Lytle, S. L. (Eds.). (1993). *Inside/outside: Teacher research and knowledge*. New York, NY: Teachers College Press.

Flores, A. (2017). *How the U.S. Hispanic population is changing*. Pew Research Center. Retrieved from http://www.pewresearch.org/fact-tank/2017/09/18/how-the-u-s-hispanic-population-is-changing/

García, O. (2009a). *Bilingual education in the 21st century: A global perspective*. Malden, MA: Wiley–Blackwell.

García, O. (2009b). Emergent bilinguals and TESOL: What's in a name? *TESOL Quarterly, 43*(2), 322–326. Retrieved from https://www.jstor.org/stable/27785009

García, O., & Kleifgen, J. A. (2018). *Educating emergent bilinguals: Policies, programs, and practices for english learners* (2nd ed.). New York, NY: Teachers College Press.

García, O., & Kleyn, T. (Eds.). (2016). *Translanguaging with multilingual students: Learning from classroom moments*. New York, NY: Routledge.

García, O., & Li, W. (2014). *Translanguaging: Language, bilingualism and education*. New York, NY: Palgrave Macmillan.

Garcia, O., Kleifgen, J. A., & Falchi, L. (2008). *From English language learners to emergent bilinguals. Equity matters. Research review no. 1.* Campaign for Educational Equity, Teachers College, Columbia University. Retrieved from https://eric.ed.gov/?id=ED524002

García, O., Johnson, S. I., & Seltzer, K. (2017). *The translanguaging classroom: Leveraging student bilingualism for learning*. Philadelphia, PA: Caslon.

Gay, G. (2000). *Culturally responsive teaching: Theory, research, and practice* (2nd ed.). New York, NY: Teachers College.

Halsall, R., Carter, K., Curley, M., & Perry, K. (1998). School improvement: The case for supported teacher research. *Research Papers in Education, 13*(2), 161–182. https://doi.org/10.1080/0267152980130204

Hubbard, R. S., & Power, B. M. (1999). *Living the questions: A guide for teacher-researchers*. York, ME: Stenhouse Publishers.

Jaspers, J. (2018). The transformative limits of translanguaging. *Language & Communication, 58*, 1–10. https://doi.org/10.1016/j.langcom.2017.12.001

Ladson-Billings, G. (1994). *The dreamkeepers: Successful teachers of African American children*. San Francisco, CA: Jossey-Bass Publishers.

Ladson-Billings, G. J. (2015). *Social justice in education award (2015) lecture: Justice… just, justice!* [Video file]. Retrieved from https://www.youtube.com/watch?v=ofB_t1oTYhI

Li, W. (2011). Moment analysis and translanguaging space: Discursive construction of identities by multilingual Chinese youth in Britain. *Journal of Pragmatics, 43*(5), 1222–1235. https://doi.org/10.1016/j.pragma.2010.07.035

Lincoln, Y. S., & Guba, E. G. (1985). *Naturalistic inquiry*. Beverly Hills, CA: Sage Publications.

Matsuda, P. K. (2014). The lure of translingual writing. *PMLA, 129*(3), 478–483. https://doi.org/10.1632/pmla.2014.129.3.478

Maxwell, J. A. (2013). *Qualitative research design: An interactive approach* (3rd ed.). Thousand Oaks, CA: SAGE Publications.

Nieto, S. (1992). *Affirming diversity: The sociopolitical context of multicultural education*. Boston, MA: Pearson Education.

Otheguy, R., García, O., & Reid, W. (2015). Clarifying translanguaging and deconstructing named languages: A perspective from linguistics. *Applied Linguistics Review, 6*(3), 281–307.

Robinson, E., Tian, Z., Martínez, T., & Qarqeen, A. (2018). Teaching for justice: Introducing translanguaging in an undergraduate TESOL course. *Journal of Language and Education, 4*(3), 77–87. https://doi.org/10.17323/2411-7390-2018-4-3-77-87

Rose, D., & Meyer, A. (2000). Universal design for learning: Associate editor column. *Journal of Special Education Technology, 15*(1), 67–70.

Short, D. J., & Echevarria, J. (1999). *The sheltered instruction observation protocol: A tool for teacher-researcher collaboration and professional development*. Santa Cruz, CA: UC Berkeley: Center for Research on Education, Diversity and Excellence. Retrieved from https://eric.ed.gov/?id=ED436981

Smith, L. T. (2012). *Decolonizing methodologies: Research and indigenous peoples* (2nd ed.). London, UK: Zed Books.

Tuck, E. (2009). Suspending damage: A letter to communities. *Harvard Educational Review, 79*(3), 409–428. https://doi.org/10.17763/haer.79.3.n0016675661t3n15

U.S. Census Bureau. (2017). *Language spoken at home, 2017 American community survey 1-year estimates*. Retrieved from http://factfinder.census.gov/bkmk/table/1.0/en/ACS/17_1YR/S1601?#

Wiggins, G., & McTighe, J. (2005). *Understanding by design*. Alexandria, Egypt: Association for Supervision and Curriculum Development.

Chapter 8
Pedagogical Sismo: Translanguaging Approaches for English Language Instruction and Assessment in Oaxaca, Mexico

Julio Morales, Jamie L. Schissel and Mario López-Gopar

Abstract The integration of translanguaging pedagogies in multicultural and multilingual contexts with classroom assessment introduces additional, often unaddressed, challenges. Our chapter aims to demonstrate how translanguaging can be integrated into both instruction and assessment in a university TESOL classroom for pre-service English teachers who are both learning English and learning how to be language teachers. Our participatory action research (PAR) project centers on the practices of one instructor and 28 pre-service teachers during the 2017–2018 academic year in the fifth and sixth semesters of their program at the Facultad de Idiomas at the Universidad Autónoma "Benito Juárez" de Oaxaca in Mexico. The chapter is organized into three parts. First, we provide an overview of the PAR project. In the second section, the instructor of the course gives a first-person account of his perspectives and experiences that have informed and shaped our project. In the final section, we discuss our initial analyses of our specific PAR project and the findings from the assessments used. Throughout, we aim to highlight the importance of not only drawing from bi−/multilingual resources already in use in the classroom, university, and the wider community but also the importance of connecting bi-multilingualism in teaching and assessment with events that were outstanding and contextually relevant for all those involved.

Keywords Translanguaging · Multilingualism · Interculturalism · Classroom assessment · Pre-service English teachers · Oaxaca · Mexico

J. Morales . M. López-Gopar
Universidad Autónoma Benito Juárez de Oaxaca, Oaxaca, Mexico

J. L. Schissel (✉)
School of Education, University of North Carolina at Greensboro, Greensboro, NC, USA
e-mail: jlschiss@uncg.edu

© Springer Nature Switzerland AG 2020
Z. Tian et al. (eds.), *Envisioning TESOL through a Translanguaging Lens*,
Educational Linguistics 45, https://doi.org/10.1007/978-3-030-47031-9_8

1 Introduction

Working under the assumption that students are capable of understanding and performing better during activities developed in classes using bi−/multilingual practices (Blackledge & Creese, 2010; Flores & Schissel, 2014; Lin, 2014; Leung & Valdes, 2019; López-Gopar, Núñez-Méndez, Sughrua, & Clemente, 2013; Otheguy, García, & Reid, 2015, 2018; Palmer, Martínez, Mateus, & Henderson, 2014; Sayer, 2013; Turner & Lin, 2017; Vaish & Subhan, 2015), our chapter aims to presents the integration of translanguaging in instruction and especially within assessments in a university TESOL classroom for pre-service English teachers in Oaxaca, Mexico. This study has been conducted amongst a team of individuals which includes university professors from the United States, the United Kingdom, and Mexico, graduate students in the United States, and undergraduate students in the United States and Mexico. In this project, we have worked toward developing shared understandings through debates and consensus building through our decision-making processes and actions.

In our collaborative project, we emphasize the need to understand different contextual factors inside and outside of the classroom setting. In other words, we see our study of integrating translanguaging in English teaching and assessment as intertwined with policies, histories, ideologies, and myriad additional influences that are present in the lives of those who are participating in the research project. Importantly, our project has been conducted in tension with dominant monoglossic language ideologies in English teaching and learning. For our work in Oaxaca, monoglossic language ideologies represent neoliberal, colonial, and linguistic purist views and actions that reify and further entrench hierarchies and modes of oppression (Heller, 2008; Kubota, 2014; López Gopar, 2016, 2019; McKinney, 2016; Rosa & Burdick, 2016).

The project described in this chapter is an outgrowth from our previous work (De Korne, López Gopar, & Rios Rios, 2018; López Gopar, 2016; Schissel, De Korne, & López-Gopar, 2018; Schissel, Leung, López-Gopar, & Davis 2018). In our past and current experiences as English educators in Oaxaca and other contexts, we have sought to understand how translanguaging approaches could enhance English learning in assessments. We have done so understanding that the popular adage "what gets tested gets taught" is often used to argue for an alignment for monoglossic classroom practices connected with monoglossic assessments. Thus, our project is designed to contest monoglossic language ideologies to effect change through integration and recognition of translanguaging in teaching and especially assessment.

Our chapter is organized into three different parts. First, we describe the participatory action research (PAR) project. Then, the instructor of the course—Julio Morales—gives a first-person account of his perspectives and experiences that have informed and shaped our project, including an introduction to the research contexts in Oaxaca. As a research team, we view Julio's insights as a driving force in shaping the directions of our PAR project and thus have dedicated this section of the chapter to documenting his views. In foregrounding Julio's perspective, we purposefully want to draw attention to and highlight the importance of his role in the project and the contributions that his views hold for future endeavors. Without the commitments from Julio and the students, this project would not have been possible.

In the final section, we return to a jointly-authored discussion of our project. We describe our initial analyses of our specific PAR project, in particular, the findings from the particular assessments used. In the analyses, we discuss how understanding the importance of using translanguaging in teaching and assessment as beneficial by looking at how students performed on the assessments. As such, our analyses focus on the grades assigned to students, as the students faced consequences based on the grades given on the assessments and thus were extremely important as a unit of analysis for them. We aim to highlight the importance of not only drawing from bi−/multilingual resources already in use in the classroom, university, and the wider community but also the importance of connecting bi-multilingualism in teaching and assessment with events that were outstanding and contextually relevant for all those involved. Title of our chapter, for example, captures our connection with local events that impacted the lives of those involved in this work. The *sismo* or earthquakes in Oaxaca and Mexico City in September 2017 impacted the lives directly and indirectly of students, teachers, administrators, and others involved in the study. We also address the limitations and new complications that accompany these changes in the classroom. The chapter ends with implications of how our research project on translanguaging in instruction and assessment opens new pathways for TESOL in Oaxaca, Mexico, that is responsive to the multicultural and multilingual context.

2 Project Design

Our study centers on the practices of one instructor, Julio, and 28 pre-service teachers during the 2017–2018 academic year in the fifth and sixth semesters of their training program at the Facultad de Idiomas (FI, henceforth) at the Universidad Autónoma "Benito Juárez" de Oaxaca (UABJO, henceforth) in Mexico. The students in these classes were both studying English as a content area and also studying English as part of their teacher education program. The project looked broadly at the research question: *How can translanguaging be integrated into instruction and assessment in a university TESOL classroom for pre-service English teachers?* In our project, we have worked together to leverage translanguaging practices in this English language class purposefully. The assessments used in this classroom incorporated translanguaging design tools such as Spanish and English reading and listening materials and support of bi−/multilingual responses in classroom interactions and the assessment. Importantly, these bi−/multilingual materials focused on culturally relevant events as well.

Our project is steeped in the assumption that *language teachers and students play crucial roles* in implementing classroom language assessments and in the contingent ways in which the assessment can be (re)oriented or presented (Davison &

Leung, 2009; Rea-Dickins, 2004). Further, we seek to understand the social implications of our work in connection with the people involved in the research project (Hornberger, 2001), in particular, the consequences attached to assessments, tests, and other forms of evaluation (Chalhoub-Deville, 2016; Schissel, 2019; Shohamy, 2001, 2006). In our study, we have actively sought out to re-inscribe traditional (power) dynamics in research between the researchers and the researched or participants. We look to ways in which interactions between researchers and participants have been conceived, in particular, the fluid boundaries of the various roles that different team members have occupied, and the positionality of the researchers in motivating collaborative project efforts. What this has meant is that each member of the team contributes to the decisions of how to proceed through ongoing conversations or negotiations amongst various members of the team.

2.1 Background of Oaxaca, UABJO, and the Research Team

Multiculturalism and multilingualism are common community practices for students who attend FI at UABJO in Mexico. The state of Oaxaca is located southeast of Mexico and with Guerrero, Puebla, Veracruz, and Chiapas as neighboring states. According to Instituto Nacional de Estadística, Geografía e Informática, Oaxaca comprises of 4.8% of Mexico territory (INEGI, n.d.). Despite this relatively small proportion of land, Oaxaca is the most linguistically and culturally diverse state in Mexico with eight distinct regions: Costa, Sierra Norte, Sierra Sur, Cañada, Cuenca del Papaloapam, Mixteca, Valles Centrales, and Istmo. These regions are home to 16 different ethnic groups in Oaxaca that speak over 100 different Indigenous languages, which is the most diverse linguistic and cultural state in Mexico. At UABJO, a large number of students represent these different backgrounds, so much so that the university has dedicated resources to support the academic success of students from Indigenous communities.

UABJO represents the only public university in the state of Oaxaca. As such, students at UABJO—like students throughout the country—are required to take an admissions test, the Exámenes Nacionales de Ingreso (EXANI) for admissions to public universities in Mexico. This test does not have an English section, and the FI has purposely not required students to take another test to demonstrate a specific proficiency level. Additionally, FI does not require specific educational experience with English learning before being admitted as a major. These choices about admissions requirements by the administrators at the FI were made to ensure that many students from Indigenous communities who have not had access to English education in their previous schools can enroll in the FI. Seventy-six percent of individuals in Indigenous communities in Oaxaca live in poverty and have limited access to English secondary education (Enciso, 2013).

At the FI, there are two options for the bachelor's degree in Language Teaching: one program, the Escolarizado program, consists of daily classes from Monday to Friday and the other program, Semiescolarizado program, consists in courses only on Saturdays. Both programs last eight semesters, and students receive the preparation needed to become language teachers specialized in English and one of the other offered languages. These different languages available for the major are world languages of Italian, French, Japanese and Portuguese and more recently the Indigenous language Zapotec, have begun the program in a second Indigenous language, Mixe, in fall of 2018. During these eight semesters, students have to study English at different levels, which are classified from basic to advanced levels.

The authors of this chapter—Julio, Jamie, and Mario—met online and in-person and regularly messaged about different decisions around the process of the project. Julio is an English instructor in the FI at UABJO. Jamie is a university professor in the United States in TESOL who has been collaborating with colleagues at UABJO on multiple projects. Mario is a university professor in the FI at UABJO who also leads the critical applied linguistics research group. Julio led the day-to-day actions of the project as he was the teacher of the course.

Julio and Jamie worked together to co-construct the assessments that were used in the classes. Another key member of the team is a university professor in the United Kingdom, Constant Leung, who met with Julio, Jamie, and Mario in person and online. He has worked with us on previous projects, and we continue to collaborate. Additionally, graduate students in the United States and undergraduate students in the United States and Mexico have assisted with our project in co-authoring articles, data analysis, data collection, and transcriptions and translations. Further, the students in the courses were consulted during informal conversations with Julio inside and outside the classroom and through semi-structured interviews and member check interviews. Students knew that they were participating in a study and that their perspectives would be taken into account throughout the project. Julio as well was in the position of developing the research project and also investigating his actions. These malleable boundaries around who was being researched and who was the researcher helped to shape the direction of the project throughout the year. Our work is based on PAR methods that also draw from the critical ethnographic approaches.

2.2   Participatory Action Research

To develop and sustain our project, we have been building a collaborative team with each member contributing to the process of creating translanguaging approaches to classroom language assessment, which aligns with PAR methodologies. PAR is research *with* participants, rather than *for* (Whyte, 1991). Within these methods is the ontological assumption that involvement of participants in all critical aspects of the research process is crucial because their knowledge is intrinsic to the production of the work (Borda, 2001; McIntyre, 2008). Engaging in participatory methodology is essential to construct translanguaging assessment approaches with scores inferences guided by teacher and student purposes. Julio's commitment to the project, and his insights, experiences, and reflections presented here reflect how PAR studies value the perspectives of teachers and their understandings of their students.

PAR methodology, for this study, has meant the close collaboration that included continued dialogues, co-planning, and building trust amongst each other. Drawing from the recursive PAR process (McIntyre, 2008), we engaged in questioning, reflecting, investigating, developing, implementing, and refining our project goals (Balakrishnan & Claiborne, 2017). Collaboration, we argue, increased the likelihood of effective translation of research question to successful data collection and analysis. That is to say, it is an approach to research where the participation of the community in the research process, thereby more closely reflects their social realities (Rahman, 2008). Our project has focused specifically on adapting McIntyre's (2008) tenets of PAR as we engage in (1) a collective commitment to the issues being researched, (2) valuing of self- and collective reflection to more clearly understand the issues being investigated, (3) work towards consensus building and joint-decision making for the benefit of those impacted by the issue, and (4) developing a team that works together in the planning, implementation, and dissemination of the work.

For our project, we shared a collective commitment to understanding how to develop translanguaging approaches to classroom language assessment. We did so with the shared perspective that a translanguaging approach in conjunction with choosing topics or themes that were connected to students' lives and interests could effect change to benefit the lives of students in these classes. Part of our valuing of self and collective reflection has centered around how we conduct our projects and the experiences and viewpoints of our different team members. For example, Julio noted throughout our study that—in integrating this approach not only in teaching but also with assessments—students' bi−/multilingual identities were being valued and sustained. Deficit positioning of bi−/multilingual identities (in particular those of Indigenous students) meant that bi−/multilingual identities were often erased, ignored, or seen as something to be embarrassed about (López Gopar & Clemente, 2011). Julio had made remarks about the general impression of the cultural shift around students' embracing bi−/multilingual identities. For example, Julio observed in his classes that students were more eager to participate or talk in class and less embarrassed about their English. Students also used English, Spanish, other languages taught in the FI (e.g., French, Italian, Portuguese), and Indigenous languages that they knew from home in the classes. They would compare linguistic forms (e.g., sounds, morphemes, cognates, syntactic structures) or use the other languages to clarify meanings in English. Often students at the FI—regardless of their knowledge of other languages from studies at the FI or speaking Indigenous languages in their communities—do not use languages other than the Spanish[1] and/or do not identify as bi−/multilingual.

---

[1] In the case of students who are return migrants (from the United States to Oaxaca), they generally use only English (Kleyn, 2017).

Although our project did not collect empirical evidence to support this claim, for us, Julio's understandings of his experiences are valid. In collaborating closely with each other, we debated the meanings behind his experiences and the issues that arise when working to understand whose truths or methods of understanding "count." Dismissing Julio's views due to paradigmatic research constraints to a certain degree, present themselves problematic and antithetical to PAR methods. Thus, we are working to include empiricist perspectives while also creating space to conduct research that accepts knowledge production through modes which include Julio's experiences. Directly stated, we back Julio and his views about the impact on this work in valuing and sustaining the bi−/multilingual identities of students. We have worked specifically in this chapter to include and appreciate Julio's views as the teacher.

We are using translanguaging in assessments aimed to move past monoglossic language ideologies—ideologies that indexed modes of oppression steeped in neo-liberal, colonial, and linguistic purist forms of oppression (De Korne et al., 2018; Heller, 2008; Kubota, 2014; McKinney, 2016; Rosa & Burdick, 2016). These methods and our modes of interaction and communication among the different team members allowed for us to discuss various viewpoints throughout our study, to question our assumptions, to create spaces for others to question our process and interpretations, all with a focus that returned to understanding the social consequences of our work. Our work on assessment in Oaxaca exists in tension and conversation with prominent paradigms of evaluation similar to most other regions of the world. As such, there have been constraints such as developing assessments to meet with the standard grading schema for higher education in Oaxaca and Mexico. These constraints also inform the design of our studies and the importance that we place on understanding the implications of the grades that are assigned to students' performances on assessments. As a team, we find PAR methods to be essential in identifying areas within these constraints to enact change that is meaningful and beneficial to those impacted by the research work. Critical ethnographic methods have also served to support such efforts.

2.3   Critical Ethnographic Methods

Within critical ethnographic methodologies are shifting perspectives about relationships between researchers and participants. Often presented these relationships have focused on the role of the research with respect to as an insider/outsider dichotomy (Noblit, Flores, & Murillo, 2004), researching the Other (Flores, 2004; Villenas, 1996), or performances and perceptions of credibility and approachability (Mayorga-Gallo & Hordge-Freeman, 2017). In his work, Ibrahim (Ibrahim, 1999; Ibrahim, 2008; Ibrahim, 2011) has developed methodological approaches that intentionally engage with, rather than observe, participants. We have found his approaches to be informative in cultivating our collaborations. His theoretical and methodological positionings are connected with critical ethnography and understanding how research needs to attend to the interactional relationships among the researcher and participants, in particular, questioning notions of objective observation and subjective interpretations (Madison, 2011).

Ibrahim (1999) engaged in "hanging out" methodology in his interactions with participants. He has described what hanging out methodology entails in a footnote[2]:

> This [hanging out] means staying somewhere to familiarize oneself with the place, its people, and their ways of 'being' in that space. In schools, these are informal sites (e.g., hallways, school yards, school steps, the cafeteria and the gymnasium) where people feel comfortable enough to speak their minds. (p. 355)

In our use of hanging out methodology, we want to stress the preposition that most often follows hanging out methodology in his work, *with*. And what's more, we emphasize the individuals or people that follow the *with*, namely each other, positioning each member of the team as holding various valuable roles. What has consistently risen to the forefront of our work together is having not only the collaborations of work bring us together, but also the sharing of experiences, our histories, our world views to gain a better understanding of each other inside and outside of these collaborations. *Hanging out with each other*, for us, means sharing physical and virtual spaces. For our team, hanging out with each other translates into being in consistent communication both concerning the demands of the project as well as allotting for understanding other aspects of our lives. Thus, hanging out is inclusive of sharing different aspects of ourselves and our lives with each other both within research situations as well as social engagements in casual settings.

In presenting our work as an ongoing PAR project, we want to emphasize the joint decision making that is infused throughout our process. As such, at times our project takes on the qualities of what is found more traditionally in research on language assessment, which may seem at odds with PAR but we argue that is it is congruent with the PAR process. For example, our first study (described in more detail below) used a quasi-experimental design at the explicit request of members of the research team, teachers, and administrators at UABJO. The design ensured that we had some evidence to make changes to assessments because we wanted to ensure that our research was being done in a way to work towards the benefit of students' learning, rather than for the sake of promoting our agendas or interests in translanguaging approaches to assessment. We wanted to effect change, but we also need to understand the social implications of our work. And in particular with assessments, we continually reflect and analyze our work with an additional lens to address any potential negative consequences that students may face that is related to this work.

---

[2] We quote from his 1999 seminal article, though we want to acknowledge that he is consistent in his definition throughout his work (e.g., Ibrahim, 2008, 2011).

3 Instructor Insights, Experiences, and Reflections

In this section, Julio provides a first-person account of his perspective, experiences, and engagement with translanguaging, teaching, assessment, and research collaborations.

3.1 Personal Trajectory

Language instructors at the FI are in charge of designing their classes, and therefore, they design their assessment tools to evaluate progress made by students throughout the semester. The first time that I (Julio) worked with students in the FI at UABJO was 2013. At that time, the methods for teaching and assessing English were different than what I have come to use now as part of this collaboration. My background in English teaching developed from my varied experiences, and all of the experiences that I had in different classes have shaped my teaching practices. During my high school and BA classes, most teachers tried to maintain an English-only policy and practice. For instance, I had to put some money in the jar if I spoke Spanish in class. In addition, all my English tests were entirely in English. Among my classmates, it was a widespread belief that the best teachers were the ones that used English only in the classroom, which would consequently mean that this would be expected from us as future English teachers. In my teaching, this has meant that I have tried to maintain an English-only policy for my instruction, students' responses, and assessments.

In 2015 I began a master's program in Critical Language Studies at the FI. In this program, I was asked to consider how translanguaging had been present throughout my life, including my previous studies and teaching practices. Upon reflection, I realized that I have been, most of my life, involved in this practice of translanguaging, not only as a linguistic practice in my communities but also as a classroom practice. I remembered how my language teachers had also used translanguaging in a classroom. My language teachers used our shared language of Spanish and the language that was the subject of the course. I, as a language learner, felt comfortable since this allowed us to be more confident with the language which we were learning. These practices were always presented, but I had largely ignored them in favor of working towards an English-only ideal, erasing the presence and utility of these translanguaging practices. However, even as I began to reflect on this in my own experiences and practices, I remained skeptical about the integration of translanguaging practices, in particular in communicating with my students about the potential pedagogical benefits of translanguaging for teaching and learning. Moreover, concerning assessments, they remained English-only.

In 2016 I met Jamie and started collaborating with her and Mario on a research project. At that point in my teaching career, I felt increasingly comfortable with my general approach to and interested in expanding translanguaging in teaching. Mario put me in contact with Jamie—who previously co-taught a class at the FI with Mario on translanguaging and assessment—because it seemed like my classrooms would be the appropriate spaces to see how translanguaging in assessment functioned with respect to students' performances on tests. In our collaboration, translanguaging practices began to take shape in my mind as a new concept that was *rooted in shared experiences.*

Mario pointed out the importance of this study to me and asked me to support it by providing Jamie the space and the opportunity of talking with potential participants or students in my classes. In December 2016, near the end of the semester, 44 pre-service English teachers in their fifth and seventh semesters of English language studies took the assessment designed in collaboration with Schissel, Leung, et al. (2018). Rather than using the traditional grammar-based assessments that were commonplace in my classroom, in this study, community and classroom language practices were explored through a task-based assessment approach. The assessment focused on the culturally relevant topics of diabetes and litter because they are some of the most common problems found in everyday interaction in Mexico. Through two different tasks, one with readings in Spanish and English and one with texts in English, students had to create their own opinion about the topic, and they had to explain information on the topic about which they were reading. Task 1 asked participants to provide advice to prevent the onset of type II diabetes, which is more common among the Mexican population due to a variety of factors such as sedentary lifestyles and diet. In this reading exercise, students had to underline key words or write comments about the content of the reading. Participants of this study had to synthesize and analyze both sources, in Spanish and English, to give advice in the form of an email to a friend. Task 2 asked participants to make a recommendation for a litter clean-up program for a campus. Participants had to repeat the same process of reading, annotating comments, and making any comment; however, this time, they had to address a letter with recommendations about litter management to the university administration.

In both tasks, analyzing cause and effect and evaluating the situation involved high-order thinking skills. After completing both tasks and analyzing students' written responses, Jamie interviewed some students to ask about their thinking process during task performance. We planned for her to interview students in pairs because I felt that would make them more comfortable. Together this project provided parameters to understand how translanguaging could be integrated into the design of an assessment and the repercussions that it has on assessment performance with implications for language learning and language teaching. This study offered some empirical evidence of an assessment approach that is consistent with the broadly supported principle of making use of all students' linguistic resources for teaching and learning. Students performed better at a level of statistical significance on the multilingual task in comparison to the monolingual task. According to Schissel, Leung, et al. (2018) the findings "pointed to not only an improved performance when using readings in English and Spanish as opposed to English-only, but also may hold implications for performance on higher-order processing skills" (p. 177).

This study also helped me understand better and think more in-depth about the teaching methods which I was using in my classes.

3.2 Recognizing and Integrating Translanguaging

After this first research project, I had started using the languages that I know, Spanish and English, to teach the learning objectives that were part of the course syllabuses at the FI. Previously I had tried to teach using only English. However, I started to wonder if my students would understand what I was planning to teach them. I looked for some information on how to address my class to basic level students, and I found out that according to Abdelilah-Bauer (Abdelilah-Bauer, 2007), bilingualism was a very complex phenomenon and researchers are still far away of having explored all the aspects of various languages coexistence in a person's mind. As I was starting to know my students at a deeper level, I began to question myself about the assumptions I had regarding bilingualism. As I understood, it was the ability to use two *separate* languages. It did not really matter at what extent I was able to use them, but they remained or were used *separately*. Using both languages at the same time for one purpose was beyond my own beliefs. Not only did I have this question in mind, but also my students who also speak more than one language. The idea of using more languages than English and Spanish in my English class then emerged.

The first time that I taught English to the group of students who participated in this year-long PAR was during the fall semester of 2016–2017, from August to January, which was the same semester when I began talking with and then met Jamie about the previous research project. At this time, the students were in the third semester of the Language Teaching program at FI. Also, the same group of students is studying the languages offered by the program in Language Teaching such as Japanese, French, Italian, and Portuguese, information that is common knowledge within the FI. At first, students seemed a bit confused since they did not understand the translanguaging methodology used in class.

Mixing languages at the moment of teaching happened to be very useful. For content explanation, I used both English and Spanish, not as echo translation, but as I way to give further examples. Furthermore, for instructions and classroom language phrases (e.g., Did you finish? Do you have any questions), I used all the languages at my disposal and the ones I knew some students would understand, Italian and French, for instance. For my students, some were surprised about the shift in language use in the classroom because they were accustomed to having English-only or discussions about the benefits of English-only instruction in class. For language education received at lower educational levels, such as middle-school and high-schools, the ideal is to teach solely in the goal language, in this case, English. Thus, I felt that taking on this translanguaging approach in early 2017 helped students to become more familiar with this approach during classes.

Linguistics and other related courses demand that students speak at least two languages so they could be compared or used in class to achieve different learning objectives. One of these courses is Comparative Linguistics in which students have to use two languages so they can study differences and similarities of the languages they speak. Spanish and English then helped students understand the different goals of the course as they are the basis of the major. At the same time that I taught English using a bilingual methodology, I taught Comparative Linguistics to a different group. That time, I focused on using different languages which my Linguistics students knew: they were Italian and French. After having learned some phrases and useful vocabulary from students, some phrases were used to compare different grammar topics.

All this made me wonder about the possibility of asking my students if they spoke a native Indigenous language; hence, and their potential in the learning process. I asked questions about not only the languages they studied at the FI but also Indigenous languages. During this semester with these students, I worked to learn more about the places from which students come from the university and the languages which they speak. At first, students did not tell me that they spoke Indigenous languages. Instead, I learned about this over time through a variety of methods and interactions across classes. Firstly, students had to become familiar and confident with each other and of course, the teacher. That is because even though the FI, UABJO, and the city and state of Oaxaca work to recognize and value Indigenous languages and Indigenous peoples, there remains a stigma of being Indigenous or a view that Indigenous languages are dialects. Because of different discourses now accepted by society, speaking an Indigenous language can mean that people feel embarrassed and occasionally, students tend to omit that information, so no one knows that they speak an Indigenous language and we, as teachers, assume that they speak Spanish as L1. Figure 8.1, for example, is a meme created by students at the FI that depicts some of the ongoing tensions—with humor—around the acceptance of Indigenous languages.

That was the beginning of an environment change during the class. Indigenous language speakers then told me which languages they spoke, and their use in the class was a proposal with which students agreed. In this group, six students speak Indigenous languages such as Zapotec, Chatino, Triqui, Mixe, and Amuzgo, along with Spanish. These students told me that they sometimes used their mother language to compare grammar and language structures. This comparison was useful for them as they understood, in a more natural way, the grammar and language points present in class, according to their words. More languages in the class were used and, therefore, students could use the languages which they study as speakers of Indigenous languages used theirs. These ideas helped me secure some thoughts in my mind about translanguaging and how I could continue using it in my other classes.

Having this landscape before my eyes made the idea of incorporating all the linguistic repertoire of my students in the teaching-learning process seem increasingly relevant. This information helped to shape cultivating and incorporating multicultural and multilinguistic characteristics of the existing environment in classes.

Fig. 8.1 Meme about how Indigenous languages are devalued
[Gloss: T: Language. Ss: Language. T: Indigenous. Ss: Indigenous. T: All together. Ss: Dialect. T: Damn it!]
[Translation: T: Indigenous. Ss: Indigenous. T: Language. Ss: Language. T: All together (*students are supposed to say "Indigenous language"*). Ss: Dialect. T: Damn it!]
(Memes Idiomas UABJO, https://www.facebook.com/298663324198532/posts/322858138445 717/?substory_index=0)

To move outside of language practices that reflected monoglossic language ideologies in the course, instructions, and questions in the teaching space were made using all languages known by the students. However, English and Spanish continued to be spoken a high percent of the time. Theories of language as a dynamic linguistic repertoire, which reflect individual and community-based language use (González,

Moll, & Amanti, 2006; Otheguy et al., 2015, 2018) support such efforts. These teaching practices are seen as reflective of community-based language practices, as some students tended to speak Indigenous languages at home in daily interactions; they use these languages with their families when talking on the phone or just talking at home. For two of the students in this course involved in the study, these practices also include negotiating meaning across different varieties of an Indigenous language. In a class discussion, they tried to interact using their language, Chatino, but it was not possible in the first try. After more attempts and interactions, they found a way to build on some of the mutual intelligibility across the language varieties to understand each other. The students later explained that although they come from the same region, their language differs significantly in the way it is spoken in different communities. After having discovered these facts, similar questions were made to the other speakers of Indigenous languages. They explained that the same phenomena happen in their languages. Triqui, Amuzgo, Mixe, and Zapotec experience a comparable situation concerning understanding a different variant of the same language.

Sismos literal y metafórico [Literal and Metaphorical Earthquakes] The above description of events was the backdrop for the linguistic aspects that impacted our project. One further and significant event that shaped the direction of our collaboration was developing pedagogies and assessments that were receptive to the earthquakes in Mexico occurred in September of 2017. On September 7, 2017, one of the strongest Earthquakes ever registered in Mexican history, 8.2 in Richter scale, hit southern Mexico states. It was a huge surprise since it happened almost at midnight. Panic could be felt in the air as some students come from the isthmus of Tehuantepec, Oaxaca, and it was one of the most affected regions in Mexico. After only 2 weeks of having started the semester, the class environment was affected by this phenomenon. Some students from the FI were absent since they decided to visit their family and relatives to help in recovering from this event. Classes were suspended for a couple of days to evaluate the damage to school buildings at UABJO. Once all schools were evaluated, and authorities guaranteed security, it was decided to continue with classes as usual, however, a few days after, September 19, 2017, another strong earthquake hit Mexico severely around 1:15 p.m. This time, epicenters were located in Puebla, which is a neighboring state with Oaxaca, and Morelos, near Mexico City. This earthquake hit southern Mexico again severely. Major affectations happened in the states of Mexico, Puebla, Morelos, Oaxaca, and Guerrero and Mexico City. This event shocked Mexican society as minor earthquakes continued happening during September, and despair was reflected in the faces of everyone.

Students in classes were still focused on the earthquakes, and constant questions about earthquake-related vocabulary started to arise among students in fifth semester. Jamie returned to Oaxaca in October 2017 to explore the possibility of conducting a study together. In light of these events around the earthquakes, we decided instead of conducting research similar to the previous. We developed translanguaging approaches for ongoing classroom assessments that were responsive to the situations that students were facing after the massive earthquakes. After discussing the findings of Schissel, Leung, et al. (2018) as well, I felt more strongly that translanguaging was a potent tool in English classes. The shift in research methodologies, in turn, has meant that we are striving to understand the social implications of our work, and how the different ideological and historical contexts and perspectives of participants shape our efforts. Having this major event as background, it was time to start designing our first assessment tool.

Balancing the needs to hold classes while communities were beginning the recovery process were taken into consideration as we started this project. Having an assessment designed those days was a slightly tricky situation since tension was present in the school environment. In a conversation with Jamie, we agreed how we should address this situation and use this information, and we decided the kind of activities which would be part of our first assessment designed together would be reflective of and responsive to the recent events of the earthquakes. In addition, I continued having regular classes with my students. In our talk, we also continued to discuss the potential benefits of using translanguaging in teaching and assessment. And thus, we decided to start searching for material in both languages, Spanish and English, so that we could generate a new kind of perception and processing of information in students. We found information about the earthquake in Spanish and English from news reports so that it could be used for our assessment design; we also took on the task of mixing it with the topics learned during the first unit of the semester.

When the exam was administered, students' reactions were new. Students were used to having a translanguaging approach in instruction, but having it in an assessment was something that they did not expect. Hence, they did not know how to react. The complete exam was designed for students to write in English, but using materials that were in both Spanish and English. Students had to evaluate the content of both texts and also use their perspectives and experiences to write their opinion about what happened during the earthquake events. Culturally relevant events were used to trigger students' responses in English due to the importance of using contextualized material so they could express their most objective opinion about their context. Having the content in both languages was fairly innovative for students. Thus, we could expect a new type of answers in which more than a language could be used.

The analysis presented on the first assessment was necessary to determine the feasibility of continued efforts. After having students do the exams, we worked together to grade the assessments, which in turn helped us understand the implications of using both languages in assessing and in the teaching-learning process. As I read students' responses while grading, I noticed that students used their full linguistic repertoire to accomplish the task, so, they used the languages shared and known amongst the students: English and Spanish. They came up with responses to what they read using both languages. "reconstruction form *de* buildings" and "the authorities *por* them" were some of the examples (Schissel, Morales, López-Gopar, & Leung, 2019).

The general goal of all assessments in the course was to have students demonstrate English learning in alignment with the learning objectives from the course syllabus. As the first unit ended up being irregular due to the events mentioned before, I was somewhat worried about students' performance. However, they completed the task at a relatively satisfactory level. They showed their understanding of what was happening in Mexico by then and could communicate and describe it to an imaginary, foreign friend. In other words, students were capable of performing at and achieving a different level of communication by using the languages shared by the majority of students at the FI, that is, Spanish and English. Moreover, with this information, we embarked on a year-long study.

4 Translanguaging in Assessments

In this section part of the chapter, we return to our collaborative research and writing process to discuss findings from initial analyses of our year-long project. The results presented are then followed by understanding the implications of our study regarding Julio's insights and the data in this investigation.

4.1 Assessment Design

Over the course of one academic year, we created assessments that incorporated translanguaging in the design of the assessment. In each semester, there were three tests. For the first semester of the study, our first assessment had translanguaging tasks, our second was English-only, and our third contained translanguaging tasks. As part of our ongoing reflection within the iterative PAR process, we wanted to monitor the impact of our research approach to see if the intended benefits were

Table 8.1 Translanguaging assessment approaches

Semester	Exam #	Grammar point	Translanguaging approach	Topical connection
Fall	1	Passive voice	New headings in Spanish	Current news events
Fall	1	Reported speech	Recorded news stories, one in English, one in Spanish	September 2017 earthquakes in Mexico
Fall	3	Quantifiers	Watch two videos with baking fails, one in Spanish, on in English	*Rosca de reyes* [three king's cake]
Fall	3	Modal verbs of speculation	Watch a video that had English and Spanish audio and subtitles and read an article in English	Rebuilding and misuse of earthquake aid
Spring	1	Conjunctions and inversions	One reading in Spanish, one reading in English	Technology in the classroom
Spring	2	Modal verbs of possibility	Reading in Spanish, video in English	Health
Spring	3	Present perfect	Reading in Spanish	Teacher strike from 2006

being achieved. For the second semester of our project, all three of the assessments used translanguaging tasks. Table 8.1 describes the translanguaging tasks for each of the assessments. The tests focused on assessing different grammar points in English. The tests were administered at the end of each unit and graded on a 10-point scale.

The grammar points were aligned with objectives on the course syllabus. The translanguaging approach was often based on the availability of resources. The topical connection was based on events that were co-occurring during the time of the test. For each of the tests, 2–4 additional grammar points were tested using English-only readings or audio. Some of the English-only parts of the assessment, for example, included cloze or fill-in-the-blank items. Some also included writing longer passages. Except for the passive voice task on assessment 1 in the fall semester, all of the translanguaging tasks asked students to write longer passages. We present assessment performances to several of the tasks below, in particular highlighting the importance of using translanguaging materials that focused on events that were the most outstanding and contextually relevant for the students during the period of the research. In the final section, we present samples of the assessments and performances from students that point to some of the advantages and reservations in viewing linguistic practices more holistically through translanguaging in instruction and assessment. We conclude with implications of how our research project on translanguaging in instruction and assessment opens new pathways for TESOL in Oaxaca, México that is responsive to the multicultural and multilingual context.

4.2   Assessment Performances

We have included two representative examples of our translanguaging tasks below. We are focusing on the third assessment of the fall semester for this analysis. This assessment, in particular, lends important information because half of the test used translanguaging tasks, and the other half used English-only, which lends itself well to making some comparisons of students' performances. First, we provide descriptive statistics reporting trends in assessment scores for the first three assessments in Table 8.2.

Table 8.2 Student scores on fall 2017 semester tests (on a 10-point scale)

	Test 1	Test 2	Test 3
Mean (n = 28[a])	7.214	7.928	8.714
Standard deviation	1.397	1.303	0.896
Median	7	8	9
Minimum	5	5	7
Maximum	9	10	10

[a]Number is reflective of the 28 students who remained in the course with Julio for the entire 2017-2018 academic year

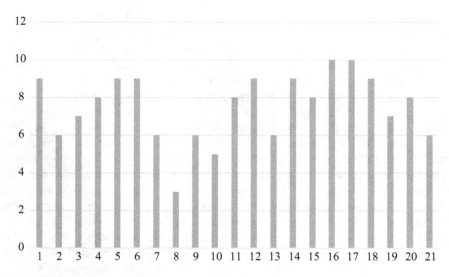

Fig. 8.2 Individual student scores on the third assessment of the fall 2017 semester

Table 8.2 reports an increase in overall average scores. The notable difference within test performance is the difference in standard deviation from tests one and 2 with test three. We attributed this difference to the potential benefits of using translanguaging in assessment for the majority of the students. The increase in test one and two is particularly relevant in a Mexican context where an "8" score or above is commonly accepted as good performance. For instance, many BA or MA programs accept students with an "8" GPA average. Hence, almost the entire class performed well.

In looking more closely at the third assessment, there were two translanguaging tasks and two English-only tasks. The requirements for the translanguaging assessments are reported in Table 8.1. For the English-only tasks (1) students needed to listen to audio and describe the item that people were talking about in 1–2 sentences using relative clauses and (2) complete sentences using the words *other(s), the other(s)*, and *another*. Figure 8.2 presents the students' overall scores on the assessment (n = 21[3]).

We can see in these scores some of the variability in test scores with one student (student 8) performing poorly on the assessment. If we look at the comparison of scores on the monolingual tasks and the multilingual tasks, we see more information in Table 8.3 about the general differences within this class.

Table 8.3 illustrates a few differences overall in the performances on the translanguaging and English-only tasks, with a slightly higher performance on the translanguaging tasks. This overall trend was not universal across students. In looking at the student-level data, we see that 13 students performed better on the

---

[3] Number is reflective of the 21 students who returned their test to make it available for closer analysis.

Table 8.3 Comparison of student scores on translanguaging and English-only tasks on the third assessment of the fall 2017 semester (on a 10-point scale)

	Translanguaging	English-only
Mean	7.81	7.14
Min	5	4.06
Max	10	9.38
SD	1.53	1.54

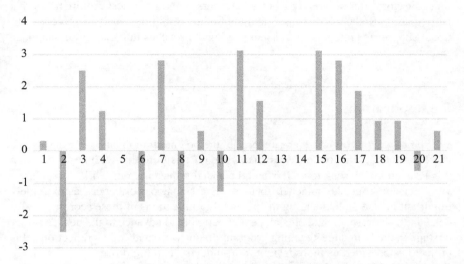

Fig. 8.3 Individual student scores differences between scores on translanguaging and monolingual tasks on the third assessment of the fall 2017 semester

translanguaging tasks, three students did not perform better or worse on either task type, and four students performed better on the English-only tasks. Figure 8.3 reports these scores.

Overall, we continue to see the trend that students performed better or got a higher score on the translanguaging tasks than on the English-only tasks, with five students performing at least 2 points better on the translanguaging tasks, and two students performing better on the English-only assessment tasks by at least two points. With these data, we make the case that there is evidence for continuing to develop, refine, and implement translanguaging assessment approaches. If, for example, we did not see any difference in the scores between English-only and translanguaging tasks, or students overall performing worse on the translanguaging tasks we would need to revisit and question the equity of our assumptions about the potential benefits of including translanguaging in language teaching assessments.

We see these findings as presenting evidence about the possibilities and potential of using translanguaging in assessment. In particular, we feel that the PAR approach and working closely amongst the different members of the research team and taking into account the views of the students has helped us to understand effect change in a way that seeks to understand the social consequences of our work. For example, students were more supportive of this approach when it meant that they received higher grades. Moreover, for the research team, we feel that the tests showed what students were learning that was being missed with English-only assessments. Further, as part of the PAR approach, we were working to make sure that participating in research did not place additional burdens on the students. The assessments, thus, did not differ so greatly from other courses and other test requirements that participating. Rather, PAR project and the findings from this analysis present additional support for integrating translanguaging approaches into classroom language assessments.

5   Implications

We do not want to overstate nor understate the potential implications of these findings. First of all, our work on assessments and the positions that we have taken using this PAR approach seek to understand the social impacts of our work. As such, we view the consequences attached to these assessment performances as extremely important in also understanding the potential ramifications of these scores. For students in this course, their scores made them eligible to advance to the next semester or stage in the Language Teaching program. In our work and Julio's reflections, this project has provided us more insight into students' learning processes and skills in English. Our purposes for working with these different assessments approaches are balanced with how students are positioned as (successful) language learners—as indexed mainly by their performance on classroom assessments. In the PAR project, the design has sought to use and analyze data that would prove to be informative to the teacher and researchers by looking at the scores that were meaningful to the students. In doing so, during the project process, we were able to check in with the social consequences of integrating translanguaging into assessments during the semester and retrospectively in this and subsequent analyses.

Julio's insights, experiences, and reflections have also significantly contributed to this work and deeper understandings of the importance of teachers' involvements in efforts to integrate translanguaging into pedagogy and assessment in TESOL classrooms. The information Julio included here around his understandings and experiences around monoglossic language ideologies and translanguaging in his life were integrated throughout the PAR project and his work with students. We hoped that the assessment approach could also contribute to troubling or pushing back against monoglossic ideologies around English-only instruction and assessments as the ideal model for the classroom. Julio's journey detailed in this chapter illustrates how he moved away from these ideologies. However, such perspectives persist, and we position our project as exploring the dynamic ways in which different individuals can come together to begin such work.

Our study has potential implications for the field of TESOL as a whole as well. As translanguaging is taken up in instruction in TESOL classrooms, we also need to see translanguaging reflected in the assessments. As we stated at the beginning of this chapter in terms of *what gets tested gets taught,* making space for translanguaging in assessments can help to contest monoglossic language ideologies and practices in the classroom. The pressure to perform well on an assessment remains a looming factor in most classes, which makes the need for assessments to become inclusive of translanguaging practices increasingly important. From these small efforts in classroom language assessment, we hope to see momentum for other forms of assessment, including more standardized forms of assessment.

References

Abdelilah-Bauer, B. (2007). *El desafío del bilingüismo*. Madrid, Spain: Morata.

Balakrishnan, V., & Claiborne, L. (2017). Participatory action research in culturally complex societies: Opportunities and challenges. *Educational Action Research, 25*(2), 185–202.

Blackledge, A., & Creese, A. (2010). *Multilingualism: A critical perspective*. London, UK: Bloomsbury Publishing.

Borda, O. F. (2001). Participatory (action) research in social theory: Origins and challenges. In *Handbook of action research: Participative inquiry and practice* (pp. 27–37). London, UK: Sage.

Chalhoub-Deville, M. (2016). Validity theory: Reform policies, accountability testing, and consequences. *Language Testing, 33*(4), 453–472.

Davison, C., & Leung, C. (2009). Current issues in English language teacher-based assessment. *TESOL Quarterly, 43*(3), 393–415.

De Korne, H., López Gopar, M. E., & Rios Rios, K. (2018). Changing ideological and implementational spaces for minoritised languages in higher education: Zapotequización of language education in Mexico. *Journal of Multilingual and Multicultural Development*. https://doi.org/10.1080/01434632.2018.1531876

Enciso, A. (2013). En México, 56% de los niños menores de cinco años viven en la pobreza [In Mexico, 56% of children under five years of age live in poverty]. *La Jornada*. Retrieved from http://www.jornada.unam.mx/2013/04/04/sociedad/040nlsoc

Flores, N., & Schissel, J. L. (2014). Dynamic bilingualism as the norm: Envisioning a heteroglossic approach to standards-based reform. *TESOL Quarterly, 48*(3), 454–479.

Flores, S. Y. (2004). Observing the observer. In G. W. Noblit, S. Y. Flores, & E. G. Murillo (Eds.), *Postcritical ethnography: Reinscribing critique* (pp. 187–188). Cresskill, NJ: Hampton Press.

González, N., Moll, L. C., & Amanti, C. (Eds.). (2006). *Funds of knowledge: Theorizing practices in households, communities, and classrooms*. New York, NY: Routledge.

Heller, M. (2008). Language and the nation-state: Challenges to sociolinguistic theory and practice 1. *Journal of SocioLinguistics, 12*(4), 504–524.

Hornberger, N. H. (2001). Educational linguistics as a field: A view from Penn's program on the occasion of its 25th anniversary. *Working Papers in Educational Linguistics, 17*, 1–26.

Ibrahim, A. (2008). Operating under erasure: Race/language/identity. *Comparative and International Education/Éducation Comparée et Internationale, 37*(2), 56–76.

Ibrahim, A. (2011). When life is off da hook: Hip-Hop identity and identification, BESL, and the pedagogy of pleasure. In *Negotiating the self in another language: Identity formation in a globalized world* (pp. 221–238). Berlin, Germany: Mouton de Gruyter.

Ibrahim, A. E. K. M. (1999). Becoming black: Rap and hip-hop, race, gender, identity, and the politics of ESL learning. *TESOL Quarterly, 33*(3), 349–369.

INEGI. (n.d.). *Instituto Nacional de Estadística, Geografía e Informática*. Retrieved from https://www.inegi.org.mx/

Kleyn, T. (2017). Centering transborder students: Perspectives on identity, languaging and schooling between the US and Mexico. *Multicultural Perspectives, 19*(2), 76–84.

Kubota, R. (2014). The multi/plural turn, postcolonial theory, and neoliberal multiculturalism: Complicities and implications for applied linguistics. *Applied Linguistics, 37*(4), 474–494.

Leung, C., & Valdes, G. (2019). Translanguaging and the transdisciplinary framework for language teaching and learning in a multilingual world. *The Modern Language Journal, 103*(2), 348–370.

Lin, A. (2014). Hip-hop heteroglossia as practice, pleasure, and public pedagogy: Translanguaging in the lyrical poetics of "24 Herbs" in Hong Kong. In *Heteroglossia as practice and pedagogy* (pp. 119–136). Dordrecht, The Netherlands: Springer.

López Gopar, M. (2016). *Decolonizing primary English language teaching*. Bristol, Inglaterra: Multilingual Matters.

López Gopar, M. (Ed.). (2019). *International perspectives on critical pedagogies in ELT*. Hampshire, Inglaterra: Palgrave.

López Gopar, M., & Clemente, A. (2011). Maestros de inglés de origen indígena en México: Identidad y multilingüismo. In A. M. Mejía & C. Hélot (Eds.), *Empowering teachers across cultures* (pp. 207–225). Frankfurt, Germany: Peter Lang.

López-Gopar, M. E., Núñez-Méndez, O., Sughrua, W., & Clemente, A. (2013). In pursuit of multilingual practices: Ethnographic accounts of teaching 'English'to Mexican children. *International Journal of Multilingualism, 10*(3), 273–291.

Madison, D. S. (2011). *Critical ethnography: Method, ethics, and performance*. Los Angeles, CA/ Thoudand Oaks, CA: Sage.

Mayorga-Gallo, S., & Hordge-Freeman, E. (2017). Between marginality and privilege: Gaining access and navigating the field in multiethnic settings. *Qualitative Research, 17*(4), 377–394.

McIntyre, A. (2008). *Participatory action research*. Thousand Oaks, CA: Sage.

McKinney, C. (2016). *Language and power in post-colonial schooling: Ideologies in practice*. London, UK: Routledge.

Noblit, G. W., Flores, S. Y., & Murillo, E. G. (2004). Introduction. In G. W. Noblit, S. Y. Flores, & E. G. Murillo (Eds.), *Postcritical ethnography: Reinscribing critique* (pp. 1–52). Cresskill, NJ: Hampton Press.

Otheguy, R., García, O., & Reid, W. (2015). Clarifying translanguaging and deconstructing named languages: A perspective from linguistics. *Applied Linguistics Review, 6*(3), 281–307.

Otheguy, R., García, O., & Reid, W. (2018). A translanguaging view of the linguistic system of bilinguals. *Applied Linguistics Review*.

Palmer, D. K., Martínez, R. A., Mateus, S. G., & Henderson, K. (2014). Reframing the debate on language separation: Toward a vision for translanguaging pedagogies in the dual language classroom. *The Modern Language Journal, 98*(3), 757–772.

Rahman, M. A. (2008). Some trends in the praxis of participatory action research. In *The Sage handbook of action research: Participative inquiry and practice* (pp. 49–62). London, UK: Sage.

Rea-Dickins, P. (2004). Understanding teachers as agents of assessment. *Language Testing, 21*(3), 249–258.

Rosa, J., & Burdick, C. (2016). Language ideologies. In *Oxford Handbook of Language and Society* (pp. 103–123). Oxford, UK/New York, NY: Oxford University Press.

Sayer, P. (2013). Translanguaging, TexMex, and bilingual pedagogy: Emergent bilinguals learning through the vernacular. *TESOL Quarterly, 47*(1), 63–88.

Schissel, J. L. (2019). *Social consequences of testing for language-minoritized*. Bristol, UK: Multilingual Matters.

Schissel, J. L., De Korne, H., & López-Gopar, M. (2018). Grappling with translanguaging for teaching and assessment in culturally and linguistically diverse contexts: Teacher perspectives from Oaxaca, Mexico. *International Journal of Bilingual Education and Bilingualism*, 1–17.

Schissel, J. L., Leung, C., López-Gopar, M., & Davis, J. R. (2018). Multilingual learners in language assessment: Assessment design for linguistically diverse communities. *Language and Education, 32*(2), 167–182.

Schissel, J. L., Morales, J., López-Gopar, M. E., & Leung, C. (2019). Insights and reflections on multilingual approaches to classroom-based language assessment. *Bilingual Basics.* http://newsmanager.commpartners.com/tesolbeis/issues/2019-07-08/2.html

Shohamy, E. (2001). *The power of tests: A critical perspective on the uses of language tests.* Harlow, UK/New York, NY: Routledge.

Shohamy, E. (2006). *Language policy: Hidden agendas and new approaches.* London, UK/New York, NY: Routledge.

Turner, M., & Lin, A. M. (2017). Translanguaging and named languages: Productive tension and desire. *International Journal of Bilingual Education and Bilingualism*, 1–11.

Vaish, V., & Subhan, A. (2015). Translanguaging in a reading class. *International Journal of Multilingualism, 12*(3), 338–357.

Villenas, S. (1996). The colonizer/colonized Chicana ethnographer: Identity, marginalization, and co-optation in the field. *Harvard Educational Review, 66*(4), 711–732.

Whyte, W. F. E. (1991). *Participatory action research.* Sage.

Chapter 9
Incorporating Australian Primary Students' Linguistic Repertoire into Teaching and Learning

Marianne Turner

Abstract Leveraging students' languages as a resource for learning has been advocated in TESOL literature for the past three decades. This focus has recently been catalysed by a translanguaging perspective which challenges deficit understandings of the 'English language learner' and promotes the idea of a holistic linguistic repertoire (García, 2017). Confronting beliefs related to the institutional centrality of English in a country like Australia is an important step in leveraging students' language resources at school. This chapter reports on research that aimed to encourage teachers in three linguistically diverse primary schools to draw on students' repertoires in the classroom. Seven generalist teachers attended professional learning in which they worked to incorporate students' language practices into their lessons. Data were collected from interviews, teachers' group discussions, lesson plans, written reflections and students' work samples. Thematic analysis evidenced a shift in teachers' thinking of what it meant to be bi/multilingual. Further, the affirmation of linguistic identities was found to be less challenging for the teachers than the leveraging of students' linguistic repertoire for specific learning objectives.

Keywords Professional learning · Primary · Language-as-resource · Mainstream education · Language maintenance · Australia

1 Introduction

Language separation is a traditional and well-established norm in the field of TESOL (e.g., Cummins, 2007). Monolingual forms of education for minority language speakers, such as mainstreaming with or without the provision of majority language support, are also very common, and are included in typologies of program

M. Turner (✉)
Monash University, Clayton, VIC, Australia
e-mail: marianne.turner@monash.edu

© Springer Nature Switzerland AG 2020
Z. Tian et al. (eds.), *Envisioning TESOL through a Translanguaging Lens*,
Educational Linguistics 45, https://doi.org/10.1007/978-3-030-47031-9_9

models for bilingual students (Baker & Wright, 2017; García, 2009). In mainstream English-speaking contexts, despite research on the incorporation of minority languages as a resource for learning and teaching (e.g., Cummins & Swain, 1986; Moll, Amanti, Neff & Gonzales, 1992; Moll, Soto-Santiago, & Schwartz, 2013; Paris, 2012; Schecter & Cummins, 2003), competence at school still appears to be overwhelmingly understood in relation to English (Gee, 2004; Lankshear & Knobel, 2003). An exclusively English focus can position other languages as having no real role to play in teaching and learning, and can ultimately threaten the maintenance of speakers' other languages through its assimilationist orientation (see Baker & Wright, 2017).

Research on translanguaging in educational contexts has challenged deficit understandings of language practices that do not fit with English as a dominant named language, and propose that students should be encouraged to use their full linguistic repertoire flexibly in order to support and develop their understanding (e.g., García, 2009, 2017; García & Li, 2014). From a translanguaging perspective, the aim of TESOL can thus be understood as enrichment: the language practices of students are valued and leveraged in class. In the Australian state of Victoria, the context of the research discussed in this chapter, 27 percent of students attending government schools identify as coming from language backgrounds other than English (LBOTE) (Department of Education and Training, Victoria, 2018). These students include children (born to immigrant parents) who are fluent in English and range from having limited to extensive exposure to other languages at home.

The chapter reports on a study which investigated the professional learning of seven in-service generalist primary school teachers who had a high number of LBOTE students in their classes. The professional learning focused on the incorporation of other languages in the classroom – a new approach for the teachers – and translanguaging was used as a conceptual tool. The professional learning took place over the course of 3 days, interspersed with the trialling of two lesson sequences (series of lessons). It was found to have a marked influence on teachers' understanding of what it means to be bi/multilingual and on their perceived capacity to leverage students' linguistic repertoires for learning. In the chapter, translanguaging, the principal theoretical frame, will be discussed in relation to languages as a resource for learning. The relationship between translanguaging and the performance of bi/multilingual identity will also be explained because this relationship was used to interpret the findings. The study and findings will be detailed and the final discussion will address the way the valuing of bi/multilingual identities can be a catalyst to encourage other pedagogical goals that teachers (and students) might find more challenging.

2   Languages as a Resource for Learning

The study was framed by translanguaging theory as it relates to teaching and learning. Translanguaging takes a holistic view of language (e.g., García, 2009; García & Li, 2014; Otheguy, García & Reid, 2015); "the language practices of bilinguals are complex and interrelated; they do not emerge in a linear way or function separately since there is only one linguistic system" (García & Li, 2014, p.14). The sophistication of what bi/multilinguals do (when given a choice) is emphasised, as is the repertoire of the speaker from the speaker's point of view (Otheguy, García & Reid, 2015). This speaker-centred lens, or a shifting away from the idea of L1 and L2 can be beneficial in contexts of diversity, where speakers do not fit neatly into categories. For example, a child may have a mother who speaks to her in Japanese, a father who does not understand Japanese and speaks in English and different friendships where she either speaks Japanese, English or draws on her complete linguistic repertoire in interactions with friends who speak both. She may also choose to draw only on English with Japanese heritage friends who are exposed to Japanese but are far more confident speaking English. Understanding students' language practices in order to leverage these practices in the classroom was an objective of the study discussed in this chapter and translanguaging was therefore considered to be useful.

Translanguaging pedagogy aims to guide teachers to think about their students' linguistic repertoire as a resource for learning (e.g., García & Li, 2014; García, Ibarra Johnson & Seltzer, 2017). A pedagogy has been developed for which goals include the adaptation of instruction for students with different kinds of language experiences, metalinguistic and cross-linguistic awareness, flexibility of language practices, the development of background knowledge, the development and extension of knowledge, the engagement of students through identity work, and interrogating and disrupting linguistic hierarchies (García & Li, 2014). All the goals prioritise meaning-making: directly translating is not considered translanguaging if there is not some additional purpose to the translation, such as metalinguistic awareness or making connections to other goals.

3   The Performance of Multilingual Identities

As indicated above, the affirmation of multilingual identities is considered to be central to translanguaging pedagogical goals. Translanguaging can be understood – in the same way as language in general – as identity performance (cf Creese & Blackledge, 2010; García & Kleifgen, 2010). The extent to which bi/multilingual students who are fluent in English make visible multilingual identities in Australian schools can be influenced by the value ascribed to their extended linguistic repertoire in class. Students choosing whether to perform aspects of their identity based on perceived worth in a particular setting relates to Bourdieu's (1977) and Bourdieu and Passeron's (1977) theorisation of cultural capital, in which a particular kind of knowledge is considered to have value or 'capital' in a social group. As Norton (2000, p.11) pointed out in the case of learning English in Canada, the relationship between a speaker and a language is socially and historically constructed, and deeply influenced by structures of power. In its explicit interrogation of linguistic hierarchies, translanguaging places these power dynamics as central to what we do with language (Flores & García, 2017; García & Li, 2014).

Another translanguaging pedagogical goal, the development of background knowledge, is also inclusive of multilingual identities, or the idea that speakers' representations of their linguistic and cultural world can help them interpret their own experiences (e.g., Dagenais & Jacquet, 2008; Prasad, 2015). This idea extends to the way teachers can use identity texts, or any kind of student creation that engages them with their linguistic and cultural repertoires (Cummins, 2006; Cummins & Early, 2011). Identity texts can take many forms. For example, Prasad (2018) discussed collage as a kind of identity text. In Australia, language maps have been implemented as a way to leverage students' language resources in the classroom (D'Warte, 2014, 2015; Somerville, D'Warte & Sawyer, 2016). D'Warte et al. facilitated LBOTE students' visual mapping of their everyday language practices to leverage these practices in ways that linked directly to curriculum content. Students were found to engage in the process, the quality of their English improved, and there was evidence of positive attitudinal change by the students towards their home language (Somerville, D'Warte & Sawyer, 2016).

Similar to D'Warte and her colleagues, identity texts were used as a pedagogical tool in the study discussed in this chapter to assist the teachers in leveraging their students' language practices in class. The teachers in the study were accustomed to encouraging their students to maintain their home language(s), but in the community domain rather than at school, and language separation was the classroom norm. The active advocation of language maintenance in the home – and for parents to speak to their children in the language they knew best – whilst continuing with an English-only message at school can be categorised as an additive approach to languages. García (2009) considered an additive framework to fit into a monolingual view of language because languages are compartmentalised, and learning is conceptualised to be occurring within a separatist framework. However, although the relegation of language to the community domain is suggestive of a subtractive typology (see Baker & Wright, 2017), parents were traditionally instructed by teachers and school leaders to speak English to their children in Australia. In its focus on transition to the majority language at school, a subtractive orientation does not necessarily make visible a shift in institutional practices whereby languages and, by extension multilingual identities, are actively promoted in the community domain. The main point of investigation in the study was a blurring of the lines between institutional and community domains, and this was found to be assisted by the institutional move towards an additive mindset.

4 The Study

The qualitative study reported in this chapter was conducted in 2017 and investigated teachers' leveraging of linguistic repertoire in primary school settings where a majority of students were born in Australia to parents who spoke at least one language other than English. The study used a design-based research framework (e.g., Anderson & Shattuck, 2012; Cobb, Confrey, diSessa, Lehrer & Schauble, 2003), which involves collaboration between the researcher and practitioners and 'tests' instructional hypotheses. The hypothesis for the research discussed in this chapter was:

> Students' creation of visual representations of their linguistic repertoires – how, where, when and with whom they speak particular languages and how they feel about them – can assist in the leveraging of the students' language practices as a resource for their learning.

Because the approach of incorporating students' language resources was new for the generalist primary teachers, the collaboration with the researcher was conceptualised as a form of professional learning in which the teachers would be introduced to translanguaging and to ways to (and objectives for) inviting students' language practices into the classroom. As part of this professional learning, the teachers would also implement two lesson sequences (or series of lessons) and regroup to reflect on these sequences.

Three Victorian primary schools in the Catholic sector – given the pseudonyms Madison, Hampton and Campbell PS – took part. All three schools had a very large proportion of children who lived in low socioeconomic areas, and over 80% of students were LBOTE (Australian Curriculum, Assessment and Reporting Authority, 2017). In all three schools, students came from diverse backgrounds, with no dominant ethnicity at Madison PS and Hampton PS. At Campbell PS, diversity of student

Table 9.1 Teachers participating in the study

School	Teacher participants[a]	Year level	Teaching experience	Years teaching at the school
Madison PS	Frida	1/2	- 18 years (primary) - 3 years (early childhood)	8 years
	Sam	1/2	- 37 years (primary)	7 years
	Jasmine	3/4	- 10 years (middle school in India) - 4.5 years (primary in Kuwait)	1st year
Hampton PS	Sophie	3/4	- 21 years (primary)	17 years
	Cassandra (support)	3/4	- 29 years (primary)	8 years
Campbell PS	Anne	3	- More than 30 years (mostly primary and also English to adults)	7 years
	Helen (support)	3	- 15 years (primary)	6 years

[a]All names are pseudonyms

background was also conspicuous, but the principal reported that the number of Indian and Vietnamese families had been increasing.

The researcher worked with seven teachers in the study – six women and one man. Details of the teachers and the school at which they taught can be viewed in Table 9.1. Five classes in total took part – two Year 1/2 classes and one Year 3/4 class at Madison PS, one Year 3/4 class at Hampton PS and one Year 3 class at Campbell PS. (In Australia, it is common to have classes with combined grades). Frida, Sam, Jasmine, Sophie and Anne were the main teachers in charge of teaching the classes, and Cassandra and Helen participated in a supporting role. Six teachers identified as solely English-speaking and one – Jasmine – also spoke Hindi, Marathi and some Konkani.

Teachers attended an initial seminar day in which they were introduced to translanguaging, and also learned how to conduct a language mapping lesson sequence in a way that would affirm students' linguistic repertoire (D'Warte, 2013; see also Turner, 2019 for more detail on this lesson sequence). After delivering the sequence, teachers regrouped with the researcher to discuss how to leverage what they had learned about their students in a way that fitted with planned curriculum objectives. The teachers then implemented this second lesson sequence, and came together once more to reflect on the process. The findings reported in this chapter are drawn from the second lesson sequence, and how different teachers chose to incorporate their students' language practices once they were more aware of what those practices entailed.

Data were collected from teachers' individual (written) and group (oral) reflections, lesson plans, student work, and end-of-project teacher interviews. All seven teachers were interviewed for 20 min. Twenty-one students in total were also interviewed for 10 min – six students each at Campbell and Madison Primary and three students from each of the three participating classes at Madison Primary. All students interviewed were from LBOTE backgrounds. Interview questions for both teachers and students focused on the visual mapping and leveraging of the students' linguistic repertoires with an additional question for teachers on whether the way they thought about bi/multilingualism and how it was recognised at school had changed over the course of the project. Work produced in the two lesson sequences by the 21 students interviewed was also sighted for the study. Thematic analysis (see Braun & Clarke, 2006) was used to analyse the data. For example, similarities and differences between the way teachers understood bi/multilingualism, choices and implementation of lesson sequences, and student engagement were cross-referenced and analysed through a translanguaging lens.

5   Findings

Teachers' understanding of what it means to be bi/multilingual was found to shift over the course of the study and this appeared to be strongly connected to the translanguaging pedagogical goal of bi/multilingual identity affirmation. The five main teachers, with the assistance of the two supporting teachers, also demonstrated a capacity to leverage their students' language resources for specific learning objectives, either by making them central to the students' learning of content, or making them relevant to this learning. This shift in thinking around bi/multilingualism will be addressed first, followed by the strategic leveraging of students' linguistic repertoire.

5.1   Teachers' Understanding of What It Means to Be Bi/Multilingual

For teachers – six of whom identified as monolingual in English – a shift in thinking around what it means to be bi/multilingual was found to occur most conspicuously as a result of a greater understanding of the linguistic experiences of their students. The teachers' focus appeared to shift from *being* bi/multilingual to *doing* bi/multilingualism or to the children's actual language practices. Helen at Campbell Primary summed this up in interview when asked whether her understanding of bilingualism[1] had changed – see the excerpt below:

> *I think particularly when [Anne] with her students did some background work to prepare for the language mapping, she found out to whom the children spoke particular languages and where they spoke it, and I think that has really added to my understanding of what bilingualism means.[…] Because I hadn't stopped to think about speaking to a grandparent in one [language] versus a parent in another, versus at school it's different.[…] It's something quite sophisticated that perhaps I'd underrated to a degree. (Helen, interview)*

The complexities around language use and how increased (linguistic) knowledge of their students was helping the teachers understand these complexities was also evidenced in another interview excerpt, this time from Anne. In the excerpt, Anne referred to Punjabi as her student's first language but demonstrated an emerging awareness of the way an idea of L1 and L2 can fail to capture lived realities through the content of what she was saying.

> *Well there was one little girl in my room that, English is not her first language, and so I thought she would find the activity of translating quite easy. But she actually found the activity difficult, I'm not really too sure, because I taught her brother when he was in prep and he came just speaking Punjabi. She came speaking more English than him, and I think her brother speaking English influenced her a lot when she was growing up. (Anne, interview)*

This shift to thinking about language practices also appeared to help overcome the notion that, although a good idea in principle, encouraging bilingualism required a daunting degree of expertise on the part of the teacher. For example, when asked

---

[1] The word 'bilingual' rather than 'bi/multilingual' is used here because this was the word used by teachers to refer to more than one language. An understanding of bilingualism as shorthand that includes multilingualism is evident in the data shown in this section.

why she had not brought children's home languages into her teaching after she studied this idea in a Masters course, Frida reported:

> *I wasn't using it because I probably didn't feel I had the expertise to use it. [...] Logistically how do I include everyone's language, even though I had studied it, I wasn't quite sure how to put it into place I suppose. (Frida, interview)*

Sam, the other Year 1/2 teacher at Madison Primary reinforced this idea when he reported:

> *We can help these children in a way we never thought about. And really, we want them to be bilingual but I think it was all just pie-in-the-sky stuff, now we can probably do something to achieve that goal for them. (Sam, interview)*

The understanding of achieving a 'bilingual goal' was underpinned by the recognition that the inclusion of languages in class would send a positive message about knowing languages other than English. For example, in the second group reflection Anne said:

> *It's a real way of valuing language, isn't it? We can say we value people's languages, but by actually getting people at home to send something, you know, send something back to us, we're showing that we are actually valuing it, because we're [going to] use this to do this activity. (Anne, Group Reflection 2)*

This idea of valuing language underscored the way teachers were affirming bi/multilingual identities in the classes. When they spoke of student engagement, they all used very positive language, for example, the students *'absolutely loved it'* (Jasmine), *'It was a really, really positive experience'* (Sophie) and *'I have to say, they loved it'* (Frida). Students' pride in what they knew, shared language-related experiences, writing about themselves and finding out about each other were the principal reasons given by the teachers for this enjoyment. Students also gave overwhelmingly positive feedback in interview and in written or oral reflections. Only one student was reported by the teacher (Sophie) to consider it boring because he couldn't speak another language. This feedback helped to show the extent to which exposure to other languages at home was being valued in the classroom, and also the need to consider translanguaging pedagogy in relation to monolingual students. This will be taken up in the discussion at the end of the chapter.

Along with the shift in focus to using languages came a shift in awareness of students' literacy practices. At the beginning of the study, Jasmine – the only teacher who spoke more than one language – included the idea of literacy in her response to what she understood bilingualism to be: *'Bilingual, to me, is being able to speak, write and understand more than one language'*. Frida, Anne and Sophie understood bilingualism in terms of communication and Sam's answer was: *'Bilingual, to me, means being able to talk in two or more languages'*. Sam evidenced the greatest shift in thinking, but other teachers, most notably Helen, also showed a shift in thinking around home language literacy.

In the second lesson sequence in particular, all the teachers delivered lessons in which students needed either to read or read and write their home language. Jasmine demonstrated that she did not assume students would be equally proficient in their languages, or in both oracy and literacy. The interview excerpt below is illustrative of her lack of assumption that the students would be literate in their language:

> *[I was] just trying to tap into what their language ability was. So, just getting to know if they spoke any language besides English, and how fluent they were. And there were some [...] who said they could **even** read and write the language. So, just getting to know all that. (Jasmine, interview, emphasis added)*

Sam, on the other hand, appeared to have had an expectation that the children would be literate in the language(s) they spoke at home because he reported it as interesting when this was not the case. In his activity, seven children were able to read what their parents had written while three were not. He reported that no one was able to write. He spoke of the importance of literacy in the second group reflection and also in interview. An excerpt from the interview is below.

> *I think if [the children] want to be bilingual it'll be a benefit for them to be able to write. Probably they concentrate on the language more when they're writing it down, probably learn more about the language, and it may have some impact on them learning English as well. (Sam, interview)*

Helen from Campbell PS also discussed the issue of home language literacy in the second group reflection. At the beginning of the study, she did not write down her understanding of bilingualism, but she did write that she understood a strong grounding/proficiency in the first language would make learning English easier. In the second group reflection, she appeared to add literacy to this idea of a strong grounding, something she had not necessarily considered previously:

> We find people were speaking English at home, it wasn't very high standard English, and we felt that was holding children back. Whereas if they were speaking their own language, the concepts, [...] the language itself is richer [...] so, that would help the child academically [...] but we hadn't ever talked about doing the reading and writing. [...] This project has given that pull, [...] something we can add to something we're already pushing, and doing. (Helen, GR2)

From the above quotation, the idea of language separation, or the parents using a particular language rather than their complete linguistic repertoire to help their children is in evidence. However, the valuing of parents' knowledge and the idea that becoming literate in another language is something that will help children improve their learning in English, rather than detract from it, is also clear.

5.2   *Leveraging Linguistic Repertoire as Central for Learning*

Although the affirmation of students' bi/multilingual identities was a clear finding for all the seven participating teachers, teachers differed as to whether or not they positioned their students' linguistic repertoire as central to the learning of content. Evidence from students' work samples showed that two teachers – Frida and Sophie – were able to leverage their students' repertoire in this way. Both teachers embedded meaning-making into activities, most conspicuously through the

Fig. 9.1 Examples of
puppets created by Frida's
Year 1/2 students

translanguaging pedagogical goal of metalinguistic and cross-linguistic awareness. Content was related to the English Curriculum: the teachers chose an English focus for their Year 1/2 class at Madison PS and Year 3/4 class at Hampton PS respectively. Frida chose a Level 2 speaking and listening curriculum content description[2]:

> Understand that spoken, visual and written forms of language are different modes of communication with different features and their use varies according to the audience, purpose, context and cultural background (Victorian Curriculum and Assessment Authority, 2017).

After completing the identity texts, and discussing language practices, the children in Frida's class taught each other the word 'hello' in their language and created puppets with speech bubbles (see Fig. 9.1). This approach led to the incorporation of more words as children were very enthusiastic about sharing what they knew. It also led to a student-initiated activity in which the students created speech bubbles for themselves, writing down what they wanted to say in their choice of language(s) and scripts.

At the end of the lesson sequence Frida asked the children to reflect orally on their learning and wrote down their responses. In these responses, the children

---

[2] The levels of the curriculum approximately equate to the grade level but teachers are expected to work at the level of the students. Classes with more than one grade are common in Australia and give teachers the opportunity to work with different levels both to reinforce and extend knowledge for students in both grades. For the study, all the teachers chose one curriculum content description and sometimes this equated with one level and sometimes with two levels. The levels are indicated in the text.

evidenced an awareness that: (1) spoken and written forms of language vary between languages, (2) they could have some influence on the language that family members spoke to them (or used with them) by showing an interest, and (3) language use needed to be varied sometimes in order to communicate with people. Two of the children's oral reflections (written down by Frida) evidencing these points appear below.

Student 1 (Year 2)
I learnt how to say different words in different people's languages. I learnt how to say 'hi' in Bari and I learnt how to say 'hi' in Arabic. [Child S] speaks her language at her grandmother's house because her grandmother doesn't speak English and she wants to talk to her. I learnt that 'Madan' (Bari) is spelt like 'Madan' and I learnt how to count up to 30 in Bari. I learnt that my uncle speaks Bari and he taught us to say the months and the days.

Student 2 (Year 2)
I loved the language project. I said to my mum we are doing a really fun language project at school. I'm going to learn how to say 'hello' in other people's language. After the language project, I asked my grandmother to teach me how to write my name in Russian. I learnt how to say 'hello' in Chinese and that's my friend's language. I learnt that Russian letters have different sounds to English letters. I learnt that [Child A] talks a little bit of Arabic when he plays soccer.

At Hampton PS, Sophie also chose to relate language incorporation for her Year 3/4 class to a specific Level 3 speaking and listening English curriculum content description:

Understand that languages have different written and visual communication systems, different oral traditions and different ways of constructing meaning (Victorian Curriculum and Assessment Authority, 2017).

She further related the lesson sequence to the writing of an information report and to an inquiry unit on geography. Her class took a sheet with geography-related words home so their parents/grandparents could translate the words into a home language. When the sheets came back to class, words were cut up and put on a word wall at the back of the classroom next to corresponding words in other languages, along with an illustration and definition in English. This word wall was then used as a springboard for discussion. Figure 9.2 is taken from a work sample of a student who completed the homework activity in Telugu.

It was clear from the students' written reflections at the end of the sequence of lessons that what they understood themselves to have learned corresponded directly

Word in English	Word in My Language	Word in English	Word in My Language
anthem	జాతీయ గీతం	melting	కరిగి పోవడం
climate	వాతావరణం	North Pole	ఉత్తర ధృవం
coat of arms	మనదు సింహలు ముద్ర	polar	ధృవ

Fig. 9.2 Extract from geography vocabulary activity in Sophie's class

to the content description and was made possible by the incorporation of different languages in the classroom. Two student reflections appear below:

Student 1 (Year 4)
I liked that when my mum wrote the words in Vietnamese she actually taught me how to say them. I learnt that all different countries have different letters and you can actually write Australian words using the different letters from other countries.
Student 2 (Year 4)
It was fun working in a small group for matching the meanings to the words and pictures. I liked thinking of sentences about Cambodia and telling my partner. I noticed some words in different languages looked the same but they aren't actually because some of the letters look the same as the letters in other words like [student S's] language and [student V's]. [Student S's] language is Telugu and [student V's] language is Khmer. Some aren't the same because they have Australian letters. Some of them are spelt with Australian letters. [Student S] taught me a bit of letters in her language and we did 'Heads, Shoulders, Knees and Toes' in her language.

5.3 Making Linguistic Repertoire Relevant for Learning

Making linguistic repertoire relevant, but not so central, to chosen curriculum content was found in the three remaining classes in the study. In these classes, as with Frida and Sophie, students' home languages were incorporated into class via translation, but the next step of connecting this translation to active meaning-making linked to content objectives was not so visible. For Jasmine at Madison PS, there was an extra step, or invitation for students to reflect on what they were hearing, but their use of extended language practices did not appear to play a pivotal role in meeting the chosen objectives. For Anne at Campbell PS and for Sam, also at Madison PS, the activity was only the translation. Jasmine and Anne both decided to incorporate the children's languages into inquiry topics, and Sam into the same English curriculum content description as Frida.

First, in her Year 3/4 class, Jasmine chose the inquiry topic of values and identity and the relevant Personal and Social Capability Level 3 and 4 curriculum content description was:

– Identify personal strengths and select personal qualities that could be further developed (Victorian Curriculum and Assessment Authority, 2017).

Students were instructed to bring a text in their language into class – this could be, for example, a poem, a song, a prayer, or a self-introduction – and an English translation. They then presented their text by reading it out loud, their classmates were given time to try to guess what it had been about and then the same student read the English translation. In their written reflections, Jasmine's students demonstrated learning of the relevant content description by identifying personal strengths. Two students' samples appear below.

Student 1 (Year 3/4)

> *My personal reflection:*
> *At the start of my presentation I was nervous. When I started I was getting more and more confident. When I finished presenting I was proud of my presentation.*

Student 2 (Year 3/4)

> *My personal reflection:*
> *I felt really nervous and oozy. It was really cool and fun presenting. I was really proud that I did it. After my presentation my friends were happy for me.*

In Jasmine's class, the incorporation of students' languages in class fitted very well with the content description, but the students appeared to consider their personal strengths in relation to public speaking rather than to having a rich linguistic repertoire. Languages were positioned as something interesting and fun but did not appear to be central to the students' personal reflections on their confidence and pride, perhaps because they took speaking their language for granted, or perhaps because there was no real exploration – or significance attached to – the content of what they were presenting.

In the Year 3 class at Campbell Primary, Anne also chose to link the leveraging of students' linguistic repertoire to an inquiry unit on living things and sustainability, addressing two science (biology) Level 3 and 4 curriculum content descriptions:

– Living things can be grouped on the basis of observable features and can be distinguished from non-living things
– Different living things have different life cycles and depend on each other and the environment to survive (Victorian Curriculum and Assessment Authority, 2017).

She gave the students a list of questions to be answered in a home language by parents/ grandparents about an animal in their country of origin: for example, 'where does the animal live?' 'What do they need to survive?' and 'what do they look like? (features)'. Students interviewed their parents/grandparents at home and recorded the interview. Back in class, they then needed to translate what their parents/ grandparents had said into English. Figure 9.3 is an example of a Year 3 student's translation of her mother's oral Vietnamese (spoken on video) into written English.

Again, this activity was relevant to the content description but students' oral reflections at the time of translation and later interviews did not evidence the incorporation of languages as central to the teaching and learning objectives of the chosen content descriptions. Although only one of the six students interviewed at Campbell Primary – a boy who attended a Punjabi language school every Saturday – explicitly stated that he could not see how using another language in class at school could help him learn, other students found it difficult to elaborate on how other languages helped them when prompted, and this may have been a result of the lack of focus on content-related meaning-making beyond that of the direct translation.

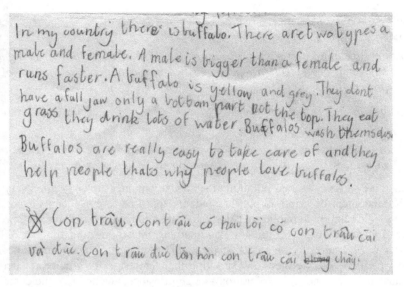

In my country there is buffalo. There are two types a male and female. A male is bigger than a female and runs faster. A buffalo is yellow and grey. They dont have a full jaw only a bottom part not the top. They eat grass they drink lots of water. Buffalos wash themselves

Buffalos are really easy to take care of and they help people thats why people love buffalos.

⊠ Con trâu. Con trâu có hai loài có con trâu cái và đực. Con trâu đực lớn hơn con trâu cái ~~không~~ chạy.

Fig. 9.3 Extract from science animal activity in Anne's class

In his Year 1/2 class at Madison Primary, Sam chose the same Level 2 speaking and listening English curriculum content description as Frida – the other participating Year 1/2 teacher at the school:

> Understand that spoken, visual and written forms of language are different modes of communication with different features and their use varies according to the audience, purpose, context and cultural background (Victorian Curriculum and Assessment Authority, 2017).

Sam incorporated students' linguistic repertoire into his teaching by writing out sentences, such as 'I'm going home today', 'how are you?' and 'what are you doing?' and asking parents and/or grandparents to write the sentences in a language they knew in order to be read and translated by their children in class. Similar to Campbell PS, from the data collected, students' learning of the content description as a result of the incorporation of their extended language practices was not evidenced, but the activity was relevant to the chosen subject matter.

Thus, the leveraging of students' linguistic repertoire and a deeper understanding of students' extracurricular language practices did not necessarily lead to the kind of meaning-making that is considered to be an element of translanguaging pedagogy (see García & Li, 2014). However, given that the approach of incorporating students' language practices was so new for the teachers, direct translation with no follow-up activity could be considered to be a positive preliminary step towards the inclusion of activities which position students' repertoire as central to the learning of content, especially given the important finding of bi/multilingual identity affirmation.

6   Discussion and Conclusion

Shifting from a language-centred lens, or asking what language a child speaks at home, to the speaker-centred lens of translanguaging, or asking instead in what ways/ contexts the child uses her/his linguistic resources, was found to be key to shifting teachers' perception of bi/multilingualism and also to their incorporation of students' language practices into teaching and learning. Understanding their students more deeply appeared to lie at the heart of the teachers' desire to engage with translanguaging pedagogy, and the affirmation of bi/multilingual identities – as an extension of who their students were in general – was the most conspicuous translanguaging goal for all the teachers. They reported that they were perceiving the LBOTE students as more sophisticated language users and also showed a growing understanding of the context-sensitive nature of students' linguistic experiences. A focus on students' linguistic repertoire (rather than the monolingual nature of their own) also appeared to take the mystique out of bi/multilingualism for the six monolingual teachers, allowing them to incorporate languages into student learning without feeling that they were not qualified enough, or did not have the relevant expertise.

Translanguaging pedagogy and its clear relationship to identity performance (see Creese & Blackledge, 2010) thus appeared to be a useful vehicle for the incorporation of students' home language practices in the classroom, and the identity texts (cf D'Warte, 2014, 2015; Somerville, D'Warte & Sawyer, 2016) created by the students provided a useful springboard. However, the extent to which the active meaning-making aspect of translanguaging was incorporated by the teachers into their lessons was found to be uneven, and this was found to affect the leveraging of students' repertoire for specific objectives. Teaching curriculum content appeared to be more conceptually challenging than the affirmation of bi/multilingual identities.

The two teachers who were found to be the most successful in meeting desired content descriptors via making students' extended linguistic repertoires central to learning focused on the English curriculum and the translanguaging pedagogical goal of metalinguistic and cross-linguistic awareness. In their reflections, the students of these two teachers showed what they had learned was directly related to the inclusion of home language practices in the classroom. The other three main teachers who made the incorporation of languages relevant to their objectives but not central appeared to have a sole focus on the affirmation of students' language practices in the community domain, and translation – with no subsequent meaning-making – was the main tool for doing this.

The extent of value, or cultural capital (Bourdieu, 1977; Bourdieu & Passeron, 1977), teachers ascribed to the language practices of their students therefore appeared to be important. The capital of students' linguistic repertoire can be considered to be higher in a class where this linguistic repertoire is positioned as central to students' learning, and it was in one of these classes where a monolingual student reported disengagement with the translanguaging pedagogy in the classroom. From his comment about not being able to speak another language, it appeared to be having a language to share with the class that was positioned as valuable, rather than learning from one's peers. This finding indicates that the translanguaging pedagogical goal of disrupting linguistic hierarchies might be achieved through not differentiating instruction for bilinguals, emergent bilinguals and monolinguals (see García & Li, 2014) in that *everyone* is expected to interact with multilingual practices. However, giving monolingual students a more active role in the process by providing them with something to share, or placing importance on their positioning as a learner of language, may make translanguaging pedagogy more sustainable in a country such as Australia that takes institutional monolingualism for granted (e.g., Clyne, 2005; Scarino, 2014).

Viewing the attribution of capital, or value, to students' extended language practices in the classroom on a continuum may also be useful. In Australia, even though still an additive and compartmentalised view of language (García, 2009), there is evidence of an institutional appreciation of the languages students speak at home and the importance of maintaining them (see Department of Education and Training, Victoria, 2018). This can be viewed as a positive step towards addressing the view of language deficit, or only understanding that English is important. Heritage languages in the community domain do not always thrive with such a strong institutional emphasis on English. Students' language practices can be brought into class as a way to affirm students' participation in that domain. Translation with no follow-up activities can be considered a bridge between formal and informal domains, and translanguaging pedagogy in the form of active meaning-making can then be considered as the next step in raising the cultural capital of an extended linguistic repertoire.

Another important element of cultural capital that arose in the study is that of literacy. Literacy has an enormous amount of capital in Australia, and this was reflected in all the teachers choosing to include a literacy component in their incorporation of their students' language practices in the classroom. This then sparked an interest in the relationship between bi/multilingualism and bi/multiliteracy among the monolingual teachers. The centrality of literacy in formal education systems is worthy of attention when applying translanguaging pedagogy in the classroom because teachers may (perhaps unwittingly) prioritise the incorporation of reading and writing over oral activities, thereby marginalising languages with rich oral traditions, and/or family members who are not literate in their home language.

In sum, using translanguaging as a conceptual tool to blur the lines between institutional and community domains in a country like Australia, where language maintenance is supported, but usually only in principle, has the potential to help embed home language practices in everyday school-based learning in ways that are of direct benefit to students. A translanguaging lens can also give teachers the confidence to experiment. If the teachers think that they need to find and comprehend the language resources themselves in order to transmit information/knowledge to the students, this may feel overwhelming. Providing a space for students to work with (and explain) material that the teacher does not understand may feel more feasible. However, translanguaging as an end in itself in the classroom is likely to require a shift in thinking in settings where language separation is the norm. In the study, one way some teachers were able to engage with a holistic view of language was to draw on their students' language practices in order to achieve English curriculum teaching and learning objectives. If TESOL is conceptualised broadly as Teaching English (language arts) to Speakers of Other Languages, the study demonstrated that teachers' engagement with translanguaging has the potential to improve students' learning of English as well as to increase the cultural capital of multilingual practices. This may be a preliminary way to shift the focus from English-only to using and developing linguistic repertoire as a worthwhile goal in its own right at school.

References

Anderson, T., & Shattuck, J. (2012). Design-based research: A decade of progress in education research? *Educational Researcher, 41*(1), 16–25.

Australian Curriculum, Assessment and Reporting Authority (ACARA). (2017). *My school.* Retrieved from https://www.myschool.edu.au/

Baker, C., & Wright, W. E. (2017). *Foundations of bilingual education and bilingualism* (6th ed.). Bristol, UK: Multilingual Matters.

Bourdieu, P. (1977). The economics of linguistic exchanges. *Social Science Information, 16*(6), 645–668.

Bourdieu, P., & Passeron, J. (1977). *Reproduction in education, society, and culture.* London, UK/ Beverly Hills, CA: Sage Publications.

Braun, V., & Clarke, V. (2006). Using thematic analysis in psychology. *Qualitative Research in Psychology, 3*(2), 77–101.

Clyne, M. (2005). *Australia's language potential.* Sydney, Australia: UNSW Press.

Cobb, P., Confrey, J., diSessa, A., Lehrer, R., & Schauble, L. (2003). Design experiments in educational research. *Educational Researcher, 32*(1), 9–13.

Creese, A., & Blackledge, A. (2010). Translanguaging in the bilingual classroom: A pedagogy for learning and teaching? *The Modern Language Journal, 94*, 103–115.

Cummins, J. (2006). Identity texts: The imaginative construction of self through multiliteracies pedagogy. In O. Garcia, T. Skutnabb-Kangas, & M. E. Torres-Guzman (Eds.), *Imagining multilingual schools: Language in education and Glocalization* (pp. 51–68). Toronto, Canada: Multilingual Matters.

Cummins, J. (2007). Rethinking monolingual instructional strategies in multilingual classrooms. *Canadian Journal of Applied Linguistics (CJAL), 10*(2), 221–240.

Cummins, J., & Early, M. (2011). *Identity texts: The collaborative creation of power in multilingual schools.* Staffordshire, UK: Trentham Books.

Cummins, J., & Swain, M. (1986). *Bilingualism in education: Aspects of theory, research and practice.* Harlow, UK: Longman.

D'Warte, J. (2013). *Pilot project: Reconceptualising English learners' language and literacy skills, practices and experiences.* University of Western Sydney. Retrieved from http://researchdirect. westernsydney.edu.au/islandora/object/uws:23461

D'Warte, J. (2014). Exploring linguistic repertoires: Multiple language use and multimodal literacy activity in five classrooms. *Australian Journal of Language and Literacy, 37*(1), 21–30.

D'Warte, J. (2015). Building knowledge about and with students: Linguistic ethnography in two secondary school classrooms. *English in Australia, 50*(1), 39–48.

Dagenais, D., & Jacquet, M. (2008). Theories of representation in French and English scholarship on multilingualism. *International Journal of Multilingualism, 5*(1), 41–52.

Department of Education and Training, Victoria (2018). *Languages.* Retrieved from http://www.education.vic.gov.au/school/teachers/teachingresources/discipline/languages/Pages/default.aspx?Redirect=1

Flores, N., & García, O. (2017). A critical review of bilingual education in the United States: From basements and pride to boutiques and profit. *Annual Review of Applied Linguistics, 37,* 14–29.

García, O. (2009). *Bilingual education in the 21st century: A global perspective.* Malden, MA: Wiley-Blackwell.

García, O. (2017). Reflections on Turnbull's reframing of foreign language education: Bilingual epistemologies. *International Journal of Bilingual Education and Bilingualism, 22*(5), 628–638.

García, O., Ibarra Johnson, S., & Seltzer, K. (2017). *The translanguaging classroom: Leveraging student bilingualism for learning.* Philadelphia, PA: Caslon.

García, O., & Kleifgen, J. (2010). *Educating emergent bilinguals: Policies, programs, and practices for English language learners.* New York, NY: Teachers College Press.

García, O., & Li, W. (2014). *Translanguaging: Language, bilingualism and education.* New York, NY: Palgrave Macmillan.

Gee, J. P. (2004). *Situated language and learning: A critique of traditional schooling.* New York, NY: Routledge.

Lankshear, C., & Knobel, M. (2003). *New literacies: Changing knowledge and classroom learning.* Buckingham, UK: Open University Press.

Moll, L., Amanti, C., Neff, D., & Gonzales, N. (1992). Funds of knowledge for teaching: Toward a qualitative approach to connect homes and classrooms. *Theory into Practice: Qualitative Issues in Educational Research, 3*(2), 132–141.

Moll, L., Soto-Santiago, S., & Schwartz, L. (2013). Funds of knowledge in changing communities. In K. Hall, T. Cremlin, B. Combre, & L. Moll (Eds.), *The Wiley Blackwell international handbook of research on children's literacy, learning and culture* (pp. 172–183). London, UK: Wiley Blackwell.

Norton, B. (2000). *Identity and language learning: Gender, ethnicity and educational change.* Essex, UK: Pearson Education.

Otheguy, R., García, O., & Reid, W. (2015). Clarifying translanguaging and deconstructing named languages: A perspective from linguistics. *Applied Linguistics Review, 6*(3), 281–307.

Paris, D. (2012). Culturally sustaining pedagogy: A needed change in stance, terminology and practice. *Educational Researcher, 4*(3), 93–97.

Prasad, G. (2015). Beyond the mirror towards a plurilingual prism: Exploring the creation of plurilingual 'identity texts' in English and French classrooms in Toronto and Montpellier. *Intercultural Education, 26*(6), 497–514.

Prasad, G. (2018). 'How does it look and feel to be plurilingual?': Analyzing children's representations of plurilingualism through collage. *International Journal of Bilingual Education and Bilingualism.* https://doi.org/10.1080/13670050.2017.1420033

Scarino, A. (2014). Situating the challenges in current languages education policy in Australia: Unlearning monolingualism. *International Journal of Multilingualism, 11*(3), 289–306.

Schecter, S., & Cummins, J. (Eds.). (2003). *Multilingual education in practice: Using diversity as a resource.* Portsmouth, UK: Heinemann.

Somerville, M., D'Warte, J. & Sawyer, W. (2016). *Building on children's linguistic repertoires to enrich learning: A project report for the NSW Department of Education.* Retrieved from http://www.uws.edu.au/centre_for_educational_research

Turner, M. (2019). *Multilingualism as a resource and a goal: Using and learning languages in mainstream schools.* Cham, Switzerland: Palgrave Macmillan.

Victorian Curriculum and Assessment Authority (VCAA). (2017). *Victorian Curriculum: English.* Retrieved from https://victoriancurriculum.vcaa.vic.edu.au/english/english/curriculum/f-10.

Chapter 10
Translanguaging as a Decolonization Project?: Malawian Teachers' Complex and Competing Desires for Local Languages and Global English

Sunny Man Chu Lau

Abstract This chapter describes an action research project with a group of Malawian teachers in exploring critical approaches to ESL education that challenge neocolonial ideologies and valorize all communicative repertoires for maximized learning and performance. Elaborating on the findings, the chapter discusses the teachers' changing perspectives about translanguaging as a legitimate means of knowledge construction and affirmation of both students' and their own ethnolinguistic identities. Yet class interactions and interview responses continued to show an ingrained coloniality that disrupted our attempt to "decolonize" language educa- tion. The study raises the question of what critical language approaches are possible in postcolonial or other similar contexts where English hegemony continues to thrive in the global discourse of quality education and world citizenship. The findings point to the need for international development researchers to exercise vigilance to understand what decolonization means to local communities and how new theories/insights might facilitate or hinder local agentive efforts to find creative solutions to education contexts faced with severe socio- political and economic demands.

Keywords Translanguaging · Bilingual education · Malawi · International development · Decolonization · ESL · Teacher training and preparation

1 Introduction

In my view language is the most important vehicle through which the power fascinated and held the soul prisoner. (Thiong'o, 1986, p. 9)

Translanguaging (García & Li, 2014) and other multi/plural lingual approaches to language/education are gaining ground in the fields of second language and bilingual education in the Global North as cultural and linguistic diversity is

S. M. C. Lau (✉)
Bishop's University, Sherbrooke, QC, Canada
e-mail: sunny.lau@ubishops.ca

© Springer Nature Switzerland AG 2020   203
Z. Tian et al. (eds.), *Envisioning TESOL through a Translanguaging Lens*,
Educational Linguistics 45, https://doi.org/10.1007/978-3-030-47031-9_10

increasingly recognized as resources for teaching and learning. As the multilingual turn (May, 2014) energizes new understandings of language, we are reminded of the long-standing history of these multilingual views and of not treating them as a contemporary urban phenomenon (Canagarajah, 2013). Multilingualism existed in a pre-modern and precolonial times in fluid language ecologies of contact zones, whether in port cities for trade and migration purposes, or in daily markets or temples in rural areas where multiethnic groups from all walks of life congregated (Canagarajah, 2013; Pennycook, 2012). Diverse and hybrid language practices circulated and self-regulated through everyday micro-interactions, often competing and conflicting, yet dynamic and consensual, as individuals negotiated their local, national and transnational identities (Sabatier, 2010). While cautioning against an over-romanticized view of the vibrant sociolinguistic practices of the past, Canagarajah (2013) points out that colonization has imposed monolingual standards and vilified translingual practices. Despite the end of political colonialism in Asia, Africa and the Middle East, colonial mono-lingual/modal ideologies continue to thrive, fueled and bolstered by the transnational neoliberal script of global socioeconomic development, reinforcing English hegemony and posing great barriers to efforts in indigenous language maintenance (Phillipson, 2009). Spivak (1990) suggests using the term *neocolonial* (rather than *postcolonial*) to indicate the perpetuation of colonial ideologies albeit in new forms. In Malawi, despite its independence from the British colonial rule in 1964 and its subsequent efforts to promote mother-tongue[1] instruction, English continues to enjoy its ESL—"English as a superior language"–status (Pennycook, 1998). Teachers, especially those in rural villages, are wrestling with the implications and contradictions of local-language instruction and the enduring symbolic dominance of English for higher education and upward social mobility.

This chapter describes an action research project with a group of Malawian elementary teachers to investigate the extent to which their engagement in a professional development (PD) course on critical approaches to English language (EL) education facilitated a critical awareness of its neocolonial sociopolitics and of the value of multilingual and multicultural resources for EL teaching and learning. Elaborating on the research findings, the chapter aims to discuss the Malawian teachers' changing perspectives on EL and on translanguaging as a legitimate way of meaning-making and affirming both students' and their own ethnolinguistic identities. Their responses, however, reflected an ingrained coloniality that disrupted our attempt to "decolonize" language education, further illustrating the irony of our critical efforts. Particularly, the study raises the question of what critical approaches to language education are possible in postcolonial countries like Malawi and other educational contexts when English hegemony continues to thrive in the global

---

[1] While Malawians are multilingual, the word "mother-tongue" is used categorically to refer to the local and/or vernacular language(s) used in the household, commensurate with its usage in the language policy introduced in 1996 in Malawi (Kamwendo, 2008a). To avoid having too many labels, I use "mother tongue" (MT), rather than the more commonly used term "first language" (L1), throughout even for the Canadian and Chinese volunteers.

neocolonial discourse of quality education and world citizenship. The findings beg the question of the extent to which decolonization is possible through international development efforts given the existing socioeconomic disparities between the local community and the researchers/volunteers from the Global North.

2   Disrupting Raciolinguistics: Decolonization of the Mind

Theories on decolonization (Kumaravadivelu, 2016; Mignolo, 2007; Motha, 2006) and critical approaches to language policy (Phillipson, 1998, 2009), as two important strands in critical applied linguistics, illuminate how the global growth of English is steeped in its colonial histories of empire building. The promotion of English as the language for enlightenment and modern civilization was accomplished and consolidated through EL policy and English-managed finance and trading companies (Morrison & Lui, 2000) with its access strictly regulated and limited to upper and middle class elites who then served as intermediaries between the colonial government and the local people (Kamwendo, 2010; Lin, 2001). By contrast, indigenous languages were seen as signs of intellectual and cultural backwardness that perpetuated chaos and disunity. The promise of English linguistic capital for upward mobility, however, was conflated because colonial subjects were often kept from going beyond support or clerical positions (Canagarajah, 2004) or lower civil service ranks (Moto, 2002) because of their race.

The dominance of English continues to grow despite the end of colonialism. With the burgeoning reach and control of transnational finanicial, technological and media corporations. English hegemony has been injected with a renewed neocolonial and neoliberal discursive boost as the gateway to world-class socioeconomic and technological advancement. Revering English as the language of international communication further threatens the global ethnolinguistic ecology whereby some minority languages and cultures are marginalised to the brink of extinction (Phillipson, 2009; Skutnabb-Kangas, 2000). English exerts its hegemonic dominance through a number of intersecting fundamental beliefs and practices, namely monolingualism, language standards and hierarchies, native-speakerism, and the racialization of English language speakers. In the case of Malawi, despite postcolonial efforts in promoting mother-tongue instruction at the lower grades, local languages continued to be viewed as the culprits for producing "inferior learners and encourag[ing] tribalism" (Chauma et al., 1997, as cited in Kretzer & Kumwenda, 2016, p. 31). The deep-seated belief in the symbolic value of English as tantamount to modernization, prosperity and quality education (Kamwendo, 2010) continues to pressurize educators to adhere strictly to the English-only policy in secondary and higher education. Many former Anglo-American colonies, Malawi included, continue to look upon the *Inner Circle* (e.g., UK, USA, Canada, etc.) for language standards (Kachru, 1990, 1997). Decades of research on perceptions of native and non-native English-speaking teachers (NES & NNES) point to the racialization of English competence as native-speakerism is fundamentally grounded in Whiteness

(Moussu & Llurda, 2008; Pennycook, 2001). *Raciolinguistic ideologies* uphold imagined language standards and norms that are marked by Whiteness rather than objective linguistic practices (Flores & Rosa, 2015). English used by racialized bodies is often considered inferior and their accents are marked while their White counterparts' is exempted from scrunity and their accents unmarked.

Decolonization efforts, hence, should not be just about decolonizing the political and economic structure, but more importantly about decolonizing *the mind* (Thiong'o, 1986). Coloniality often survives colonialism, meaning despite the end of the colonial rule, the ingrained inequitable colonial power relations find themselves replicated and maintained in how "culture, labour, intersubjective relations, and knowledge production" (Maldonado-Torres, 2010, p. 97) are defined. For example, Dr. Hastings Banda, the first post-independent Malawian president was ironically the embodiment of coloniality as evident in his continual imposition of English for government administration and education, as well as his private elite English-medium school, Kamuzu Academy, where European languages such as Latin and Greek were promoted while use of any indigenous languages including Chichewa was absent from the curriculum and disallowed within school (Kamwendo, 2010).

Mignolo (2007) argues that decolonizing the mind requires an epistemic shift that "brings to the foreground other epistemologies, other principles of knowledge and understanding and, consequently, other economy, other politics, other ethics" (p. 453). The epistemic shift or *de-linking* can be effectuated by an active challenge to the "pretended universality" of the knowledge and worldviews that European colonialism has imposed and propagated. The focus is to uncover the origin of the myths of modernity, including the very idea of liberation and decolonization:

> In this complexity, we need a relentless critical exercise of awareness of the moments when the guiding principle at work is liberation/decoloniality and when, on the other hand, the irrational myth directs social actors in their projects for political, economic and spiritual (epistemic, philosophical, religious) decolonization. (p. 458)

In essence, the project of liberation/de-coloniality includes a remapping of the very rational concept of liberation, being cognizant of the fact that no one has access to an ultimate truth nor universal solutions for all problems, and of the need to be highly vigilant and critical of the orientation and location from which the decolonization project operates. Any decolonization project, as Fanon describes (1967), is hence a *double operation* (Mignolo, 2000, p. 458) involving decolonization of the colonizer as well to ensure the inclusion of the perspectives from the colonized and their active involvement in their own decolonization, rather than waiting for a "gift" from the colonizer to free them. De-linking involves not just an active challenge of the conversation content but also the very terms of the conversation themselves so as to push for an epistemic shift to *other-versality* and *pluri-versality* where totalizing truths are replaced by the co-existence of different worlds but the appreciation of shared goals and works.

3   Translanguaging: Legitimizing and Promoting Heteroglossic and Pluri-versality

Translanguaging, a term first coined in the Welsh educational context, describes a pedagogical use of two languages in the classroom to reinforce conceptual and linguistic connections for better learning and performance (C. Williams, Lewis, & Baker, 1996). The premise of the concept is built on an integrated view of bi/multilingual competence, treating languages in individual minds and in communities as an "eco-system of mutual interdependence" (Cook, 2016), all changing and evolving in dynamic, interconnected ways. It embraces the Bakhtinian notion of *heteroglossia* (1981), viewing language as a cacophony of styles, varieties, voices, ideas, and expressions that overlap and intermix, indexing diverse sociopolitical and cultural contexts and purposes, rather than being unitary, compartmentalized and assigned to different territories or functions (Blackledge & Creese, 2014; García, 2009). Western colonialization and its legacies have pushed on top "the European layer of languages, and definitions of languages and diversity" (Pennycook, 2012, p. 7) and imposed a totalizing view of what history and knowledge look like, giving privilege to *monolingual* (the language of the European colonizer), *monosemiotic* (alphabets over other sign systems such as symbols or images) and *monomodal* (visual over oral, aural, spatial, etc.) ways of knowledge construction (Canagarajah, 2013).

In Malawi, there are 12–16 indigenous languages,[2] with Chichewa and/or Chinyanja (the two often considered as the same language) spoken by almost 70% of the population, followed by Chiyao, Chitumbuka, Chisena, etc. (the prefix "Chi" refers to "the language of") (E. Williams, 2007). There are also non-Malawian languages such as Portuguese, Arabic and Swahili adopted through ivory and slave trade from 1840s onwards as well as English through first missionary and commerce from 1860s, then political colonization in 1891 (Kayambazinthu, 1998). Massive migration, intermarriage, economic expansions, trade and political decentralization might have created geographical distance among ethnic groups and their languages, which in turn contributed to the dialectal distance between people who originally shared the same language and culture, but these socio- economic and political factors had also allowed for language contact and mutual influence among languages. Despite the apparent linguistic divide, Malawian languages all belong to the Bantu family and share different degrees of comprehnsibility (E. Williams, 2007). People in the region speak their own mother tongue(s) and belong to "a larger national or continental geography" by speaking one or two regional lingua franca (Thiong'o, 1986, p. 23). People in multilingual/ethnic areas tend to hold more open, accepting and fluid attitudes to language, and their communication

---

[2] The number of languages varies depending on the sociopolitical and linguistic considerations ethnologists use to classify and distinguish languages from dialects (Kretzer & Kumwenda, 2016). The 1998 Census of Malawi (National Statistics Office, 2000) lists only 12 Malawian languages (E. Williams, 2007).

practices often involve non-exclusive use of languages and non-graphocentric, multimodal literacies such as ideographs, pictographs, and collective oral traditions
(McCarty, 2013).

When English became the main official language in colonial Malawi in 1891,
Chichewa and Chitumbuka, the respective regional lingua franca for the central-
southern and the northern parts of Malawi, were elevated as auxiliary languages for
minor local administration and early years education. With the colonial language
policy in place, local administration and missionaries made attempts at educational
planning that were in line with the government ideologies (Kayambazinthu, 1998).
This not only redefined the relations among the different ethnolinguistic groups in
terms of their status and prestige but also created artificial boundaries between
them, inside and outside Malawi, removing itself from the same ethnolinguistic
groups in its neighboring countries: Chichewa in eastern Zambia and western
Mozambique, Chiyao and Chilomwe in Mozambique, and Chitumbuka in eastern
Zambia (Kayambazinthu, 1998) (see Fig. 10.1).

When President Banda in 1968 made English the official language and Chichewa
the only auxiliary official language for administration and early years education, the
policy further displaced other local languages such as Chilomwe and Chiyao as
liabilities to socio-economic advancement (Kayambazinthu, 1998).

Translanguaging as a practical theory of language recognizes and valorizes the
plurality and intermixing of languages, cultures and semiotic systems as normal
everyday practices among bi/multilinguals for communication and knowledge-
making (Li, 2017). This heteroglossic notion of language underscores the agency of
individuals, particularly racialized minorities as they actively and creatively

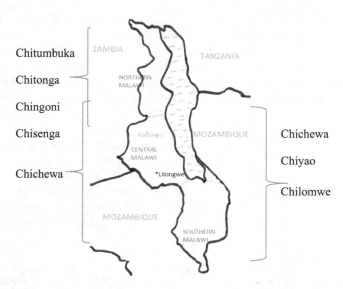

Fig. 10.1 Map of Malawi & its neighboring countries – a rough representation of a few main local
languages spoken in different regions

transfer, resemiotize and recontextualise *pluri-versal* knowledge, thinking, and being in diverse social and cultural contexts. Translanguaging pedagogy articulates a *political stance* (García, Johnson, & Seltzer, 2017) to value and mobilize minoritized languages and identities for effective and meaningful knowledge construction and performance (García & Kleyn, 2016). It disrupts monolingual norms inherent in raciolinguistic ideologies (Flores & Rosa, 2015) and seeks to reposition bi/multilinguals based on an asset-orientation. It aims to recover and legitimize the "subaltern knowledge" that is the "knowledge conceived from the exterior borders of the modern/colonial world system" (Mignolo, 2000, p. 11). Engaging in "border thinking" (Mignolo, 2000) for language education is to not only reconceptualize language and literacy as multilingual, multisemiotic, multisensory, and multimodal (Li, 2017), but also valorize minoritized and racialized languages and cultural resources as legitimate pluri-versal ways of knowing, thinking and being.

4   Malawian Education Scenario

As mentioned earlier, English language policy remained intact in post-independent Malawi even though Chichewa was made the medium of instruction from Grades 1–4 during the three-decade Banda era (1964–1994) (Kamwendo, 2010). Students outside of the central region had to master a second and third language (Chichewa and English) in order to have access to education. Although various efforts were made by the post-Banda governments to promote the use of mother tongues (local languages, other than just Chichewa) for earlier grades (Kamwendo, 2008b), the expensive and expansive nature of the local-language policy, coupled with the lingering negative neocolonial attitudes towards local languages and the concerns about national unity (Kamwendo, 2008b, 2013), made this initiative difficult to implement and enforce.

In Malawi, primary education (Grades 1–8) is free but not compulsory. At present, the national drop-out rate continues to be a serious concern, averaging at 10.5% with only 58.5% of school going children finishing the first 4 years (UNICEF Malawi, 2016). Enrollment in fee-paying secondary and tertiary education is strikingly low, respectively at 33.8% and 0.77% in 2011 (Global Economy, 2018a, b). UNICEF (2016) data show current average teacher to student ratio as 1:92, with a higher rate in rural areas because of teacher shortage due to challenges in access, accommodation, and infrastructure such as classrooms, water and electricity (Japan International Cooperation Agency, 2012, p. 58). These are the same realities faced by the teachers in the rural Kasungu village (see Fig. 10.1) in central Malawi where this action research took place.

5   Research Context

The action research study was on a professional development (PD) course for a group of Malawian teachers to explore critical approaches to English education. The guiding research question was: To what extent does the PD program facilitate a critical awareness of the sociopolitical dimensions of English education and promote teachers' valorization and mobilization of students' full communicative repertoires for learning and performance?

The action research was part of an international experiential learning project (ELP) headed by one of my colleagues, Christopher Stonebanks, who started the project around 10 years ago. Working within the principles of decolonization (Fanon, 1966) and critical pedagogy (Freire, 1970), the ELP largely adopts a community action research model (Senge & Scharmer, 2006) whereby multidisciplinary university participants, in conjunction with professors, engage in collaborative inquiry with local community members on education, heath, and socioeconomic development for capacity building (Stonebanks, 2013). As part of the ELP, the university students enroll in a credited International Situated Learning Project course, which examines works from Fanon (1966), Freire (1970), Easterly (2006), and other critical works on international development. The project strives to embody Fanon's idea of "double operation" of decolonization (1967) and challenges our assumed role as world "saviors" to seek genuine transformative partnerships and mutual commitment for sustainable development.

The first year joining the project, I worked alongside Christopher to deliver a PD program on curriculum design to meet the teachers' self-reported needs for critical and creative instructional strategies. Given the teachers' positive response, we delivered a second PD the year following, focusing on EL education. The Practice Teaching Director from our university came on board, working on this study with me while assisting with the teaching on the side. Apart from the Malawian teachers' learning, the study also examined that of the university volunteers from this international experience. Yet given the limited space, this chapter focuses mainly on the Malawian teachers' perspectives and their changes in the process towards language education.

5.1   PD Program and Participants

The PD program was comprised of 1-h workshops over 10 days whereby we examined topics including language, race and identity, neocolonialism, neoliberalism, and critical approaches to language teaching (e.g., translanguaging). The participants included 3 head teachers (i.e., principals), 1 deputy head teacher and 2 teachers from 3 primary schools. Our teacher participants had completed a 2-year Teachers Certificate after 4 years of high school. Among the university volunteers from Canada, there were 3 undergraduate education students and 4 international Masters of Education students from China (Table 10.1):

Table 10.1 Participant profiles

Name	Age/Sex	Origin	Languages MT = mother tongue	Education/Teaching experience
1. Lucas	40/M	Kasungu, Central Malawi	Chichewa (MT); English	Taught for 12 years Head teacher for 2 years
2. Celine	34/F	Northern Malawi	Chitonga (MT but not confident in writing); Chitumbuka (learned from friends & relative; English; Chichewa	Taught for 10 years Teaches standards 7 & 8 English & Life Skills
3. Caleb	54/M	Northern Kasungu, Central Malawi	Chichewa & Chitumbuka (MTs); Chingoni; English; studied French & Latin for 2 years in secondary school	Head teacher for 15 years Teaches English & Science
4. Fara	45/F	Kasungu, Central Malawi	Chichewa (MT); English; Chisenga (learned from husband who was from the Mchinji district close to Zambia)	Taught for 24 years Teaches Math & Expressive Arts Second year as deputy head teacher
5. Anthony	46/M	Kasungu, Central Malawi	Chichewa (MT); English	Taught for 23 years Teaches standard 3; all subjects
6. Harry	49/M	Kasungu, Central Malawi	Chichewa (MT); English	Taught for 25 years Head teacher for 5 years Teaches social environmental sciences
7. Ling	35/F	North-Western China	Mandarin (MT), Shanghainese, Cantonese, English, learning French	BA in EL Taught EL at elementary for 2 years; worked as EL tutor and teaching assistant (TA) at college First year MEd
8. YuZhi	28/F	North-Western China	Mandarin (MT); English; started learning French in university in China	BA in EL TA in an EL school First year MEd
9. Nuo	25/F	Central-eastern China	Mandarin & Nanjing dialect (MTs), English; just started learning French	TA in an EL school First year MEd
10. Yi	27/F	North-eastern China	Mandarin (MT); English; just started learning French	TA in an EL school First year MEd
11. Kiera	22/F	Nova Scotia, Canada	English (MT); French as a second language – Functional	BA in educational studies Just completed BEd in elementary education
12. Lennie	22/F	Quebec, Canada	English (MT); French (comfortable in all skills except speaking)	Last year BEd in secondary education and teaching EL
13. Maguire	22/M	Quebec, Canada	English (MT); French (social & work); just started learning Spanish	2nd year BA in educational studies (social studies/history) Coaching soccer & ski in French

Our design was to have these local educators and university students jointly take the PD program as co-learners to examine neocolonial influences on language education as manifested in language policy, native-speakerism, and monolingual dominance, and to learn about translanguaging pedagogy to transform EL teaching for contextualized needs. These 13 participants were formed into three triads, with at least one Malawian educator, and a Canadian and Chinese international student in each group. Two of the Canadian volunteers were returnees and all three of them were able to obtain an award through the university to fund their participation of the project. The international students joined the project out of their volition and interest and paid their own way. Although comparatively less experienced in teaching, these international students enriched the class discussions and lesson planning by relating personal stories of English learning in second/foreign language contexts, which helped sensitize their Canadian counterparts to the complex challenges in EL learning outside Canada. During the 10-day period, the triads team-taught in local classrooms during school hours, exploring and experimenting with some critical, linguistically and culturally responsive pedagogies learned in the afternoon PD sessions.

I positioned myself as a researcher and educator who advocates for socially just language education. I was drawn to the project because, being born and raised in Hong Kong, I felt I shared a similar colonial background with the Malawian teachers. As a non-native English speaker and an adult Chinese immigrant to first English-speaking Canada (Ontario), then to French-speaking Quebec, I recognized and intimately experienced the impact from neocolonial values and hegemony of dominant language policies. These minoritized identities and experiences of mine, to a certain degree, helped create mutual trust and prompt honest sharing from the Malawian participants. However, I was also aware of my privileged status afforded by my Canadian academia identity, which in some way reinforced the narratives of "success" from colonial education and immigration and integration, adding certain contradictions in our decolonizing effort (to be discussed further).

6   Research Methodology and Data Collection

Adopting a critical action research model (Kemmis, 2001), this study aimed to connect research with practice through recursive cycles of reflexive planning, teaching and evaluation to effectuate socially responsive engagements to best address the situated needs of the community. Core to this interpretive approach to research is an integration of the three audiences and voices: *me, us* and *them* (Coghlan & Brannick, 2009; Reason & Bradbury, 2006). Integral to action research is self-study (first person) with the researcher actively interrogating one's actions and choices in daily practices while engaging in inquiry with others (second-person) on issues of mutual concern through dialogue and/or joint action, all contributing to the creation of broader communities (third person) of inquiry to develop "living theories" intimately grounded in lived realities.

A range of qualitative data were collected for triangulation (Cohen, Manion, & Morrison, 2000): pre- and post- program interviews (30-min individual semi-structured), field notes on PD sessions, teachers' journal entries based on class discussions, and work samples collected throughout the workshop. The field notes also included daily debriefings with our university volunteers about their team-teaching experience with the teachers. I and my co-researcher (the Canadian practicum director) visited each classroom at the end of the program for approximately 6 h to observe their teaching in action and application of learning. Member checking was done throughout with the director as we read and discussed the ongoing data for clarity and validity.

Data analysis involved First Cycle coding (Saldaña, 2013) of both pre- and post-interviews using *structural coding* (Namey, Guest, Thairu, & Johnson, 2008) with question-based codes to label and initially categorize the data in order to identify commonalities, differences and relationships across the comparable segments or topics, including teacher perceptions on the challenges of teaching (in) English, strategies to support learning, broader sociopolitical forces that affect English education, etc. (See Appendix 1 for pre and post- interview protocols). The data were then recursively analyzed using *eclectic coding* (Saldaña) with a mix of in vivo coding and emotion coding to capture the participants' voice and gain insight into their felt experience of English teaching and learning as well as the PD sessions. For the other data sets (journal entries, work samples, field notes, etc.), descriptive coding was used to establish the basic topics of data segments, which were then recursively analyzed using the same eclectic coding approach to capture participants' perspectives regarding their teaching practice and PD experience. Through iterative clustering, chunking, and reconfiguring, Second Cycle coding generated pattern codes on which the narrative description of the findings were based (Saldaña) (See Appendix 2 for an example of the data analysis process).

7 Findings

In this section, I will first report the findings on the initial interviews to provide a baseline for the teacher participants' developing learning from the PD and their collaborative teaching experience.

7.1 Initial Interviews: English Dominance, Making Do, Hidden Tactics

All teachers reported in the pre-program interviews that they found the biggest challenge to be their students' "lack" of English proficiency. The perceived low levels of students' language competencies made teaching and learning almost impossible, as

Anthony reported: *"You speak, you talk, but they just don't get it. They don't listen to what you're saying."* As for Lucas, he emphasized the contextual constraints of his and the students' rural backgrounds leading to limited exposure to and usage of English. Celine found most of her students' sentence construction was so poor that it gave *"teachers a tough time of translating [the learners'] English into simple Chichewa"* just to try to understand their writing. Caleb opined that cross-language interference was one main problem faced by the learners. He illustrated by quoting some common mispronunciations such as sounding /r/ in English as /l/ because both consonants share the same phoneme in Chichewa. Also, given that some Chichewa consonants are followed by an extra vowel, many learners pronounce the word "against" (/əgenst/), for example, as /əgensɪtɪ/, with an extra /ɪ/ after consonants /s/ and /t/.

These comments about students' lack of abilities and their home language and cultures as interference and barrier reflected a deficit-orientation towards the learners and a monolingual preference for English, accepting English education and English-only policy as the default good teaching practices. As Fara asserted, it was the mother-tongue instruction policy in lower grades that had contributed to declined student achievements:

> It is difficult when they [the learners] moved from lower primary to upper classes; it is difficult for the learners to grasp what the teachers are trying to explain.

She believed English-medium instruction should be carried out across levels. Apart from language policy, teachers mentioned other broader sociopolitical influences on education, including poverty, lack of teaching materials, HIV epidemic, and the activities of a local cult, *Gule Wamkulu*, which allegedly spread non-Christian values and lured young boys away from school.

To support student learning, Lucas said, "We come to mix with Chichewa a little bit so that we get to say what's important", to which, he added "but it's not allowed to do that." Apart from this covert practice of language mixing, he and other teachers mentioned a range of strategies that went beyond monosemiotic restrictions, such as miming, use of drawings and pictures, real objects from local environment including plants, animals, and material objects (e.g., stones, earth or even packaging of daily products) as relia for table displays or manipulatives for numeracy and literacy learning. This expansive view of meaning-making was fully in line with government curricular guideline, *Teaching and Learning Using Locally Available Resources* (TALULA) (Malawi Institute of Education, 2004). However, we could not ascertain the extent to which these TALULA strategies were regularly employed. As Celine divulged, "sometimes [teachers] don't use it [TALULA] even though by laws, [teachers] are asked to do so". Based on class observations from the previous trip and reports by the university volunteers during this PD, teachers adopted the TALULA approach in varying degrees–some seemed to be more comfortable than the others in tapping into different modalities to support learning. For example, Fara, a dancer, singer, and teacher of Expressive Arts, routinely used a plurality of art forms to aid student comprehension:

> We use drama... we also demonstrate either by singing or dancing [...] I am good at singing because I'm so creative in the songs. You teach them and then you create a song so it can help them grasp [the concepts].

With all these strategies in place, she believed she could make English-only instruction intelligible to everyone. Lucas, on the other hand, employed real-life situations to creatively make English come to life. For example, when he taught the adverb "only", instead of simply giving a dictionary meaning, he used contextualized examples to highlight its usage:

> "My brother gave me <u>only</u> 200 Kwacha for my birthday". Only 200 Kwacha. Then another sentence: "My <u>only</u> brother gave me 200 Kwacha for my birthday". My <u>only</u> brother gave me 200. Then the last sentence sounds like this: "<u>Only</u> my brother gave me 200 Kwacha".

For Caleb, to raise students' awareness of language interference, he explicitly compared and contrasted English and Chichewa sounds to help them master the different pronunciation and spelling, for example, by reminding students that /ka/ in English is spelt as "ca" but "ka" in Chichewa and not to add an extra vowel after consonants in English words, such as "bad" (/bad/); not /badɪ/ and "food" (/fuːd/), not /fuːdu/.

The initial interviews and observations showed teachers' conformity toward English dominance and the urgency they felt to address their students' perceived lack of English proficiency for better learning. Although expressing a certain level of helplessness in face of the immense challenges posed by poverty and scarcity of resources, most teachers mentioned using creative ways to make do with the circumstantial and language demands through the hidden practices of language mixing and the utilization of multimodalities to support meaningful learning. Below, I describe the three main findings from the data gathered during and after the PD.

7.2   Findings Related to the PD

7.2.1   Recognizing and Vocalizing Monolingual Hegemony

One focus of the PD program was to expand participants' understanding of language as social practice tied to culture and identity. In reading Pavlenko's (2006) work on the emotional dimensions of bilingual minds, we discussed whether speaking a different language made us feel differently. Lucas, who had so far been soft-spoken and quiet in class, shared emphatically, *"I felt my voice is taken away."* Celine also recounted her early learning experience in Chichewa and English. Her family was originally from Northern Malawi and spoke Chitumbuka. Moving to central Malawi meant she was taught in Chichewa (in early grades) while learning English as a subject. She said she could understand nothing in class and had to secretly use a Chichewa-Chitumbuka bilingual dictionary to help herself learn.

These discussions were followed up by a language portrait assignment (Busch, Jardine, & Tjoutuku, 2006) whereby students marked on a body template different emotions they attached to own languages and cultures using different colors. This autographical approach served to promote participants' critical awareness and reflections on their diverse sociolinguistic identities and associated emotions as shaped by broader complex socio- political and economic forces. I shared my own language portrait as a model and then the participants (including our university volunteers) took turns to present their portraits to class over a few sessions.

Lucas added a write-up to his portrait in his journal (Fig. 10.2). He used blue to represent his being Black, orange for mother tongue Chichewa and red for English that he used in "office and educational purposes". Recounting his language learning experience, he highlighted one critical incident in Grade 6. His teacher drew an owl on a piece of paper with the words "I am an English failure" below it, which students being caught speaking Chichewa had to put around their neck. Lucas shared his feelings of humiliation when he was once caught using Chichewa and how spent the rest of that class desperately trying to find another offender to replace him.

Despite this traumatic experience, he ended his portrait by reinscribing it as a blessing in disguise: "In so doing, I was learning English little by little. And now here I am".

The sharing of the language portraits encouraged a mutual reinforcement of an affirmative attitude towards linguistic diversity, with some of them showcasing their multilingual talents by doing their greetings in a number of languages/dialects. Commenting on the overall learning from the PD, Caleb said:

> I've learnt a lot that we can develop English as a second language, without throwing away the mother language. And if we do that, our learners will really catch English as a second language quickly.

This changing attitude towards one's home language was also shown in teacher participants' gradual adoption of translanguaging pedagogy and a more asset-oriented view towards their students as well as of themselves as teachers.

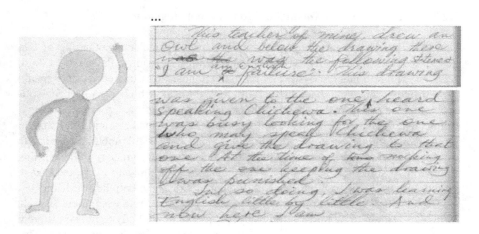

Fig. 10.2 Lucas' language portrait and journal excerpts

7.2.2 Embracing a Translanguaging Perspective

As the course progressed, Malawian teacher participants and university volunteers co-designed and tried out different teaching ideas that mobilized students' full communicative resources to promote interactive learning and comprehension. In our daily debriefing sessions with the university volunteers, we explored dialogic ways to engage teachers in practices that went beyond the safe perimeters of the prescriptive ministry teaching guide, while reminding each other of the importance to respect teachers' local expertise and knowledge of contextualized needs as well as their varied levels of comfort and readiness for change. Our program-end class observations showed a different range of employment of translanguaging pedagogy. Lucas focused on improving his use of gestures and facial expressions to convey meaning. We observed his Grade 5 English lesson in which he taught how to express likes and dislikes using the structures "I (dis)like ___. What do you (dis) like?". He effectively used his facial expressions to promote understanding of different key vocabulary without relying on verbal explanation: "Even though I didn't tell them 'this means this one', through expressions, they knew the meaning." He also allowed his students to use L1 in pair work and came to adopt translanguaging as not only an effective tool but also as a socially just means to democratize the learning process:

> We were just lecturing, as if we were preaching. The learners were just being quiet, without producing even a word. […] I knew that my learners were left behind; they were not getting what I was trying to make them learn. […] When we are not allowed to use the mother tongue […], we fail to deliver the message to the learners. […]. But now, when you mix the languages, I think the learners are learning a lot.

Similarly, Celine employed translanguaging in her Grade 8 Life Skills class, allowing students to use Chichewa in group discussions and then role-play to show their knowledge of mediation, arbitration and negotiation strategies. She said role-play in English only was too demanding and impossible for her students; yet with Chichewa, they were able to interactively co-construct meaning. She attributed this pedagogical change to her improved appreciation of multilingualism from the PD as assets rather than barriers to student learning. Fara also creatively used translanguaging in her Grade 3 Math class to teach shapes (*circle*, *rectangle*, *square* and *triangle*) in Chichewa and English at the same time. She was supposed to use Chichewa only at this level, but she thought with translanguaging, she could do both at the same time. The observed lesson was the second class when she taught shapes, with teaching ideas co-constructed with the university volunteers in her team. The day before she brought in used cereal and cardboard boxes and asked students to cut out different shapes as she introduced the vocabulary. Her follow-up activity was to match the cut-outs back to the missing segments of original cardboard. She started the next class by hanging the same cut-outs with the corresponding word in English from a stick which she used to do a quick review and as a visual reminder of the concepts they had learned. To engage her class with over 50 students, she had them work in groups to come up with creative ways to form different shapes using their bodies. To form a rectangle, for example, students discussed how many people they needed to place on the four sides to represent the difference in lengths and widths. This embodied learning engagement not only heightened their motivation but also deepened learning. Fara shared emphatically that her learning of translanguaging pedagogy further affirmed her use of multimodal and multisensory resources to ensure student attainments. As for her attitude towards English, she said,

> I might say I was one of the teachers who did not like the learner to mention a word in mother language when I'm teaching English. [...] I'm really changed now and I'm going to accommodate the learner even though they mention the word in their mother language and help him or her to mention it in English.

Caleb also demonstrated a great level of creativity in his Grade 2 Bible Knowledge class. After brainstorming with his teammates, he decided to reenact the story of Noah's ark using props. As he was telling the story, he stopped periodically to sing a related song and do the dance steps the class had previously learned, and invited the students to join in. Soon, the whole class was gathered around, listening to Caleb recount the story while singing and dancing along with him.

Caleb was very satisfied with the result, particularly with the translanguaging method. Bible Knowledge at Grade 3 should be taught in Chichewa, but he thought students would have a hard time understanding the Chichewa word "chombo" (ark) without help from a concrete object, so he used the English word "canoe" to explain, a word students already knew. Caleb found these multilingual and multimodal means engaging particularly "the passive ones were able to participate." He added that translanguaging made sense and made teaching more effective because all teacher's guides were in English (including subjects taught in Chichewa).

Caleb reported that the PD made him realize that he was on the right track by using the cross-language methods to bridge students' Chichewa and English language learning. Now knowing these strategies were actually theory-based and had a legitimate name, he felt much relief and excitement in applying them more extensively and effectively in teaching, which he did since beginning the PD, even at home. He shared an example of assisting his 6-year-old grandson to decode the English word "carpenter" by sounding it out using his Chichewa phonetic knowledge. The child first read it as "kalipenitala". With Caleb highlighting the cross-language spelling and pronunciation differences, this Grade 1 child was able to read, spell and write the word correctly in English. This further confirmed Caleb's belief in the efficacy of employing mixed language features to maximize learning and performance.

7.2.3 Adopting an Asset-Oriented Mindset Towards Students and Themselves

Teacher participants overall expressed a more asset-oriented view towards their students in their exit interviews. Caleb articulated the value of students' home literacy experiences, which to him should be effectively harnessed for school learning:

> I was reading about Pennycook, [...] I have understood, that a learner from home is not empty-headed; the learner has something. We only just need to guide what he has at home, or we need to link what is at home and the school life. [...] and when we see that, we will discover a lot, and a lot will be unveiled.

Lucas previously saw students' (and his own) lack of exposure to English as a determining factor for poor learning. Now he came to see their mother tongue as a resource and recognize his agency in employing translanguaging to establish an inclusive learning environment:

> When I see my learners stuck, I definitely change the language so that we will move together, with the lesson, without leaving them behind. [...]

Similarly, Fara recognized the value of her rich cultural and linguistic resources for pedagogical purposes:

> Before [the language portrait], I could not know that I have so many languages in me, though I could not maybe speak well or read well. But with the combination of the aspects [...] I feel now I can accommodate the languages which I have, and I can use them in my class, and even allow the learners to use their languages in a classroom situation, without burying them [...].

She expressed a great sense of agency to effect change through translanguaging together with the teaching tools she already had, highlighting the professional transformation she underwent:

> On the first day you were interviewing me, I'm not the same as I am now, I'm a changed person. [...] as I was teaching with my partner, we could say the word in English as well as in Chichewa. It was combined, so I've learned much on this.

The Malawian teachers revealed in the post interview that they were much inspired by the project, particularly by the university volunteers' myriad ethnolinguistic backgrounds. Not only did some of them come from humble, rural backgrounds, they all took pride in their multilingual identities, especially the Chinese students who held a strong affirming attitude towards Mandarin and other local dialects, on top of their proficient mastery of English as second or third language. For example, Celine said she was moved by one Chinese volunteer's sharing about her poor rural background and parents' lack of access to education, which changed her views about these overseas volunteers:

> I feel we are sharing almost the same stories. [...] we feel that our friends who are abroad [...], all of them were coming from well to-do families. [yet] they might share the same world [...] if you are working hard, you can still progress in life.

Another major identity shift was seen in their view towards the opportunity to work with professors as well as the undergraduate and graduate student volunteers. All of them expressed that the sharing of their language portraits was one of the best moments in the PD. As Fara shared, she had "never had the chance of interacting with teachers or students from the international level", so to her, the co-learning experience represented a global learning community of which she could now claim membership. This newly acquired global identity constituted a desire for continual growth in professionalism: "[The PD] made me think critically …from where I was, where I am, and where I want to be."

For Lucas, the newly acquired global identity comprised an elevated status as an equal to the White:

> We were taught that only the president, ministers can speak with the White men. […] I am interacting with you [Sunny], while I am a black person. I have never gone abroad, I'm born in Malawi, but I'm now able to communicate with you.

While it was not sure if Lucas was positioning me as being White here, nonetheless, he could be associating my Canadian professional identity and global mobility as Whiteness. The cross-cultural collaborations signaled a global partnership in which he saw himself an equal, legitimate member, albeit peripheral.

8   Discussions and Conclusions

The findings show some positive outcomes; however, their persistent colonial mind-set reverberated throughout the study. On one hand, teachers became more aware of (or at least felt more comfort in sharing) how monolingual ideologies and English hegemony had imposed restrictive regulations on who they were and how they taught. This was evident in Lucas' assertion of his being silenced and positioned as a failure under English-only education and in Celine's divulging of her hidden independent practice of seeking Chitumbuka dictionary meaning for Chichewa in order to keep up with school work. Some came to question more openly the totalizing neocolonial discourse on pedagogical effectiveness of lingualism and language separation and allow their intuitive "subaltern knowledge" to make sense and find solutions to contextual needs. This was shown in Caleb's Noah's ark lesson, Celine's L1 role-play in her Life Skills lesson, as well as Lucas' and Fara's English and Math classes where a range of multilingual, multisemiotic, multisensory, and multimodal resources (Li, 2017) were mobilized for enhanced motivation and comprehension. They all expressed a positive attitude towards translanguaging practices, a new term they came to know and identify with the hybrid practices some of them had already adopted, albeit covertly, as pedagogical strategies for learning support.

On the other hand, however, the fact that their sense of guilt was only assuaged by their Canadian partners' reassurance of the legitimate nature of multilingual and multimodal means of knowledge construction points to the power differential in claiming authority to the validity of translanguaging pedagogy. Teachers like Caleb and Lucas were already intuitively employing some language mixing and Fara a range of creative multi-semiotic means for sense-making. But the fact that they deferentially counted on a nod of approval from their academic partners from the west suggested a degree of persistent coloniality, relegating knowledge and authority to the Global North. Although most teachers in the exit interview acknowledged the pedagogical efficacy of teacher- and student-directed translanguaging practices (Lewis, Jones, & Baker, 2012), so far we only saw Lucas' and Celine's employment of these practices in their respective classes for student discussions and role-play. Teachers such as Caleb and Fara who though incorporated translanguaging in their respective lesson on Noah's ark and shapes, their incorporation of English was in classes that were supposed to have been taught in Chichewa. It is therefore not certain if they would have felt the same degree of comfort in applying translanguaging practices in English-mandated subject areas, reflecting a possible continued coloniality in valuing English over local languages. Undoubtedly, effective use of translanguaging strategies for contextualised needs requires prolonged experience and practice; it was not something that one could master just through a 10-day workshop.

Many of them, though came to see the negative impact of academic monolingualism on their identities, attributed their success as a member in the teaching profession to the restrictive and constrictive English-only policy; for example, Lucas took his teacher's humiliating punishment to delegitimize Chichewa use as an effective way to improve his English. Further, on one hand, the Canadian and Chinese international students' life stories disrupted the Malawian teachers' stereotyped image of overseas volunteers' assumed wealth. On the other, they attributed these students' multilingual abilities, particularly their mastery of English, to diligence and industry, hence reinscribing "success" within the long-standing neocolonial, capitalist narrative of meritocracy.

The teachers' appreciation of the collaborative inquiry, though genuine and immense, lay mainly in its constitution of an imagined global learning community in which they felt they could claim equal membership. Did this newly acquired/imagined global identity (Kanno & Norton, 2003) effectively enhance their self-efficacy as perseverant and creative professionals in dealing with educational and social inequalities? Or did this imagined global identity further reinscribe them into the global script that revels in the superior value of English education? All participating teachers took pride in collaborating with professors and students from overseas, particularly in having an international audience to their life stories. The same can be said with our university volunteers and us as professors. International development work has become a symbol of quality education for the twenty-first century that encompasses border-crossing experiences and global perspectives necessary for global citizenry (Pence & Macgillivray, 2008; Sahin, 2008). However, Lucas' revelation of his pride as derived from being in the company of the White suggests a persistent degree of coloniality and raciolinguistic ideologies (Flores & Rosa, 2015). His associating my Canadian professional identity and global mobility with Whiteness adds an interesting layer and nuance to raciolinguistic ideologies. Though being Chinese, my English linguistic capital and institutional identity

afforded certain authority and privilege close to Whiteness in the context of rural
Malawi. This points to the need to understand raciolinguistic ideologies through an
intersectionality lens (Carbado, Crenshaw, Mays, & Tomlinson, 2013), taking into
consideration of how these ideologies and power relations play out in micro-
interactions situated within particular socio- political, historical and economic
structures. The Malawian teachers' persistent hierarchical understanding of our
partnership, coupled with the short-term, uni-directional nature of the project (North
to South), made us wary of the affirmative claims they made about the PD as well
as their understanding of translanguaging. It remains a question whether their overwhelmingly positive responses were merely amplified by their politeness and
respectfulness as Malawians and/or a certain degree of entrenched coloniality in
deferring to authority and knowledge claims to their foreign/White "bwanas"
(bosses).

Trudell (2016) argues that researchers working in African countries like Malawi
have to understand the diametrical co-existence of pro-local language policy and the
enduring preference for English in the region, which speaks to the complex entan-
glements between two competing desires: (1) the ideological and political motivations to preserve and promote the country's ethnolinguistic realities and identities,
and (2) the longing to belong to the "global community" where English is believed
to hold prominent linguistic currency. Our efforts to engage the local teachers in
decolonizing English education reveals an imperative need to recognize the "access
paradox" (Janks, 2010) inherent in critical language education, i.e., while the promotion of English sustains its dominance and curtails efforts in multilingualism,
denying minoritized students' access to its prestigious linguistic capital further perpetuates their marginalization. Given the prevailing global language hierarchies
with English and other named languages dominating over other minoritized and
indigenous languages, any language education has to be done in tandem with critical engagements that destabilize and demystify dominant languages' privileged status. As Flores and Rosa (2015) argue, "[a] critical heteroglossic perspective that
both legitimizes the dynamic linguistic practices of language-minoritized students
while simultaneously raising awareness about issues of language and power marks
an important starting point for developing this alternative approach" (p. 167).

Researchers on international development also need to exercise vigilance and
humility in our understanding of what decolonization means to local communities
(Darroch & Giles, 2014) and how our new theories and insights on language and
language education might facilitate or hinder local agentive efforts to find creative
solutions to make do with varied severe socio- political and economic demands.
While disrupting English monolingual dominance, we should not lose sight of its
material impact on local people's access to education and upward mobility and be
vigilant of the power deferentials so that the reintroduction or the relegitimization
of translanguaging practices does not become another cyle of symbolic violence
(Bourdieu, 1995) on the locals who have grown to become economically dependent
on foreign aid. Decolonization as a *double operation* points to the need for "a relent-
less critical exercise of awareness" (Mignolo, 2000, p. 458) on the part of

researchers from the Global North as the ongoing guiding principle to their actions and reflections on any decolonization project.

Appendices

Appendix 1: Interview Protocols

Pre-program

1. Personal information: name, age, languages, education, teaching experience, subject areas, etc.
2. What are some of the challenges in teaching (in) English?
3. What teaching strategies do you use to support students' learning of/in English?
4. What are some of the broader sociopolitical forces that affect teaching of/in English?
5. What are the main qualities of an ideal EL teacher?
6. What was the best second language lesson that you have experienced or taught and why?
7. What are your expectations of the PD and your co-learning (challenges & benefits) with our student teachers and MEd students?

Post-program

Questions 2–6 – changes if any from the pre-program interview

8. Describe one of the best (and worst) moments in your PD sessions and explain why.
9. Describe one of the best (and worst) moments in your teaching (placement) with your partners and explain why.
10. You were asked to design and try out a lesson with your Canadian partners using culturally and linguistically responsive strategies. In your opinion, how did it go? What could be improved? What did you learn in the process?

Appendix 2 – An Example of Data Analysis Process

Source	Data	First Cycle Coding		Second Cycle Coding
Interviews – pre & post		Structural Coding	Eclectic coding: **Descriptive coding** **In vivo codes** - in " __ " **Emotion codes** - in capitals	**Pattern Coding**
In your opinion, what are some of the challenges of teaching in/of English?	It is true that in Malawi, English teachers are very few. Even in secondary schools. Maybe [it's because of] our background because in the villages, we probably speak Chichewa throughout, so even if you go to secondary school, you don't become a fluent speaker. […] if some people are to respond in English it becomes a challenge. Because of our, our background. **(Lucas, pre-interview on June 10, 2017)**	challenges	lack of English teachers "villages" "speak Chichewa" "not …a fluent speaker" "background" HELPLESSNESS	**Contextual constraints & challenges** - Teacher shortage - Poor rural background - Limited exposure to & practice in English
	Yeah, so pronunciation is a big challenge […] maybe just let me give an example, like 'problem'. You get this one said like, "What is the *ploblem*?"--"What is the *ploblem*?" instead of 'problem'. So it's those things. […]So there's also a mixture of the mother language, always can be a challenge to teaching English. **(Caleb, pre- interview on June 10, 2017)**	challenges	mis-pronunciation "mixture of the mother language"	**Deficit orientation** -students' poor level of language proficiency & comprehension -Interference from mother tongue - Chichewa language & culture as barriers rather than assets
	Most learners do not understand English as their second language. Since they do not comprehend, it is difficult to answer comprehension questions. And even, writing compositions, […], learners do fail. And even in sentence construction again, it's too hard to most Malawian learners. In so doing, it gives us teachers a tough time of translating this English into simple Chichewa for better understanding between me as a teacher and the learners. **(Celine, pre- interview on June 10, 2017)**	challenges	"do not understand" "do not comprehend" "fail" "too hard" FRUSTRATION	

Source	Data	First Cycle Coding		Second Cycle Coding
PD	Field notes	Descriptive Coding	Eclectic coding: In vivo codes - in " " / Emotion codes - in capitals	Pattern Coding
	When we came to discussions about whether they felt being different speaking a different language, all teachers and Chinese international students were nodding their heads emphatically. Lucas even turned towards me and said, "*I felt my voice is taken away.*" Lucas seldom spoke up in class; he came across as a very gentle and soft-spoken person. This came as a surprise since he spoke so emphatically about his loss of voice. It was really the first time him talking like this. Caleb added that he felt a bit nervous speaking in front of the Canadian student teachers. I commended them all, saying how brave it was for them to share such intimate thoughts and that we aimed to create an inclusive environment so we all felt safe to take risks, just as what we should all do in our EL classrooms. **(Researcher, Class 2 on June 14, 2017)**	identity English-only policy learning environment teaching strategies	"felt different" "my voice is taken away" "NERVOUS" "inclusive environment"	**Improved understanding of interconnections between language, culture & identity** - Think & feel differently when speaking an L2 **Heightened awareness in English hegemony:** -deprivation of own voice -internalization of native-speakerism **Instructional strategies** - inclusive classroom

References

Blackledge, A., & Creese, A. (Eds.). (2014). *Heteroglossia as practice and pedagogy.* Dordrecht, The Netherlands: Springer Netherlands Imprint.

Bourdieu, P. (1995). *Language and symbolic power* (G. Raymond & M. Adamson, Trans. E. a. I. b. J. B. Thompson Ed.). Cambridge, MA: Harvard University.

Busch, B., Jardine, A., & Tjoutuku, A. (2006). *Language biographies for multilingual learning* (PRAESA Occasional Papers no. 24). Retrieved from http://web.uct.ac.za/depts/praesa/all%20andy%20pdf%20feb07mar11/Paper24-600dpi.pdf

Canagarajah, A. S. (2004). Language rights and postmodern conditions. *Journal of Language, Identity & Education, 3*(2), 140–145.

Canagarajah, A. S. (2013). *Translingual practice: Global Englishes and cosmopolitan relations.* London, UK: Routledge.

Carbado, D. W., Crenshaw, K. W., Mays, V. M., & Tomlinson, B. (2013). Intersectionality: Mapping the movements of a theory. *Du Bois Review: Social Science Research on Race, 10*(2), 303–312.

Coghlan, D., & Brannick, T. (2009). *Doing action research in your own organization* (3rd ed.). Thousand Oaks, CA: Sage Publications.

Cohen, L., Manion, L., & Morrison, K. (2000). *Research methods in education* (5th ed.). London, UK: Routledge Farmer.

Cook, V. (2016). Premises of multi-competence. In V. Cook & L. Wei (Eds.), *The Cambridge handbook of linguistic multi-competence* (pp. 1–25). Cambridge, UK: Cambridge University Press.

Darroch, F., & Giles, A. (2014). Decolonizing health research: Community-based participatory research and postcolonial feminist theory. *Canadian Journal of Action Research, 15*(3), 22–36.

Easterly, W. R. (2006). *The white man's burden: Why the West's efforts to aid the rest have done so much ill and so little good*. New York, NY: Penguin.

Fanon, F. (1966). *The wretched of the earth* (C. Farrington, Trans.). New York, NY: Grove Press (Original work published in 1961).

Fanon, F. (1967). *Black skin, white masks* (C. L. Markmann, Trans.). New York, NY: Grove. (Original work published in 1952).

Flores, N., & Rosa, J. D. (2015). Undoing appropriateness: Raciolinguistic ideologies and language diversity in education. *Harvard Educational Review, 85*(2), 149–171.

Freire, P. (1970). *Pedagogy of the oppressed*. New York, NY: Herder & Herder.

García, O. (2009). *Bilingual education in the 21st century: A global perspective*. Oxford, UK: Wiley-Blackwell.

García, O., & Kleyn, T. (Eds.). (2016). *Translanguaging with multilingual students: Learning from classroom moments*. New York, NY: Routledge.

García, O., & Li, W. (2014). *Translanguaging: Language, bilingualism and education*. Hampshire, UK: Palgrave Macmillan.

García, O., Johnson, S. I., & Seltzer, K. (2017). *The translanguaging classroom: Leveraging student bilingualism for learning*. Philadelphia, PA: Calson.

Global Economy. (2018a). *Malawi: Secondary school enrollment*. Retrieved from: https://www.theglobaleconomy.com/Malawi/Secondary_school_enrollment/

Global Economy. (2018b). *Malawi: Tertiary school enrollment*. Retrieved from: https://www.theglobaleconomy.com/Malawi/Tertiary_school_enrollment/

Janks, H. (2010). *Literacy and power*. New York, NY: Taylor & Francis.

Japan International Cooperation Agency. (2012). *Basic education sector analysis report*. Retrieved from http://openjicareport.jica.go.jp/pdf/12083275.pdf

Kachru, B. B. (1990). World Englishes and applied linguistics. *World Englishes, 9*, 3–20. https://doi.org/10.1111/j.1467-971X.1990.tb00683.x

Kachru, B. B. (1997). World Englishes and English-using communities. *Annual Review of Applied Linguistics, 17*, 66–87.

Kamwendo, G. H. (2008a). The bumpy road to mother tongue instruction in Malawi. *Journal of Multilingual and Multicultural Development, 29*(5), 1–11.

Kamwendo, G. H. (2008b). The bumpy road to mother tongue instruction in Malawi. *Journal of Multilingual and Multicultural Development, 29*(5), 353. https://doi.org/10.2167/jmmd547.0

Kamwendo, G. H. (2010). Denigrating the local, glorifying the foreign: Malawian language policies in the era of African renaissance. *International Journal of African Renaissance Studies - Multi-, Inter- and Transdisciplinarity, 5*(2), 270–282. https://doi.org/10.1080/18186874.2010.534850

Kamwendo, G. H. (2013). Malawi: Contemporary and critical issues. In C. Harbor (Ed.), *Education in Southern Africa* (pp. 103–122). London, UK: Bloomsbury.

Kanno, Y., & Norton, B. (2003). Imagined communities and educational possibilities: Introduction. *Journal of Language, Identity & Education, 2*(4), 241–249.

Kayambazinthu, E. (1998). The language planning situation in Malawi. *Journal of Multilingual and Multicultural Development, 19*(5 & 6), 369–439.

Kemmis, S. (2001). Exploring the relevance of critical theory for action research: Emancipatory action research in the footsteps of Jürgen Habermas. In P. Reason & H. Bradbury (Eds.), *Handbook of action research: Participative inquiry and practice* (pp. 91–102). London: SAGE.

Kretzer, M. M., & Kumwenda, J. I. (2016). Language policy in Malawi: A study of its contexts, factors for its development and consequences. *Marang: Journal of Language and Literature, 27*, 20–36.

Kumaravadivelu, B. (2016). The decolonial option in English teaching: Can the subaltern act? *TESOL Quarterly, 50*(1), 66–85.

Lewis, G., Jones, B., & Baker, C. (2012). Translanguaging: Developing its conceptualisation and contextualisation. *Educational Research and Evaluation, 18*(7), 655–670.

Li, W. (2017). Translanguaging as a practical theory of language. *Applied Linguistics, 39*(1), 9–30.

Lin, A. M. Y. (2001). Symbolic domination and bilingual classroom practices in Hong Kong. In M. Heller & M. Martin-Jones (Eds.), *Voices of authority: Education and linguistic difference* (pp. 139–168). West Port, CT: Ablex.

Malawi Institute of Education. (2004). *TALULAR – A user's guide: Teaching and learning using locally available resource*. Domas, Malawi: Malawi Institute of Education.

Maldonado-Torres, N. (2010). On the coloniality of being: Contributions to the development of a concept. In W. Mignolo & A. Escobar (Eds.), *Globalization and the decolonial option* (pp. 94–124). London: Routledge.

May, S. (Ed.) (2014). *The multilingual turn: Implications for SLA, TESOL and bilingual education*. New York/London: Routledge.

McCarty, T. L. (2013). *Language planning and policy in Native America: History, theory, praxis*. New York, NY: Multilingual Matters.

Mignolo, W. (2000). *Local histories/global designs: Coloniality, subaltern knowledges, and border thinking*. Princeton, NJ: Princeton University Press.

Mignolo, W. (2007). Delinking: The rhetoric of modernity, the logic of coloniality and the grammar of de-coloniality. *Cultural Studies, 21*(2–3), 449–514.

Morrison, K., & Lui, I. (2000). Ideology, linguistic capital and the medium of instruction in Hong Kong. *Journal of Multilingual and Multicultural Development, 21*(6), 471–486.

Motha, S. (2006). Decolonizing ESOL: Negotiating linguistic power in U.S. public school classrooms. *Critical Inquiry in Language Studies, 3*(2–3), 75–100.

Moto, F. (2002). African language and the crisis of identity: The case of Malawi. In F. R. Owino (Ed.), *Speaking African languages for education and development* (pp. 33–44). Cape Town, South Africa: CASAS.

Moussu, L., & Llurda, E. (2008). Non-native English-speaking English language teachers: History and research. *Language Teaching, 41*(3), 315–348. https://doi.org/10.1017/S0261444808005028

Namey, E., Guest, G., Thairu, L., & Johnson, L. (2008). Data reduction techniques for large qualitative data sets. In G. Guest & K. M. MacQueen (Eds.), *Handbook for team-based qualitative research* (pp. 137–161). Lanham, MD: AltaMira Press.

National Statistics Office (Malawi). (2000). *Malawi population and housing census, 1998*. Zomba: National Statistics Office.

Pavlenko, A. (Ed.) (2006). *Bilingual minds: Emotional experience, expression and representation*. Clevedon, UK: Multilingual Matters Ltd.

Pence, H. M., & Macgillivray, I. K. (2008). The impact of an international field experience on preservice teachers. *Teaching and Teacher Education: An International Journal of Research and Studies, 24*(1), 14–25.

Pennycook, A. (1998). *English and the discourses of colonialism*. London, UK/New York, NY: Routledge.

Pennycook, A. (2001). *Critical applied linguistics: A critical introduction*. Mahwah, NJ: Lawrence Erlbaum Associates.

Pennycook, A. (2012). What might translingual education look like? *Babel, 47*(1), 4–13. Retrieved from https://search.informit.com.au/documentSummary;dn=859716477022294;res=IELAPA

Phillipson, R. (1998). Globalizing English: Are linguistic human rights an alternative to linguistic imperialism? *Language Sciences, 20*(1), 101–112.

Phillipson, R. (2009). *Linguistic imperialism continued*. New York, NY/London, UK: Routledge.

Reason, P., & Bradbury, H. (2006). *Handbook of action research: Participative inquiry and practice*. Los Angeles, CA: SAGE.

Sabatier, C. (2010). Plurilinguismes, représentations et identités: des pratiques des locuteurs aux définitions des linguistes. *Nouvelles perspectives en sciences sociales, 6*(1), 125–161.

Sahin, M. (2008). Cross-cultural experience in preservice teacher education. *Teaching and Teacher Education, 24*(7), 1777–1790. https://doi.org/10.1016/j.tate.2008.02.006

Saldaña, J. (2013). *The coding manual for qualitative researchers*. Los Angeles, CA: SAGE Publications.

Senge, P. M., & Scharmer, C. O. (2006). Community action research: Learning as a community of practitioners, consultants and researchers. In P. Reason & H. Bradbury (Eds.), *Handbook of action research* (pp. 195–206). Los Angeles, CA: Sage.

Skutnabb-Kangas, T. (2000). *Linguistic genocide in education – Or worldwide diversity and human rights?* Mahwah, NJ: Lawrence Erlbaum Associates.

Spivak, G. (1990). Gayatri Spivak on the politics of the subaltern. *Socialist Review, 20*(3), 85–97.

Stonebanks, C. D. (2013). Cultural competence, culture shock and the praxis of experiential learning. In E. Lyle & G. Knowles (Eds.), *Bridging the theory-practice divide: Pedagogical enactment for socially just education* (pp. 249–277). Nova Scotia, Canada: Backalong Books.

Thiong'o, N. w. (1986). *Decolonising the mind: The politics of language in African literature.* London, UK: James Currey.

Trudell, B. (2016). Language choice and education quality in Eastern and Southern Africa: A review. *Comparative Education, 52*(3), 281–293. https://doi.org/10.1080/03050068.2016.1185252

UNICEF Malawi. (2016). *Basic quality education.* Retrieved from: https://www.unicef.org/malawi/development_15943.html

Williams, E. (2007). Extensive reading in Malawi: Inadequate implementation or inappropriate innovation? *Journal of Research in Reading, 30*(1), 59–79. https://doi.org/10.1111/j.1467-9817.2006.00328.x

Williams, C., Lewis, G., & Baker, C. (1996). *The language policy: Taking stock. Interpreting and appraising Gwynedd's language policy in education.* Llangefni, Wales: CAI.

Part III
Translanguaging in TESOL Classrooms

Chapter 11
Tower of Babel or Garden of Eden? Teaching English as a Foreign Language Through a Translanguaging Lens

Mirjam Günther-van der Meij and Joana Duarte

Abstract This chapter discusses the use of translanguaging pedagogy for learning English with young learners (kindergarten and elementary school level) in the context of the officially bilingual Province of Friesland, the Netherlands (with Dutch and the regional minority language Frisian). First, a holistic model for multilingualism in education (Duarte, 2017 (Meer Kansen Met Meertaligheid) NHL Stenden University of Applied Sciences, Leeuwarden, The Netherlands; 2017) and its relation to teaching English to speakers of other languages (TESOL) is presented. The model places pedagogical practices along a continuum, oscillating between the acknowledgement of languages and their full use in education. Then examples of multilingual activities for TESOL – combining a translanguaging approach with several multilingual approaches such as language awareness and Content and Language Integrated Learning (CLIL) methodologies – will be discussed, drawn from two research projects set in the Province of Friesland. Exemplary transcripts from English classrooms will also be presented and discussed in which we focus on the role of translanguaging in interaction, distinguishing three types of functions: *symbolic*, *scaffolding* and *epistemological*. The chapter ends with a reflection on the extent to which translanguaging within the context of TESOL in primary education causes a Tower of Babel or is perceived by schools to be a Garden of Eden.

Keywords TESOL · Translanguaging · Multilingual approaches · Holistic approach

M. Günther-van der Meij (✉) · J. Duarte
Research group on Multilingualism & Literacy, Department of Primary Teacher Education, NHL Stenden University of Applied Sciences, Leeuwarden, The Netherlands
e-mail: mirjam.gunther@nhlstenden.com; joana.da.silveira.duarte@nhlstenden.com

© Springer Nature Switzerland AG 2020
Z. Tian et al. (eds.), *Envisioning TESOL through a Translanguaging Lens*, Educational Linguistics 45, https://doi.org/10.1007/978-3-030-47031-9_11

1 Introduction

English is growingly taught as a foreign language at early ages within European school systems. This often means teaching English as an early foreign language (EFL) or teaching English to speakers of other languages (TESOL) (Cenoz & Gorter, 2013) (for this chapter we will use the term TESOL). For example, for pupils living in the Netherlands whose family language differs from the majority language Dutch – as in the case of a migrant language (e.g. Arabic or Polish), a regional minority language (e.g. Frisian) or a dialect (e.g. Low Saxon) – the foreign language English might be the third or fourth language they acquire at an early age, as most of these pupils are proficient in their home language(s) and the majority language (Duarte & Günther-van der Meij, 2018a). Traditionally, the didactic approach to teaching English as a foreign language is immersion, which is based on the separation of the English language from the other languages of instruction by using the 'one person one language' approach (Melo-Pfeifer, 2018). In early language learning programs across Europe (Nikolov & Mihaljević Djigunović, 2011) this has been mostly operationalized in three ways: schools will engage either (a) a class teacher, (b) a (near) native-speaker specialist teacher, or (c) have the class and specialist teachers co-teach English (Unsworth et al., 2015).

With the increase of multilingual pupils in European schools and new insights from research claiming that language skills are transferable across languages, varieties and registers (Cenoz & Gorter, 2015; Cummins, 2008; Duarte & Gogolin, 2013), the exclusive use of this approach is being questioned. Latest research suggests, in fact, that both multilingual and monolingual pupils would benefit from an educational approach in which several languages are used in instruction. Conteh and Meier (2014) speak of the multilingual turn in language education, May (2014) and Flores and Beatens-Beardsmore (2015) describe the benefits of so-called heteroglossic approaches in which regional minority, and immigrant languages as well as dialects are incorporated in instruction. Specifically for foreign languages, Melo-Pfeifer discusses the implications of the multilingual turn in foreign languages education (Melo-Pfeifer, 2018). She argues that the multilingual turn "legitimizes the use of pluralistic approaches to languages and cultures, as well as the development of an integrated language learning curriculum (namely for the L3 or additional languages), that fully acknowledges pupils' linguistic biographies and previous knowledge" (2018, p. 207).

In recent years, reinforced attention has been given to the use of translanguaging (García & Kano, 2014; García & Li Wei, 2014) in TESOL classrooms. Since the topic is broadly discussed in this volume, we will only highlight a few relevant findings in relation to translanguaging. Translanguaging is based on the idea that different chunks of language(s) form a single integrated system in which languages are fluid (Canagarajah, 2011; Duarte, 2016; García et al., 2017). In a translanguaging approach the learner's full language repertoire is used in teaching and learning (García & Li Wei, 2014; García et al., 2017). Or as García and Kano (2014, p. 261) describe it: "a process by which students and teachers engage in complex discursive practices that include ALL the language practices of ALL students in a class in order to develop new language practices and sustain old ones, communicate and appropriate knowledge, and give voice to new socio-political realities by interrogating linguistic inequality". Different studies have shown the importance of the use of translanguaging in the classroom for both migrant and regional minority languages, for example resulting in better achievement (Arthur & Martin, 2006; Lin & Martin, 2005), for protecting and promoting regional minority languages (Cenoz, 2017) or even for raising participant confidence and motivation (Creese & Blackledge, 2010).

Including multiple languages in mainstream instruction is not a new phenomenon. A concept that is widely accepted in foreign language classes is *Content and Language Integrated Learning* (CLIL). It refers to teaching subjects such as science, history and geography to students through a foreign language (Cenoz, 2013), focusing on both content and language. *CLIL* approaches are often implemented as a means to provide instruction in recognized foreign languages, such as English, French or German.

Several other pedagogical approaches for including multiple languages have been put forward, such as language awareness. Four dimensions of language competence can be distinguished in language awareness approaches (Andrade et al., 2003, p. 489) which aim at helping individuals to:

1. reflect upon and reveal some degree of awareness of their own dispositions and motivations regarding languages (socio-affective dimension);
2. be capable of managing their linguistic and communicative biography in new interaction situations (management of linguistic and communicative repertoires dimension);
3. enable them to manage acquisition processes (management of learning repertoires dimension);
4. reflect upon the interactive processes which characterize language contact situations, (management of interaction dimension).

According to Candelier (2010) activities that foster language awareness have the following features: (a) integrated language learning, aimed at establishing associations between different languages (regional minority, immigrant, instruction and foreign languages); (b) intercomprehension, which particularly works with various languages within the same language family; (c) a pedagogy for awakening to languages, implying attempts to break with the segmentation and isolation of the language teaching methods at schools. Earlier results achieved by teaching programs aimed at raising the levels of language awareness were very positive (e.g. Hélot & Young, 2006; Oliveira & Ança, 2009; Wildemann, 2013).

These issues of translanguaging, CLIL and language awareness all play a role in the Province of Friesland. Friesland is a bilingual province in the North of the Netherlands, with Frisian as a regional minority language and Dutch as the majority language. About 55% of the 646.000 inhabitants of Friesland has Frisian as their mother tongue whilst 30% has Dutch and 15% has another language as their mother tongue (Province of Fryslân, 2015). Frisian is typically spoken in the rural areas and to a much lesser extent in the urban areas where Dutch or dialects are spoken

(Province of Fryslân, 2015). Native Frisian speakers are also proficient in Dutch, since Dutch is the dominant language. English is the most commonly taught foreign language. English has been a compulsory subject in primary education from 1986 onwards in the Netherlands (Unsworth et al., 2015). At primary level English is mostly taught in grades 7 and 8 (ages 10–12) for one lesson per week. English is almost always taught as a subject only and not used as a language of instruction. There is however a still rising trend for trilingual education (Frisian, Dutch and English) where English is used as a language of instruction for approximately 20% of the teaching time in the higher grades next to 40% Dutch and 40% Frisian (Inspectie van het Onderwijs, 2010). About 18% of the 445 primary schools are officially certified Trilingual Schools. The attainment targets for English for primary school pupils are limited to simple oral communication, listening and speaking and being able to read simple texts (Duarte & Günther-van der Meij, 2018a).

Our setting is thus a typical case of a region still in the process of consolidating the position of a regional minority language in education, while at the same time dealing with increasing migration-induced diversity (Duarte & Günther-van der Meij, 2018a). In this context a holistic model for multilingualism in education was developed and implemented in two research projects aimed at primary education. While the 3M-project (*Meer kansen Met Meertaligheid* – More Opportunities with Multilingualism) works with 12 schools in order to develop multilingual activities for pupils aged 8–10, the Languages4all-project (*Talen4all*) focuses on pupils aged 10–12 in 8 schools. The projects focus on different school types such as trilingual Frisian-Dutch-English schools, refugees / newcomer schools, schools with a high percentage of migrant language speakers and schools with a high percentage of Dutch speakers. All (home) languages that are present at the school are involved in the activities developed. In some activities, a translanguaging (García, 2009; García & Li Wei, 2014) lens is used to achieve less separation between the languages of instruction, while in others language awareness (Young & Hélot, 2003) is implemented to acknowledge and explore migrant languages in relation to the languages of instruction. At the core of the projects' methodology is a design-based approach (Cobb et al., 2003), in which tailored didactical units are developed in co-construction between teachers and researchers through iterative development rounds.

The aims of this chapter are (a) to present the holistic model for multilingualism in (primary) education and (b) to discuss examples of multilingual activities that were developed within the two research projects. It also discusses transcripts of classroom interaction, zooming in on the different functions of pedagogical translanguaging (García & Li Wei, 2015): *symbolic, scaffolding* and *epistemological* (Duarte, 2018). The chapter first presents the principles behind the holistic model for multilingual education. This is followed by the methodology section and examples of activities developed within the projects. Last, translanguaging scenes from classroom interaction will be discussed in relation to the model. The chapter ends with a reflection of the extent to which translanguaging within the context of TESOL in primary education causes a tower of Babel or is perceived by teachers to be a garden of Eden.

2 A Holistic Approach Towards Multilingual Education

Recently, multilingual approaches have arisen in which languages are learnt in relation to each other based on the idea of transferable language skills (Cenoz & Gorter, 2015; Cummins, 2008; Duarte & Gogolin, 2013). It is assumed that languages share an underlying cognitive proficiency (interdependence hypothesis, Cummins, 1979) which enables learners to transfer their language skills from one language to the other (Cummins, 2007; Nortier, 2009). Stepping away from strict language separation pedagogies and adopting a multilingual approach has so far yielded positive results. For example, through using cross-linguistic transfer for raising academic achievement (Duarte, 2011; Duarte & Pereira, 2011; Francis & Lesaux, 2006) or using multilingualism as a resource for learning (Bourne, 2013; Bührig and Duarte, 2014; Creese & Blackledge, 2010; Moodley, 2007; Rolff, 2006). Different studies have also shown that using multiple languages in the classroom has no negative effect on the achievement in the majority language (Cummins, 1979; Slembrouck et al., 2018). Specifically for TESOL, Cenoz and Gorter (2013) make a critique of the policy of language isolation and propose a multilingual approach to the teaching of English that softens the boundaries between languages.

In terms of pedagogical implications for the TESOL classroom, multilingual approaches consider language learning as a dynamic process that perceives all existing linguistic and communicative resources as sources of transfer (Melo-Pfeifer, 2018). It defines the foreign language classroom as an intrinsically multilingual learning space, highlighting the value of interconnecting languages and language learning across the curriculum, fostering collaborative work among pupils and teachers at different school levels (Krumm & Reich, 2013). According to Melo-Pfeifer (2018, p. 200) "pluralistic approaches challenge the myth of both the native speaker and of pre-available linguistic norms; they abandon the idea of the classroom being a monolingual locus of teaching and learning; and they accept that interaction does not need to occur in just one language".

Against this backdrop and in order to develop teacher's professionalization, a holistic model for multilingualism in education (Fig. 11.1) was developed (Duarte,

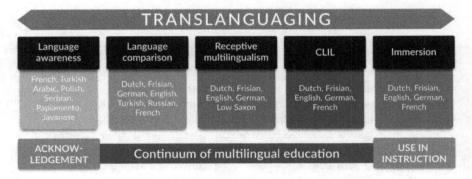

Fig. 11.1 Holistic model for multilingualism in education (Duarte, 2017; Duarte & Günther-van der Meij, 2018b).

2017; Duarte & Günther-van der Meij, 2018b). This model was originally developed for schools in the Province of Friesland where language separation in trilingual models is still common and mainstream regular primary schools use mostly the majority language Dutch as the only language of instruction.

Research on multilingual approaches has recently called for the development of such holistic or integrative models that "recognize that language learning and teaching is more than the sum of the elements of that equation seen as isolated units – language, learning and teaching – and should therefore be seen from a more holistic and ecological perspective" (Melo-Pfeifer, 2018, p. 193). Within our setting, there was the need for such a model in which (1) both migrant and regional minority languages of pupils would be acknowledged and used in education, next to the majority languages and (2) that was suitable for different school types (e.g. trilingual, mainstream, newcomer schools). Next, the model had to incorporate different approaches towards multilingual education. This was done by placing five approaches along a continuum that oscillates between the acknowledgement of different languages and their actual use in instruction. By doing so, teachers can choose whether to focus on, for example, language awareness with activities in which languages and dialects in the classroom and the environment are explored, or language comparison in which typologically related and unrelated languages are compared or on conveying content-knowledge through a foreign language using the CLIL approach. Finally, the model addresses attitudes, knowledge and skills of both teachers and pupils (Herzog-Punzenberger et al., 2017) within a multilingual approach. Language awareness, language comparison and receptive multilingualism approaches focus more on attitudes whilst CLIL and immersion focus more on knowledge and skills in the language(s). As the model shows, translanguaging is a feature that appears in each of the five approaches and is mostly manifested in interaction. Translanguaging is thus also an interactional manifestation of transfer processes. For more detailed information about the model see Duarte and Günther-van der Meij (2018b). The present chapter examines how these approaches are actively applied in interaction during the implementation of multilingual teaching activities in TESOL classes. In the following section, we will first provide examples of activities developed for each of the five approaches in the model.

2.1   Classroom Activities Within a Multilingual Approach

For raising *language awareness* of languages in the environment and reflecting on the term language, pupils filled in a language portrait (Busch, 2006). The portrait shows which languages they already know, which they would like to learn and where in their body's language has a place, for example in their heads, heart or hands. The language portrait in Photo 1 is of 9-year-Ruba from Palestine who has been living in the Province of Friesland since a few years with her family. At home the family mainly speaks Arabic, which Ruba has placed mainly in her head, mouth and heart (in red, dark blue and dark green with the labels 'Palestina', 'Afghanistan'

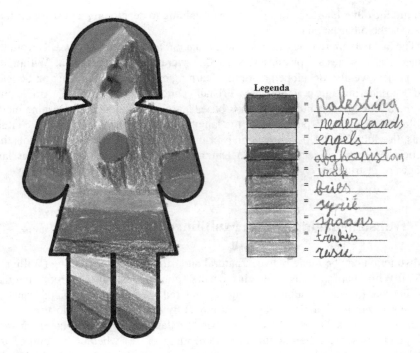

Photo 1   Example of a language portrait

and 'Syrië'). Interestingly, she writes down the names of the countries and not the language (Arabic) spoken. This is different compared to the other languages she places in her portrait. The whole family is learning Dutch which Ruba speaks at school and in the portrait has placed in her head, mouth and hands (in orange with the label 'Nederlands'). Ruba has a lot of Frisian-speaking friends and she places the language in her shoulders and ankles (in light blue with the label 'Fries') and she is interested in English which she places close to her heart and in her throat and knees (in yellow with the label 'Engels'). Furthermore, she names a few other languages she wants to learn, such as Spanish and Turkish.

For promoting *language comparison* several activities were developed focusing on similarities and differences between languages at orthographic, phonetic and/or semantic levels. For example, through using cognate tables which are suitable to use for every subject to summarize core concepts in as many languages as desired. *Receptive multilingualism* (ten Thije, 2010) is a communication strategy in which interlocutors use different languages but are able to understand each other by means of sufficient receptive skills in the language of the other person. In the projects, several cooperative activities were created in which pupils with different language backgrounds each communicated in their own language whilst trying to solve different assignments (e.g. finding a treasure in a maze). The goals of the activities were to receptively recognize words and structures in the other language and to acquire the other language in a playful way, adding to developing a positive attitude towards the other language.

The last two approaches are *CLIL* and *Immersion*. An example of CLIL from the projects is a series of physics lessons that were taught in English. Within the 3M-project we also developed an online learning environment focusing on Science and Engineering in six languages: Frisian, Dutch, English, Polish, Arabic and Tigrinya. The lessons integrate inquiry-based learning with language learning methodologies focusing on pupils using the language in concrete communicative situations. In addition to CLIL, immersion is primarily used by the trilingual schools that participate in the projects, in which Dutch, Frisian and English are used as languages of instruction.

3   Translanguaging Within Multilingual Interaction

A distinction can be made between natural and official translanguaging (Williams, 2012). While natural translanguaging occurs spontaneously in classroom interaction in order to enhance subject or language-related understanding, official translanguaging refers to explicit strategies employed by teachers in order to use several languages in class. Duarte (2018) described translanguaging spaces, in which various practices serve different functions depending on (a) whether the aim of the teachers is to acknowledge or actively use the different languages; (b) whether the teachers are proficient in the languages involved in the translanguaging moment, and (c) the types of languages involved. Instances of official translanguaging (see Table 11.1) with a *symbolic function* are aimed at recognising and valorising migrant languages within mainstream education and require no proficiency in those languages from the teacher. A *scaffolding function* is achieved when temporary but systematic bridges towards other languages are incorporated in everyday teaching attributing equal value to all languages. Teachers require no knowledge of migrant languages to do this, as long as pupils are perceived as the experts for their own family languages. Similar aims can be reached by scaffolding the acknowledgement of various instruction languages present within the teaching model (such as Dutch, Frisian and English). Finally, official translanguaging also fulfils an *epistemological*

Table 11.1 Functions of official translanguaging (Duarte, 2018)

Functions of official translanguaging	Aims (acknowledgement or use)	Proficiency of teacher in the language	Types of languages
Symbolic function	Acknowledgement	No proficiency is needed	Migrant
Scaffolding function	Acknowledgement and use in daily routines	No proficiency is needed (except in instruction languages)	Migrant, regional minority and foreign
Epistemological function	Use for content- and language learning	Teacher (or assistant teacher) is proficient	Migrant, regional minority and foreign

function when the different languages are actively used to enhance both content- and language knowledge. This is suitable for exploring migrant, regional minority and foreign languages in their full potential as learning instruments. To this end, a teacher proficient in those languages is needed to interact with the pupils. The difference between the scaffolding and the epistemological functions is mainly in the degree of proficiency of the teacher in the languages being used. While to fulfil a scaffolding function, the teacher does not need to be proficient in the languages of the pupils (pupils are themselves the experts and use the teacher's scaffolds to make connections between languages), for an epistemological function to be achieved, the joint co-construction of knowledge takes place in the additional language, as both teacher and pupils are proficient. This may be the case with bilingual teaching assistants, for example.

4   Summary and Research Questions

In general, classroom interaction in most European schools is dominated by national languages, with the exception of foreign or, to a lesser extent, regional minority languages used in education (Duarte, 2016; Duarte et al., 2013). In addition, the typical insistence on the national languages as main languages of schooling (Kroon & Spotti, 2011) is based on the idea that immersion in each of the target languages triggers the best outcomes, thus leading to language separation pedagogies. As a result, multilingual interaction in education is (a) still largely under-researched (Araújo e Sá & Melo-Pfeifer, 2018; García, 2018), (b) mostly analysed in the context of language teaching and (c) seldomly analysed from a holistic perspective (Duarte, 2017) in which multilingualism is seen as a pre-condition and an aim, but also as an procedural part of mainstream instruction. Moreover, few studies combine different types of languages of instruction, such as migrant languages, regional minority, foreign and national languages or dialects. Against this backdrop, this chapter focuses on the analysis of translanguaging within multilingual interaction (a) at primary education, (b) for both language- and content-subjects and (c) as a result of an intervention for multilingual education in which teachers co-developed teaching approaches to actively use different types of languages in their classes. It aims at answering the following research questions:

RQ1:   What types of multilingual interaction can be found within different school types in early TESOL classes?
RQ2:   Which functions do the different languages fulfil in interaction for the learning of TESOL?

5 Methodology

In the current study videographic classroom observations were used in order to analyse multilingual interaction following a conversation analysis methodology (Heritage & Clayman, 2010). Recordings were made during the implementation of the holistic model for multilingualism in education used in both the 3M- and the Languages4all-project. We explore here excerpts of classroom interaction of TESOL classes in which a holistic perspective has been applied and focus on the different functions of translanguaging in and for English language learning in TESOL settings.

5.1 Design-Based Research (DBR)

DBR (McKenney & Reeves, 2013) tries to find 'solutions' to 'problems'. This is achieved by designing interventions for the problems which are tested and if necessary adjusted until the problem is solved. DBR acknowledges the complexity of educational contexts by carefully examining the different processes, levels and actors involved in carrying out a jointly engineered educational experiment (Cobb et al., 2003). Previously assembled theoretical knowledge is used together with an iterative cyclic design to improve the original experiment.

In both the 3M- and the Languages4all-project, DBR is used to work with teachers in order to co-develop the multilingual activities. The project schools have each formulated their own questions regarding language education and multilingualism, such as: "How can we integrate other languages in our trilingual concept without speaking those languages?" (trilingual primary school with migrant speakers) and "how can we create a didactic structure for the cross-subject application of the English language / Frisian language through CLIL lessons?" (city school with mainly majority Dutch speakers). The projects work bottom-up: teachers and researchers jointly develop multilingual activities as an "answer" to the issues of the schools. These activities are then implemented, evaluated and adjusted in several rounds until the activity is approved. Regular school visits as well as the organisation of workshops for the teachers add to their theoretical knowledge and experiences which are useful in the development and implementation of the activities. By providing teachers with knowledge, guiding them and giving them agency in the development of the activities the use of translanguaging-based approaches in the classroom is promoted.

5.2 Participants and Setting

Within both projects a large team of teachers and researchers (see Table 11.2) jointly develop the educational experiments, following the holistic model for multilingualism in education.

Table 11.2 Sample of participating schools, teachers, pupils and researchers in the study

Type	N
Schools	20
Teachers	40
Pupils	1000
Researchers	4
Teacher educators	3
Student teachers	4

Table 11.3 Observation sample

School	Teacher	Grade	Subject	Activity	Pupils	Hours recorded
1	T1	Kindergarten	Math	More or less	20	3
2	T2	1/2/3	English	It's wintertime	14	5
3	T3	5	Language	Language is communication	26	6
3	T3	5	Language	Express yourself	26	6

For the current chapter, we focus on the implementation of the projects at a trilingual primary school with migrant speakers, a city school with mainly majority Dutch speakers and a city school with a variety of majority, regional minority and migrant speakers.

5.3 Data Collection and Analysis

For the current study a total of 20 hours of videographic observations were recorded in three project schools (see Table 11.3). The recordings were conducted in classes in which English was the main language of instruction. Pupils aged 4 to 11 were observed in order to provide examples of the different types of interaction possible within TESOL classes.

After careful consideration by the research team and participating teachers, four excerpts were selected for the present chapter according to the following criteria:

(a) they show different types of interaction patterns;
(b) they illustrate the teaching of English in both language and content-subjects;
(c) they include different types of languages (national, foreign, migrant and regional minority).

The excerpts were analysed following a conversation analysis approach (Heritage & Clayman, 2010) which allows a detailed and stepwise description of events in interaction. The four selected excerpts will be discussed in terms of (1) what approaches they use from the holistic model for multilingualism in education and (2) the function of translanguaging.

6 Results

The first excerpt is from the city school with a variety of majority, regional minority and migrant speakers. The teacher teaches math for kindergarten pupils, using three languages: English, Frisian and Dutch.

Excerpt 1 – More or Less

School: city school with a variety of majority, regional minority and migrant speakers
Subject: mathematics
Grades: kindergarten (4–5 years old)
Setting: Teacher discusses what is less and more.

Actor	Utterance (English, **Frisian**, <u>Dutch</u>, *Kurdish*)	*English translation*
T1	Ok kids, we're going to talk English. Because K can talk English so well.	But T can speak Frisian. And we have other languages in the classroom. Such as Kurdish with M. Good afternoon. And C knows Turkish.
	But T kin ek Frysk. En wy hawwe oare talen yn 'e klasse. Sokas it Koerdysk mei M. *Roj baş.* **En C kin Turks.**	
	I want to do a game with <u>pepernoten</u> with you guys, cookies cookies. **Pipernuten**. And my question is, which one is more? And which one is less? You can do it with your head, you can nod. Yes or no. And I will say this one (points to left) or this one (points to right). Ok?	I want to do a game with pepernoten with you guys, cookies cookies. Peppernuts.
	<u>Ik ga aanwijzen en jij doet ja</u> (nods yes) <u>of je doet nee</u> (nods no) <u>als dat meer of minder is. Ja? Is dit minder dan deze?</u> (points at peppernuts)	I'm going to point, and you do yes (nods yes) or you do no (nods no) when it is more of less. Yes? Is this less than this? (points at peppernuts)

In this example, only the teacher speaks. She explains the activity to the pupils, using Dutch, Frisian and English. She starts in English, switching to Frisian to address a pupil that speaks Frisian. She then continues with other languages spoken by the pupils, addressing them in Frisian but also greeting the Kurdish pupil in Kurdish. She continues explaining the activity in English, using the Dutch and Frisian words for 'peppernuts'. Finally, she repeats the explanation in Dutch.

This excerpt shows several multilingual approaches. From the holistic model we see language awareness and CLIL being implemented, using knowledge about and in the languages. Translanguaging has a symbolic function by acknowledging the regional minority and migrant languages in class, while aiming at teaching the English language. It has a scaffolding function by using the other languages as a bridge, for example in explaining the word *peppernuts* and by using both Dutch and English as language of instruction. Finally, it also has an epistemological function as the languages are actively used to enhance both content- and language knowledge.

The second excerpt was observed at the trilingual school with regional minority and migrant speakers. Since this is a small school, grades 1, 2 and 3 are put together in one class. The recording is from an English class in which the theme 'winter' is discussed, using English, Dutch and Frisian.

Excerpt 2 – It's Wintertime

School: trilingual school with regional minority and migrant speakers

Subject: English, theme 'winter'

Grades: 1/2/3 (6–8 years old)

Setting: The theme of the English lesson is winter. T2 starts of by making a word cloud on the whiteboard, using a different colour of pen for each of the languages used: English, Frisian and Dutch.

Actor	Utterance (English, **Frisian** and <u>Dutch</u>)	*English translation*
T2	Well, this morning I want to talk to you about winter. What do you know about winter?	
	<u>We gaan een woordveld maken over winter. Dan mag je mij vertellen wat je weet en het maakt mij niet uit in welke taal. Dus als jij het in het Fries weet, zeg jij het in het Fries. Weet jij het in het Engels, dan zeg je het in het Engels. Weet je het in het Nederlands, zeg je het in het Nederlands.</u>	We are going to make a word field about winter. You may tell me what you know and it doesn't matter in which language. So if you know it in Frisian, you say it in Frisian. If you know it in English, you say it in English. Do you know it in Dutch, you say it in Dutch.
	Winter. What do you know about winter?	
P	<u>Koud.</u>	Cold.
T2	<u>Koud.</u>	Cold.
	Does somebody know what *koud* is in English?	
P	Cold.	
T2	Cold. Very good. It is very cold in the winter. That's right.	
P	<u>Sneeuwpop.</u>	Snowman.
T2	<u>Sneeuwpop.</u>	Snowman.
Pps	**Sniepop.**	Snowman.
T2	Oh, I hear something.	Snowman.
	Sniepop.	
Pps	<u>Sneeuwballen</u>, **snieballen**, snowball.	Snowballs, snowballs
T2	Can you please raise your hand if you want to say something?	Snowball.
	<u>Sneeuwbal.</u>	
P	Snowball!	
T2	Snowball, very good.	

(continued)

P	Ijs.	Ice.
T2	Ijs.	Ice.
T2	(Pupils are talking.) Raise your hand if you want to say something.	
P	Iis.	Ice.
T2	**Dat is iis.**	That is ice.
	Now if you want to say something, please raise your hands.	
P	**In beam.**	A tree.
T2	**In beam, ja in Krystbeam miskien. In beam. Dat doch ik even yn it read. Alle Fryske wurden dogge wy yn it read.**	A tree, yes maybe a Christmas tree. A tree. I'll put that word in red. We mark all Frisian words red.
	Witte jim dit ek yn it Ingelsk, in beam? Witsto dat K?	Do you know this in English, a tree? Do you know it K?
P	Ik weet een ander woord.	I know a different word.
T2	**Oh dat mei ek.**	Oh that is also fine.
P	Snowman.	
T2	Snowman. Very good.	
T2	Who knows this word in English? (points at the word 'beam')	Tree.
	Beam.	
P	*Beem.	Tree.
P	Boom.	Tree.
T2	Boom. In het Nederlands. Goed zo.	Tree. In Dutch. Well done.
T2	(A pupil raises his hand.) C?	
P	Tree.	
T2	Tree. Very good!	
Pps	Oh ja, tree. Van one two three. Tree tree tree.	Oh yes, tree. From one two three. Tree tree tree.

The activity continues with pupils saying words around the theme winter in the three languages.

The teacher starts by using English to explain the activity in this English class. She then switches to Dutch to explain that the pupils are allowed to use Dutch and Frisian as well. The first step of the activity is to make a trilingual word cloud around the winter theme. Although the teacher translanguages to Frisian and Dutch to expand what she herself or a pupil just said, for example by saying "Who knows this word in English? *Beam*", she keeps returning to English as the main language of instruction of the lesson. The pupils also use all three languages.

This excerpt also shows several multilingual approaches. From the holistic model we see language comparison being used to compare the three languages to each other, for example in the word cloud activity. Receptive multilingualism is used as pupils and teacher use different languages but are able to understand each other. Furthermore, both CLIL and immersion are implemented, using knowledge about and in the languages. Translanguaging has two functions in this excerpt. Firstly, it is used as a scaffolding function by using the Frisian and Dutch as a bridge to English and using Dutch, Frisian and English as languages of instruction. For example, in the first utterance the teacher asks: "What do you know about winter?" and then explains in Dutch that they will make a word field about winter: *"We gaan een woordveld maken over winter"* and that it does not matter which language the pupils use: *"Dan mag je mij vertellen wat je weet en het maakt mij niet uit in welke taal."* Secondly, translanguaging is used in an epistemological function as the languages are all actively used to enhance both content- and language knowledge since the topic of the lesson is winter and the language of instruction is English.

The third excerpt is from grade 5 from a mainstream city school with primarily Dutch speakers. The subject is 'language' and the teacher discusses the theme 'communication' using English, Frisian and Dutch.

Excerpt 3 – Language is Communication

School: mainstream city school with Dutch speakers

Subject: language

Grade: 5 (10–11 years old)

Setting: The theme of the English lesson is communication. The class discusses what language is. The teacher uses Dutch, Frisian and English as languages of instruction.

Actor	Utterance (English, **Frisian** and <u>Dutch</u>)	*English translation*
T3	I wanted to talk about language today. (writes down 'language' on smartboard) Language. It has to do with communication. I'm going to talk in English, Dutch and sometimes in Frisian. So let's see how that goes and whether you can understand what I'm saying. And sometimes I will explain in your mother language. Can someone try and translate what I've just said?	Who knows what I've just said? N?
	<u>Wie weet wat ik nu heb gezegd? N?</u>	
T3	(Pupil who raised her hand doesn't know.) Maybe T knows.	
P	<u>Je zei dat eh ik ga eh misschien een beetje in het Engels praten, een beetje in het Nederlands en een beetje in het Fries.</u>	You said that eh I'm maybe going to talk a little bit in English, a little bit in Dutch and a little bit in Frisian.
T3	Ok. So we're going to look at our own language and languages from other countries or from our own province, Friesland. Yes? So, language. Why do we use language?	Why do we use language? Why do we use language? E?
	<u>Waarom gebruiken we taal?</u> **Wêrom brûke wy taal?** E?	
P	<u>Om te praten in andere talen en om met elkaar te communiceren.</u>	To talk in other languages and to communicate with each other.
T3	Ok, to communicate. Communication. Eh, to talk with each other. To understand each other. What does that mean, understand each other, G?	
P	<u>Dat je het verstaat.</u>	That you understand it.

The main language of instruction in this excerpt is English. However, the teacher switches to Dutch and Frisian to explain and expand. For example, by translating to Dutch "Can someone try and translate what I've just said? *Wie weet wat ik nu heb gezegd?*" in his first utterance or repeating himself in Dutch and Frisian in the third utterance: "Why do we use language? *Waarom gebruiken we taal? Wêrom brûke wy taal?*". The pupils answer in Dutch.

If we look at the holistic model for multilingualism in education, this excerpt is an example of the use of receptive multilingualism as the teacher speaks primarily English and the pupils respond in Dutch. It is also an example of immersion in English as it is the language that is mainly used as language of instruction. Translanguaging has a scaffolding function in this excerpt, it is used as a bridge between English on the one hand and Frisian and Dutch on the other hand.

Excerpt 4 stems also from the city school with primarily Dutch speakers. It is in the same lesson as excerpt 3. In this excerpt the class discusses what language can be used for.

Excerpt 4 – Express Yourself

School: mainstream city school with Dutch speakers

Subject: language

Grade: 5 (10–11 years old)

Setting: The theme of the English lesson is communication. The class discusses what language can be used for. The teacher uses Dutch, Frisian and English as languages of instruction.

Actor	Utterance (English, **Frisian**, <u>Dutch</u> and *French*)	*English translation*
T3	Eh, language can be very handy if you want to … (writes 'express yourself' on smartboard) express yourself. <u>Wat zou ik daarmee bedoelen?</u> If you want to express yourself, it can be very interesting to know how. T?	What would I mean with that?
P	Nou eh, ik wou zeggen van eh als je bijvoorbeeld iets hebt gedaan wat niet goed was van je en je wou daarvoor sorry zeggen dan is het wel fijn als je weet hoe je dat moet zeggen.	Well eh, I wanted to say that if for example you did something which wasn't right and you wanted to say sorry for it than it is nice if you know how to say so.
Teacher repeats and expands in Dutch on what the pupil just said. And then adds 'jezelf uiten' (express yourself) on the smartboard.		
T3	Eh, ik zou het ook op kunnen schrijven als jezelf uiten.	Eh, I could also write it down as express yourself.
T3	Uiten is misschien een beetje een lastig woord maar het omschrijft zo dat je leert om te zeggen hoe je je voelt en wat je ervan vindt. **Mar do kinst ek dysels uterje** en dat is in het Fries. Dat je jezelf kunt uiten, dat je kunt duidelijk maken hoe je je voelt.	Express is perhaps a bit of a difficult word but it describes so that you learn to say how you feel and what you think of something. But you kin also express yourself and that is in Frisian. That you can express yourself, that you can make clear how you feel.

(continued)

The class then discusses how language can be expressed: through singing, rapping, mail, etc.		
T3	For language we use words.	We use words. What do we say in Frisian? What do we say in Frisian?
	Wij gebruiken woorden. Wat zeggen we in het Fries? **Wat sizze wy yn it Frysk?**	
T3	(Pupils all talk) **Ien ien.** Ssst. Niet allemaal tegelijk. Vinger even omhoog doen. N?	One one. Ssst. Not all at once. Raise your finger. N?
P	Eh, een **wurd** ofzo?	Eh, a word or something?
T3	**In wurd. Mar at wy, eh, it mearfâld dêrfan is dan wurden.**	A word. But if we, eh, the plural of that is words.
	And lets try and go to French.	
	Weet iemand wat het woord 'woorden' in het Frans betekent?	Does somebody know what the word 'words' is in Frans?
T3	(Pupils all talk) Ssst. Ik zal hem erbij schrijven. *Les mots.* We're going to have a look at words today and we're going to play with language. We're going to look at several languages to express yourself. How can we express ourselves? By singing, writing, talking but also drawing for instance.	Ssst. I'll write him down. The words.
	Je kunt ook iets tekenen. **En eh, ast dudlik meitsje wolst hoe'st dy fielst, dan binne der dus in hiele protte dingen wêr'st dat mei dwaan kinst. En dat gean wy hjoed even besjen.**	You can also draw something. And eh, if you want to make clear how you feel, then there are lots of ways to do this. And that is what we're going to look at today.
The class continues with a multilingual poster with several assignments attached to it.		

The main language of instruction here is still English, but the teachers switches more to Dutch and Frisian to explain and expand, for example by translating and discussing the expression *express yourself* to and in Dutch and Frisian. The pupils still primarily speak Dutch with the exception of naming the Frisian term for *word* (*wurd*).

In terms of the holistic model for multilingualism in education, this excerpt is an example of language comparison comparing English, Dutch, Frisian and also French words. As in excerpt 3, it is also an example of receptive multilingualism in which teacher and pupils speak different languages but are able to understand each other. It is also an example of immersion in the English, Dutch and Frisian languages as they are all used as language of instruction. Translanguaging has a symbolic function, by including French. It also has a scaffolding function, using the languages as languages of instruction but also as a bridge between the languages. Finally, it also has an epistemological function as the languages are actively used to enhance both content knowledge about the function of language as well as knowledge in the language.

The four excerpts show different facets of multilingual approaches to TESOL teaching and learning. Also, all three teachers show a very conscious way of using translanguaging in several functions: symbolic, scaffolding or epistemological. They play with the languages available, intertwining them and using Frisian and Dutch to expand, elaborate and explain and as a lever to and from English. It is however mostly the teachers that use all languages, the pupils are free to choose the language they wish to use, and they primarily use Dutch. It must be noted that, before participating in the projects, these teachers rarely mixed languages in their teaching and almost never included regional minority (with the exception of T2) or migrant languages. For this reason, pupils might not yet be used to using translanguaging in official classroom communication, whereas they do it spontaneously in group work or in one-to-one interaction with the teacher.

7 Discussion and Conclusion

This chapter aimed at discussing examples of the implementation of a holistic multilingual approach towards the TESOL in primary education, with the aim of identifying different functions of official translanguaging within a TESOL setting. The model used was specifically developed for the professional development of teachers in using different languages in official classroom communication. The focus was thus on the teacher's role in orchestrating translanguaging-based interaction within foreign language classes. According to García and Li Wei, 'adopting a translanguaging lens means that there can be no way of educating children inclusively without recognising their diverse language and meaning-making practices as a resource to learn' (2015, p. 227). This could be seen in the discussed excerpts. Teachers consciously used different functions of translanguaging to enhance the content and English language learning of the pupils (RQ1). The described activities and functions of translanguaging in the different abstracts oscillated between the acknowledgement of languages and their full use in education (RQ2). Regarding the implementation of translanguaging-based pedagogies, design-based research offered the necessary support for teachers to progressively operationalize the concept of translanguaging for their own contexts. Bottom-up and tailored approaches owned by the teachers themselves can thus be a way to promote translanguaging-based approaches within multilingual approaches.

This chapter has shown that English alongside other languages is used in TESOL classes but also in other subjects and that the use of the different language(s) can have different functions, enhancing both content- and language knowledge. Although the holistic approach towards multilingual education (Duarte, 2017; Duarte & Günther-van der Meij, 2018b; Melo-Pfeifer, 2018) as adopted in the two research projects (3M and Languages4all) is so far perceived as positive by the project schools, we do identify some shortcomings. The first shortcoming is that pupils primarily speak Dutch in class and, as can be seen from the excerpts, are not encouraged to use their languages. The pupils seem to have a high language threshold to use their languages and should be encouraged to use the(ir) other languages as well. By making them language ambassadors of their own language(s), this threshold could be turned into a stepping stone. The second shortcoming is that the activities are so far mainly focused on oral skills whilst developing literacy skills in several languages have proven to add to developing language knowledge (Sanz, 2000). Since both projects are still in their beginning stages (developmental phase), we aim at focusing more on this in the years to come in which the developed activities and approaches are implemented in new schools.

Nonetheless, in the excerpts showed here, we could identify two relevant trends in the context of early TESOL teaching from a multilingual perspective; (a) the realization that English is not the only language to be favoured in the practices and curricula but that it can easily co-exist with different languages; and, (2) the active promotion of multilingualism in mainstream English education by doing away with the chronological addition of separate languages.

Lastly, we wish to reflect on whether the holistic model for multilingualism in education and the different translanguaging functions are transferable to other contexts than in the Province of Friesland, focusing on TESOL classes. We do believe that this is the case. Firstly, relating and incorporating other languages in the TESOL classroom can enhance content and language learning and this is not only applicable for the Province of Friesland. Even more so, the *societal and education challenge* of catering for needs of migrant, regional minority and majority pupils in relation to their language development and scholastic achievement is a worldwide phenomenon. Secondly, we believe that the holistic approach of the model is transferable to other contexts as it steps away from isolating and separating several multilingual approaches and combines all in a more fluid and more natural learning approach (Cenoz & Gorter, 2013), which is something that can be adapted in other contexts. For this to succeed, adequate teacher professionalisation for TESOL classes is needed, using official translanguaging within different multilingual approaches. We do need more work on the topic, for example by comparing and exchanging ideas and developments between countries and continents to learn what does and does not work. This way we will learn whether translanguaging within the context of TESOL teaching in primary education worldwide is a Tower of Babel – symbolising the confusion of tongues – or can be a Garden of Eden – symbolising the ideal state in which there is mutual intelligibility.

References

Andrade, A. I., Araújo e Sá, M. H., Bartolomeu, I., Martins, F., Melo, S., Santos, L., & Simões, A. R. (2003). Análise e construção da Competência Plurilingue – Alguns percursos didácticos. In A. Neto, J. Nico, C. J. Chouriço, P. Costa, & P. Mendes (Eds.), *Didácticas e metodologias de educação – percursos e desafios* (pp. 489–506). Évora, Portugal: Universidade de Évora, Departamento de Pedagogia e Educação.

Araújo e Sá, M. H., & Melo-Pfeifer, S. (2018). Introduction: Multilingual interaction – Dynamics and achievements. *International Journal of Bilingual Education and Bilingualism, 21*(7), 781–787.

Arthur, J., & Martin, P. (2006). Accomplishing lessons in postcolonial classrooms: Comparative perspectives from Botswana and Brunei Darussalam. *Comparative Education, 42*, 177–202.

Bourne, J. (2013). "I know he can do better than that": Strategies for teaching and learning in successful multi-ethnic schools. In I. Gogolin, I. Lange, U. Michel, & H. H. Reich (Eds.), *Herausforderung Bildungssprache – und wie man sie meistert* (pp. 42–54).

Bührig, K., & Duarte, J. (2014). Zur Rolle lebensweltlicher Mehrsprachigkeit für das Lernen im Fachunterricht – ein Beispiel aus einer Videostudie der Sekundarstufe II. *Gruppendynamik und Organisationsberatung, 44*(3), 245–275.

Busch, B. (2006). Language biographies – approaches to multilingualism in education and linguistic research. In B. Busch, A. Jardine & A. Tjoutuku (Eds.), *Language biographies for multilingual learning* (pp. 5–18).

Canagarajah, S. (2011). Translanguaging in the classroom: Emerging issues for research and pedagogy. *Applied Linguistics Review, 2*, 1–28.

Candelier, M. (Ed.). (2010). *FREPA/CARAP: Framework of reference for pluralistic approaches to languages and cultures*. Strasbourg, France: Council of Europe.

Cenoz, J. (2013). Discussion: Towards an educational perspective in CLIL language policy and pedagogical practice. *International Journal of Bilingual Education and Bilingualism, 16*(3), 389–394.

Cenoz, J. (2017). Translanguaging in school contexts: International perspectives. *Journal of Language, Identity and Education, 16*(4), 193–198.

Cenoz, J., & Gorter, D. (2013). Towards a plurilingual approach in English language teaching: Softening the boundaries between languages. *TESOL Quarterly, 47*(3), 591–599.

Cenoz, J., & Gorter, D. (Eds.). (2015). *Multilingual education. Between language learning and Translanguaging*. Cambridge, UK: Cambridge University Press.

Cobb, P., Confrey, J., diSessa, A., Lehrer, R., & Schauble, L. (2003). Design experiments in educational research. *Educational Researcher, 32*(1), 9–13.

Conteh, J., & Meier, G. (2014). *The multilingual turn in languages education. Opportunities and challenges*. Bristol, UK: Multilingual Matters.

Creese, A., & Blackledge, A. (2010). Translanguaging in the bilingual classroom: A pedagogy for learning and teaching? *The Modern Language Journal, 94*(1), 103–115.

Cummins, J. (1979). Linguistic interdependence and the educational development of bilingual children. *Review of Educational Research, 49*(2), 222–251.

Cummins, J. (2007). Rethinking monolingual instructional strategies in multilingual classrooms. *Canadian Journal of Applied Linguistics/Revue Canadienne de Linguistique Appliquée, 10*(2), 221–240.

Cummins, J. (2008). Teaching for transfer: Challenging the two solitudes assumptions in bilingual education. In N. H. Hornberger (Ed.), *Encyclopedia of language and education* (pp. 1528–1538). New York, NY: Springer.

Duarte, J. (2011). *Bilingual language proficiency. A comparative study*. Münster, Germany: Waxmann Verlag.

Duarte, J. (2016). Translanguaging in mainstream education: A sociocultural approach. *International Journal of Bilingual Education and Bilingualism*, 1–15. https://doi.org/10.1080/13670050.2016.1231774

Duarte, J. (2017). *Project proposal 3M project (Meer Kansen Met Meertaligheid)*. Leeuwarden, The Netherlands: NHL Stenden University of Applied Sciences.

Duarte, J. (2018). Translanguaging in the context of mainstream multilingual education. *International Journal of Multilingualism*. https://doi.org/10.1080/14790718.2018.1512607

Duarte, J., & Gogolin, I. (2013). Linguistic superdiversity in educational institutions. In J. Duarte & I. Gogolin (Eds.), *Linguistic superdiversity in urban areas. Research approaches* (pp. 1–24). Amsterdam, The Netherlands/Philadelphia, PA: John Benjamins Publishing Company.

Duarte, J., Gogolin, I., & Siemon, J. (2013). Sprachliche Interaktion im Unterricht – erste Ergebnisse der LiViS-Videostudie. *OBST – Osnabrücker Beiträge Zur Sprachtheorie, 83*, 79–94.

Duarte, J., & Günther-van der Meij, M. T. (2018a). Drietalige basisscholen in Friesland: een gouden greep in tijden van toenemende diversiteit? In O. Agirdag & E.-R. Kambel (Eds.), *Meertaligheid en onderwijs: Nederlands plus* (pp. 90–102). Amsterdam, The Netherlands: Boom.

Duarte, J., & Günther-van der Meij, M. T. (2018b). A holistic model for multilingualism in education. *EuroAmerican Journal of Applied Linguistics and Languages Special Issue, 5*(2), 24–43.

Duarte, J., & Pereira, D. (2011). Didactical and school organisational approaches in bilingual schools: The cases of Portuguese-creole in Lisbon and Portuguese-German in Hamburg. In B. Hudson & M. Meyer (Eds.), *Beyond fragmentation: Didactics, learning and teaching* (pp. 319–328). Opladen, Germany/Framington Hills, MI: Barbara Budrich.

Flores, N., & Baetens-Beardsmore, H. (2015). Programs and structures in bilingual and multilingual education. In W. Wright, S. Boun, & O. García (Eds.), *Handbook of bilingual and multilingual education* (pp. 205–222). Oxford, UK: Wiley-Blackwell.

Francis, D. J., & Lesaux, N. (2006). Language of instruction. Developing literacy in second-language learners. In D. August & T. Shanahan (Eds.), *National Literacy Panel on language-minority children and youth* (pp. 365–413). Mahwah, NJ: Erlbaum.

García, O. (2009). Education, multilingualism and Translanguaging in the 21st century. In A. Mohanty, M. Panda, R. Phillipson, & T. Skutnabb-Kangas (Eds.), *Multilingual education for social justice: Globalising the local* (pp. 128–145). New Delhi, India: Orient Blackswan.

García, O. (2018). The multiplicities of multilingual interaction. *International Journal of Bilingual Education and Bilingualism, 21*(27), 881–891.

García, O., Johnson, S. I., & Seltzer, K. (2017). *The translanguaging classroom. Leveraging student bilingualism for learning*. Philadelphia, PA: Caslon.

García, O., & Kano, N. (2014). Translanguaging as process and pedagogy: Developing the English writing of Japanese students in the US. In J. Conteh & G. Meier (Eds.), *The multilingual turn in languages education: Opportunities and challenges* (pp. 258–277). Bristol, UK: Multilingual Matters.

García, O., & Wei, L. (2014). *Translanguaging: Language, bilingualism, and education*. New York, NY: Palgrave Macmillan.

García, O., & Wei, L. (2015). Translanguaging, bilingualism, and bilingual education. In W. Wright, S. Boun, & O. García (Eds.), *The handbook of bilingual and multilingual education* (pp. 223–240). Malden, MA: Wiley-Blackwell.

Hélot, C., & Young, A. (2006). Imagining multilingual education in France: A language and cultural awareness project at primary level. In O. García, T. Skutnabb-Kangas, & M. Torres-Guzmán (Eds.), *Imagining multilingual schools. Languages in education and glocalization* (pp. 69–90). Clevedon, UK/Buffalo, NY/Toronto, Canada: Multilingual Matters.

Heritage, J., & Clayman, S. (2010). *Talk in action: Interactions, identities and institutions*. Boston, MA: Wiley-Blackwell.

Herzog-Punzenberger, B., Le Pichon-Vorstman, E., & Siarova, H. (2017). *Multilingual education in the light of diversity: Lessons learned*. Luxembourg, Luxembourg: Publications Office of the European Union.

Kroon, S., & Spotti, M. (2011). Immigrant minority language teaching policies and practices in the Netherlands: Policing dangerous multilingualism. In S. Domovic, M. Krüger-Potratz, & A. Petravic (Eds.), *Europsko obrazovanje: Koncepti i perspektive iz pet zemalja* (pp. 80–95). Zagreb, Croatia: Kolska Knjiga.

Krumm, H. J., & Reich, H. H. (2013). *Multilingualism curriculum: Perceiving and managing linguistic diversity in education*. Münster, Germany: Waxmann Verlag.

Lin, A., & Martin, P. (Eds.). (2005). *Decolonisation, globalisation: Language-in-education policy and practice*. Clevedon, UK: Multilingual Matters.

May, S. (Ed.). (2014). *The multilingual turn: Implications for SLA, TESOL and bilingual education*. New York, NY/London, UK: Routledge.

McKenney, S., & Reeves, T. (2013). Systematic review of design-based research Progress: Is a little knowledge a dangerous thing? *Educational Researcher, 42*(2), 97–100.

Melo-Pfeifer, S. (2018). The multilingual turn in foreign language education. In A. Bonnet & P. Siemund (Eds.), *Foreign language education in multilingual classrooms* (pp. 192–2013). Amsterdam, The Netherlands/Philadelphia, PA: John Benjamins Publishing Company.

Moodley, V. (2007). Code-switching in the multilingual English first language classroom. *International Journal of Bilingual Education and Bilingualism, 10*, 707–722.

Nikolov, M., & Mihaljević Djigunović, J. (2011). All shades of every color: An overview of early teaching and learning of foreign languages. *Annual Review of Applied Linguistics*, (31), 95–119.

Nortier, J. (2009). *Nederland, meertalenland: feiten, perspectieven en meningen over meertaligheid*. Amsterdam, The Netherlands: Amsterdam University Press.

Oliveira, A. L., & Ançã, M. H. (2009). 'I speak five languages': Fostering plurilingual competence through language awareness. *Language Awareness, 18*(3–4), 403–421.

Provinsje Fryslân. (2015). *De Fryske Taalatlas*. Ljouwert, The Netherlands: Provinsje Fryslân.

Rolff, H.-G. (2006). *Qualität in multikulturellen Schulen (QUIMS). Schulentwicklung mit System und im System. Eine evaluative Würdigung des QUIMS-Projektes*. Retrieved from http://www.volksschulamt.zh.ch.

Sanz, C. (2000). Bilingual education enhances third language acquisition: Evidence from Catalonia. *Applied PsychoLinguistics, 21*, 23–44.

Slembrouck, S., Van Avermaet, P., & Van Gorp, K. (2018). Strategies of multilingualism in education for minority children. In P. Van Avermaet, S. Slembrouck, K. Van Gorp, S. Sierens, & K. Maryns (Eds.), *The multilingual edge of education* (pp. 9–39). London, UK: Palgrave Macmillan.

ten Thije, J. D. (2010). Lingua receptiva als bouwsteen voor de transnationale neerlandistiek. *Internationale Neerlandistiek: tijdschrift van de internationale vereniging voor Neerlandistiek, 4*, 5–10.

Unsworth, S., Persson, L., Prins, T., & de Bot, K. (2015). An investigation of factors affecting early foreign language learning in the Netherlands. *Applied Linguistics, 36*(5), 527–548.

van het Onderwijs, I. (2010). Tussen wens en werkelijkheid. In *De kwaliteit van het vak Fries in het basisonderwijs en het voortgezet onderwijs in Fryslân*. Utrecht, The Netherlands: Inspectie van het Onderwijs.

Wildemann, A. (2013). Sprache(n) thematisieren – Sprachbewusstheit fördern. In S. Galiberger & F. Wietzke (Eds.), *Handbuch Kompetenzorientierter Deutschunterricht* (pp. 321–338). Berlin, Germany: Beltz Verlag.

Williams, C. (2012). *The national immersion scheme guidance for teachers on subject language threshold: Accelerating the process of reaching the threshold*. Bangor, UK: The Welsh Language Board.

Young, A., & Hélot, C. (2003). Language awareness and/or language learning in French primary schools today. *Language Awareness, 12*(0), 1–13.

Chapter 12
"Colibrí" 'Hummingbird' as Translanguaging Metaphor

Brian Seilstad and Somin Kim

Abstract This chapter explores translanguaging as theory and practice by first introducing superdiversity as a phenomenon that leads to the creation of adolescent newcomer programs and then discussing how translanguaging intersects with these spaces in terms of sociolinguistic and pedagogical exploration. Relevant theoretical and empirical studies engage translanguaging as an important framework for supporting bi/multilingual adolescents. Drawing on ethnographic and classroom discourse analysis, the chapter then analyzes a key moment from a "Bilingual Biomes" project in a 10th grade Biology classroom at a Central Ohio adolescent newcomer program in which a "*colibrí*" 'hummingbird' becomes a salient metaphor for translanguaging as theory and practice. Specifically, this metaphor explores translanguaging's potential to destabilize national/named borders between languages, create opportunities for shared understanding, and evoke moments of unexpected joy.

Keywords Adolescents · Newcomers · Language programs · Translanguaging · Superdiversity

1 Introduction

The United States and Central Ohio, this article's geographic focus, has been experiencing a demographic shift from relatively homogenous to "superdiverse" (Vertovec, 2007). A key element of superdiversity is that it is not simply "more diversity" but rather a specific type of shift summarized by Blommaert's (2013)

B. Seilstad (✉)
American College Casablanca, Casablanca, Morocco
e-mail: bseilstad@aac.ac.ma

S. Kim
Department of Teaching and Learning, College of Education and Human Ecology,
The Ohio State University, Columbus, OH, USA
e-mail: kim.6110@osu.edu

© Springer Nature Switzerland AG 2020
Z. Tian et al. (eds.), *Envisioning TESOL through a Translanguaging Lens*,
Educational Linguistics 45, https://doi.org/10.1007/978-3-030-47031-9_12

"mobility, complexity, and unpredictability" or Meissner and Vertovec's (2015) "spread, speed, and scale" indexing challenges to "governmentality" (Budach & Saint-Georges, 2017, pp. 66–69) and public services, including education (e.g., King & Carson, 2016). In the U.S., superdiverse changes have occurred for manifold reasons, including shifts in national migration policy and refugee resettlement patterns. These manifest in various data; for example, from 1980 to 2013 the nationalities represented by refugees increased from 11 to 64 (Capps et al., 2015, p. 1) in addition to a 70% increase in the number of immigrants arriving in 1995–2014 compared to a 20% increase in the U.S-born population. Moreover, the National Academies of Sciences, Engineering, and Medicine (2017) note, "Geographic settlement patterns have changed since the 1990s, with immigrants increasingly moving to states and communities that historically had few immigrants" (p. 3). The Midwest has particularly felt these changes across multiple domains (Longworth, 2009), including the education of adolescent newcomers, this article's focal topic.

Returning to governmentality and the educational system, debates about the best way for schools to receive and educate migrant students have existed for centuries, waxing and waning during periods of tolerance or opposition (Gándara & Hopkins, 2010). Although academic research has consistently shown that bilingual approaches have the best outcomes (Baker, 2011; Collier & Thomas, 2004; Crawford, 2004; García, 2008; Umansky & Reardon, 2014), the reality is that these programs or related supports are depressingly rare in the U.S. (Lewis & Gray, 2016). Moreover, the evidence supporting bilingual approaches is most robust when considering young learners (Valentino & Reardon, 2015), leaving a certain lack in clarity for adolescents (Faltis & Wolfe, 1999) who must do "double the work" of acquiring the language and content necessary for mainstream schooling (Short & Fitzsimmons, 2007). This may be one explanatory factor in the data demonstrating that many adolescent newcomers struggle in schools and dropout at a higher rate than their native-born peers (Fry, 2005; Suárez-Orozco et al., 2010).

Although American schools have been wrestling with the question of how to support immigrant students in schools for centuries (Hood, 2003), a relatively new educational model, adolescent newcomer programs, has emerged to address the challenges of superdiversity and support equity for this population. These programs started in the U.S. as early as the 1970s, gained prominence in the 80s and 90s, and have been defined as "specialized academic environments that serve newly arrived, immigrant English language learners for a limited period of time" (Constantino & Lavadenz, 1993; Short & Boyson, 2012, p. vii). The focus on these programs is largely English language learning although a small percentage of programs are integrated with bilingual programs (Center for Applied Linguistics, 2014). Moreover, programs may have additional criteria for identifying a student as a "newcomer" such as time in the U.S., home language or English literacy, income, and documentation of prior educational experiences (Custodio, 2010; Custodio & O'Loughlin, 2017; Faltis & Coulter, 2007, pp. 51–61; Short & Boyson, 2012, pp. 11–13).

Thus, adolescent newcomer programs arise from superdiverse conditions and, despite the dominant focus on English language acquisition rather than bilingual education (Center for Applied Linguistics, 2014; Short & Boyson, 2012), are potent sites to explore both the phenomenon and the potential of translanguaging in language and content learning (Bajaj & Bartlett, 2017; Bartlett, 2007; García & Sylvan, 2011; Sylvan, 2013). On the one hand, researchers active in these environments have the opportunity to observe the translanguaging processes and practices that educators and students deploy. On the other hand, teachers, especially those sensitive and receptive to translanguaging have an opportunity to learn about it and its contribution to, among many, the fields of sociolinguistics and education. Specifically, many teachers in multilingual spaces with a central target language are aware of terms such as code-switching or code-mixing but may have not wrestled with the monolingual assumptions underlying these terms (García, 2008). Translanguaging explicitly addresses and destabilizes these assumptions by questioning the national/named basis for languages and, by so doing, is a political act aimed at expanding educational and societal possibilities for people, particularly linguistically minoritized students (Flores, 2014).

This chapter explores a 10th grade Biology class in an urban Ohio district's adolescent newcomer program serving students from more than 100 national/named languages with five—Spanish, Somali, Arabic, Nepali, and French—being the most common due to migration from Mexico/Central America and refugee resettlement of Iraqis, Syrians, Nepali-speaking Bhutanese, Congolese, and other Francophone groups. Thus, the program was English-centric in that English is the target language and instructional medium, but it is not English-only due to the multilingual students and teachers and realities of everyday discourse (Pacheco, 2016).

This chapter's focal teacher is a multilingual (Spanish/Somali/English) white American male with an M.Ed in Science and a Teaching English to Speakers of Other Languages (TESOL) endorsement who, at the time of the research, had previously served in Peace Corps in Honduras, taught in the newcomer program for 4 years, worked with local refugee-support organizations, and had been expanding his TESOL knowledge by taking a continuing education course about bilingual education at the Ohio State University. This class, drawing in educators from the English as a Second Language (ESL) and bilingual programs in the school district, explored the history of bilingual education, relevant pedagogies, and, critical to this chapter, key aspects of translanguaging as an emerging framework for supporting language learners. As a result of this class and dialogue with the researchers, this teacher developed not only his theoretical understanding of translanguaging but also pedagogies to draw on students' "full linguistic repertoire" and decenter English as they acquired key science knowledge, prepared for the mainstream environment, and took standardized assessments (García, Johnson, & Seltzer, 2017; Otheguy, García, & Reid, 2015, 2018).

Another key actor in newcomer programs and bi/multilingual schools relevant for this chapter are bilingual instructional assistants/paraprofessionals (Connally & Dancy, 2016; Dalla, MoulikGupta, Lopez, & Jones, 2006; Ernst-Slavit & Wenger, 2006). In the history of the program, the development of this cadre was essential to ensuring that most, if not all, students have access to staff or teachers who speak their languages. Although this type of support is still depressingly rare in the U.S. (Lewis & Gray, 2016), it is a strong feature of the focal program in that most classes have a bilingual assistant present. The focal classroom had a bilingual

Serbian-English assistant with a master's degree in science from a U.S. university. Thus, she was a strong fit to support the classroom's science and language learners; however, one salient issue is that this assistant often said in interviews that her specific linguistic repertoire with Serbian was of little use in the classroom because very few, if any, students came from that region.

This chapter focuses on this context and classroom and proposes a new metaphor for translanguaging, the "*colibrí*" 'hummingbird.' Metaphors are helpful for consolidating and demonstrating important concepts. For example, García and colleagues have proposed at least two relevant metaphors for translanguaging as an all-terrain vehicle (2008) or a river with the *translanguaging corriente* (García et al., 2017). This chapter describes the classroom context and an activity, the Bilingual Biomes, a research and presentation project that the teacher developed and deployed over several weeks as the culminating activity of the school year (Seilstad, Braun, Kim, & Choi, 2019). This dovetailed with and accentuated an array of practices described below that the teacher used to support the students' English learning by engaging their linguistic repertoires. The "*colibrí*" 'hummingbird' metaphor arose from a specific moment that occurred during the presentations of the Bilingual Biomes that exemplifies translanguaging as both theory and practice, particularly for TESOL-oriented spaces.

2   Theoretical Framework: Translanguaging's Unexpected Contexts and Moments

In this context, this chapter's engagement with translanguaging is connected to "empirical efforts to document and better understand the languaging practices of bilinguals in schools and communities" as well as "the ways that teachers leverage emergent bilingual students' complex discursive practices to develop new understandings, expand students' linguistic repertoires and metalinguistic awareness, and incorporate and build on student knowledge and expertise" (Gort, 2015, pp. 2–3). Essential here, particularly in the TESOL context, are the structural and ideological barriers students and teachers face when trying to engage home or community language practices in spaces dedicated to English-language learning (Alim, Rickford, & Ball, 2016; Flores & Schissel, 2014; Rosa & Flores, 2017).

To elaborate further, from a sociolinguistic perspective, if "there is no such thing as Language, only continual languaging, an activity of human beings in the world" (Becker, 1991, p. 34) or, as Blommaert (2016) notes, "capital" L- language such as "English" is "*real* as an ideological artifact because people believe it exists" whereas regular l- language is "language as observable social action—the specific forms people effectively use in communicative practice" (p. 6, italics in original), then translanguaging is perhaps a special extension used to describe what people, particularly bi/multilingual people, do as part of "doing being bilingual" (Gort, 2015). Thus, the language(s) people know and use are not separate cognitively but rather part of a unitary system even if the sociopolitical reality is that these languages may be divided and described variably in terms of time, space, intention, or power/politics (e.g. first/second, home/school, target, or minority/national) (MacSwan, 2017; Otheguy et al., 2015, 2018).

In terms of schools and learning, translanguaging pushes educators to address the pedagogical implications that emerge when students' full linguistic repertoires are recognized and actively engaged in learning—from the overall school environment to the individual classroom. This can be challenging for teachers who exist in policy and pedagogical contexts where the target language is powerful and privileged in manifold ways—including but not limited to the allocation of local resources, the training of teachers, and the ideologies associated with the language. English, at the current moment and in the U.S. particularly, creates an intense field in this regard. However, both superdiversity and translanguaging have emerged and exist to, in part, resist these hegemonic demographic or linguistic forces by offering theoretical vocabulary that is consciously positive and accessible with the ultimate goal of creating more political and pedagogical opportunities to support minoritized peoples. Figure 12.1 demonstrates this relationship.

Thus, translanguaging and engaging languages other than English and students' full linguistic repertories can seem transgressive. However, a key goal of translanguaging pedagogy is to diffuse these tensions and help teachers and learners work together with and across languages more productively and equitably even when the focus is on learning specific target languages considered essential for academic or

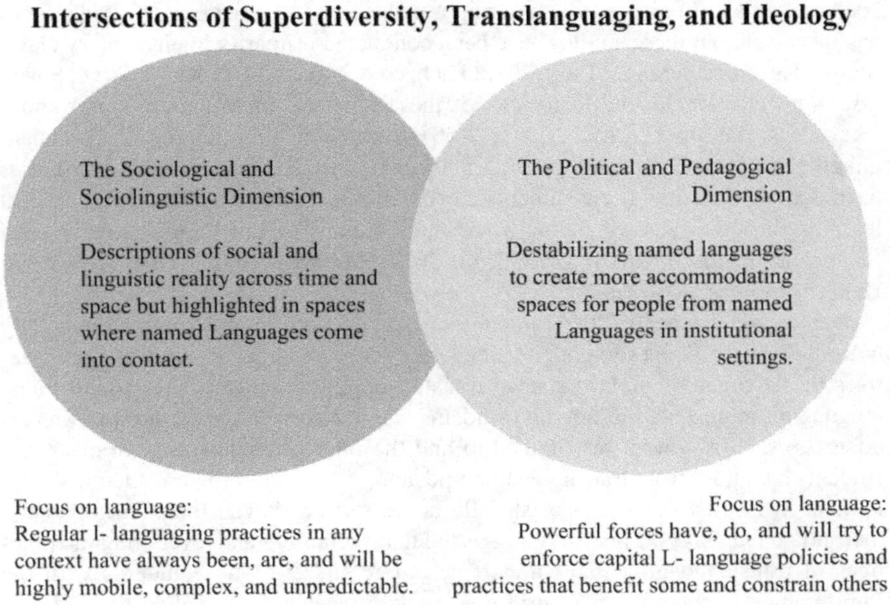

Intersections of Superdiversity, Translanguaging, and Ideology

The Sociological and Sociolinguistic Dimension

Descriptions of social and linguistic reality across time and space but highlighted in spaces where named Languages come into contact.

The Political and Pedagogical Dimension

Destabilizing named languages to create more accommodating spaces for people from named Languages in institutional settings.

Focus on language:
Regular l- languaging practices in any context have always been, are, and will be highly mobile, complex, and unpredictable.

Focus on language:
Powerful forces have, do, and will try to enforce capital L- language policies and practices that benefit some and constrain others

Fig. 12.1 Interplay between superdiversity and translanguaging

professional success in the local society (Daniel, Jiménez, Pray, & Pacheco, 2017; García et al., 2017). This indexes not only the political struggle but is aspirational, even metaphysical/ontological, envisioning times/spaces when such debates may be irrelevant:

> "Trans" suggests a movement *beyond* borders, a transcendence or transformation of things that were being held apart, or artificially constructed as separate and distinct. This is not the same as hybridity, which presumes an even and presumably equitable blend of different forms. Nor is it the erasure of difference. Rather, it is about questioning the ontologies that hold things apart. It involves the resolution of dialectic tensions and the emergence of something new—something that we perhaps cannot even imagine. (Orellana, 2016, p. 91, italics in original)

This chapter is founded on these three pillars—that translanguaging is the natural state for bi/multilingual people, schools and educators should make all efforts to engage with translanguaging and peoples' full linguistic repertoires, and, if they do, something new and unexpected can emerge.

3 Literature Review: Translanguaging Pedagogy and Practice

As discussed above, this research project examined adolescents in the newcomer program using multiple languages strategically, or translanguaging, to make meaning, learn additional language(s), acquire content-based knowledge, and accomplish academic goals. Research documenting translanguaging practices and pedagogies has increased, but these studies have been conducted primarily in elementary classrooms (e.g., Hornberger & Link, 2012; Pacheco & Miller, 2016; Rowe, 2018; Sayer, 2013) or "provide general overviews of these practices in secondary classrooms" (Stewart & Hansen-Thomas, 2016, p. 450). Among existing literature on translanguaging practices and pedagogies, particularly at the secondary level, most studies have documented how these students engage productively in language and content learning through translanguaging by drawing upon their full linguistic repertoires (Daniel & Pacheco, 2016; Li & Luo, 2017; Martin-Beltrán, 2014; Stewart & Hansen-Thomas, 2016).

Daniel and Pacheco (2016) documented how multilingual teens strategically used multiple languages to understand class content and how the students' perspectives on language ideologies shaped translanguaging practices. They found translanguaging represented in how the students adapted their language use to different contexts, such as whom they talked to and the interactional setting. In class, the students benefited from translanguaging pedagogy to support their academic development in English, which also partially addressed or allayed their fear of losing their home languages. This study suggested that promoting and leveraging the practices of translanguaging may support academic success when students with the same home language are placed in classes with teachers who value the students' translanguaging practices and "encourage the development of the full range of students' linguistic resources" (p. 661).

In line with Daniel and Pacheco's (2016) suggestion, Stewart and Hansen-Thomas (2016) asserted that multilingual adolescents' learning opportunities were manifested "when a space for translanguaging was sanctioned" (p. 450). They found that not only the space but also the use of literature in both English and the student's home language allowed a student to make individual linguistic decisions. While engaging in writing assignments, one student chose Spanish words to enhance her English poem, which demonstrated her criticality and creativity that, according to García and Wei (2014) and Wei (2011), are available for multilingual students through translanguaging. This study also showed that translanguaging practices "facilitate students' use of higher-order thinking to make decisions and evaluate all linguistic options available to them in their writing" (Stewart & Hansen-Thomas, 2016, p. 467).

Enhancing linguistic decisions in writing through translanguaging was also observed in Martín-Beltrán's (2014) study, in which she examined how adolescents' translanguaging practices mediated language learning opportunities. While engaging in collaborative literacy activities, the students drew upon their linguistic knowledge to discuss meanings of the given text as they co-constructed knowledge. These practices enhanced their understanding of the text and broadened their linguistic repertoires as they chose words more appropriate in academic writing and defended their choices. Martín-Beltrán's (2014) findings suggest that translanguaging draws on students' full linguistic repertoires while engaged in academic tasks and creates learning contexts in which multilingual adolescents can be "recognized as legitimate participants" (p. 226).

Finally, and relevant to this chapter, to create a space for translanguaging and implement its pedagogies in classes, teachers do not necessarily need to know all the languages of their students. Li and Luo (2017) proposed three pedagogical methods that educators can use in their classrooms. First, teachers can place students into homogeneous groups and provide them with collaborative activities that involve high-order thinking, and the students can be encouraged to draw on the practices of translanguaging to accomplish the activities. Second, teachers can incorporate appropriate multilingual resources such as books, images, or videos that encourage students to engage in translanguaging. Third, teachers can implement translanguaging pedagogies such as providing important materials in different languages or asking students to demonstrate their content knowledge through translanguaging (pp. 156–157).

Taken together, these studies represent what García et al.'s book *The Translanguaging Classroom* (2017) argues: Teachers must have a stance of affirming and supporting home language and translanguaging in the classroom, design appropriate and engaging activities, and shift instruction as necessary. In this way, the practices of translanguaging enable multilingual adolescents to draw on and even expand their linguistic repertoires, create learning opportunities for themselves, achieve academic success, and strengthen their criticality and creativity. These studies suggest that to maximize the benefits of translanguaging practices, schools and teachers should create environments where the practices are welcomed and allowed. To take into account the suggestions and the need for research at the secondary level (Martin-Beltrán, 2014; Stewart & Hansen-Thomas, 2016), this chapter examines how the teacher implemented pedagogies in his instruction in a way "that leverages students' transnational lived experiences, their culturally embedded knowledge and skills, and their full linguistic repertoires" (Stewart & Hansen-Thomas, 2016, p. 467).

4 Methodology

This study is theoretically and methodologically framed by the ethnographic and discourse analytic approaches to understanding the complex daily life of a particular classroom (Blommaert & Jie, 2010; Bloome, Carter, Christian, Otto, & Shuart-Faris, 2005; Spindler & Spindler, 1987). The data analyzed here are part of a corpus collected at the school district's adolescent newcomer program during the 2015–2016 academic year. This program has existed for nearly 20 years and seeks to address the superdiverse shifts happening in Central Ohio. The program has also evolved considerably during this period, from relatively small Welcome Centers in the early 2000s, to a full middle/high school in the late 2000s/early 2010s, and now as a 1–2 year transitional program with up to 800 students per year, forming the hub of the district's ESL program that serves around 8000 students, roughly 15% of the district's total.

Teachers in this program all must have content area certification and TESOL endorsements to ensure that students receive expert language and content instruction. The focal 10th grade Biology class is part of the second year course designed to both provide regular academic credit to the adolescent newcomers and also prepare them to transition to more "mainstream" schools where they, it is hoped, will succeed and graduate. Thus, in terms of English language development, the students, aged 15–21 collectively, were generally able to communicate socially and engage with appropriately moderated academic tasks; however, the students and instructors used home languages often to help students make meaning of the English-language material.

The data corpus for this chapter was gathered by the two researchers, the lead author and co-author, as well as the teacher. The data were collected over 8 months and include 20 classroom observations with fieldnotes, simultaneous audio-video recordings of the whole classroom, interviews with the teacher, students, and instructional assistant, and artifact collection of quizzes, handouts, and student work. The focal data are drawn from a year-end "Bilingual Biomes" project that the teacher developed to move to a translanguaging pedagogy challenging the monolingual habitus of the school and, by extension, TESOL (Auerbach, 1993; Cummins, 2007, 2009; Seilstad et al., 2019).

This move by the teacher was also commensurate with the broader aim of the research, which was to work with a teacher recognized in the school and community for his efforts to support refugee and other migrant students, particularly in his daily classroom pedagogy of engaging the students' linguistic repertoires. Thus, during the course of our observations, the teacher consistently deployed a number of strategies such as:

- Speaking to students in their home languages when addressing the whole class, small groups, or individuals, drawing on his Spanish/Somali proficiency in addition to linguistic features he knew in other home languages.
- Encouraging students of similar backgrounds to make meaning together through their home languages.
- Using Google Translate to provide target vocabulary in the home languages.
- Inviting students to explain an activity to each other, either in small groups or from the front of the room, in their home languages.
- Providing home language learning materials whenever possible. For example, referring students to New York University's Metropolitan Center for Research on Equity and the Transformation of Schools' bilingual glossaries (NYU Steinhardt, 2018).
- Showing instructional videos in the home languages or with home language subtitles whenever possible. For example, presenting BrainPOP videos in both English and BrainPOP Español or Français, in addition to providing the written materials from those websites. In addition, using YouTube's automatic translate feature to subtitle English language videos in the home language.
- Informing students of their right to take bilingual or translated versions of standardized tests and actively preparing students for those versions.
- Inviting former students to come speak to the class about educational options beyond the newcomer program; these speeches were often delivered bilingually or in the home languages at the teacher's suggestion.

Beyond these efforts to engage and support the linguistic repertoires of the students, the teacher also made more subtle moves such as wearing clothes relevant to the students' home cultures or playing music suggested by the students during warm-ups or group work. Thus, although García et al.'s book *The Translanguaging Classroom* (2017) had not been published at the time of the research, the teacher demonstrates the principles of translanguaging pedagogy's stance, design, and shifts. The students, in turn, drew on their linguistic repertoires throughout the class to make social and academic connections and, in interviews, mentioned that the teacher's actions helped them learn English language and science content and subtly validated their previous knowledge and home languacultures.

However, during the course of the semester, the teacher and research team reflected on the phenomenon that despite these generally supportive practices, home language use remained hierarchically positioned as something that students could do in their seats with each other or in short talks with the teacher but not something that came to the front of the class or was a pedagogical goal per se. Thus, as a result of these discussions and in parallel to the knowledge the teacher was gaining about bilingual education and translanguaging in his Ohio State University course, he decided to modify his previous year's culminating activity from a monolingual focus to a bilingual. Specifically, previous students had ended the year with a unit on biomes, and the teacher would place the students in heterogeneous language groups and ask them to choose a global biome, research it, and present their findings in English to the class. This final project took approximately 2 weeks and was the most significant group activity of the academic year. Although the teacher generally found that the students completed this activity well, he was troubled by the English-centric nature of the task in addition to the fact that the students were forced to choose a biome that they may be unfamiliar with.

Thus, to adapt this activity to a more bilingual and languaculturally-affirming approach, the teacher decided to place the students into linguistically homogeneous groups and ask them to research a biome from their home countries. To achieve this with the focal classroom, the teacher placed students in four groups intentionally by home language, with Spanish, Somali, and Nepali the dominant languages in the class. However, due to the demographics of the class, only the Spanish and Nepali groups were composed of solely speakers of these languages. Thus, one Somali group had a Zomi/Burmese speaker, and another had a Wolof/Fulani-speaker from Senegal and a French/Kirundi/Swahili-speaker from Burundi. In addition, some of the speakers, particularly those from Somalia had a linguistic repertoire that included Arabic and Swahili due to their religious and migration backgrounds. Moreover, students across the groups varied in their home language literacy and prior schooling. For example, in the Nepali group, there were three students who were literate in Nepali script and two who were not; despite the fact that they communicated in Nepali using Latin characters on social media, the relative unfamiliarity with Nepali scripts was a challenge. In addition, some groups had students who had not received formal education prior to arriving in the U.S. whereas others had parallel or even advanced educations. For example, one Somali female had been raised on a farm in Northern Somalia and never attended school before coming to the newcomer program whereas a French/Kirundi/Swahili speaker had already been already pursuing a B.A. in Kenya before resettlement with his family to the U.S. in 2015. Regardless, both students were placed in the same collaborative group, illustrating some of the pedagogical challenges to translanguaging in superdiverse contexts. However, this need not be seen through a deficit lens; indeed, the Somali woman was recognized by the other Somali speakers who had lived in refugee camps in Kenya as having deeper knowledge of Somali due to her longer residency in Somalia.

The goal of the activity was for the students to (1) choose a biome representative of their home country and (2) prepare a presentation about the biome in the students' home language using Google Slides. The presentation required the students to identify the biome's location with a map, the temperature range and annual precipitation, common producers, primary/secondary consumers, and three interesting additional facts. This task was easier with the homogeneous Spanish and Nepali groups, but the mixed Somali-Zomi/Burmese and Somali-Wolof/Fulani-French/Kirundi/Swahili groups had to negotiate and come to somewhat uncomfortable compromises about the choice of the biome and how to organize the Google Slides and present in their home languages and English in a coherent way. Despite these challenges, this activity not only engaged the students' home languages and supported a translanguaging pedagogy but indexed multimodality and the affordances that digital and online tools can bring to English-learning or bilingual education (Choi & Yi, 2016). During the presentation itself, the students would first speak in their home language(s) and then a designated team member would interpret sequentially into English. Preparation for the presentations unfolded over several weeks, with instruction about the science of biomes per se occurring in the first 2 weeks of May. Then, on May 17–18, 2016, the teacher reorganized the students into the aforementioned groups and introduced the activity. However, the teacher was forced to introduce the project, in shorter forms, on the 18th and 19th because many students were absent on the 17th. Indeed, absenteeism is a chronic issue in the program and, more generally, with adolescent newcomers who frequently have other demands or concerns, including supporting their families, work, or dealing with the U.S. justice system (Allard, 2015; Fry, 2005; Short & Boyson, 2012; Suárez-Orozco et al., 2010). Despite this challenge, the teacher conveyed the activity structure and requirements during this period and addressed student concerns. Initially, some students were either confused or resisted, asking questions such as "What other language?" or simply asking the teacher "Why?" These statements challenged the assignment's validity in their English-centric context and raised questions about the students' ability to perform the task given some perceived weaknesses with literacy or academic abilities in their home languages in addition to the fact that their schooling in the U.S. had been highly English-centric. Thus, the teacher had to rationalize the activity to the students, explaining that the goal was to use both English and the home language to learn the science content. When these issues were addressed, the students worked in their groups during the five school days between May 19–25 and presented on May 26–27, 2016.

5   Findings and Discussion

The findings and subsequent discussion will focus on a relatively small section of classroom talk that emerged during the presentation of the Spanish-speaking group. However, this is not meant to elide the complexities and complications in each group's preparation processes. Indeed, in terms of learning and translanguaging, this was where the majority of the activity occurred that illustrated the engagement with the students' linguistic repertoires and some of the challenges of superdiversity. These included a variety of issues such as students debating what biome to select, discussing appropriate terms for flora and fauna in that region, finding home language support online, working with Google Slides, and writing in home languages using scripts or standardized spellings that students were unpracticed in using despite having strong oral proficiency. In many cases, these struggles (or lack thereof) indexed the students' prior education or home language literacy. In general, challenges with these issues were most prevalent for the Nepali, Zomi, Somali, and Wolof/Fulani speakers whose home language education had been adversely impacted by migration to countries where their home language was not dominant, long-term education in UNHCR refugee camps that often use English as a medium of instruction, or personal family circumstances that prevented the student's access to education before coming to the U.S. In contrast, the Spanish-speaking group, comprised of one young man, Manuel[1] who took the role of group interpreter, and two other young women, was able to work on the task relatively smoothly, drawing on their own prior educations, the available resources on the internet, and their own experiences working in collaborative groups. Thus, this group's presentation was one of the most polished, and they presented last among all groups.

This section, rather than focusing on the presentation process, analyzes an aspect of the final presentations themselves and a moment that illustrates the theoretical concerns related to translanguaging above. After each presentation, the class would be invited to ask questions to the group, offering therefore some experience with question and answer formats. If students did not ask questions initially, the teacher or bilingual assistant would typically engage the presenters. Thus, prior to the focal section of talk below, the teacher had asked the students a question in Spanish, further demonstrating his commitment to the bilingual approach. Then, before the group concluded, the bilingual assistant engaged the presenters with some general comments and the specific one here in Table 12.1.

Prior to this section, the bilingual assistant had briefly commented on the presentation slides themselves but then, in lines 1–3, quickly moved to comment on the students' translation of *"colibrí"* 'hummingbird.' Although she seemed to criticize in lines 7–14 the groups' not using "hummingbird," in point of fact, Manuel had said "hummingbird" during the presentation but his pronunciation revealed some hesitation with the term so that the bilingual assistant perhaps did not hear it clearly. Regardless, the focal moment occurred in lines 4 and 19 when the bilingual assistant recognized that the Serbian term she knows for hummingbird is the same as Spanish *"colibrí."* This provoked an emotional response from the students, who said "oh yeah" and smiled at line 6. The assistant repeated her surprise at this connection, saying "I'm like 'hello!'" in line 22 before connecting this term in lines 24–27 to her own experience seeing hummingbirds in her backyard, which prompted the students to move the slides to the *colibrí*/hummingbird picture in line 28 before the bilingual assistant complimented the group one final time and the whole audience clapped.

This moment exemplifies the three elements of translanguaging focal to this chapter. First is the relatively mundane sociolinguistic aspects of translanguaging in that, during both the preparation and the presentations, the students, teachers, and bilingual assistant drew on their unitary linguistic repertoires to make and negotiate meanings important to the activity. These included selecting an appropriate biome, agreeing on team roles, researching basic information, and debating correct translations, drawing on their own linguistic repertoires as well as digital multimodal tools such as Google Translate. Then, during each presentation, the audience listened to presentations in a variety of national/named languages and engaged in question and

---

[1] All names pseudonyms.

Table 12.1 Section of talk from the question-answer portion of the Spanish group's presentation

1	Bilingual assistant (BA)	Now just to add to the animals, I noticed one animal, it's your primary consumer
2		you actually see the bird flying as well, it's one of my favorite, a teeny tiny bird, it's considered a small bird I think
3		and um, I'm always learning from you
4		cause in my language, my first language, Serbian, we call that bird the same as in Spanish, I just learned that
5		colibrí
6	Presenting students	Oh yeah *smiling*
7	BA	But when you interpreted that word, and this is gonna be something to ask the teacher
8		I thought in English a different thing, hummingbird?
9		or you said, do you know the word in English, or maybe I don't
10	Teacher	um for hummingbird, you mean the colibrí
11	BA	Yes, and when you translated that word you called that colibrí
12		I'm not sure that word, can that word be used in English or not?
13	Manuel	*Shakes his head 'no'*
14	BA	cause I thought that was called a hummingbird in English
15	Manuel	Hummingbird, yeah
16	Other students in presenting group	Hummingbird, yeah
17	BA	Can they also be called colibrís, colibrí, no, so that
18	Teacher	Um, I had heard that word before, um
19	BA	Because in my language they are called colibri as well
20	Teacher	Yeah
21	BA	I think that you translated, you said it was colibrí
22		and I'm like 'hello!' but um
23		for students, that's called hummingbird
24		the teeny tiny bird can really fast spin, you know, um wings
25		I see sometimes in my back yard
26		it drinks nectar from beautiful flowers and stuff
27		and stops just like that
28	Presenting students	*Move slide to back to the image of the hummingbird*
29	Manuel	A hummingbird
30	BA	It's a beautiful, it's considered a small bird
31		you guys have beautiful uh images
32		I would say my favorite part of this is the flowers
33		great job
34	Other students in class	*Clapping*

N.B. line number on left, speaker in column 2, text in regular font, paralinguistic items in italics answer sessions. For the Spanish group, the students drew on their linguistic repertoires and prior educations to prepare the slides and deliver the presentation, the teacher responded before the focal section in Spanish and English, and the audience listened to the presentation and asked questions before the focal moment. The focal moment of the bilingual assistant noticing a cognate between two languages, Serbian and Spanish, that seem quite dissimilar on the surface, is, in itself unsurprising in that Serbian and Spanish are part of the Indo-European language family and therefore have a number of lexical and grammatical similarities. Moreover, this noticing of cognates happened frequently in the class between, for example, the Nepali, Somali, and Arabic speakers discovering that "*kursi*" 'chair' is shared in their respective languages, the Somali and Wolof/Fulani speakers connecting over shared religious vocabulary such as "*Allahi*" 'my God,' or the Spanish and French speakers discovering that many features were shared in their languages in addition to English. On the other hand, due to the English-centric focus of the classroom and school, these connections were rarely formally explored, which leads to the second point regarding pedagogical design.

Perhaps more substantial than the first point is the layered contexts and activities that were necessary for this moment to emerge. First is the creation of newcomer programs themselves. Although some may rightly question whether these schools are another form of segregation (Feinberg, 2000), their broad goals of supporting students doing "double the work" of language and content learning is admirable and sometimes effective (Fine, Stoudt, & Futch, 2005; Short & Boyson, 2012; Short & Fitzsimmons, 2007). In addition, these spaces remain interesting as multilanguacultural spaces despite the fact that very few of them employ bilingual approaches (Center for Applied Linguistics, 2014). In this vein, what is notable is the factors and processes involved in the teacher developing this activity—his ideological stance, personal multilingualism, continuing education, engagement with translanguaging, and willingness to decenter English in his classroom. In other words, as mentioned above, the teacher's stance towards translanguaging, which was becoming more explicit during the semester with his continuing education course, led to the pedagogical design of the activity, and the question and answer session provoked an important shift in the discussion through the destabilization of the presumed distance/borders between two national/named languages. However, the activity itself was a first for the students in the school, and initially they questioned or resisted along various lines but ultimately created presentations that displayed their home languages and connections to English and the content knowledge. The students' reactions to the task varied, as explored in interviews and a short survey, with most expressing general satisfaction but a few critical voices underlining that the task was difficult due to their perceived shortcomings with home language literacy and academic register.

The third point invokes "the emergence of something new—something that we perhaps cannot even imagine" (Orellana, 2016, p. 91) and underlines that this moment was, in fact, quite unexpected and surprising. None of the actors—the teacher, students, bilingual assistant, or researchers—could have predicted that the Spanish group would have selected tropical biome for their presentation much less included a picture of a "*colibrí*" 'hummingbird' that would have been noticed and remarked upon by the Serbian bilingual assistant. The fact that she did provoked both a "hello!" moment of realization for her and an emotional reaction from the students and audience which raises important issues about translanguaging, namely efforts to destabilize the national/named orientation towards language that undergirds and often undermines efforts towards greater equity for minoritized students.

The fact that Serbian and Spanish both share the use of *colibrí* may have been surprising to the students and bilingual assistant, but this term is widely shared among many national/named languages. For example, Google Translate gives *colibrí* or a close variant as a translation of "hummingbird" for many named/national languages such as:

- Belarussian, Bosnian, Bulgarian, Catalan, Corsican, Czech, Danish, Dutch, Esperanto, Estonian, Finnish, French, Galician, German, Greek, Haitian Creole, Hungarian, Indonesian, Italian, Kyrgyz, Latvian, Lithuanian, Luxemboughish, Malagasy, Mongolian, Polish, Romanian, Russian, Serbian, Slovak, Slovenian, Spanish, Swedish, Ukranian, Welsh

Of course, the validity of Google Translate for this term is suspect; nevertheless, the general point holds that *colibrí* is a quite common term that spans multiple named/national languages and language families. This may be partially explained and extended with reference to the actual biome of hummingbirds, which are located solely in South and North America.

Figure 12.2's image, part of broader efforts to map Earth's biodiversity for the purpose of understanding and conserving habitat (Jenkins, Pimm, & Joppa, 2013), reveals that *colibrí* 'hummingbirds' are not extant in Serbia or Spain although certainly in many countries where Spanish is a common national language. However, the use of the term and the actual habitats of the birds transcend the national/named

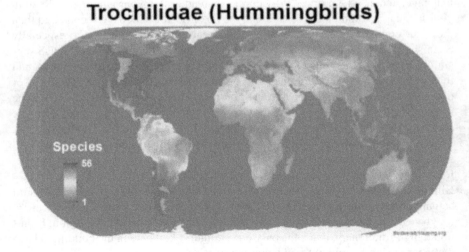

Fig. 12.2 Image with the biome of *colibrí*/hummingbird (Jenkins, 2018)

boundaries that the students and bilingual assistant were accustomed to living within. In this specific case, it was indeed unlikely that the bilingual assistant, in contrast to the students, would have grown up with "*colibrí*" 'hummingbird' in her home county. However, when she moved to the U.S., she was able to see and enjoy these birds in her backyard, a pleasant experience that the students may also have had in their lives. Although it is impossible to know exactly the impact of this "*colibrí*" 'hummingbird' moment on the bilingual assistant's stance towards translanguaging, an interview with her the following year, when her role had shifted to a small group reading intervention leader, reveals that she remained committed to studying and applying translanguaging in her superdiverse instructional context.

Lead Author: What do you think about bilingual classes? We've talked about this before, how could the school support the L1 more aggressively or more systematically?

Bilingual assistant: That's a great question and I wish you could give me the answer because I am thinking of it as well. I am thinking of writing my research project based on using the L1, and thinking of the way how to utilize it and that's something, again, I don't have the good answer. I Google things for instance, what I do in my class, I find some articles, I find some websites that can translate articles from one language to another, from English and my kids love them. They love them and I give them those in both languages. They want to take it home, most of the time we keep all the work in school. But I thought, the kids can take this home, they really want, they love to see something great in their life. I ask them do you feel they are learning. Especially these kind of students of course because my students will say, "I know this in my language." Once they read in their language.

Lead author: Do you do this especially in any specific language or for all languages?

Bilingual assistant: I would print in all their languages. Because I have small groups, I would print in Arabic, I give them both two versions English and their language, and ask them first, "Why don't you read first in your language?" Read in your language, and then for the first maybe do only their language second and then they can compare, they can highlight, they can underline the words, especially Spanish because there's so many common words they are going to find English very simple. They'll figure out, "Oh this is this. Acrobat is acrobat." A zillion words, and then at the end we only read in English. Once they maybe going to spend two or three days looking at it, it depends how long that article is, but the final day will be in English. It's not like they are going to get mixed. They will just use it, maybe some translate some of them not. Some of them don't even, there are a few students. There are some students who don't read nor write in their language and that's all right. Some of the students.

Lead author: What have you been doing in that situation?

Bilingual assistant: In that situation I have one student [who speaks Kinyarwanda] actually. She would just use English, she would like, "Can I use English word?" Maybe use a dictionary maybe some words she can look in dictionary. Again, I can't find it in the dictionary, that's the only one I couldn't find here in the building. I have dictionaries, but I could not find a dictionary.

Lead author: They exist but I mean. Because in Rwanda the whole national curriculum is in Kinyarwanda, I mean that there are resources out there in the world but there you know we'd have to go kind of get them, and [Lead Author offers to connect her with a friend who speaks Kinyarwanda], but like when I think about the answer to your question like you know for bilingual resources for students that I might, my main concern is you know the kids who are not literate in their home language, they have a big challenge to do that transfer.

Bilingual assistant: That's a good point, I agree actually another student who is even less because she told me she speaks Fulani and when I gave her, I'm sorry Swahili, I'm mixing up, Swahili. I gave her the dictionary and then the kids are telling me "Miss she couldn't" because this was another activity, they gave him something and they were supposed to look for the words in their language, like use the dictionary, it's also practice because that's the only accommodation they can get during the state testing so I want them to have that skill, and she couldn't use the dictionary but she was using I didn't even know, and then students were telling her, but she cannot read or write. I agree, that's a challenge. (bilingual assistant, personal communication, March 3, 2017)

This section demonstrates the bilingual assistant's stance towards translanguaging, some of the aspects of instructional design she employed in her small group, and the important shifts she made to accommodate the wide range of national/named languages and student backgrounds. These, in a fashion similar to the teacher, emerge from a number of factors including her personal bilingualism, migration history, educational background, and the unique sociolinguistic and pedagogical demands of the newcomer program. What emerges is a realization that translanguaging, whether as theory or pedagogy, is not a panacea in that challenging situations remain for specific groups or individuals, but it certainly does open up new perspectives and possibilities that, if nourished, can lead to unexpected and even joyful connections and insights.

6   Conclusion

This chapter, drawing on the focal moment above in the context of the broader research project in an adolescent newcomer program in superdiverse Central Ohio, proposes that "*colibrí*" 'hummingbird' may be an appropriate metaphor for translanguaging, complementing other existing metaphors such as the all-terrain vehicle or river. Certainly the hummingbird's specific nature with its quick yet steady movements and beautiful plumage evoke aspects of the flexible and creative language use of bi/multilngual peoples. However, this should not elide the fact that challenges remain. For example, recently a new species of hummingbird was discovered in the Ecuadorian Andes that was, due to its "restricted distribution, apparently low population size, and lack of protection of its habitat," immediately considered critically endangered (Sornoza-Molina, Freile, Nilsson, Krabbe, & Bonaccorso, 2018). These conditions connect to the aforementioned political struggle of bi/multilingual peoples to have their experiences and skills recognized, validated, and supported in spaces such as schools or the broader society. Thus, the hummingbird as translanguaging metaphor may be summarized in the following way:

- First, although it is relatively common in some parts of the world, not all have direct experience with it.
- Second, despite the lack of direct experience, a number of shared yet distinct vocabularies exist to describe it.
- Third, new discoveries about it continue to emerge but may be almost immediately endangered.
- Finally, when directly observed and experienced, it evokes pleasure and joy.

In conclusion, this relatively brief classroom moment indexes multiple levels of translanguaging theory and practice. The school, teacher, bilingual assistant, and students are ripe sites for exploration of translanguaging as a sociological and pedagogical phenomenon. The focal activity drew on translanguaging pedagogy in an English-centric space, resulting in presentations that decentered English and produced an unexpected moment that, while fleeting, destabilized the national/named divisions between languages and created a positive response between the students and bilingual assistant. This moment affirms the power and importance of translanguaging people and pedagogies in TESOL-oriented educational spaces.

References

Alim, H. S., Rickford, J. R., & Ball, A. F. (Eds.). (2016). *Raciolinguistics: How language shapes our ideas about race*. Oxford, UK/New York, NY: Oxford University Press.

Allard, E. C. (2015). Undocumented status and schooling for newcomer teens. *Harvard Educational Review, 85*(3), 478–501. https://doi.org/10.17763/0017-8055.85.3.478

Auerbach, E. R. (1993). Reexamining English only in the ESL classroom. *TESOL Quarterly, 27*(1), 9–32.

Bajaj, M., & Bartlett, L. (2017). Critical transnational curriculum for immigrant and refugee students. *Curriculum Inquiry, 47*(1), 25–35. https://doi.org/10.1080/03626784.2016.1254499

Baker, C. (2011). *Foundations of bilingual education and bilingualism* (5th ed.). Bristol, UK: Multilingual Matters.

Bartlett, L. (2007). Bilingual literacies, social identification, and educational trajectories. *Linguistics and Education, 18*(3–4), 215–231. https://doi.org/10.1016/j.linged.2007.07.005

Becker, A. L. (1991). Language and languaging. *Language & Communication, 11*(1), 33–35. https://doi.org/10.1016/0271-5309(91)90013-L

Blommaert, J. (2013). *Ethnography, superdiversity and linguistic landscapes: Chronicles of complexity*. Bristol, UK: Multilingual Matters.

Blommaert, J. (2016). Superdiversity and the neoliberal conspiracy. *Ctrl+Alt+Dem*. Retrieved from https://alternative-democracy-research.org/2016/03/03/superdiversity-and-the-neoliberal-conspiracy/

Blommaert, J., & Jie, D. (2010). *Ethnographic fieldwork: A beginner's guide*. Bristol, UK: Multilingual Matters.

Bloome, D., Carter, S. P., Christian, B. M., Otto, S., & Shuart-Faris, N. (2005). *Discourse analysis and the study of classroom language and literacy events: A microethnographic perspective*. New York, NY: Routledge.

Budach, G., & de Saint-Georges, I. (2017). Superdiversity and language. In *The Routledge handbook of migration and language*. London, UK: Routledge. https://doi.org/10.4324/9781315754512.ch3

Capps, R., Newland, K., Fratzke, S., Groves, S., Auclair, G., Fix, M., & McHugh, M. (2015). *The integration outcomes of U.S. refugees*. Washington, DC: Migration Policy Institute.

Center for Applied Linguistics. (2014). *Secondary newcomer programs in the U.S.* Retrieved November 20, 2016, from http://webapp.cal.org/Newcomer/

Choi, J., & Yi, Y. (2016). Teachers' integration of multimodality into classroom practices for English language learners. *TESOL Journal, 7*(2), 304–327. https://doi.org/10.1002/tesj.204

Collier, V. P., & Thomas, W. P. (2004). The astounding effectiveness of dual language education for all. *NABE Journal of Research and Practice, 2*(1), 1–20.

Connally, K., & Dancy, K. (2016, May 12). *Are paraprofessionals the answer to the nation's shortage of bilingual teachers?* Retrieved December 5, 2016, from The Hechinger Report website: http://hechingerreport.org/paraprofessionals-answer-nations-shortage-bilingual-teachers/

Constantino, R., & Lavadenz, M. (1993). Newcomer schools: First impressions. *Peabody Journal of Education, 69*(1), 82–101.

Crawford, J. (2004). *Educating English learners: Language diversity in the classroom* (5th ed.). Los Angeles, CA: Bilingual Education Services.

Cummins, J. (2007). Rethinking monolingual instructional strategies in multilingual classrooms. *Canadian Journal of Applied Linguistics, 10*(2), 221–240.

Cummins, J. (2009). Multilingualism in the English-language classroom: Pedagogical considerations. *TESOL Quarterly, 43*(2), 317–321.

Custodio, B. (2010). *How to design and implement a newcomer program*. Boston, MA: Pearson.

Custodio, B., & O'Loughlin, J. B. (2017). *Students with interrupted formal education: Bridging where they are and what they need*. Thousand Oaks, CA: Corwin.

Dalla, R. L., MoulikGupta, P., Lopez, W. E., & Jones, V. (2006). "It's a balancing act!": Exploring school/work/family interface issues among bilingual, rural Nebraska, paraprofessional educators. *Family Relations, 55*(3), 390–402. https://doi.org/10.1111/j.1741-3729.2006.00410.x

Daniel, S. M., Jiménez, R. T., Pray, L., & Pacheco, M. B. (2017). Scaffolding to make translanguaging a classroom norm. *TESOL Journal, 10*, e361. https://doi.org/10.1002/tesj.361

Daniel, S. M., & Pacheco, M. B. (2016). Translanguaging practices and perspectives of four multilingual teens. *Journal of Adolescent & Adult Literacy, 59*(6), 653–663. https://doi.org/10.1002/jaal.500

Ernst-Slavit, G., & Wenger, K. J. (2006). Teaching in the margins: The multifaceted work and struggles of bilingual paraeducators. *Anthropology & Education Quarterly, 37*(1), 62–82. https://doi.org/10.1525/aeq.2006.37.1.62

Faltis, C. J., & Coulter, C. A. (2007). *Teaching English learners and immigrant students in secondary schools*. Upper Saddle River, NJ: Pearson.

Faltis, C. J., & Wolfe, P. M. (Eds.). (1999). *So much to say: Adolescents, bilingualism, and ESL in the secondary school*. New York, NY: Teachers College Press.

Feinberg, R. C. (2000). Newcomer schools: Salvation or segregated oblivion for immigrant students. *Theory Into Practice, 39*(4), 220–227. https://doi.org/10.1207/s15430421tip3904_5

Fine, M., Stoudt, B., & Futch, V. (2005). *The Internationals Network for public schools: A quantitative and qualitative cohort analysis of graduation and dropout rates*. Retrieved from The Graduate Center, The City University of New York website: http://www.internationalsnps.org/pdfs/FineReport.pdf

Flores, N. (2014, July 19). *Let's not forget that translanguaging is a political act*. Retrieved April 1, 2018, from The Educational Linguist website: https://educationallinguist.wordpress.com/2014/07/19/lets-not-forget-that-translanguaging-is-a-political-act/

Flores, N., & Schissel, J. L. (2014). Dynamic bilingualism as the norm: Envisioning a hetero-glossic approach to standards-based reform. *TESOL Quarterly, 48*(3), 454–479. https://doi.org/10.1002/tesq.182

Fry, R. (2005, November 1). *The higher drop-out rate of foreign-born teens*. Retrieved June 21, 2017, from Pew Research Center's Hispanic Trends Project website: http://www.pewhispanic.org/2005/11/01/the-higher-drop-out-rate-of-foreign-born-teens/

Gándara, P., & Hopkins, M. (Eds.). (2010). *Forbidden language: English learners and restrictive language policies*. New York, NY: Teachers College Press.

García, O. (2008). *Bilingual education in the 21st century: A global perspective*. Malden, MA: Wiley-Blackwell.

García, O., Johnson, S. I., & Seltzer, K. (2017). *The translanguaging classroom: Leveraging student bilingualism for learning*. Philadelphia, PA: Caslon Publishing.

García, O., & Sylvan, C. E. (2011). Pedagogies and practices in multilingual classrooms: Singularities in pluralities. *The Modern Language Journal, 95*(3), 385–400. https://doi.org/10.1111/j.1540-4781.2011.01208.x

García, O., & Wei, L. (2014). *Translanguaging: Language, bilingualism, and education*. Palgrave Pivot.

Gort, M. (2015). Transforming literacy learning and teaching through translanguaging and other typical practices associated with "doing being bilingual". *International Multilingual Research Journal, 9*(1), 1–6. https://doi.org/10.1080/19313152.2014.988030

Hood, L. (2003). *Immigrant students, urban high schools: The challenge continues* (p. 15). New York, NY: The Carnegie Corporation.

Hornberger, N. H., & Link, H. (2012). Translanguaging and transnational literacies in multilingual classrooms: A biliteracy lens. *International Journal of Bilingual Education and Bilingualism, 15*(3), 261–278. https://doi.org/10.1080/13670050.2012.658016

Jenkins, C. N. (2018). *Mapping the world's bird diversity*. Retrieved December 6, 2018, from BiodiversityMapping.org website: https://biodiversitymapping.org/wordpress/index.php/birds/

Jenkins, C. N., Pimm, S. L., & Joppa, L. N. (2013). Global patterns of terrestrial vertebrate diversity and conservation. *Proceedings of the National Academy of Sciences, 110*(28), E2602–E2610. https://doi.org/10.1073/pnas.1302251110

King, L., & Carson, L. (Eds.). (2016). *The multilingual city: Vitality, conflict and change*. Bristol, UK: Multilingual Matters.

Lewis, L., & Gray, L. (2016). *Programs and services for high school English learners in public school districts: 2015–16*. Washington, DC: National Center for Education Statistics.

Li, S., & Lui, W. (2017). Creating a translanguaging space for high school emergent bilinguals. *CATESOL Journal, 29*(2), 139–162.

Longworth, R. C. (2009). *Caught in the middle: America's heartland in the age of globalism*. New York, NY: Bloomsbury USA.

MacSwan, J. (2017). A multilingual perspective on translanguaging. *American Educational Research Journal, 54*(1), 167–201. https://doi.org/10.3102/0002831216683935

Martin-Beltrán, M. (2014). "What do you want to say?" How adolescents use translanguaging to expand learning opportunities. *International Multilingual Research Journal, 8*(3), 208–230. https://doi.org/10.1080/19313152.2014.914372

Meissner, F., & Vertovec, S. (2015). Comparing super-diversity. *Ethnic and Racial Studies, 38*(4), 541–555. https://doi.org/10.1080/01419870.2015.980295

NYU Steinhardt. (2018). *Glossaries for ELLs/MLLs accomodations—Resources*. Retrieved December 7, 2018, from https://steinhardt.nyu.edu/metrocenter/resources/glossaries

Orellana, M. F. (2016). *Immigrant children in transcultural spaces: Language, learning, and love*. New York, NY: Taylor & Francis.

Otheguy, R., García, O., & Reid, W. (2015). Clarifying translanguaging and deconstructing named languages: A perspective from linguistics. *Applied Linguistics Review, 6*(3), 281–307. https://doi.org/10.1515/applirev-2015-0014

Otheguy, R., García, O., & Reid, W. (2018). A translanguaging view of the linguistic system of bilinguals. *Applied Linguistics Review*, Advance online publication. https://doi.org/10.1515/applirev-2018-0020.

Pacheco, M. B. (2016). *Translanguaging in the English-centric classroom: A communities of practice perspective*. Nashville, TN: Vanderbilt University.

Pacheco, M. B., & Miller, M. E. (2016). Making meaning through translanguaging in the literacy classroom. *The Reading Teacher, 69*(5), 533–537. https://doi.org/10.1002/trtr.1390

Rosa, J., & Flores, N. (2017). Unsettling race and language: Toward a raciolinguistic perspective. *Language in Society, 46*(05), 621–647. https://doi.org/10.1017/S0047404517000562

Rowe, L. W. (2018). Say it in your language: Supporting translanguaging in multilingual Classes. *The Reading Teacher, 72*(1), 31–38. https://doi.org/10.1002/trtr.1673

Sayer, P. (2013). Translanguaging, TexMex, and bilingual pedagogy: Emergent bilinguals learning through the vernacular. *TESOL Quarterly, 47*(1), 63–88. https://doi.org/10.1002/tesq.53

Seilstad, B., Braun, D., Kim, S., & Choi, M.-S. (2019). Bilingual biomes: Revising and redoing monolingual instructional practices for multilingual students (10th grade). In M. A. Stewart & H. Hansen-Thomas (Eds.), *Engaging research: Transforming practices for the high school* (pp. 111–126). Alexandria, VA: TESOL Press.

Short, D. J., & Boyson, B. A. (2012). *Helping newcomer students succeed in secondary schools and beyond* (p. 78). Washington, DC: Center for Applied Linguistics.

Short, D. J., & Fitzsimmons, S. (2007). *Double the work: Challenges and solutions to acquiring language and academic literacy for adolescent English language learners. Carnegie Corporation of New York*. Washington, DC: Alliance for Excellent Education.

Sornoza-Molina, F., Freile, J. F., Nilsson, J., Krabbe, N., & Bonaccorso, E. (2018). A striking, critically endangered, new species of hillstar (Trochilidae: Oreotrochilus) from the southwestern Andes of Ecuador. *The Auk, 135*(4), 1146–1171. https://doi.org/10.1642/AUK-18-58.1

Spindler, L., & Spindler, G. D. (Eds.). (1987). *Interpretive ethnography of education at home and abroad*. Hillsdale, NJ: Psychology Press.

Stewart, M. A., & Hansen-Thomas, H. (2016). Sanctioning a space for translanguaging in the secondary English classroom: A case of a transnational youth. *Research in the Teaching of English, 50*(4), 50.

Suárez-Orozco, C., Gaytán, F. X., Bang, H. J., Pakes, J., O'Connor, E., & Rhodes, J. (2010). Academic trajectories of newcomer immigrant youth. *Developmental Psychology, 46*(3), 602–618. https://doi.org/10.1037/a0018201

Sylvan, C. E. (2013). Newcomer high school students as an asset: The internationals approach. *Voices in Urban Education, 37*, 19–24.

Umansky, I. M., & Reardon, S. F. (2014). Reclassification patterns among Latino English learner students in bilingual, dual immersion, and English immersion classrooms. *American Educational Research Journal, 51*(5), 879–912. https://doi.org/10.3102/0002831214545110

Valentino, R. A., & Reardon, S. F. (2015). Effectiveness of four instructional programs designed to serve English learners: Variation by ethnicity and initial English proficiency. *Educational Evaluation and Policy Analysis, 37*(4), 612–637.

Vertovec, S. (2007). Super-diversity and its implications. *Ethnic and Racial Studies, 30*(6), 1024–1054. https://doi.org/10.1080/01419870701599465

Wei, L. (2011). Moment analysis and translanguaging space: Discursive construction of identities by multilingual Chinese youth in Britain. *Journal of Pragmatics, 43*(5), 1222–1235. https://doi.org/10.1016/j.pragma.2010.07.035

Chapter 13
Translanguaging and Task Based Language Teaching: Crossovers and Challenges

Corinne A. Seals, Jonathan Newton, Madeline Ash, and Bao Trang Thi Nguyen

Could it be that all our current pedagogic methods in fact make multilingual development more difficult than it need be, simply because we bow to dominant political and ideological pressures to keep languages pure and separate?

-Lemke, 2002, p. 85

Abstract The current chapter explores what opportunities exist theoretically and empirically for two of the currently most popular approaches in language pedagogy to work together: Task Based Language Teaching (TBLT) and translanguaging. The chapter begins with an overview of research in TBLT, examining where more of the full linguistic repertoire, instead of just the target language, is brought into focus. Through this examination, we make the argument that there is room for translanguaging in TBLT research, but it has for the most part been filtered out in TBLT research to date. We then look to the guiding principles of translanguaging pedagogy and TBLT to see what differences and similarities exist between the two. Following this analysis of theory, we illustrate how TBLT research can make room for translanguaging by applying this interwoven analysis to data from a TBLT English language class in Vietnam. Finally, we follow this illustration with a discussion of what can be gained through joining translanguaging and TBLT moving forward.

Keywords TBLT · Theoretical comparison · Pedagogical methods · Translanguaging · Vietnam · EFL

C. A. Seals (✉) · J. Newton · M. Ash
School of Linguistics and Applied Language Studies, Victoria University of Wellington, Wellington, New Zealand
e-mail: corinne.seals@vuw.ac.nz; jonathan.newton@vuw.ac.nz

B. T. T. Nguyen
Faculty of English, University of Foreign Languages, Hue University, Hue, Vietnam
e-mail: ntbtrang@hueuni.edu.vn

© Springer Nature Switzerland AG 2020
Z. Tian et al. (eds.), *Envisioning TESOL through a Translanguaging Lens*,
Educational Linguistics 45, https://doi.org/10.1007/978-3-030-47031-9_13

1   Introduction

Translanguaging has been defined as 'the ability of multilingual speakers to shuttle between languages, treating the diverse languages that form their repertoire as an integrated system' (Canagarajah, 2011, p. 401). While theoretically exciting, language teachers have reported struggling with how to make use of learners' full linguistic repertoire within the popular task based language teaching (TBLT) approach in the language classroom (e.g. Carless, 2004, 2008). This chapter examines the relationship between translanguaging and TBLT in depth, answering the question of how both approaches can co-exist in the language classroom. The translanguaging paradigm shift is beginning, and this is a time for the well-established TBLT to work with and alongside it.

We take an applied sociolinguistics approach,[1] asking what roles learners' full linguistic repertoires, including first languages and affiliated first acquired linguistic resources (L1s), play in oral task performance in the language classroom. This is a key question when language teachers use interactive classroom tasks, especially in the many EFL contexts in which learners often share a common L1 (Storch & Wigglesworth, 2003; Storch & Aldosari, 2010). We have decided to use the term "L1" to encompass all of an individual's naturally acquired linguistic resources during youth, and we contrast this with "L2" to mean any socially defined 'language' that is purposefully learned in addition to L1. By utilising this terminology, we maintain a bridge between TBLT and translanguaging, using TBLT recognised terminology while making room for translanguaging conceptualisations of the linguistic repertoire, a bridge which encompasses the essence of this chapter. We then illustrate our discussion with data from Vietnamese learners of English participating in classroom speaking tasks, as well as interviews with the students.

Finally, this chapter provides a mandate for TBLT to embrace 'the intuitive communicative strategies multilinguals display in everyday life' (Canagarajah, 2011, p. 401). We maintain that TBLT has space for translanguaging. Furthermore, actively making and maintaining space for translanguaging in TBLT will both enrich TBLT's research agenda and extend the impact of TBLT beyond its typical second/foreign language education sphere of influence.

2   Situating L1 in Translanguaging and TBLT Research

In education, traditional codeswitching analysis (where the respective authors have used the term "codeswitching" and consider languages to be discreet, definable, and separable linguistic systems) and the monolingual bias result in "L1" use (or use of the full repertoire, as described in the section above) often being overlooked or

---

[1] considering both language pedagogy and the influence of larger social structures on language practices, ideologies, and identities in language learning

discouraged (May, 2014). However, since translanguaging considers use of the full repertoire highly beneficial and argues that when learners use their existing linguistic resources they can better acquire new linguistic resources (García & Wei, 2014; Weber, 2014), there is an inherent challenge posed to dominant views of a monolingual norm in education. Where learners are cut off from portions of their linguistic repertoire, either through social or other factors, growing the rest of their repertoire is harder. Due to its grounding in a sociocultural framework, translanguaging further emphasises that use of the full linguistic repertoire is natural: speakers naturally use whatever features best suit the social and linguistic situation (Canagarajah & Wurr, 2011; García & Wei, 2014).

However, this exciting approach to languages education hits some barriers when it comes to applying it in one of the most popular forms of language teaching today – Task Based Language Teaching (TBLT), which traditionally sits within a cognitivist/psycholinguistic paradigm (Skehan, 1998). TBLT is, simply put, teaching through tasks.[2] As explained further by Ellis (2003, p. 16),

> A task is a workplan that requires learners to process language pragmatically in order to achieve an outcome that can be evaluated in terms of whether the correct or appropriate propositional content has been conveyed… A task is intended to result in language use that bears a resemblance, direct or indirect, to the way language is used in the real world. Like other language activities, a task can engage productive or receptive, and oral or written skills and also various cognitive processes.

Questions concerning the role of L1 in the teaching and learning of additional languages have occupied language teachers and applied linguistics for as long as either has existed (Hall & Cook, 2012; Howatt, 1984; Cook, 2001). However, the field of TBLT has been relatively slow to engage with this question directly, especially in the formative years of the development of the field from the 1980s to early 2000s (although more recent research shows promise, cf. Moore, 2017).

One explanation for the reluctance in TBLT research to engage with the L1 question can be found in TBLT's roots in communicative language teaching (CLT), an approach that privileged the native speaker teacher and tended to adopt a subtractive view of L1 use in the classroom. Traditional CLT discouraged L1 use because it reduced opportunities for L2 input processing and communicative practice (Cook, 2001). The theoretical roots of TBLT in Long's Interaction Hypothesis (1996) and Krashen's Input Hypothesis (1985) gave credence to this subtractive view.

A second contributing factor involves the 'second language' settings (c.f. foreign language or multilingual settings) in which TBLT research in its formative years was carried out and which typically involved research participants drawn from classes of adolescent or young adult pre-sessional 'English as a Second Language' (ESL) students at universities or colleges in North American or the United Kingdom (e.g. Bygate, 1996; Doughty & Pica, 1986; Gass & Varonis, 1985). Students in such classes do not always share common L1s with each other and/or with the teacher and so their L1s are often denied a role in classroom discourse. In research

---

[2] Although we are aware that Long (2015) argues for a rather more precise definition of TBLT.

conducted in such contexts, researchers often choose to conveniently avoid L1 use by placing learners in groups with learners from other L1 backgrounds to perform communication tasks (e.g. Doughty & Pica, 1986; Newton, 2013). Given this situation, it is hardly surprising that native speakerism has dominated much of the research and theorising around TBLT, with the monolingual native speaker treated, by default, as the ideal model or target, and the full linguistic repertoire of learners made all but invisible.

However, there are notable exceptions. For example, Antón and DiCamilla (1998) examined the socio-cognitive functions L1 played in collaborative dialogue between learners engaged in a writing task. L1 was used to maintain intersubjectivity (i.e. to establish a shared perspective on the task), to scaffold work on the task, and to regulate mental activity (i.e. through private speech). L1-use has also been a consistent theme in task-related research conducted in Canadian bilingual and immersion contexts, notably by Merrill Swain and colleagues. Swain & Lapkin (2000), for instance, investigated the ways that grade 8 French immersion students in Canada used L1 to perform a jigsaw and Dictogloss task. While L1 was shown to be used most frequently for the purpose of task management, it was also used to clarify aspects of grammar and vocabulary, and to a lesser extent for interpersonal talk.

A small collection of TBLT studies over the last 10–15 years has continued this tradition of investigating L1 use in task-based interaction. Storch and Aldosari (2010) found a 'modest' amount of L1 use in pair work by EFL students at a Saudi Arabian college, with the type of task having a stronger influence of L1 use than proficiency pairing. L1 was used primarily for task management and deliberations over vocabulary. Lasito and Storch (2013) compared L1 use in pair and small group work by adolescent Indonesian EFL learners, finding greater L1 use in pairs where it was primarily used for task management and for dealing with unfamiliar vocabulary. Moore (2013, 2017) investigated L1 use by university-level Japanese EFL learners as they worked in pairs to prepare for an oral presentation. Moore found a relatively high level of L1 use (28% in the 2013 data), although with individual learners displaying consistently high or low L1 use patterns. L1 talk occurring across all categories of talk, though, particularly focused on procedural matters and off-task talk. Additionally, in a study which drew on interviews with English teachers and teacher educators in Hong Kong, Carless (2008) highlighted the complexity of the issues surrounding L1 use in task-based classrooms in this context, concluding that "a balanced and flexible view of MT [mother tongue] use in the task-based classroom" (p. 336) is needed.

While the studies discussed above typically focus on adolescents or young adults performing tasks, there is also an emerging strand of TBLT research that is concerned with the viability of TBLT for young learners in pre-school or primary school contexts. In this research, L1-use in peer-peer interaction is a noticeably more consistent theme. For example, Tognini and Oliver (2012) reported on the use of L1 in primary and secondary foreign language classrooms in Australia, with a subset of their data focused on tasks. They found that, predictably, L1 use increased as tasks became more demanding, and was used more in pair or group work in which students had to work collaboratively to construct a text, such as a role play or arguments for a debate. Azkarai and García Mayo (2017) investigated the use of L1 by Spanish primary school EFL learners, with a particular focus on the effect of task repetition on L1 use. They found relatively modest L1 use (although more than has been reported in studies involving adult participants), with its main functions being to appeal for help (i.e. to find a word), for metacognitive talk, or as borrowings from Spanish to keep the task flow. L1 use fell significantly in task repetitions. Additionally, Shintani (2014) showed how beginners in pre-school used L1 during input-based tasks to complete the tasks successfully. The learners used L1 for meta-talk and to communicate with the teacher. Over the five weeks of data collection, the learners began to rely less on their L1 and to use English more.

The consistent orientation in all of these studies is towards the productive functions played by L1 in task performance, especially its role in metacognitive talk, task management and appeals for help. It is interesting to note that the topic of L1 use features so prominently in research involving young learners (and by default, often beginners). To put it another way, L1 use appears to be infrequently reported in task-based research except when it involves young learners, which is an interesting emerging trend. This is also possibly why TBLT and translanguaging studies have not spoken to each other much, as the majority of translanguaging research to date has focused on teenage or adult learners (see Seals and Olsen-Reeder, 2019 for notable exceptions to this).

The TBLT studies reviewed above have all deliberately focused on L1 use. It is possible that other studies may report L1 data without it being a main research focus (e.g., Ellis and Yuan, 2004). However, Plonsky and Kim's (2016) meta-analysis of 85 TBLT studies involving learner production found that only six explicitly accounted for L1 use in the data. We conclude that the majority of TBLT studies involving learner production either design L1 use out of the data (e.g. by requiring tasks to be performed in L2 only), do not report it, or exclude it from analysis when it does occur. The third of these options is illustrated in Park's (2010) study on pre-task planning and task-based interaction in which examples of language related episodes containing both L1 and L2 are supplied but with no mention of this L1 data, or indeed any reference to L1 use.

Given this situation, it is not surprising that our search for TBLT studies which adopt an explicit translanguaging view of language has come up almost empty handed. There are positive signs in this direction however. Moore's research (2013, 2017), for example, draws on the concepts of languaging (Swain, 2009) and translanguaging (García, 2009) to frame L1 use as 'situated discursive practice' (p. 240). Moore's (2013) conclusion that L1 use is a 'naturally occurring phenomenon in the L2 classroom as in bilingual communication' (2013: 251) points promisingly to the synergistic relationship between TBLT and translanguaging that we are advocating for in this paper. In addition, recent years have seen researchers engaging with TBLT across a much broader range of contexts, including primary school language classrooms (e.g., García Mayo & Imaz Agirre, 2016; Newton & Bui, 2017), bilingual and multilingual classrooms (e.g., Álvarez & Pérez-Cavana, 2015) and English Medium instruction settings (e.g. Moore, 2017). We are hopeful that, as a consequence, the field will continue to engage more critically with a broader range of orientations and perspectives on the nature of language than has traditionally been the case.

3   Similarities and Differences in Principles

We have established that there is room for translanguaging in TBLT empirical research and that it likely is indeed present but often not focused on. But what about its fit theoretically? In investigating the characteristics of a translanguaging-friendly pedagogy, García & Sylvan (2011) established that there are eight guiding principles:

1. Celebrating heterogeneity and singularities in plurality
2. Collaboration among students
3. Collaboration among faculty
4. Learner-centred classrooms
5. Language and content integration
6. Plurilingualism from the students up
7. Experiential learning
8. Localised autonomy and responsibility

These can then be compared to the guiding principles of TBLT. Predictably, TBLT treats 'a task' as the core element in classroom language teaching and learning. Definitions of tasks have proliferated over the years but centre around the key elements in Ellis's (2003: 4) definition of a task as "an activity which requires learners to use language, with an emphasis on meaning in order to attain an objective". More recently however, Ellis (Ellis, 2018; Ellis & Shintani, 2013) has argued that this and other similar definitions fail to make a crucial distinction between 'task' as an educational unit of planning (task-as-workplan) and 'task' as the activity that learners engage in when they perform a task (task-in-process). Ellis argues that the starting point for TBLT should be the former - task-as-workplan, which is defined with respect to four key features:

1. The primary focus on meaning; learners are primarily focused on comprehending and/or producing messages (Ellis, 2018, p. 12).
2. There is some kind of gap. The task-as-workplan presents the learners with a gap which needs to be filled with information, reasoning or opinions.
3. Learners need to use their own linguistic and non-linguistic resources. Rather than the task-as-workplan providing learners with the language resources they need to complete the task learners need to "draw on their own existing linguistic resources *(potentially both L1 and L2)* [emphasis added] and their non-linguistic resources (e.g. gesture; facial expressions) for comprehension and/or production" (Ellis, 2018, p. 12).
4. There is an outcome other than the display of language. The task-as-workplan specifies what communicative outcome the task is designed to accomplish, and

learner performance is measured not in whether language is used correctly but on whether this outcome is established (Ellis, 2008, p. 12).

Furthermore, the following ten methodological principles (MPs) for TBLT were proposed by Michael H. Long (2009, 2015). He claims that these are "universally desirable instructional design features motivated by theory and research findings" (Long, 2009, p. 376).

MP1:   Use task, not text, as unit of analysis
MP2:   Promote learning by doing
MP3:   Elaborate input
MP4:   Provide rich input
MP5:   Encourage inductive "chunk" learning
MP6:   Focus on form
MP7:   Provide negative feedback
MP8:   Respect learner syllabi and developmental processes
MP9:   Promote cooperative collaborative learning
MP10:   Individualise instruction

As the guiding principles above show, there are divergent areas in the focus of translanguaging and TBLT that pose challenges when finding how they might work together. This is reflective also of the hesitancy that often accompanies discussions of translanguaging and TBLT in the same space. When examining TBLT and translanguaging's divergent areas with respect to theory, there are two main areas of difference. Firstly, translanguaging has a broadly descriptive focus when looking at qualities of dynamic plurilingual pedagogies, while TBLT has a more granular focus on pedagogy – what to do and how to do it. Second, translanguaging has a much more explicit agenda of learner empowerment and metacognitive awareness of language and power, while, traditionally at least, TBLT has situated itself with a broadly cognitive orientation to SLA and focused on the impact of generalizable features of task design on language acquisition.

Where then is the common ground? In fact, when conducting a comparative analysis between the guiding principles of both TBLT and translanguaging, it may be surprising to some to find that two approaches that have developed in two such seemingly different directions (one socioculturally and one cognitively) actually have a *lot* in common, as elaborated in the bulleted list below:

• Both translanguaging and TBLT align in their focus on student collaboration. Students working together to negotiate meaning is key to both approaches.
• TBLT and translanguaging advocate for the importance of content and language integration. Stemming from a historical background in communicative language teaching for both has led to this recognised need of language learning's usefulness to understand meaningful material.
• TBLT and translanguaging advocate for experiential learning. It is not enough to merely receive language instruction passively; learners must actively take part in their acquisition of sociolinguistic knowledge.

- Both approaches recognise the criticalness of learner-centred classrooms. Long gone are the days where a teacher-centred approach was deemed the most appropriate to language learning. Now it is understood that successful language learning and teaching must take place in an environment in which learners own their learning.
- Pedagogy must be more fluid and needs-responsive. This recognition of learner differences emphasises both inter-learner and intra-learner difference across time. In order for learners to keep growing their sociolinguistic repertoire, language teaching must be adaptable to their needs.
- There is a need to focus on functional, communicative language use. Similar to the second and third commonalities, language use must have a communicative purpose, and the material that is being taught in language classrooms must be functional for the learners (i.e. teaching to learners' communicative needs).

In all, based on the literature and on these six principles, it seems evident that translanguaging and TBLT are not as far apart as they first may seem, and in fact have quite a lot in common. To illustrate how the two approaches can work together, we present an analytical illustration in the next section of this chapter.

4 Applying Theory to Practice

In this section of the chapter we explore the potential for complementarity in the analysis of classroom task-interaction data from a TBLT perspective and from a translanguaging perspective. The data we use here are drawn from a study carried out in EFL classrooms at a secondary school in Hanoi, Vietnam (Nguyen, 2013; Newton & Nguyen, 2019). The original purpose of the study was to understand how the EFL teachers in this school went about teaching with tasks in the speaking lessons, and how learners engaged with and performed the tasks. The researchers identified the well-established practice shared by all the EFL teachers in the school of giving learners the opportunity to first rehearse a speaking task in pairs or groups, and then for as many pairs or groups as time allowed to perform the task again publicly in front of the class. Data included video and audio recordings and field notes from observations of 45 lessons from nine Grades 10, 11 & 12 classes (15–18 year old learners) taught by nine different teachers. Interviews were conducted with the teachers and with selected students. One of the research questions addressed in the study concerned the quantity and purpose of L1 use in task rehearsal, which brought our attention to the presence of this data for a qualitative translanguaging analysis as well. We are aware that terminology is a challenge here, but that is in the nature of trying to start a conversation across approaches. As explained near the beginning of this chapter, we use the terms L1 and L2 here in a way that attempts to bridge understandings across TBLT and translanguaging research: "L1" refers to all of an individual's naturally acquired linguistic repertoire in their youth, while "L2" refers to the socially defined 'language' that is the current target of the language learning taking place.

The entire data set from which the following excerpts come contains many examples of what we see as translanguaging behaviours, although none of the data were originally collected for translanguaging analysis. This reinforces that translanguaging is a natural response and practice that can be located in much TBLT research. Further, these data were originally analysed through a codeswitching lens. The behaviour termed 'translanguaging' below and 'codeswitching' originally, on the surface, look similar in form. However, there is an important distinction between codeswitching and translanguaging found in the applied theoretical lens. As explained by Seals (forthcoming, p. 3):

> Chiefly, translanguaging is a macro lens through which language use can be viewed that acknowledges all parts of the linguistic repertoire as connected and equally valid. It is a position actively aligned with critical pedagogy... Within a translanguaging lens, it is entirely possible to have micro units of analysis such as codeswitching/codemeshing, etc. Therefore, a translanguaging lens does not preclude the existance or use of codeswitching and codemeshing. However, naming translanguaging is also naming an activist position."

Through a re-analysis of the data below (originally analysed via a TBLT lens), we found that translanguaging (incorporating L1) was used by speakers for three key purposes: task management, giving or seeking assistance, and negotiation of meaning. Translanguaging therefore fulfils a crucial function in TBLT practice – it allows students to manage the task, to collaborate, and to extend their control over the language and forms used.

A summary of L1 use is presented in its original quantitative form in Tables 13.1 and 2. Data for both turns and words are presented because the turns varied considerably in length. Table 13.1 shows that L1 turns constituted around 43% (964 turns) of the total; L2 made up 38% (860 turns) and the use of both together made up 19% (422). On average, in each task rehearsal, the students produced 20 L1 turns ($M = 20.08$), 18 L2 turns ($M = 17.91$), and 9 translanguaged turns ($M = 8.79$). A *Friedman* test showed a significant difference in the size of the different types of turns ($\chi^2 = 21.027, p = .000$). A follow-up *Wilcoxon signed ranks* test indicated that the mean of L1 turns and L2 turns was significantly different from translanguaged turns ($Z = -5.117, p = .000$ and $Z = -3.958, p = .000$), but L1 and L2 turns did not differ statistically from each other ($Z = -1.085, p = .278$). This indicates that in task rehearsal, students produced L1 and L2 turns in similar amounts.

Table 13.1 Amounts of L1 and L2 use by turn in task rehearsal

Rehearsal (n = 48)	Turn					
	n	%	Min.	Max.	Mean	SD
L1	964	42.92	1	59	20.08	15.19
L2	860	38.29	3	56	17.91	14.04
Both L1&L2	422	18.79	0	25	8.79	5.75
Total	2246	100.00				

Table 13.2 Amounts of L1 and L2 use by word in task rehearsal

Task rehearsal (n = 48)	Word					
	n	%	Min.	Max.	Mean	SD
L1	7890	55.8	25	473	164.37	122.49
L2	6251	44.2	19	522	130.22	93.13
Total	14,141	100.0				

With regards to the amounts of L1/L2 use by word, Table 13.2 shows that in total students produced more L1 words (55.8%) than L2 words (44.2%). On average, in each rehearsal, students used more L1 words ($M = 164.37$; $SD = 122.49$) than L2 words ($M = 130.22$; $SD = 93.13$). A paired-samples t-test showed no significant difference between these two means, $t(47) = 1.643$, $p = .107$. This again shows that the students used L1 in roughly equal amounts to the L2 target.

It is clear from these data that during dialogic rehearsals, the students used L1 substantially. This finding contrasts with findings of other studies on the amount of L1 use during pair and group work.[3] For example, Storch and Aldosari (2010) found a limited amount of L1 use with 15 pairs of EFL Arabic learners (7% for L1 words, and 16% for L1 turns). Other studies also found similar low proportions of L1 use. For example, Swain and Lapkin (2000) found that in their talk in preparation for a written task, Grade 8 French immersion students used L1 for 29% of the turns in the jigsaw task and 21% in the dictogloss task. However, the considerable amount of L1 use in Vietnamese classroom data reported above echoes Guk and Kellogg's (2007) finding that the Korean EFL learners in their study used L1 in 47% of their utterances. Alegría de la Colina and García Mayo (2009) also found high L1 use – 55–78% depending on the tasks (jigsaw, dictogloss, text reconstruction). Alley (2005) also found students used English L1 predominantly in group work (71%), though for different mediating functions.

The considerable amount of L1 in the rehearsal stage in the present study can be explained in several ways. First, the students used L1 extensively because they treated public performance as final, and rehearsal as preparatory. Second, under time pressure (there were time limits for task rehearsal, on average 5 min), the students used L1 to sort out their ideas and marshal language resources to express the messages they wanted to convey. The following excerpt (translated into English) between the researcher (R) and students (focus group interview) illustrates these points.

Excerpt 1 Interview with Students About L1 Use

R: Do you use Vietnamese when you work with each other?

---

[3] It should be noted that in the present study, the data on L1/L2 use were gathered in the context of task rehearsal in preparation for the subsequent performance of the same task, which was different from all the studies cited here where there was no rehearsal and only a single task performance (cf. Swain & Lapkin, 2001). Another note was that student groups varied greatly in amounts of L1 use and this also found support in previous studies (Storch & Aldosari, 2010; Storch & Wigglesworth, 2003; Swain & Lapkin, 2000).

S1:   Yes, a lot.
R: Why?
S1:   Time for preparation [rehearsal] is often limited, if we use English right away, it is very time-consuming. So we use Vietnamese first to be quick to prepare ideas and find English words later.
S2:   Also my friends might not understand all that I say if I say all in English.
R: Umh huh. Do you think when you use Vietnamese, you'll lose opportunities to speak English?
S1:   Not really, because the final thing is to speak up there in front of everyone.
R: When you are up there, you can use only English?
S3:   Yes, because we have already prepared for it!

(Student focus group interview- 11D)

The students' use of L1 also reflects their familiarity and comfort working with each other. Research into pair talk in EFL contexts (e.g., Storch & Aldorsari, 2010) has shown that when students become comfortable working with each other, they tend to use more L1 in their interaction. Crucially though, whether it was considered acceptable to use L1 was largely set by teachers. In these classes, by implementing a rehearsal phase in the first half of each of the speaking lessons in which L1 use could occur freely, the teachers had adopted an ideology which permitted translanguaging.

5   Functions of L1 and Translanguaging

In line with studies on L1 use in pair/groupwork, the current data show the students using L1 for a variety of functions. One such function was to discuss and resolve language problems. For example, students use L1 to explicitly ask for assistance concerning English words/phrases to express their intended meanings, weighing language solutions and giving explanations. Excerpt 2 displays this. Furthermore, this excerpt allows us to qualitatively analyse the discourse to investigate the use of translanguaging in this space.

Excerpt 2 Translanguaging to Request and Provide Metalinguistic Assistance

S3:   Air chi hèo?*(Air what?)*
S1:   Air pollute … air pollute phải không?*(is it air pollute?)*
S3:   Air polluted
S4:   Air pollution. Pollution là sự ô nhiễm
(Pollution is the state of being polluted)
S2:   Polluted là bị ô nhiễm *(Polluted is passive)*

Here S3 uses L1 to ask for the word that collocates with *'air'*. S1 provides the answer in English L2 but is uncertain and shifts back to L1 for a confirmation check. S4 and S2 then offer solutions and metalinguistic explanations, translanguaging as they do so, drawing upon L1 to provide deeper meaning while highlighting the focus word through L2.

Students also translanguaged to generate ideas, scaffold, and self-regulate as illustrated in Excerpt 3. In this task rehearsal, translanguaging is used by students as a form of bridging and negotiation of meaning. Bridging, like scaffolding, is where a gap exists in a student's linguistic repertoire and they then acquire a corresponding lexical item from another language. However, unlike scaffolding, the use of translanguaging to fill the gap with a new lexical item is intended to retain lexical items in *both* languages, not simply in a target language and then to discard the other feature.

Excerpt 3 Translanguaging to Generate Ideas During Rehearsals

01 S2: Bởi vì khi đau ốm … khi ill

(Because when they are sick … when ill)
02 S1: They old (.) when they old (.) they old (.) they are old chứ! *(should be they are old!)* … sick or old!
03 S2: They are sick (.) or old (.) their children will nuôi dưỡng *(take care of)* will erm
04 S1: Take care of
05 S2: Take care of
06 S1: Them. Nếu có nhiều con thì erm nguồn lao động sẽ nhiều *(If they have many children, they will have a good labour force)* … if they have many children
07 S2: Công nhân là workers *('Workers' is workers)* … have workers
08 S1: Then their family sẽ có nhiều người làm việc *(will have many workers)*

Gia đình họ (.) *(Their family)* their family will have nhiều *(a lot of)* a lot of

S2 starts by providing metalinguistic commentary in line 01, almost entirely in L1. S1 then connects this meaning to English L2, but with false starts. S1 later reflects on his language use by self-correcting, saying 'they are old' instead of 'they old', with the emphatic Vietnamese 'chứ' directed to himself. This indicates his obvious noticing of the difference between the target-like form and his language production, showing the triggering of mental processes that lead to modified output (Swain & Lapkin, 1995, pp. 372–373). In other words, S1 has utilised translanguaging to extend his analysis beyond semantic processing to syntactic processing (Swain, 1995). Through this process, S1 is using translanguaging between L1 and L2 as a useful cognitive tool for accessing performance output in English L2.

S2 continues his contribution by starting from what S1 has said, and in line 03, mid-turn, he uses Vietnamese 'nuôi dưỡng' to regulate his L2 search. Sensing his interlocutor is having difficulty finding the needed word, S1 translanguages across speaker turns, offering the correct phase 'take care of', which S2 uses in his talk. At line 06, S1 completes S2's utterance by adding the pronoun 'them' after the verb and keeps generating content in L1, followed by mapping that L1 meaning to L2 words via translanguaging. In lines 3–6, S2 is seen bridging, with input from S1 to acquire the feature "take care of" in L2.

Similarly, in lines 7–8, S2 and S1 translanguage to build upon meaning from L1 to retrieve L2 resources to express the message they want to convey. In brief, Excerpt 2 shows translanguaging being used as a sociocognitive mediating tool (Lantolf &Thorne, 2007), lending support to other studies that show how learners translanguage to mediate their use of L2 (Algería de la Colina & García Mayo, 2009; Alley, 2005; Antón & DiCamilla, 1998, Brooks & Donato, 1994; Guk & Kellogg, 2007; Storch & Aldorsari, 2010; Storch & Wigglesworth, 2003; Swain & Lapkin, 2000).

Excerpt 3 also demonstrates the collaboration and negotiation of meaning. The discussion in lines 02–03, 03–04, and 06–07 involves students refining, clarifying and negotiating meaning through all the linguistic resources they have, therein showing the usefulness of a positive stance towards translanguaging in the language learning space. The students are actively searching to find what they want to say, and how they want to say it, using every skill at their disposal, without the reservations that the monolingual bias brings. The task is better completed through students' accessing their full linguistic repertoires.

Finally, Excerpt 4 below shows an example of what occurred when the students devised the opening and closing for the performance before acting it out.

Excerpt 4 L1 for Metadiscursive Commentary

S1:   Xí lên bắt tay đồ rứa nghe chưa. How are you đồ rứa nghe.

(When we are up there, remember to shake hands and the like. Also remember to ask 'how are you', and the like.)
S2:   Hi teacher, hi kids. You look very beautiful today! [Laugh] [Joking]
S1:   Oh, thank you! [Laugh] [Joking]

Excerpt 4 shows the use of students' full linguistic repertoires to give voice to the metadiscussion. S1 uses L1 features to discuss how to proceed. The return to the performance is then signalled by S2 through the use of L2, the target language. Through using their full linguistic repertoire and translanguaging, the students are able to shift their conversation between task preparation and task performance.

While previously a codeswitching analysis within TBLT research might have viewed the excerpts above as "resorting" to the L1, a translanguaging analysis encourages a more nuanced view, while simultaneously drawing upon critical pedagogy framing. The use of L1 during L2 task preparation allows for a much more sophisticated negotiation of meaning to take place. Additionally, as shown in Excerpt 4, students are able to take on multiple "voices", therein constructing two distinct but connected discussions simultaneously: the task performance in L2, with task preparation and discussion incorporating L1. Though some may argue this is due to a gap in the students' English proficiency, translanguaging posits that this is actually a complex negotiation of the linguistic and social setting, without which students would lose an important tool to discursively negotiate and complete the task.

The learners' verbal reports further confirm the roles of translanguaging as demonstrated above. For example, 29 of the 54 students said that they use L1 to prepare ideas or meanings first and then connect these established meanings to L2 forms:

1. *Thinking in Vietnamese is powerful. I can think of millions of ideas that my limited English cannot express them all. My friends can help translate what I think into English. (HVT-10A)*
2. *I speak in Vietnamese first to search for and present ideas, and after that I turn those ideas into English. It's like matching meanings to the English words. (NKHH-11F)*

This indicates that the students view L2 as a bridge that connects meaning to L2 forms, which in turn convey that meaning across the bridge. Students further said they use L1 to sustain communication during L2 negotiation of meaning:

3. *For example, in the middle of communication, I don't know to express certain ideas, I don't know what else to do but use Vietnamese to move on; I cannot let ideas flow out in English, only Vietnamese can help. (HDH-12I)*
4. *Sometimes we have to stop talking in English to use Vietnamese to give explanations. Sometimes we have very brilliant ideas but can't express them in English, so using Vietnamese enables us to speak out ideas, which we later translate into English, and move on with our communication. (TTHL-10B)*

Seen from a traditional TBLT perspective, the students' comments above would indicate that students use L1 because they lack L2 resources, or are unable to access their L2 resources quickly enough. However, via translanguaging, the script is flipped, and instead, L1 is seen to be beneficial in bridging students' cognition. Taken together, the students appear to view L1 as a mediating tool to support producing meaning in L2. This result corroborates the findings of previous research (e.g., Alley, 2005; Brooks-Lewis, 2009; Kim & Petraki, 2009) where students perceived the usefulness of using L1 in learning L2. As V. Cook (2001) argues:

> Bringing the L1 back from exile may lead not only to the improvement of existing teaching methods but also to innovations in methodology. In particular, it *may liberate* the task-based learning approach so that it can foster the students' natural collaborative efforts in the classroom through their L1 as well as their L2. (p.419, italics added)

The examples above, as well as corroborating prior research, show that TBLT pedagogy must accept the "fact of life" (Stern, 1992, cited in V. Cook, 2001, p.408) that "two [or more] languages are permanently present" (V. Cook, 2001, p.418). It then follows that if students are prohibited from using L1 in classrooms, they will be denied access to this useful tool (see Alegría de la Colina & García Mayo, 2009; Brooks-Lewis, 2009; Storch & Aldosari, 2010; Swain & Lapkin, 2000). Given that L1 use has been reported as one of the deterrents to the implementation of TBLT in EFL Asian contexts (e.g., Carless, 2008; Pham, 2007) and as one of the teachers' 'fears' (Alley, 2005), the findings here concerning translanguaging as a cognitive tool further highlight the need to rehabilitate L1 in the TBLT space.

Overall the students' positive perceptions of task performance following rehearsal were in line with the teachers' dedication to bringing the task through to the public performance, which they described as the 'happy ending' of the task-based speaking lessons. In the current study, students made use of translanguaging to a considerable extent, and this played an important mediating function. By translanguaging between their available linguistic resources, students were able to successfully negotiate the task and perform it in the still required target form (i.e. English L2), therein taking nothing away from the TBLT agenda and instead assisting students through access to their full linguistic repertoire. This additionally shows that there is space for both TBLT and translanguaging in the language classroom, both empirically and theoretically. This illustrative analysis shows a beginning to how we might integrate TBLT and translanguaging in research and practice.

6   Concluding Discussion: What Is Gained from Integrating Translanguaging and TBLT?

As the above discussion of principles and illustrative analysis have shown, much is to be gained from integrating translanguaging and TBLT instead of pursuing differing research and pedagogical tracks. The above illustration showed how a focus on a TBLT pedagogy drove a shift to a learner-centric pedagogy (e.g. group work). This in turn opened up space for translanguaging. Consequently, translanguaging became a critical tool by which learners were able to successfully negotiate and perform the speaking tasks, therein further developing their sociolinguistic gains. The learners themselves also expressed the necessity and usefulness of translanguaging, particularly during the task rehearsal phase. The learners were empowered in their language learning and built up their confidence for the task performance, having already metadiscursively discussed how they would perform the task and why.

This empowerment of learners is further highlighted through a focus on translanguaging, making sure that this crucial element of learning is not lost in the classroom. For teachers, a translanguaging perspective offers a socially accountable and theoretically justifiable basis for harnessing learners' full linguistic repertoires in the classroom, even if the ultimate aim is proficiency in target language (as is often the case in TBLT classrooms). That being said, through the adoption of a translanguaging perspective, teachers and learners are also more fully able to realise the meaning making goals of TBLT, freed from the constraint of only making meaning in the target language.

Additionally, translanguaging in the classroom more closely mirrors actual real-world language use, particularly in multilingual settings (which is indeed the majority of the world). This helps TBLT classrooms to maintain a more functional purpose, better suiting learners for the real communicative practices they will encounter outside of the classroom.

In sum, translanguaging issues a challenge to TBLT. It asks what TBLT is doing to challenge the status quo and to offer more opportunities to more learners, particularly those from minority communities and contexts who are trying to navigate the dominant systems of learning. As stated by Long (2015, p. 4) in discussing TBLT: 'a responsible course of action… is to make sure that language teaching (LT) and learning are as socially progressive as possible.' Engaging with translanguaging is one way that TBLT might more fully realise this socially progressive goal.

References

Alegría de la Colina, A., & García Mayo, M. P. (2009). Oral interaction in task-based EFL learning: The use of the L1 as a cognitive tool. *IRAL: International Review of Applied Linguistics, 47*, 325–345.

Alley, D. C. (2005). A study of Spanish II high school students' discourse during group work. *Foreign Language Annals, 38*(2), 250–258.

Álvarez, I., & Pérez-Cavana, M. L. (2015). Multilingual and multicultural task-based learning scenarios: A pilot study from the MAGGIC project. *Language Learning in Higher Education, 5*(1), 59–82.

Antón, M., & DiCamilla, F. (1998). Socio-cognitive functions of L1 collaborative interaction in the L2 classroom. *The Canadian Modern Language Journal, 54*(3), 314–342. https://doi.org/10.3138/cmlr.54.3.314

Azkarai, A., & García Mayo, M. D. P. (2017). Task repetition effects on L1 use in EFL child task-based interaction. *Language Teaching Research, 21*(4), 480–495. https://doi.org/10.1177/1362168816654169

Brooks-Lewis, K. A. (2009). Adult learners' perceptions of the incorporation of their L1 in foreign language teaching and learning. *Applied Linguistics, 30*(2), 216–235.

Brooks, F. B., & Donato, R. (1994). Vygotskyan approaches to understanding foreign language learner discourse during communicative tasks. *Hispania, 77*, 262–274.

Bygate, M. (1996). Effects of task repetition: Appraising the developing language of learners. In J. Willis & D. Willis (Eds.), *Challenge and change in language teaching* (pp. 136–146). Oxford, UK: Heinemann.

Canagarajah, S. (2011). Codemeshing in academic writing: Identifying teachable strategies of translanguaging. *The Modern Language Journal, 95*(3), 401–417.

Canagarajah, A. S., & Wurr, A. J. (2011). Multilingual communication and language acquisition: New research directions. *Reading Matrix: An International Online Journal, 11*(1), 1–15.

Carless, D. R. (2004). Issues in teachers' reinterpretation of a task-based innovation in primary schools. *TESOL Quarterly, 38*(4), 639–662. https://doi.org/10.2307/3588283

Carless, D. R. (2008). Student use of the mother tongue in the task-based classroom. *ELT Journal, 62*(4), 331–338. https://doi.org/10.1093/elt/ccm090

Cook, V. (2001). Using the first language in the classroom. *The Canadian Modern Language Review, 57*(3), 402–423. https://doi.org/10.3138/cmlr.57.3.402

Doughty, C., & Pica, T. (1986). "Information gap" tasks: Do they facilitate second language acquisition? *TESOL Quarterly, 20*(2), 305–325. https://doi.org/10.2307/3586546

Ellis, R. (2003). *Task-based language learning and teaching*. Oxford, UK: Oxford University Press.

Ellis, R. (2008). *The study of second language acquisition*. Oxford: Oxford University Press.

Ellis, R. (2018). *Reflections on task-based language teaching*. Bristol, UK: Multilingual Matters.

Ellis, R., & Shintani, N. (2013). *Exploring language pedagogy through second language acquisition research*. New York, NY: Routledge.

Ellis, R., & Yuan, F. (2004). The effects on planning on fluency, complexity and accuracy in second language narrative writing. *Studies in Second Language Acquisition, 26*(1), 59–84.

García Mayo, M. D. P., & Imaz Agirre, A. (2016). Task repetition and its impact on EFL children's negotiation of meaning strategies and pair dynamics: An exploratory study. *The Language Learning Journal, 44*(4), 451–466. https://doi.org/10.1080/09571736.2016.1185799

García, O. (2009). *Bilingual education in the 21st century: A global perspective*. Maldan, MA: Wiley.

García, O., & Sylvan, C. E. (2011). Pedagogies and practices in multilingual classrooms: Singularities in pluralities. *Modern Language Journal, 95*(3), 385–400. https://doi.org/10.1111/j.1540-4781.2011.01208.x

García, O., & Wei, L. (2014). *Translanguaging: Language, bilingualism and education.* Basingstoke, UK: Palgrave Macmillan.

Gass, S., & Varonis, E. (1985). Task variation and non-native/non-native speaker negotiation of meaning. In S. Gass & E. Varonis (Eds.), *Input in second language acquisition* (pp. 149–161). Rowley, MA: Newbury House.

Guk, I., & Kellogg, D. (2007). The ZPD and whole class teaching: Teacher-led and student-led interactional mediation of tasks. *Language Teaching Research, 11*(3), 281–299.

Hall, G., & Cook, G. (2012). Own-language use in language teaching and learning. *Language Teaching, 45*(3), 271–308. https://doi.org/10.1017/S0261444812000067

Howatt, A. (1984). *A history of English language teaching.* Oxford, UK: Oxford University Press.

Kim, Y., & Petraki, E. (2009). Students' and teachers' use of and attitudes to L1 in the EFL classrooms. *Asian EFL Journal, 11*(4), 58–89.

Lantolf, J. & Thorne, S. L. (2007). Sociocultural theory and second language learning. In B. van Patten & J. Williams (Eds.) *Theories in second language acquisition* (pp. 201–224). Mahwah, NJ: Lawrence Erlbaum.

Lasito, & Storch, N. (2013). Comparing pair and small group interactions on oral tasks. *RELC Journal, 44*(3), 361–375. https://doi.org/10.1177/0033688213500557

Lemke, J. (2002). Language development and identity: Multiple timescales in the social ecology of learning. In C. Kramsch (Ed.), *Language acquisition and language socialization* (pp. 68–87). London, UK: Continuum.

Long, M. H. (2009). Methodological principles for language teaching. In M. H. Long & C. Doughty (Eds.), *The handbook of language teaching* (Blackwell handbooks in linguistics) (pp. 373–394). Malden, MA: Wiley-Blackwell.

Long, M. H. (2015). *Second language acquisition and task-based language teaching.* West Sussex, UK: Wiley.

May, S. (2014). Disciplinary divides, knowledge construction and the multilingual turn. In S. May (Ed.), *The multilingual turn: Implications for SLA, TESOL and bilingual education* (pp. 7–31). New York, NY: Routledge.

Moore, P. J. (2013). An emergent perspective on the use of the first language in the English-as-a-foreign-language classroom. *The Modern Language Journal, 97*(1), 239–253.

Moore, P. J. (2017). Unwritten rules: Code choice in task-based learner discourse in an EMI context in Japan. In *English medium instruction in higher education in Asia*-Pacific (pp. 299–320): Springer.

Newton, J. (2013). Incidental vocabulary learning in classroom communication tasks. *Language Teaching Research, 17*(2), 164–187. https://doi.org/10.1177/1362168812460814

Newton, J., & Bui, T. (2017). Teaching with tasks in primary school EFL classrooms in Vietnam. In M. Ahmadian & M. D. P. G. Mayo (Eds.), *Current trends in task-based language teaching and learning* (pp. 259–278). Boston, MA: Mouton de Gruyter.

Newton, J., & Nguyen, B. T. (2019). Task rehearsal and public performance in task-based language teaching at a Vietnamese high school. *Language Teaching for Young Learners, 1*(1).

Park, S. (2010). The influence of pretask instructions and pretask planning on focus on form during Korean EFL task-based interaction. *Language Teaching Research, 14*(1), 9–26. https://doi.org/10.1177/1362168809346491

Pham, H. H. (2007). Communicative language teaching: Unity within diversity. *ELT Journal, 61*(3), 193–201.

Plonsky, L., & Kim, Y. (2016). Task-based learner production: A substantive and methodological review. *Annual Review of Applied Linguistics, 36*, 73–97.

Seals, C. A. (forthcoming). Classroom translanguaging through the linguistic landscape. In D. Malinowski, H. Maxim, & S. Dubriel (Eds.), *Language teaching in the linguistic landscape: Mobilizing pedagogy in the public space.* New York, NY: Springer.

Seals, C. A., & Olsen-Reeder, V. I. (Eds.). (2019). *Embracing multilingualism across educational contexts*. Wellington, New Zealand: Victoria University Press.

Shintani, N. (2014). Using tasks with young beginner learners: The role of the teacher. *Innovation in Language Learning and Teaching, 8*(3), 279–294. https://doi.org/10.1080/1750122 9.2013.861466

Skehan, P. (1998). *A cognitive approach to language learning*. Oxford, UK: Oxford University Press.

Storch, N., & Aldosari, A. (2010). Learners' use of first language (Arabic) in pair work in an EFL class. *Language Teaching Research, 14*(4), 355–375. https://doi.org/10.1177/1362168810375362

Storch, N., & Wigglesworth, G. (2003). Is there a role for the use of the L1 in an L2 setting? *TESOL Quarterly, 37*(4), 760–770.

Swain, M. (2009). Languaging, agency and collaboration in advanced second language proficiency. In H. Burns (Ed.), *Advanced language learning: The contribution of Halliday and Vygotsky* (pp. 95–108). London, UK: Continuum.

Swain, M. (1995). Three functions of output in second language learning. In G. Cook & B. Seidlhofer (Eds.) *Principle and practice in applied linguistics* (pp. 125–144). Oxford: Oxford University Press.

Swain, M., & Lapkin, S. (1995). Problems in output and the cognitive processes they generate: A step towards second language learning. *Applied Linguistics, 16*, 371–391.

Swain, M., & Lapkin, S. (2000). Task-based second language learning: The uses of the first language. *Language Teaching Research, 4*(3), 251–274. https://doi.org/10.1177/136216880000400304

Tognini, R., & Oliver, R. (2012). L1 use in primary and secondary foreign language classrooms and its contribution to learning. In E. Alcón Soler & M.-P. Safont-Jordà (Eds.), *Discourse and language learning across L2 instructional settings* (pp. 53–77). New York, NY: Rodopi.

Weber, J.-J. (2014). *Flexible multilingual education: Putting Children's needs first*. Bristol, UK: Multilingual Matters.

Chapter 14
Translanguaging for Vocabulary Development: A Mixed Methods Study with International Students in a Canadian English for Academic Purposes Program

Angelica Galante

Abstract Translanguaging has been largely implemented in bilingual classrooms, but there is a paucity of research investigating this approach in classrooms where more than two languages co-exist. Moreover, it is still unclear what particular dimensions of language learning are positively affected by translanguaging. This chapter reports results from a mixed methods study examining whether translanguaging has positive effects on academic vocabulary compared to a traditional monolingual approach. Seven English for Academic Purposes teachers used two different approaches with their students ($n = 129$): translanguaging to a treatment group and English-only to a comparison group. Data from students' vocabulary tests, classroom observations, and learner diaries were analyzed and compared for convergence. Results show that students in the translanguaging group had significant higher scores in academic vocabulary at the end of the program compared to students in the monolingual group. Results also show that students in the translanguaging group engaged in meaning-making across languages and took an active role in language learning, suggesting that translanguaging may provide engagement in vocabulary learning in ways which monolingual practices may not. Implications for TESOL education in multilingual settings are discussed.

Keywords Translanguaging · Language pedagogy · TESOL · Vocabulary learning · Plurilingualism · EAP · ESL · Classroom research · Mixed methods research

1 Introduction

In many societies across the globe, there has been an increase in travel, migration and immigration, contributing to diversifying landscapes. Diversity is also present in many English as a Second Language (ESL) classrooms, where students already

A. Galante (✉)
McGill University, Montreal, QC, Canada
e-mail: angelica.galante@mcgill.ca

© Springer Nature Switzerland AG 2020   293
Z. Tian et al. (eds.), *Envisioning TESOL through a Translanguaging Lens*,
Educational Linguistics 45, https://doi.org/10.1007/978-3-030-47031-9_14

have one, two or more languages in their repertoire before learning English. For many years, language pedagogy, including in TESOL, has neglected the students' diverse linguistic repertoires (Cook, 1999, 2016; Cummins, 2007, 2009), despite urgent calls for a reconceptualization of effective pedagogy and the need for a multilingual/plurilingual turn (Conteh & Meier, 2014; Kubota, 2016; May, 2014; Piccardo, 2013; Piccardo & Puozzo Capron, 2015). This much needed turn has been shown to be effective when applied in pedagogy as it validates students' plurilingual identity, particularly in multilingual settings such as Canada (Galante, 2019a; Stille & Cummins, 2013; Prasad, 2015), provides opportunities to advance language learning and creates equitable spaces in TESOL (Galante, 2020a). Thus, delivering monolingual language instruction in multilingual settings is incongruent with the present social reality. In Canada, many English for Academic Purposes (EAP) programs have classrooms with international students from different language backgrounds, and adopting pedagogy that moves away from monolingualism is much needed. This was the goal of the study reported in this chapter.

Researchers have been investigating pedagogy that overcomes the monolingual bias for quite some time, but some have emerged outside the TESOL field. Within a plurilingual framework (Council of Europe, 2001, 2018), one of the several pedagogical approaches is *intercomprehension* (Doyé, 2005), which encourages students to use their existing linguistic repertoire to mediate learning a new language they have not formally (at school) been introduced to (Melo-Pfeifer, 2014). Another approach is *comparons nos langues* (Auger, 2004), which also draws on language learners' repertoire for comparison of linguistic features between two or more languages, promoting metalinguistic awareness (Dault & Collins, 2017). *Translingual* practices consider synergies among languages and the integration of semiotic systems to communicate meaning (Canagarajah, 2016; Horner, Lu, Royster, & Trimbur, 2011), and students draw on languages, symbols and modes of communication with different degrees of language mixing (Canagarajah, 2013). *Translanguaging* is a pedagogical approach within the plurilingual framework that has gained much attention, and while it shares similarities with other strategies—i.e., drawing on students' linguistic repertoire—, it goes beyond the focus on linguistic dimensions to explore fluid and flexible language use (García & Li, 2014; Otheguy, García, & Reid, 2015) that is creative, critical and engages learning on meaning-making. These approaches support a plurilingual shift in language pedagogy and have been effectively used in multilingual contexts (Dault & Collins, 2017; Galante, 2019a) but this chapter will focus on translanguaging only.

It is important to note that plurilingualism and translanguaging share similarities. Having emerged from different epistemological traditions, both plurilingualism and translaguaging consider the notion of repertoire as central to language learning (García & Otheguy, 2020). The fact that plurilingualism has been explicitly used in European documents such as the Common European Framework of Reference for languages (CEFR) (CoE, 2001, 2018) have led to questions about its applicability in non-European contexts particularly where language learners are from minoritized and racialized communities (Flores 2013; García & Otheguy, 2020). However, the same questions could be asked about translanguaging, as it also has European origins. Of crucial importance, however, is to examine whether the pedagogical implementation of plurilingualism and/or translanguaging can ultimately benefit minoritized communities (García & Otheguy, 2020). In this chapter I report research on translanguaging as a pedagogical approach that was conceptualized within a plurilingual theoretical framework. This choice was made for two main reasons: (1) most of the research on translanguaging focus on bilingual classrooms and an examination of translanguaging in classrooms where more than two languages co-exist was much needed, and (2) a vast majority of the language learners in the research context were from different minoritized linguistic and racial backgrounds living in Canada, a non-European country, and taking the plural nature of these backgrounds (as opposed to only one or two) was deemed necessary.

This chapter therefore seeks to contribute to the growing applied linguistics literature in multilingual/plurilingual times, with a particular focus on pedagogy in TESOL. Specifically, I report results of a mixed methods study in an EAP program at a Canadian university that examined the effects of pedagogical translanguaging on academic vocabulary learning. The chapter first provides a brief overview of pedagogical translanguaging, which served as the conceptual foundation for the design of the language tasks. It then outlines the details of the study and ends with a discussion of the implications for TESOL. Finally, the chapter provides arguments for the inclusion of pedagogies that challenge monolingual ideologies and the need for more empirical studies in this area.

2   Spontaneous Translanguaging and Pedagogical Translanguaging

Translanguaging is often used to describe the natural phenomenon in which multilinguals engage using the languages in their repertoire, also called spontaneous translanguaging (Cenoz & Gorter, 2015; Li, 2011). People who are comfortable using two or more languages often use their linguistic repertoire naturally, moving from one language to another in different communicative situations (CoE, 2001, 2018; Coste, Moore, & Zarate, 2009; Marshall & Moore, 2018). Spontaneous translanguaging allows multilinguals to use language flexibly and creatively (Galante, 2019b), mixing languages and inventing new representations of language (Li, 2018). For example, a speaker of English and Spanish can use an English word in a sentence which is mostly in Spanish as in "Yo tengo que hacer un homework hoy" to mixing grammatical features of Spanish into an sentence in English as in "Can you take mi photito, please?" While spontaneous translanguaging is an observable phenomenon that occurs frequently and naturally in daily life interactions, translanguaging can also be purposefully used in pedagogy, also known as pedagogical translanguaging (Cenoz, 2017; García, Johnson, & Seltzer, 2017).

Pedagogical translanguaging can also be seen as deriving from the concept of languaging, which is an approach used in language classrooms to engage learners cognitively when using language for meaning-making (Swain, 2006, 2010; Swain,

Lapkin, Knouzi, Suzuki, & Brooks, 2009). In an English class, for example, learners can *language* (as a verb) in English to talk things through (Swain, 2010; Swain & Lapkin, 2002). For example, learners use English in discussions with classmates to try to figure out the meaning of a text or to talk about a topic in English, that is, they are using English to make meaning of particular linguistic items and/or to gain knowledge of new concepts or ideas in English texts. Translanguaging, however, goes beyond the act of languaging in that discussions are not done in the target language only. In fact, pedagogical translanguaging requires that students use the languages in their repertoire to make meaning of the target language. In this sense, the term translanguaging is used in this chapter for pedagogical purposes with the understanding that language learners will engage in *languaging* not only in one but in two or more languages.

Pedagogically, translanguaging has been heavily applied in bilingual education (Creese & Blackledge, 2010; Gort, 2015; Martínez, Hikida, & Durán, 2015; Palmer, Martínez, Mateus, & Henderson, 2014; Schwarts & Asli, 2014), but less in multilingual contexts where more languages are present in the classroom (Canagarajah, 2011; Cenoz & Gorter, 2015). In bilingual classrooms, teachers often—although not always—share the same linguistic repertoire as the students. In multilingual classrooms, however, several languages which are not always shared among students and the teacher are present, adding a more complex dimension that is unique to this context.

While translaguaging studies have contributed to the applied linguistics literature, they mostly document translanguaging as a natural phenomenon among multilinguals, with few studies examining the effects of translaguaging as pedagogy on language learning, particularly on vocabulary development. For example, a study conducted in South Africa (Makalela, 2015) with pre-service teachers shows that pedagogical translanguaging had a positive effect on learners' vocabulary development. In the study, participants were multilingual speakers of African languages and took an additional language course in Sepedi; they were divided into two groups: an experimental group that received pedagogical translanguaging and a control group that received lessons following a one-language-only approach. Over time, it was found that participants who engaged in translanguaging had increased gains in Sepedi vocabulary compared to students who did not receive the intervention. Another study conducted in the US (Infante & Licona, 2018) found that students who received translanguaging in an English/Spanish dual middle school science classroom engaged in higher and more meaningful scientific concepts and content of the curriculum. These two studies provide evidence that pedagogical translanguaging afford opportunities to explore meaning-making, increasing vocabulary learning in the target language, although more research is needed to confirm these results.

Clearly, translanguaging is a social linguistic practice in which multilinguals naturally engage for creative representations of language (Li, 2011, 2018; Bradley et al. 2017; Galante, 2019b). In the classroom, translanguaging as pedagogy can open up possibilities for meaning-making across languages and students can access knowledge by engaging their whole linguistic repertoire (García et al., 2017). In addition, creating *translanguaging spaces* (Li, 2011) where students make use of the languages in their repertoire and also learn about the languages of their peers can be a transformative experience to engage in meaning-making across languages.

3   Translanguaging and Power Among Languages

Pedagogical translanguaging cannot ignore existing monolingual expectations and power relations among languages, particularly among minoritized languages. Take the city of Toronto in the province of Ontario, for example: while Canada has official English-French bilingual policies, English is the dominant language in all Canadian provinces, with the exception of Quebec where French is the dominant language. In Toronto alone, despite the fact that nearly half of the population speaks a language other than English or French as a mother tongue (Statistics Canada, 2016), the dominant language is still English. In ESL programs, including EAP, it is important to discuss the social dominance of English with students and encourage them to continue to use and develop all of the languages in their repertoire.

The issue of language dominance is also of particular importance as language assessment is still largely done in a monolingual manner. Because of current institutional language policies and constraints, teachers are required to use monolingual models of language assessment even if they pedagogically engage students in using the languages in their repertoire (Galante et al., 2020; Schissel, de Korne, & López-Gopar, 2018). For example, in Canadian English-speaking universities, students may translanguage in the classroom but assessment is in English only. In addition, in order to be admitted into a university program, students need to take high-stakes tests (e.g., TFI for French and TOEFL and IELTS for English) and perform in a monolingual way so they can gain access to education. This conflicting situation in which tensions between pedagogy that is linguistically relevant to a multilingual population and the expectations from educational institutions of students' monolingual performance needs careful consideration.

Another concern is the extent to which translanguaging can be used in the classroom. Some teachers feel unprepared to implement pedagogy that promotes the use of other languages in the classroom (Ellis, 2013; Galante et al., 2019; Pauwels, 2014) and others, even if prepared, are concerned that the amount of exposure to other languages can limit exposure of the target language (Galante, 2020b). In contexts with language policies that promote minority languages, the use of a majority language in the classroom is seen as a threat. In the Basque context, for example, teachers have reported being worried about translanguaging, fearing that the use of Spanish, a majority language, can weaken and disempower Basque (Arocena, Cenoz, & Gorter, 2015). Thus, while translanguaging can be a transformative pedagogical approach, power relations among languages need to be examined in the context where instruction is delivered (Cummins, 2017; Jaspers, 2018; Turner &

Lin, 2017) and the dominating social perspective of deficit when languages are mixed cannot be ignored (MacSwan, 2017).

The present study adds to the research of translanguaging in a context that has linguistic tensions: an EAP program with pedagogical translanguaging in an English-speaking university in the (non-official) multilingual city of Toronto, Canada. Successful completion of this EAP program grants student admission into an undergraduate program in the same university, whose language of instruction is English. Thus, while translanguaging was used as pedagogy, it was done so within some constraints within the EAP program, which largely followed a monolingual English-only approach.

4 Methodology

This chapter reports a study that was part of larger research project investigating affordances of plurilingual instruction (Galante, 2018) in an EAP program located in the city of Toronto, Canada. The focus of this chapter is on the implementation of two sets of tasks to two different groups of students: one that received three pedagogical translaguaging tasks and the other that received three monolingual English-only tasks. The research methodology is described below.

4.1   Research Design and Sampling

This was a mixed methods study with a quasi-experimental design, with students being part of two intact groups (Creswell & Plano Clark, 2017). At the time of data collection, six teachers had two sections of the Academic Listening & Speaking course and they were asked to choose one section to be the treatment group and one the comparison group. One teacher had only one section and she chose it as a treatment group. In total, there were seven groups of students that made up the treatment group and six groups of students that made up the comparison group. The teachers were made aware that they would implement different tasks in each group and the goal of the study was to investigate the effectiveness of these tasks. No further details were given as not to affect the results of the study.

A total of seven EAP teachers and 129 adult students participated in the study. After the seven teachers chose which of their sections would be the treatment and the comparison groups, the student sample consisted of 79 in the treatment group and 50 in the comparison group, as indicated in the table below (Table 14.1).

All of the teachers were somewhat proficient in at least one additional language besides English but most of the teachers had proficiency in three or more languages. These were highly experienced teachers who had a minimum of 10 years of teaching, a Master's degree in Education or Applied Linguistics, and a TESOL certificate. Students were between 18 and 21 years old, all with international status in

Table 14.1 Student
distribution across groups

Instructor	Treatment	Comparison
Instructor 1	$n = 6$	$n = 11$
Instructor 2	$n = 11$	$n = 8$
Instructor 3	$n = 14$	$n = 8$
Instructor 4	$n = 12$	$n = 8$
Instructor 5	$n = 13$	$n = 9$
Instructor 6	$n = 10$	$n = 6$
Instructor 7	$n = 13$	–
Total	$N = 79$	$N = 50$

Canada, coming from different countries: Korea, Japan, Taiwan, Turkey, and Ecuador, with a vast majority of student participants from China (84%). All of the students had IELTS scores between 5 and 6, and had been placed in the same course after completing a placement test at the EAP program. They had all received conditional offer by the university provided that they completed the EAP program successfully.

4.2   Research Questions

Two research questions guided the study:

RQ1. Do students who engage in pedagogical translanguaging (treatment group) have more gains in academic vocabulary in the target language at the end of the EAP program compared to students who engage in traditional monolingual pedagogy (comparison group)?
RQ 2. To what extent does pedagogical translanguaging engage EAP students in meaning-making across languages?

4.3   The Tasks

As noted, both treatment and comparison groups followed the same curriculum with similar tasks but with different pedagogical orientations: the treatment group received three tasks that used translanguaging while the comparison group received three tasks that used monolingual practices (see sample of one set of tasks in the Appendix). Both sets of tasks were applied at weeks 3, 5 and 7 of a 12-week EAP program, as indicated in Table 14.2.

The two sets of tasks focused mostly on academic listening and speaking skills to suit the EAP course (see a sample of each set in Appendices 1 and 2). Below is description of the tasks:

4.3.1 Task 3 (Week 3)

The monolingual task focused on strategies to make small talk. A warm-up engaged students to think of situations and topics for small talk and a few strategies were presented. The task ended with a presentation in front of the class with role-plays created by the students. The translanguaging task, on the other hand, focused on engaging students to recognize spontaneous translanguaging. A warm-up asked students to think of situations where they would use fluid linguistic practices, followed by a video showing people from different linguistic backgrounds naturally translanguaging (Lim, 2015). Because the people in the video used the term code-switching, students often used the term code-switching—instead of translanguaging—during the data collection. Students then participated in a class discussion—with spontaneous translanguaging taking place— in which they talked about reasons for translanguaging. The task ended with a presentation in front of the class with role-plays created by the students showing situations in which they spontaneously translanguaged. While audience members watched the role-plays, they were encouraged to guess the meaning of the non-English words/sentences and possible reasons for language mixing. Task 3 was the only task that did not focus on particular vocabulary items and explored overall language use. Task 3 set the stage for the upcoming tasks, especially for students in the treatment group as translanguaging was a new pedagogical strategy used.

4.3.2 Task 5 (Week 5)

With a clear focus on vocabulary, Task 5 explored idiomatic expressions, a requirement of the EAP curriculum. In both groups, students engaged in a warm-up activity that asked them about idiomatic expressions with which they were familiar and their use in everyday conversation. A set of 18 idiomatic expressions was presented to both groups, who first tried to guess their meaning and later engaged in meaning-making. While the monolingual task asked students to work individually and use idiomatic expressions in sentences, the translanguaging task asked students to work in pairs or small groups and identify whether the expressions were present in other languages and whether they had similar/different meanings. Both sets of tasks ended with a role-play of a situation where the comparison group used some of the idiomatic expressions in English while the treatment group used idiomatic expressions in both English and other languages, while audience members guessed the meaning of the non-English idioms.

Table 14.2 Task distribution across groups

Week	Treatment	Comparison
Week 3	*Translanguaging task 3*	*Monolingual task 3*
Week 5	*Translanguaging task 5*	*Monolingual task 5*
Week 7	*Translanguaging task 7*	*Monolingual task 7*

4.3.3   Task 7 (Week 7)

Task 7 focused on discourse markers, also a requirement of the EAP curriculum. In both groups, students engaged in a warm-up activity that asked them about discourse markers in English with which they were familiar and the purposeful use in speech, but students in the treatment group were also asked about the use of discourse makers in other languages. A set of 8 discourse markers was presented to both groups. While students in the comparison group completed the task in English only, the students in the treatment group were encouraged to translanguage. Students from both groups watched videos to analyze the speakers' use of discourse markers, but with different topics: study abroad and intercultural communication to comparison and treatment groups respectively. The task ended with a group discussion of the respective topics, once again having the comparison group perform the task monolingually while the treatment group was encouraged to translanguage.

Taken together, both sets of tasks had the same vocabulary focus but different pedagogical approaches. They were all delivered in the same week and had similar length, between 30–40 min.

4.4   Data Collection

Three data collection instruments were used:

1. a monolingual (English-only) vocabulary test that was applied to students in both treatment ($n = 79$) and comparison groups ($n = 50$) at the end of the EAP course. It tested a limited amount of vocabulary items that both groups studied during the program: idiomatic expressions and discourse markers. The choice of these items stemmed from the existing curriculum and the fact that both groups had received the exact same amount of exposure to the vocabulary, but with different approaches. The test assessed students' knowledge of receptive meaning and use of idioms and discourse markers: students looked at sentences with blank spaces and were required to complete them using one vocabulary item from a list provided. The number of vocabulary items in the list was two times higher than the number of sentences;
2. three classroom observations were conducted in each of the seven treatment groups ($n = 21$). These observations were conducted at three different times: start (week 3), mid (week 5) and toward the end of the program (week 7). During the observations, I aimed to examine the extent to which students engaged with meaning-making during vocabulary learning and their overall reactions to translanguaging;
3. diary entries from learners in each of the seven treatment groups gathered their overall opinions of the translanguaging tasks, with a total of 197 entries. After completing the pedagogical translanguaging tasks, students—at home—were asked to write their perceptions of the tasks and whether they found them helpful for overall learning. Each student wrote a paragraph of approximately seven to ten lines.

4.5 Data Analyses

Following a convergent parallel design (Creswell & Plano Clark, 2017), quantitative data from vocabulary tests and qualitative data from diaries and classroom observations were first analyzed separately and subsequently mixed at the interpretation phase to look for convergence or divergence. Quantitative data from vocabulary tests were analyzed using IBM SPSS version 25, with independent samples t-tests to investigate gains in vocabulary mean scores. Qualitative data from classroom observations were analyzed through a content analysis, and a thematic analysis of learner diary entries was conducted using QSR's NVivo 11. The analysis process is described in Table 14.3.

5 Results

The goal of the study was twofold: (1) to investigate vocabulary learning in two different instructional approaches; and (2) to examine the extent to which pedagogical translanguaging engages students in meaning-making compared to monolingual English-only tasks. The results are presented under each RQ below.

5.1 RQ1: Academic Vocabulary

Students in both groups completed a test at the end of the EAP program, which required the completion of sentences with appropriate academic vocabulary in English only. This was a test applied solely for the purposes of the study and was not part of the course assessment, so students had not purposefully studied for this test. As previously noted, students in both groups received instruction of the same vocabulary items, which included idiomatic expressions and discourse markers.

First, mean scores were calculated for all items of the vocabulary test combined. Then, an independent samples t-test was conducted to investigate whether there

Table 14.3 Data sources and analytical approaches for each research question

Research question	Data sources	Data analyses
RQ1. Do students who engage in pedagogical translanguaging (treatment group) have more gains in academic vocabulary in the target language at the end of the EAP program compared to students who engage in traditional monolingual pedagogy (comparison group)?	Vocabulary tests	Independent samples t-tests
RQ 2. To what extent does pedagogical translanguaging engage EAP students in meaning-making across languages?	Classroom observation	Content analysis
	Student diaries	Thematic analysis

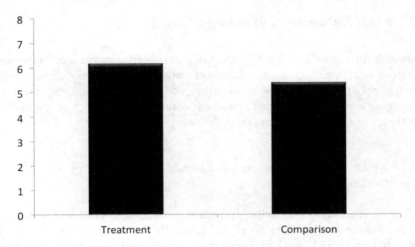

Fig. 14.1 Vocabulary mean scores for both treatment and comparison groups

would be a significant difference between scores from students in both treatment and comparison groups. The t-test revealed that there was a significant difference in vocabulary scores between treatment ($M = 6.15$, $SD = 1.50$) and comparison groups ($M = 5.36$, $SD = 1.57$) at the end of the program, $t(127) = 2.77$, $p < .01$, indicating that vocabulary gains among participants in the treatment group were significantly higher compared to participants in the comparison group. Figure 14.1 shows the difference in vocabulary scores.

While knowledge of vocabulary was limited to idioms and discourse markers, the fact that students in the treatment group did better than the students in the comparison group shows that pedagogical translanguaging may have had a positive effect on vocabulary learning. The translanguaging tasks were particularly designed with the purpose to engage students in meaning-making across languages while the monolingual tasks simply engaged in meaning in English only. It could be that with translanguaging, comparing and reflecting on concepts and use of academic vocabulary in different languages, not only between L1 or L2 but other languages spoken by students and their peers, facilitated English vocabulary learning. Although a pre-test at the start of the program (Time 1) was not applied, all of the students in both groups reported having similar English proficiency levels (i.e. IELTS scores). Thus these results compare mean scores between groups at the end of the program rather than a comparison between groups and over time. The next section provides results of the process of vocabulary engagement that emerged from the other two data sources, complementing the results of the vocabulary tests.

5.2   RQ2: Engaging in Meaning-Making

The results of content analysis of three classroom observations in each of the seven groups ($n = 21$) and of thematic analysis of student diary entries of three translanguaging tasks ($n = 197$) are included in this section and organized into four major converging results that emerged from both data sets. The names of the students reported here are pseudonyms of their choice.

5.2.1   Result 1—Translanguaging as a Gradual Process to Meaning-Making

During the classroom observations, I noted that students' level of engagement during the translanguaging tasks developed gradually. In the first round of observations, students looked surprised when teachers deliberately asked them to use their entire linguistic repertoire, including languages and dialects they spoke fluently and others in which they had limited knowledge. In all seven groups, students looked shocked but pleased when the teachers asked them to speak in another language in class. For example, in order to explore concepts in different languages, teachers explicitly asked students to go beyond the cognitive level—thinking about the concepts in the languages they spoke—to speak and even teach the concepts in other languages to both their peers and the teacher. In one class, the teacher asked a Chinese student to say an equivalent word of English in Chinese, but instead of speaking in Chinese, the student explained in English that the concept was the same. The teacher insisted and reiterated that the student could say the word in Chinese, but the student was still hesitant: she first looked at her peers to get confirmation that the teacher wanted her to speak in Chinese and asked the teacher, "*Do you want me to speak in Chinese?*" When the teacher nodded, the student had a smile on her face and immediately spoke the academic vocabulary in Chinese, explaining it to her peers with a mix of English and Chinese. This initial shock is unsurprising given that the students had probably been used to monolingual approaches only in the classroom. In my second and third round of observations, translanguaging seemed to be a common practice.

Results from the diary entries analysis converge with my observations and show that while students immediately accepted translanguaging as pedagogy, it was a novel practice to them, at least in the classroom. Kevin, a student from China, explains:

> It is funny because I use it all the time but none of us aware about it. During the activity of presenting each group's performing, it made me noticed that code-switch can be used almost every time with two people from same culture background. I feel that this task changes my attitude of code-switch. I felt weird when someone is talking in two languages but now I feel it is normal. This task is so helpful.

For Kevin, pedagogical translanguaging helped him realize that his fluid use of language was normal and not a deficiency; he also learned that spontaneous translaguaging is used by many language speakers of all cultures, and not only among Chinese-English bilinguals. Like Kevin, most students in all seven classes reported positive attitudes toward translanguaging when it was first introduced as a pedagogical approach in the classroom. At first, many students reported that their spontaneous translanguaging practices were simply being validated by the teacher, but with time their diary accounts show that they gained understandings that pedagogical translanguaging could be used for meaning-making across languages. In class, students often performed role-play scenarios that required the use of languages in their repertoire and also watched their peers perform in languages that they did not necessarily understand. These role-plays may have provided an opportunity for students to be exposed to languages that were not part of their repertoire and use all of their semiotic resources to both convey and understand the message. Rather than being afraid of the unknown, students were encouraged by the teachers to make efforts to understand the meaning of the message in other languages, even if they were not proficient in these languages. Sophie, a student from China, clearly articulated this feeling the first time translanguaging was introduced in the curriculum:

> When I talk with people from my own language background here in Toronto, I switch between Chinese and English. Here I just use the English word to express it. This class is much more interesting than the previous one. There was a role-play during the class. I really feel like being involved and getting to understand the topic.

In this account, Sophie referred to a role-play in which students mixed languages when eating at a restaurant in Toronto's Chinatown, which reflected most of the students' reality. The role-play shows that even in Toronto, where the dominant language is English, people interact in many other languages in the public realm.

A result that was not found during the observations emerged in the diary entries: the use of translanguaging gradually became more complex, with higher engagement of cognition for meaning-making. By the third diary entry, toward the end of the program, several students expressed elaborate thoughts of how they were using their linguistic resources. Momo, a student from China, explains how discourse markers are used in both English and Chinese and what they mean in different languages:

> This task makes me realize different people have different ways in terms of expressing their ideas. However, this task concentrated more on saying things "logically". In other words, how to express ideas that can make people understand. During this task, I realize that English sounds more logic than Chinese in terms of explaining things step by step. In English, people usually use "Firstly, Secondly, Lastly" these connectors to make their thoughts coherent. However, in Chinese, we do not say these connectors on casual talk. Therefore, English speakers sometimes feel confused when we explain things since we do not use transfer languages frequently. In addition to that, different cultural backgrounds shape people's way to talk. Therefore, we need to be respect and have patience to listen to understand the difference. I think this task is helpful because it shows different talking strategies for different people and it is fun to get to know about diverse cultures that behind varies talking strategies. (Momo)

This critical reflection among languages and cultures enhanced Momo's understandings of language use: translanguaging was viewed as raising metalinguistic awareness, further contributing to the development of empathy during intercultural communication. Many of the students seemed to have little awareness of the extent to which culture can influence language use, and among the Chinese speakers, results show that through translanguaging pedagogy they gained understandings of the difference between the use of discourse markers across languages.

Taken together, analyses from both classroom observations and student diary entries show that translanguaging was gradually welcomed by students in the curriculum and moved from the perception of validation of a spontaneous phenomenon practiced by multilinguals to the development of rich and complex engagement of language for meaning-making.

5.2.2   Result 2—Translanguaging in Action: Students Exercising their Agency

When students were engaged in the translanguaging tasks, they often took on the role of the teacher to explain the meaning of words across languages, which may have afforded students with opportunities to exercise their agency. During the classroom observations, I noted that teachers often invited students to explain abstract concepts, words, and language use to their peers, either standing in front of the class or in small groups. Students seemed to have high engagement in the translanguaging tasks and often volunteered to show their knowledge, putting themselves in a position of authority. While explaining, their peers and the teacher listened attentively and showed interest by asking follow-up and clarification questions. For example, during one observation, a Chinese student volunteered to explain the meaning of the idiom *burn your bridges* in English and related it to Chinese:

> In China we have the same idiom but it means that you should just move forward and not look back and imagine the future is better. You have no choice, so you must be brave. So it has a positive meaning. This is part of Chinese culture.

In this particular example, the Chinese student highlighted a difference in meaning across languages and while he was explaining it to his classmates, his Chinese classmates were nodding, all agreeing with his explanation. Students seemed to be committed to actively learning vocabulary items from their peers. The active role taken by the students can also be interpreted as a liberating experience: because students had knowledge of other languages and cultures, they did not seem to be afraid of being judged when translanguaging and explaining the cultural reasoning behind the vocabulary items. This process also provided teachers with an opportunity to be in the role of the student and to remind them that the process of language learning is complex and often rooted in culture.

In their diaries, a vast majority of the students reported that translanguaging was a linguistic practice in which they engaged, even in monolingual spaces such as the university environment, as explained by Apple:

> I often use mix language with my classmate. Sometimes, it is hard to use only one language for me. My friends also have the same problem. There is some word cannot replace by other language. It is normal for us use different language to deliver our meaning, especially in school. (Apple)

It is possible that the translaguaging tasks allowed students to feel empowered about their flexible language use, which may have strengthened agency over their repertoire. Like Apple, other students reported using different languages in conversation or even in one single sentence to facilitate the accuracy in meaning given that in some languages translations equivalents are not always the best option. Students also confidently reported that spontaneous translanguaging is effective particularly when all speakers share the same language, not requiring translations. Pipi Pig explains:

> This is an interesting phenomenon in reality, especially international students who must be speaking at least two different kinds of language. For example, "我明天有一个作业要完成", it means that "tomorrow I have an assignment needs to be done". It is the most popular sentence between us. It is useful because we don't need to translate the meaning into our own language but other could understand. However, I would not appropriate to switch in formal occasion, or when we talk to people who don't know the meaning of those words. (Pipi Pig)

Pipi Pig's account provides evidence of pragmatics awareness: he knows when translanguaging is suitable and appropriate and when the use of one language only would be more efficient. This is an important result as teachers may be afraid that if translanguaging is used in the classroom, students will not use the target language, English in this case.

In short, both diary entry and classroom observation data show that students exercised agency when using their linguistic repertoire for meaning making, developed awareness of social conventions as well as of when translanguaging is beneficial in conversations or when it should be avoided. Many students reported that certain situations require monolingual performance, including the EAP program where assessment is in English only. Nevertheless, despite the monolingual expectations, students showed appreciation for the pedagogical translanguaging used by the teachers. Thus, the provision of a translanguaging space (Li, 2011) in the classroom, where pedagogically students were encouraged to access their entire linguistic repertoire and actively engage in meaning making was transformative and may have facilitated vocabulary learning.

5.2.3   Result 3—Translanguaging for Meaning-Making across Languages: Similarities and Differences

Because pedagogical translanguaging encourages students to make meaning across languages, I observed that teachers asked students to reflect on the target English vocabulary items in other languages/dialects that students knew, with the goal of looking for similarities and differences in meaning. Students were also encouraged to observe whether some vocabulary items existed in one language only, with no equivalent translation or meaning. For example, when asked about idioms in other languages, students were required to translate the meaning of the idiom—not necessarily word by word—or provide a similar idiom in another language. From my observation, students seemed highly engaged by contributing idioms that they knew in other languages. To show students the process of pedagogical translanguaging, one teacher made comparisons of idioms in English to idioms in Japanese, two languages in her repertoire: she used one idiom in Japanese and later explained that it meant *"when you leave a place, you have to leave it in the same condition as you entered"* but also explained that the literal translation of the Japanese idiom was *"the bird that leaves the water does not make a splash."* This connection to meaning may have facilitated understanding of the idiom because some students reported in their diary that they enjoyed—what one student called—this *"new way of learning."*

While the monolingual tasks had the same vocabulary items, the translanguaging tasks may have been more beneficial as students made comparisons with other languages in their repertoire. For example, many students reported similarities between English idioms and idioms in other languages, which could have contributed to an understanding that idioms are present in many languages and may even have the same meaning. In EAP programs, it is not uncommon for students to think that learning idioms is a challenging task, especially because of the high number of existing idioms and that meaning is not literal. Typically, students learn idioms by memorizing techniques and using them in sentences, which may have been the case among students in the monolingual group. In contrast, the translanguaging tasks encouraged a certain level of awareness that idioms can have similar meanings across languages and are frequently used in daily speech, at least in English. One interesting observation was that some students indicated that learning English idioms through translaguaging was more interesting than simply attempting to memorize them, especially because they could understand how they are embedded in culture, as explained by Mavis:

> I learned many idioms from today's lecture. I think I will use the English idiom "call it a day" more often. Most idioms are easy to explain in my first language because there always have a similar idioms in my first language. The idioms show the attractive part of the language, which there always have another meaning behind the words. I realized that we use idiom in English could make the English speaking more interesting. (Mavis)

While idioms could also be a topic of interest among students in the comparison group, Mavis' account reflects what I observed in the classroom: when students made connections of idioms in their own languages, learning idioms seemed to be more meaningful.

Despite similarities across languages, another interesting finding was that translanguaging may have enhanced awareness of differences across languages, particularly in terms of language use. For example, many students reported that while discourse markers in English are often used in both spoken and written language, in Chinese, discourse markers are not used as often. In addition, some students observed that discourse markers can make their speech—in English—sound organized and have a logical flow; therefore, they concluded that they probably use discourse markers more often in English than in Chinese. Similarly, one Spanish speaker student pointed out that discourse markers in English and Spanish are nearly the same but the difference lies in the usage, especially when writing; he argued that while in English there is the need to use discourse markers to signal what is coming next, writing in Spanish does not require discourse markers as frequently.

Results show that translanguaging opened up possibilities for students to develop metalinguistic awareness about similarities and differences in meaning as well as usage across languages. This awareness raising process may have been afforded by translanguaging pedagogy, and students in the comparison group may not have been as engaged given that the monolingual tasks simply required that students reflect on meaning-making in English only.

5.2.4 Result 4—Translanguaging for Building an Inclusive Learning Community

One concern that is often raised by language teachers who are willing to use pedagogical translanguaging in a multilingual classroom is whether students will have someone with whom they can talk in the languages in their repertoire. In bilingual programs where most students share the same L1 this is rarely an issue. However, in multilingual classrooms where students have different languages in their repertoire teachers often worry that students may be isolated if no one shares the languages they speak. During my observations, students often chatted with peers who spoke the same languages to either ask about an equivalent English vocabulary in their L1, or to ask for confirmation of the meaning of vocabulary. Rather than translanguaging to exclude others, as language teachers may fear, students often reported using translanguaging for the purpose of being inclusive, as highlighted by Harden:

> Code-switching can help people establish close connections, communicate more effectively and include others in conversation. Moreover, it may also make people able to teach others about their languages and use language in a creative way. (Harden)

In this study, students were often working in small groups to complete a task and in each group a majority of the students were from China with only one student who was non-Chinese. Often, the Chinese students would translanguage, moving from English to Chinese or a Chinese dialect but always ensured to use English to include the non-Chinese students in the conversation, at least during my observations. This awareness of when and how to translanguage could be attributed to students' maturity levels— they were all adults—or to the fact that they were all multilinguals and translaguaging to include others who do not share the same language in conversation may already be a common daily practice that happens outside of class.

Several students wrote in their diary that translanguaging can also be used with people whose languages are not shared. They reported that if someone starts using a language that they do not know, this is a learning opportunity—contrary to common beliefs that translanguaging can be disrespectful if not exclusively used among people who share the same languages. Sunny, a Chinese student, explains opportunities to learn Spanish from one of her peers:

> This [translanguaging] benefits the people who are talking to me, also me, myself, because we can learn from each other. When I talk to Isabella, she suddenly speaks something I don't know but I'll ask her what's that mean so I can learn something in Spanish. (Sunny)

Teaching each other words in the languages that students spoke seemed to be a common practice in the classroom and results from both learner diary and classroom data show that students felt included—rather than excluded as some teachers might think—in conversations. Interestingly, some students engaged in their whole linguistic repertoire and did not limit their language use to L1 only by teaching their peers a few words in Spanish, French, Korean, Russian, Chinese and some Chinese dialects. Diary data provides further evidence that some students engaged in translanguaging to learn the languages of their peers, which could or not be the L1.

> The task helped me know many English idioms and also learned some idioms in Spanish and Korean. (Amber)

> This task let me know more idioms even in Korean, Spanish and English. (Christian)

It is important to note that using two or more languages in conversation was dependent on the speaker's proficiency and comfort levels using these languages, but translanguaging also occurred when students had partial competence or even knew only a few words or expressions in additional languages. In this way, students seemed aware of their limitations in knowledge of other languages but still seemed to maintain that there were benefits for learning each other's languages, even if this meant learning only one or two vocabulary words:

> I learned so many different languages such as Korean, Russian and Cantonese. As I used a few sentences in other language, I usually spoke to the native speaker in some way to show off that I knew their language. It is not systematically learning process, just a few words or sentences, but still the communication between languages without English is so comfortable, it gave me the feeling of closer relationship which English can't give. (Wei)

> We learned some special words from this class and enhanced our vocabulary. It feels good. (Ting)

Besides learning vocabulary words in languages other than English, I also observed that the students who did not speak Chinese made use of technology to mediate language learning. The teachers in this study allowed students to use their mobile phones to look up words in online dictionaries and gather information from websites in different languages. Thus, the use of technology was an added strategy that afforded translanguaging.

Concerns often raised by language teachers about the extent to which pedagogical translanguaging is inclusive are laudable; after all, they wish to use pedagogy that is suitable to their students. The results reported in this section show that allowing students to use technology and to teach words in the languages in their repertoire were effective strategies that made students feel included in classroom practices. This is an important result as it provides evidence that translanguaging can include and engage students in meaning-making.

6   Conclusion: Implications for TESOL

In countries with increasing social multilingualism, such as Canada, many language classrooms reflect this multilingual reality. In EAP classrooms in Canada and other countries, there is an urgent need to implement pedagogy that is inclusive and engages all students in language learning, but practical application is still considered a challenge among teachers (Ellis, 2013; Galante et al., 2019; Pauwels, 2014). The overarching goal of this study was to examine the extent to which pedagogical translanguaging can engage students in meaning-making across languages and whether this engagement would have a positive effect on learning vocabulary in the target language. Results show that students who engaged in translanguaging tasks had a significant increase in vocabulary at the end of the program compared to students who learned vocabulary following monolingual practices. In addition, results from students in the translanguaging group also show high engagement in meaning-making, which may have had a positive impact on vocabulary learning. This study suggests that pedagogical translanguaging offers unique opportunities for language learning that goes beyond linguistic items and transcend boundaries across languages. Affordances such as inclusion of student engagement in the tasks and opportunities for students to take an active role in vocabulary learning were found and deserve attention in TESOL.

While the results of this study are not generalizable and more research is needed to examine the extent to which translanguaging has a positive effect on vocabulary learning and other dimensions, the results obtained here are largely favorable. One recommendation for TESOL is to include pedagogical translanguaging in teacher training programs such as TESL, TEFL and TESOL professional certificates. Such change can better prepare both pre- and in-service instructors to shift their pedagogical orientations and implement translanguaging spaces (Li, 2011) in the classroom.

While translanguaging is not a new pedagogical strategy, the link between theory and pedagogy needs to be further explored, particularly in multilingual classrooms where the teacher and the students do not always have a shared language. Context-specific implementation along with existing social and institutional language tensions also deserve attention (Galante 2020a; Schissel et al., 2018). While translanguaging can be a transformative pedagogical approach, it cannot ignore the existing power relations among languages (Arocena et al. 2015; Cummins, 2017; Jaspers, 2018; Turner & Lin, 2017) in the context where it is applied. Many educational contexts, which was the case of the research site of the study reported in this chapter, require that students perform in a monolingual manner to gain access to higher education, and the language is typically the official language of the country.

Thus, while translanguaging can be successfully used as pedagogy, it may not yet be feasible to include multilingual assessment in certain contexts and students still need to be prepared academically to perform in one language only to gain access to higher education. The fact that most higher education settings, at least in North America, still require high-stakes English tests such as IELTS and TOEFL for university entry contradicts pedagogical orientations that respect and push for multilingualism. Therefore, while it is important that an analysis of the context be carried out when implementing pedagogical translanguaging, it can still be infused in the language curriculum.

Pedagogically, this study shows one manner to shift the paradigm in language teaching from the historical monolingual tradition to a multilingual/plurilingual paradigm. In TESOL, when teachers are supported and know how to apply translanguaging, they can infuse it in the language curriculum and start shifting pedagogy away from monolingualism without fearing the use of languages other than English in the classroom.

Appendices

Appendix 1: Sample of a Pedagogical Translanguaging Task

Slides	Instructions
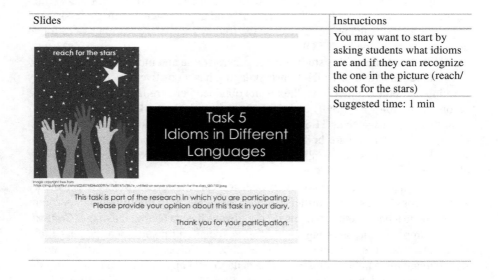	You may want to start by asking students what idioms are and if they can recognize the one in the picture (reach/shoot for the stars)
	Suggested time: 1 min

Slides	Instructions
 **Warm-up** take a 1. Why do people use idioms? 2. Can you think of some idioms in English? 3. Can you think of some idioms in other languages/dialects? picture from Kate Spade taken from https://www.katespade.com/products/rain-check-umbrella/135247.html	Ask students if they have ever heard of the idiom "take a rain check" and what it means. This task helps students reflect on the use of idioms in English and in other languages. Idioms are phrases that are fixed and have figurative or literal meaning. They can be used to represent meaning in a more accurate and creative way. Students can work in pairs or in small groups and share a few ideas about each question. Suggested time: 5 min
18 Idioms – Guessing Game 1. Reach/shoot for the stars 2. Take a rain check 3. Off the top of my head 4. Give it a shot 5. Speak your mind 6. Go out of your way to do something 7. A rip off 8. Have mixed feelings about something 9. Know your stuff 10. Get your act together 11. Play it by ear 12. Have second thoughts 13. Out of the blue 14. Have a chip on your shoulder 15. Get something off your chest 16. Burn your bridges 17. Call it a day 18. Play the devil's advocate	Hand out accompanying worksheet and show each idiom in this slide to your students. Have students work in groups (of 3 or 4) and try to find out what the idioms mean. Give them about 20 s to write the meaning of each idiom in the worksheet (page 1). Tell them that they will be able to check their answers at the end of the activity and record their score in the worksheet. Suggested time: 10 min

Slides	Instructions
18 Idioms - Worksheet 1. First, take a look a the idiom and its definition. Did you get them right? What was your score? 2. Second, choose *Yes* or *No* for an equivalent or translation of this idiom in your fist language/dialect or other languages you know. 3. Third, write two idioms in your first language/dialect or another language you know. Explain the definition in English. Decide if there is an equivalent in English. 4. Finally, share the two idioms with the class. Say the idiom in the original language and explain its meaning in English. Would you use this idiom in conversations in English?	1. On page 2 of their worksheet, students check their answers and record their score.
	2. Ask students to reflect on a possible equivalent of this idiom in their languages/ dialects. If there is an equivalent, ask them to write it and say it in the original language.
	3. Ask students to contribute with two idioms in their first language/dialect (or another language they know). They can say the idiom and have others in the group guess what idioms it is. In English conversations, students can use idioms in their first language and explain to the English speaker what this means.
	4. This question can be answered as a class so students can share the idioms in their first language/dialect with others.
	Suggested time: 10 min
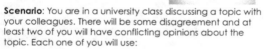**Scenario: Managing Conflict** ○ You will work in groups of 3 or 4. ○ **Scenario**: You are in a university class discussing a topic with your colleagues. There will be some disagreement and at least two of you will have conflicting opinions about the topic. Each one of you will use: ○ **1) one idiom (from the worksheet) in English and** ○ **2) one idiom in your first language/dialect** ○ One or two of you will manage the conflict and try to solve the problem. **Your audience will identify the idioms you have used.**	Get students to work in groups of 3 or 4 with (ideally) one person from a different language background.
	Give each group about 5 min to prepare their scene. Ask each student to pick one idiom in English and one idiom in their first language/dialect. When they present their scene, encourage students to speak the second idiom in their first language and explain it in English during the conversation. It is important that students understand how to use the idiom in their first language in English conversations to ensure more language and cultural diversity, even if the conversation is in English.
	Have groups present their scene in front of the class. Tell the groups that the audience will identify the idioms used.
	Suggested time: 15 min

Slides	Instructions
During this task: What English idiom do you think you will use more often? Was it easy to explain the idiom in your first language/dialect to your colleagues? In future conversations in English, you might want to use idioms from your first language for a concept or an idea that doesn't exist in English	These questions serve to wrap up the task. You can ask these two questions to the whole class and have them share a few thoughts. Suggested time: 2 min
 Task 5 **Idioms in Different Languages** Image copyright free from https://img.clipartfest.com/af2zd07682da5009f07e17b/874fb76b7e_untitled-on-emaze-clipart-reach-for-the-stars_580-750.jpeg **You have completed Task 5** This task is part of the research in which you are participating. At home, please provide your opinion about this task in your diary. **Thank you for your participation.**	This is simply a note to remind students to complete their diary entry. If you can remind them to do this when they arrive home, that would be much appreciated. Thank you for your collaboration!

Accompanying Worksheet for Pedagogical Translanguaging Task

Idiom	What do you think the meaning is?	Score
1. reach/shoot for the stars		□ 1 point
		□ 0
2. take a rain check		□ 1 point
		□ 0
3. off the top of my head		□ 1 point
		□ 0

(continued)

Idiom	What do you think the meaning is?	Score
4. give it a shot		□ 1 point
		□ 0
5. speak your mind		□ 1 point
		□ 0
6. go out of your way to do something		□ 1 point
		□ 0
7. a rip off		□ 1 point
		□ 0
8. have mixed feelings		□ 1 point
		□ 0
9. know your stuff		□ 1 point
		□ 0
10. get your act together		□ 1 point
		□ 0
11. play it by ear		□ 1 point
		□ 0
12. have second thoughts		□ 1 point
		□ 0
13. out of the blue		□ 1 point
		□ 0
14. have a chip on your shoulder		□ 1 point
		□ 0
15. get something off your chest		□ 1 point
		□ 0
16. burn your bridges		□ 1 point
		□ 0
17. call it a day		□ 1 point
		□ 0
18. play devil's advocate		□ 1 point
		□ 0
Total score		**/18 points**

Idiom	Meaning	Is there an equivalent/ translation in your first language/dialect?
1. reach/shoot for the stars	To set your goal or ambitions very high	□ Yes □ No
		If yes, write it here:
2. take a rain check	To refuse an offer/invitation but with the hope/promise that it can be postponed to a later date/time	□ Yes □ No
		If yes, write it here:
3. off the top of my head	Using only the ideas you have in your head at that moment	□ Yes □ No
		If yes, write it here:
4. give it a shot	Give it a try	□ Yes □ No
		If yes, write it here:
5. speak your mind	Say what you honestly feel	□ Yes □ No
		If yes, write it here:
6. go out of your way to do something	To take extra time to make an additional effort to do something	□ Yes □ No
		If yes, write it here:
7. a rip off	Something overpriced	□ Yes □ No
		If yes, write it here:
8. have mixed feelings	To be unsure about something	□ Yes □ No
		If yes, write it here:
9. know your stuff	To know something very well	□ Yes □ No
		If yes, write it here:
10. get your act together	Start behaving properly	□ Yes □ No
		If yes, write it here:
11. play it by ear	To improvise; to not make a plan but decide what to do as you do it	□ Yes □ No
		If yes, write it here:
12. have second thoughts	To have doubts	□ Yes □ No
		If yes, write it here:
13. out of the blue	Unscheduled, improvised	□ Yes □ No
		If yes, write it here:
14. have a chip on your shoulder	To seem angry all the time because you think you have been treated unfairly or feel you are not as good as other people	□ Yes □ No
		If yes, write it here:
15. get something off your chest	To say something serious or difficult that you have been thinking about for a while	□ Yes □ No
		If yes, write it here:
16. burn your bridges	Ruin a relationship	□ Yes □ No
		If yes, write it here:

(continued)

Idiom	Meaning	Is there an equivalent/ translation in your first language/dialect?
17. call it a day	Expression said near the end of a day which means "That's enough for today. Let's end and go home."	□ Yes □ No
		If yes, write it here:
18. play devil's advocate	To argue against somebody just so you can hear your opponent's reasoning	□ Yes □ No
		If yes, write it here:
Write an idiom in your first language/ dialect		Is There An Equivalent/ Translation In English?
		□ Yes □ No
		If yes, write it here:
Write an idiom in your first language/ dialect		Is There an equivalent/ translation in English?
		□ Yes □ No
		If yes, write it here:

Appendix 2: Sample of a Monolingual Task

Task 5
Idioms in English

image copyright free from
https://img.clipartfest.com/602d076824a500917e17bf8747b78b7e_unfilled-on-emaze-clipart-reach-for-the-stars_580-750.jpeg

This task is part of the research in which you are participating.

Thank you for your participation.

You may want to start by asking students what idioms are and if they can recognize the one in the picture (reach/shoot for the stars).

Suggested time: 1 min

Warm-up

1. Why do people use idioms?

2. Can you think of some idioms in English?

3. What do they mean?

take a

picture from Kate Spade taken from https://
www.katespade.com/products/rain-check-
umbrella/135247.html

Before starting the warm-up, ask students if they have ever heard of the idiom "take a rain check" and what it means (the meaning will be in the next activity).

This is a warm-up to help students reflect about the use of idioms in English. Idioms are phrases that are fixed and have figurative or literal meaning. They can be used to represent meaning in a more accurate and sometimes fun way.

Students can work in pairs or in small groups and share a few ideas about each question.

Suggested time: 5 min

18 Idioms – Guessing Game

1. Reach/shoot for the stars
2. Take a rain check
3. Off the top of my head
4. Give it a shot
5. Speak your mind
6. Go out of your way to do something
7. A rip off
8. Have mixed feelings about something
9. Know your stuff
10. Get your act together
11. Play it by ear
12. Have second thoughts
13. Out of the blue
14. Have a chip on your shoulder
15. Get something off your chest
16. Burn your bridges
17. Call it a day
18. Play the devil's advocate

Hand out worksheet and show each idiom in this slide to your students. Have them work in groups (of 3 or 4) and try to find out what they mean. Give them about 20 s to write the meaning of each idiom in the worksheet (page 1). Warn them not to look at page 2 because the answers are there. Tell them that they will be able to check their answers at the end of the activity and record their score in the worksheet.

Suggested time: 10 min

18 Idioms - Worksheet

1. First, take a look a the idiom and its definition. Did you get them right? What was your score?

2. Second, each one of you will be assigned one of two idioms. Write a sentence for each idiom you were assigned.

3. Third, share your sentences with the class.

Students can continue working in the same group of 3 or 4.

1. On page 2 of their worksheet, students can check their answers and record their score. If you have a competitive group, you may want to check who had the highest score and won the game.

2. Assign one or two idioms for each of your students (e.g., one student will have idioms 1 and 2, another student will have idioms 3 and 4, etc.). You might want to allow them about 5 min to complete their sentences.

3. Tell students to share their sentence with the whole class. If you want to turn this step into a listening activity, you might want to ask students to write down the sentences they hear. This could be good listening practice.

Suggested time: 10 min

Scenario: Managing Conflict

○ You will work in groups of 3 or 4.

○ **Scenario**: You are in a university class discussing a topic with your colleagues. There will be some disagreement and at least two of you will have conflicting opinions about the topic. Each one of you will use:

○ **one idiom in English**

○ One or two of you will manage the conflict and try to solve the problem. **Your audience will identify the idioms you have used.**

Get students to work in groups of 3 or 4.
Give each group about 5 min to prepare their scene. Ask each student to pick one idiom in English to use during the presentation of the scenario.
Have groups present their scene in front of the class. Tell the groups that the audience will identify the idioms used. This is also good listening practice.
Suggested time: 15 min

During this task:

What English idiom do you think you will use more often?

This question serves to wrap up the task. You can ask this question to the whole class and have them share a few thoughts.
Suggested time: 2 min

This is the end of task 5. Thank you for your collaboration!

Accompanying Worksheet for Monolingual Task

Idiom	What do you think the meaning is?	Score
1. reach/shoot for the stars		□ 1 point □ 0
2. take a rain check		□ 1 point □ 0
3. off the top of my head		□ 1 point □ 0
4. give it a shot		□ 1 point □ 0
5. speak your mind		□ 1 point □ 0
6. go out of your way to do something		□ 1 point □ 0
7. a rip off		□ 1 point □ 0
8. have mixed feelings		□ 1 point □ 0
9. know your stuff		□ 1 point □ 0
10. get your act together		□ 1 point □ 0
11. play it by ear		□ 1 point □ 0

(continued)

Idiom	What do you think the meaning is?	Score
12. have second thoughts		▢ 1 point ▢ 0
13. out of the blue		▢ 1 point ▢ 0
14. have a chip on your shoulder		▢ 1 point ▢ 0
15. get something off your chest		▢ 1 point ▢ 0
16. burn your bridges		▢ 1 point ▢ 0
17. call it a day		▢ 1 point ▢ 0
18. play devil's advocate		▢ 1 point ▢ 0
Total score		**/18 points**

Idiom	Meaning	Sentence
1. reach/shoot for the stars	To set your goal or ambitions very high	
2. take a rain check	To refuse an offer/invitation but with the hope/promise that it can be postponed to a later date/time	
3. off the top of my head	Using only the ideas you have in your head at that moment	
4. give it a shot	Give it a try	
5. speak your mind	Say what you honestly feel	
6. go out of your way to do something	To take extra time to make an additional effort to do something	
7. a rip off	Something overpriced	
8. have mixed feelings	To be unsure about something	
9. know your stuff	To know something very well	
10. get your act together	Start behaving properly	
11. play it by ear	To improvise; to not make a plan but decide what to do as you do it	
12. have second thoughts	To have doubts	
13. out of the blue	Unscheduled, improvised	
14. have a chip on your shoulder	To seem angry all the time because you think you have been treated unfairly or feel you are not as good as other people	
15. get something off your chest	To say something serious or difficult that you have been thinking about for a while	
16. burn your bridges	Ruin a relationship	
17. call it a day	Expression said near the end of a day which means "That's enough for today. Let's end and go home."	
18. play devil's advocate	To argue against somebody just so you can hear your opponent's reasoning	

References

Arocena, E., Cenoz, J., & Gorter, D. (2015). Teachers' beliefs in multilingual education in the Basque Country and in Friesland. *Journal of Immersion and Content-Based Language Education, 3*, 169–193. https://doi.org/10.1075/jicb.3.2.01aro

Auger, N. (2004). *Comparons nos langues. Démarche d'apprentissage du français auprès d'enfants nouvellement arrivés (ENA)*. Languedoc-Roussillon, France: CRDP. http://asl.univ-montp3.fr/masterFLE/n.auer/Livret_Comparons.pdf. Accessed 30 Dec 2019

Bradley, J., Moore, E., Simpson, J., & Atkinson, L. (2017). Translanguaging space and creative activity: theorising collaborative arts-based learning. *Language and Intercultural Communication, 18*(1), 54–73. https://doi.org/10.1080/14708477.2017.1401120

Canagarajah, S. (2011). Translanguaging in the classroom: Emerging issues for research and pedagogy. *Applied Linguistics Review, 2*, 1–28. https://doi.org/10.1515/9783110239331.1

Canagarajah, S. (2013). Negotiating translingual literacy: An enactment. *Research in the Teaching of English, 48*(1), 40–67.

Canagarajah, S. (2016). Translingual writing and teacher development in composition. *College English, 78*(3), 265–273.

Cenoz, J. (2017). Translanguaging in school contexts: International perspectives. *Journal of Language, Identity and Education, 16*(4), 193–198. https://doi.org/10.1080/15348458.2017.1327816

Cenoz, J., & Gorter, D. (2015). Translanguaging as a pedagogical tool for multilingual education. In J. Cenoz, D. Gorter, & S. May (Eds.), *Language awareness and multilingualism: Encyclopedia of language and education* (3rd ed., pp. 1–14). Cham, Switzerland: Springer.

Conteh, J., & Meier, G. (2014). *The multilingual turn: Opportunities and challenges*. Bristol, UK: Multilingual Matters.

Cook, V. (1999). Going beyond the native speaker in language teaching. *TESOL Quarterly, 33*(2), 185–209. https://doi.org/10.2307/3587717

Cook, V. (2016). Where is the native speaker now? *TESOL Quarterly, 50*(1), 186–189. https://doi.org/10.1002/tesq.286

Coste, D., Moore, D., & Zarate, G. (2009). *Plurilingual and pluricultural competence: Studies towards a Common European Framework of Reference for language learning and teaching*. Strasbourg, France: Council of Europe Publishing. https://www.coe.int/t/dg4/linguistic/Source/SourcePublications/CompetencePlurilingue09web_en.pdf. Accessed 30 Dec 2019

Council of Europe. (2001). *Common European framework of reference for languages*. Strasbourg, France: Council of Europe Publishing. http://www.coe.int/t/dg4/linguistic/source/framework_en.pdf. Accessed 30 Dec 2019

Council of Europe. (2018). *Common European framework of reference for languages: Learning, teaching, assessment-companion volume with new descriptors*. Strasbourg, France: Council of Europe Publishing. https://rm.coe.int/cefr-companion-volume-with-new-descriptors-2018/1680787989. Accessed 30 Dec 2019

Creese, A., & Blackledge, A. (2010). Translanguaging in the bilingual classroom: A pedagogy for learning and teaching? *Modern Language Journal, 94*(1), 103–115. https://doi.org/10.1111/j.1540-4781.2009.00986.x

Creswell, J. W., & Plano Clark, V. L. (2017). *Designing and conducting mixed methods research* (3rd ed.). Thousand Oaks, CA: Sage.

Cummins, J. (2007). Rethinking monolingual instructional strategies in multilingual classrooms. *Canadian Journal of Applied Linguistics (CJAL)/Revue canadienne de linguistique appliquée (RCLA), 10*(2), 221–240.

Cummins, J. (2009). Multilingualism in the English-language classroom: Pedagogical considerations. *TESOL Quarterly, 43*(2), 317–321.

Cummins, J. (2017). Teaching minoritized students: Are additive approaches legitimate? *Harvard Educational Review, 87*(3), 404–425.

Dault, C., & Collins, L. (2017). Comparer pour mieux comprendre: perception d'étudiants et d'enseignants d'une approche interlangagière en langue seconde. *Language Awareness, 26*(3), 191–210. https://doi.org/10.1080/09658416.2017.1389949

Doyé, P. (2005). *L'intercompréhension. Guide pour l'élaboration des politiques linguistiques éducatives en Europe—De la diversité linguistique à l'éducation plurilingue.* Strasbourg, France: Conseil de l'Éurope. https://rm.coe.int/l-intercomprehension/1680874595. Accessed 30 Dec 2019

Ellis, E. (2013). The ESL teacher as plurilingual: An Australian perspective. *TESOL Quarterly, 47*(3), 446–471. https://doi.org/10.1002/tesq.120

Flores, N. (2013). The unexamined relationship between neoliberalism and plurilingualism: A cautionary tale. *TESOL Quarterly, 47*(3), 500–520. https://doi.org/10.1002/tesq.114

Galante, A. (2018). *Plurilingual or monolingual? A mixed methods study investigating plurilingual instruction in an EAP program at a Canadian university* (Doctoral dissertation). Toronto, Canada: University of Toronto. http://hdl.handle.net/1807/91806. Accessed 30 Dec 2019

Galante, A. (2019a). Plurilingualism in linguistically diverse language classrooms: Respecting and validating student identity. In V. Kourtis-Kazoullis, T. Aravossitas, E. Skourtou, & P. P. Trifonas (Eds.), *Interdisciplinary research approaches to multilingual education* (pp. 65–78). New York, NY: Routledge.

Galante, A. (2019b). "The moment I realized I am plurilingual": Plurilingual tasks for creative representations in EAP at a Canadian university. *Applied Linguistics Review.* https://doi.org/10.1515/applirev-2018-0116

Galante, A. (2020a). Plurilingualism and TESOL in two Canadian postsecondary institutions: Towards context-specific perspectives. In S. M. C. Lau & S. van Viegen (Eds.), *Plurilingual pedagogies: Critical and creative endeavours for equitable language in education* (pp. 237–252). Cham, Switzerland: Springer.

Galante, A. (2020b). Pedagogical translanguaging in a multilingual English program in Canada: Student and teacher perspectives of challenges. *System, 92.* https://doi.org/10.1016/j.system.2020.102274

Galante, A., Okubo, K., Cole, C., Abd Elkader, N., Wilkinson, C., Carozza, N., … Vasic, J. (2019). Plurilingualism in higher education: A collaborative initiative for the implementation of plurilingual tasks in an English for academic purposes program at a Canadian university. *TESL Canada Journal, 36*(1), 121–133. https://doi.org/10.18806/tesl.v36i1.1305

Galante, A., Okubo, K., Cole, C., Abd Elkader, N., Carozza, N., Wilkinson, C., Wotton, C., & Vasic, J. (2020). "English-only is not the way to go:" Teachers' perceptions of plurilingual instruction in an English program at a Canadian university. *TESOL Quarterly Journal.* https://doi.org/10.1002/tesq.584

García, O., Johnson, S., & Seltzer, K. (2017). *The translanguaging classroom: Leveraging student bilingualism for learning.* Philadelphia, PA: Caslon.

García, O., & Li, W. (2014). *Translanguaging: Language, bilingualism and education.* New York, NY: Palgrave Macmillan.

García, O., & Otheguy, R. (2020). Plurilingualism and translanguaging: Commonalities and divergences. *International Journal of Bilingual Education and Bilingualism, 23*(1), 17–35. https://doi.org/10.1080/13670050.2019.1598932

Gort, M. (2015). Transforming literacy learning and teaching through translanguaging and other typical practices associated with "doing being bilingual". *International Multilingual Research Journal, 9*(1), 1–6. https://doi.org/10.1080/19313152.2014.988030

Horner, B., Lu, M.-Z., Royster, J. J., & Trimbur, J. (2011). Language difference in writing: Toward a translingual approach. *College English, 73*(3), 303–321.

Infante, P., & Licona, P. R. (2018). Translanguaging as pedagogy: Developing learner scientific discursive practices in a bilingual middle school science classroom. *International Journal of Bilingual Education and Bilingualism.* https://doi.org/10.1080/13670050.2018.1526885

Jaspers, J. (2018). The transformative limits of translanguaging. *Language and Communication, 58,* 1–10. https://doi.org/10.1016/j.langcom.2017.12.001

Kubota, R. (2016). The multi/plural turn, postcolonial theory, and neoliberal multiculturalism: Complicities and implications for applied linguistics. *Applied Linguistics, 37*(4), 474–494. https://doi.org/10.1093/applin/amu045

Li, W. (2011). Moment analysis and translanguaging space: Discursive construction of identities by multilingual Chinese youth in Britain. *Journal of Pragmatics, 43*(5), 1222–1235. https://doi.org/10.1016/j.pragma.2010.07.035

Li, W. (2018). Translanguaging as a practical theory of language. *Applied Linguistics, 39*(1), 9–30. https://doi.org/10.1093/applin/amx039

Lim, S. (2015, March 4). *Things bilingual people do* [Video file]. Retrieved from https://www.youtube.com/watch?v=ReHdQsB5rI8&t=6s

MacSwan, J. (2017). A multilingual perspective on translanguaging. *American Educational Research Journal, 54*(1), 167–201. https://doi.org/10.3102/0002831216683935

Makalela, L. (2015). Moving out of linguistic boxes: The effects of translanguaging strategies for multilingual classrooms. *Language and Education, 29*(3), 200–217.

Marshall, S., & Moore, D. (2018). Plurilingualism amid the panoply of lingualisms: Addressing critiques and misconceptions in education. *International Journal of Multilingualism, 15*(1), 19–34. https://doi.org/10.1080/14790718.2016.1253699

Martínez, R., Hikida, M., & Durán, L. (2015). Unpacking ideologies of linguistic purism: How dual language teachers make sense of everyday translanguaging. *International Multilingual Research Journal, 9*(1), 26–42. https://doi.org/10.1080/19313152.2014.977712

May, S. (Ed.). (2014). *The multilingual turn: Implications for SLA, TESOL and bilingual education.* New York, NY: Routledge.

Melo-Pfeifer, S. (2014). Intercomprehension between Romance Languages and the role of English: A study of multilingual chat-rooms. *International Journal of Multilingualism, 11*(1), 120–137. https://doi.org/10.1080/14790718.2012.679276

Otheguy, R., García, O., & Reid, W. (2015). Clarifying translanguaging and deconstructing named languages: A perspective from linguistics. *Applied Linguistics Review, 6*, 281–307. https://doi.org/10.1515/applirev-2018-0020

Palmer, D. K., Martínez, R. A., Mateus, S. G., & Henderson, K. (2014). Reframing the debate on language separation: Toward a vision for translanguaging pedagogies in dual language classroom. *The Modern Language Journal, 98*(3), 757–772. https://doi.org/10.1111/modl.12121

Pauwels, A. (2014). The teaching of languages at university in the context of super-diversity. *International Journal of Multilingualism, 11*(3), 307–319. https://doi.org/10.1080/14790718.2014.921177

Piccardo, E. (2013). Plurilingualism and curriculum design: Towards a synergic vision. *TESOL Quarterly, 47*(3), 600–614. https://doi.org/10.1002/tesq.110

Piccardo, E., & Puozzo Capron, I. (2015). Introduction. From second language pedagogy to the pedagogy of 'plurilingualism': A possible paradigm shift?/De la didactique des langues à la didactique du plurilinguisme: Un changement de paradigme possible? *The Canadian Modern Language Review/La revue canadienne des langues vivantes, 71*(4), 317–323.

Prasad, G. (2015). Beyond the mirror towards a plurilingual prism: Exploring the creation of plurilingual 'identity texts' in English and French classrooms in Toronto and Montpellier. *Intercultural Education, 26*(6), 497–514. https://doi.org/10.1080/14675986.2015.1109775

Schissel, J. L., de Korne, H., & López-Gopar, M. (2018). Grappling with translanguaging for teaching and assessment in culturally and linguistically diverse contexts: Teacher perspectives from Oaxaca, Mexico. *International Journal of Bilingual Education and Bilingualism.* https://doi.org/10.1080/13670050.2018.1463965

Schwarts, M., & Asli, A. (2014). Bilingual teachers' language strategies: The case of an Arabic-Hebrew kindergarten in Israel. *Teaching and Teacher Education, 38*, 22–32. https://doi.org/10.1016/j.tate.2013.10.013

Statistics Canada. (2016). Census Profile, 2016 Census: Toronto, City [census subdivision], Ontario and Canada [Country]. https://www12.statcan.gc.ca/census-recensement/2016/dp-pd/prof/details/page.cfm?Lang=E&Geo1=CSD&Code1=3520005&Geo2=PR&Code2=01&Dat

a=Count&SearchText=3520005&SearchType=Begins&SearchPR=01&B1=All&Custom=&T
ABID=3. Accessed 30 Dec 2019.

Stille, S., & Cummins, J. (2013). Foundation for learning: Engaging plurilingual students' linguistic repertoires in the elementary classroom. *TESOL Quarterly, 47*(3), 630–638. https://doi.
org/10.1002/tesq.116

Swain, M. (2006). Languaging, agency and collaboration in advanced language proficiency. In
H. Byrnes (Ed.), *Advanced language learning: The contribution of Halliday and Vygotsky*
(pp. 95–108). London, UK: Continuum.

Swain, M. (2010). Talking it through: Languaging as a source of learning. In R. Batstone (Ed.),
Sociolinguistic perspectives on second language learning and use (pp. 112–130). Oxford, UK:
Oxford University Press.

Swain, M., & Lapkin, S. (2002). Talking it through: Two French immersion learners' response to
reformulation. *International Journals of Educational Research, 37*(3–4), 285–304. https://doi.
org/10.1016/S0883-0355(03)00006-5

Swain, M., Lapkin, S., Knouzi, I., Suzuki, W., & Brooks, L. (2009). Languaging: University students learn the grammatical concept of voice in French. *Modern Language Journal, 93*, 5–29.
https://doi.org/10.1111/j.1540-4781.2009.00825.x

Turner, M., & Lin, A. (2017). Translanguaging and named languages: Productive tension and
desire. *International Journal of Bilingual Education and Bilingualism.* https://doi.org/10.108
0/13670050.2017.1360243

Chapter 15
EFL Instructors' Ambivalent Ideological Stances Toward Translanguaging: Collaborative Reflection on Language Ideologies

Christian Fallas-Escobar

Abstract In this chapter, I report findings of a qualitive study I conducted with three Costa Rican EFL instructors regarding their stances toward translanguaging. Using critical dialogues, I document the instructors' ambivalent ideological postures and the ways these shifted over time. Drawing on a language ideologies lens, I examine how their individual postures are informed by personal, institutional, and societal ideological orientations and how they manage to agentively reconfigure and appropriate them. Findings suggest that critical dialogues play an important role in providing instructors with opportunities to engage in the interrogation of the ideologies undergirding their teaching practices and the examination of the extent to which their pedagogical choices are shaped by circulating language ideologies. By and large, this study highlights (1) the potential of critical dialogues to help instructors develop agency to challenge broader ideologies, and (2) the promises translanguaging holds to serve as an entry point to resist the language ideologies currently shaping the EFL department in question.

Keywords Translanguaging · Critical dialogues · Language ideologies · Ideological work · Ideological stances · EFL instructors · Collaborative reflection

1 Introduction

In two studies I previously conducted at an English as a Foreign Language (EFL) Department at a Costa Rican university, I arrived at the conclusion that the participating EFL instructors' reported opposition to translanguaging partly arose from lack of

C. Fallas-Escobar (✉)
Department of Bicultural and Bilingual Studies, University of Texas at San Antonio,
San Antonio, TX, USA
e-mail: cristhian.fallasescobar@utsa.edu

© Springer Nature Switzerland AG 2020   329
Z. Tian et al. (eds.), *Envisioning TESOL through a Translanguaging Lens*,
Educational Linguistics 45, https://doi.org/10.1007/978-3-030-47031-9_15

opportunities to reflect upon the language ideologies underlying their language teaching practices (Fallas, 2016; Fallas & Dillard-Paltrineri, 2015). This need for opportunities to engage in reflection upon their ideological stances became even more apparent upon later noticing that these EFL instructors would often engage in fluid and dynamic language use during faculty meetings and informal exchanges in the hallways. While one alternative explanation would be to attribute such contradictions between articulated and embodied ideological stances to levels of awareness, I argue that these ambivalent stances also derive from the tensions that arise as they struggle to accommodate and resist institutionally endorsed and societal language ideologies shaping their teaching practices. Likewise, I surmise that collaborative reflection can potentially assist these (and other) EFL instructors in negotiating and challenging language ideologies embedded in personal, institutional, and societal scales.

In this chapter, I report results of a qualitative study I conducted with three instructors from the aforementioned EFL department. Drawing on a language ideologies lens (Kroskrity, 2006), this study consisted of a series of critical dialogue sessions (Marchel, 2007) I held with these EFL instructors about their posture toward their own and their students' translanguaging and toward instances of translanguaging in their classrooms. I document how these instructors' struggled to embrace translanguaging in their classrooms, as they navigated institutional and societal spaces that favor language separation. As findings suggest, even though instructors still hesitated to embrace translanguaging, dialogue about the complexities of its incorporation in their classrooms was an important step forward in collaboratively interrogating entrenched institutional and societal language ideologies and envisioning alternative pedagogical practices within their EFL classrooms.

2 Language Ideologies

While the connection between language and thought has received plenty of attention across disciplines, thoughts about language, or language ideologies, have been undertheorized until relatively recently. The various definitions following the increasing attention to language ideologies have created a tension between underscoring speakers' awareness as a form of agency and highlighting the embeddedness of these ideologies in the sociocultural spaces speakers navigate (Kroskrity, 2006, pp. 496–497). As Woolard (1998) expounds, the term language ideology bears four features that characterize the uses different scholars have given it at different points in time. First, ideology has been taken to be conceptual, and thus connected to beliefs, notions and ideas. Second, it has been understood as rooted in the experience or interests of particular groups, though constructed as universally true. Third, it has been associated with distortion, falseness, mystification or rationalization. Finally, language ideology has also been connected with the legimation of asymmetrical power relations.

Over the last three decades, scholars have critiqued long-held and pervasive language ideologies such as language hierarchy, standard language, one nation-one language, mother tongue, and language separation. All of these language ideologies can be traced back to the emergence of modern European Nation-States in the 1800s and 1900s, which created a monolingual-monocultural political imaginary (Makoni & Pennycook, 2007). Such imaginary forged ideological orientations that connect language to a sense of nationhood and citizenship, and thus language became a device to narrate and imagine the nation into being (Bhabha, 1994; Anderson, 1983; cited in Makoni & Pennycook, 2007, p. 140). However, the increasingly diverse nature of modern societies has made the monolingual-monocultural imaginary unsustainable and unethical. That is, the growing visibility of the translingual, transracial, and transnational subject (Alim, Rickford, & Ball, 2016) brought with it the need to turn to alternative pluralist ideological orientations that embrace diversity and heterogeneity, and challenge traditional conceptualizations of language use and learning.

For this study I draw on Kroskrity's (2006) conceptualization of language ideologies as being rationalizations about language that are either explicitly articulated or embedded in communication and constructed from the sociocultural experience of the speakers. As he posits, this ubiquitous set of beliefs provides speakers with frameworks upon which to judge language use (pp. 496–497). Such ideological frameworks spread and teach individuals to discriminate against certain types of language practices and the speakers who embody them (Lippi-Green, 2012). The explanatory power of Kroskrity's definition lies in that it acknowledges that language ideologies are multiple, partial, and context contingent, and that speakers may be aware, partially aware or unaware of the language ideologies they hold, ergo articulating and embodying them in a contradictory manner. Equally important, scholars have underscored central considerations for the study of language ideologies. Gal (1989, 1998) proposed focusing on *multiplicity and contention*: how language ideologies construct opposing realities that arise from multiple subjectivities within a single social formation. Irvine and Gal (2000) pointed to the *indexical nature* of language ideologies in that they connect forms of talk to social groups. Further, Blommaert (1999) pointed to the need to study the *historical (re)production* of language ideologies, as tracing the historical processes leading to the formation of ideologies can help arrive at a deeper understanding of ideological processes. For the present study, I examine the contention that arises as EFL instructors envision the implementation of translanguaging within an EFL department that largely endorses the language separation.

3   Translanguaging: Towards a Heteroglossic View of Language

In an effort to challenge deep-rooted monoglossic ideologies of language separation, numerous scholars (e.g Flores & Schissel, 2014, Li, 2011; Ortega, 2014) have advocated for a pedagogy that reflects the dynamic and fluid nature of bilingualism (García & Sylvan, 2011). In fact, the last decade has witnessed abundant studies that document the affordances of translanguaging (García, 2009). And yet, despite this push for more pluralist conceptualizations of language use and learning, ideologies that construct language as a bounded system and position monolingualism as the norm continue to be the tacit, sometimes consciously agreed upon, principles around which language curricula are structured and delivered. That is, despite efforts to dismantle this monolingual bias (Ortega, 2014), monoglossic, language separation ideologies continue to dominate in bilingual and foreign language education programs the world over (Martínez, Hikida & Durán, 2015).

The language separation ideology is so pervasive (Cummins, 2008) that languages continue to be compartmentalized, harnessed on the premise that each language works as an entirely separate system for emergent bilinguals (Grosjean, 1996). Believed to be most beneficial for learners, language programs are constructed upon monoglossic principles that "silence the ways in which [emergent bilinguals] language, thus limiting their educational and life opportunities" (Skutnabb-Kangas, 2009, p. 141) and depriving them from spaces to develop their bilingualism in spontaneous and authentic ways (Durán & Palmer, 2014). In programs that operate upon this and other ideologies, language instructors commonly enact English-only policies that force emergent bilinguals to leave what constitutes part of their intricate linguistic repertoire outside of the classroom to avoid cross-linguistic contamination (Martínez et al., 2015). Further, many of these instructors may feel compelled to compartmentalize and separate languages because allowing their students to use their mother tongue in the classroom implies returning to the widely criticized grammar-translation method (Creese & Blackledge, 2010, p. 105), thereby disregarding the documented benefits of translanguaging.

To be sure, monoglossic language ideologies suggesting "that legitimate practices are only those enacted by monolinguals" make way for ideologies of language separation, standard language, and mother tongue (Flores & Schissel, 2014, p. 457). Thus, multilingual teaching practices that allow learners to utilize all of their linguistic resources are frowned upon; so much so that instances of translanguaging are guilt-laden and attributed to laziness and carelessness (Creese & Blackledge, 2010, p. 105). As García-Mateus and Palmer (2017) explain, nonetheless, "strictly separating the language of instruction appears to inhibit both [emergent bilinguals'] development of positive identities and their willingness to take linguistic risks and engage in critical discussions that scrutinize societal issues related to equity" (2017, p. 245). Conversely, tranlanguaging creates flexible spaces where emergent bilinguals can utilize the totality of their communicative repertoire dynamically.

All in all, translanguaging holds promise to reconfigure how we understand and do language education (García, 2009). On the one hand, translanguaging has pedagogical value because it maximizes opportunities for learners to harness their compound linguistic repertoires and to take ownership of their status as bilingual speakers (Creese & Blackledge, 2010; Gort & Sembiante, 2015; Sayer, 2013; Schwartz & Asli, 2014). On the other, in-class translanguaging can potentially create spaces in which instructors and learners can challenge the ideologies implicit in English-only teaching policies (Grosjean, 1996; Sayer, 2013). As Flores (2014) stresses, however, we must not forget that translanguaging is a political act that cannot be disconnected from larger political struggles. In this sense, translanguaging is a tool that does more than scaffold bilingualism and biliteracy; it helps interrogate "…who benefits and who loses from understanding languages the way we do" (Creese & Blackledge, 2015, p. 24). In like manner, as Palmer, Martínez, Mateus, and Henderson (2014) assert, "If our goal as educators is to develop bilingual students, it seems wise to normalize translanguaging in the classroom," as it reflects the fluid and dynamic nature of language learning and use (García & Sylvan, 2011) in bilingual and EFL education settings.

Adopting translanguaging as the norm and leveraging students' translanguaging (De los Rios & Seltzer, 2017), however, requires creating and attending to ideological and implementational spaces (Hornberger, 2005), given that even in programs that construct bilingualism as a resource, instructors may develop ambivalent feelings towards dynamic and hybrid language practices (Durán & Palmer, 2014; Martinez, Hikida, & Durán, 2015). That is, while instructors think positively of translanguaging, they may at times also feel compelled to go back to monoglossic ideologies of language separation within the classroom, given institutional and societal pressures to keep languages separate and compartmentalized. Against this backdrop, language instructors' collaborative reflection on their own and institutional and societal ideological orientations promises to be a fruitful endeavor.

4 Methodology

4.1 Context and Participants

This qualitative study took place in a public Costa Rican university whose English as a Foreign Language (EFL) Department serves around 240 students; the majority of the student population being Costa Rican. The department offers a B.A. in EFL, a B.A. in the teaching of English as a foreign language (TEFL), and an M.A. in applied linguistics. As I confirmed in previous studies, instructors from this EFL Department largely favor ideologies of language separation in that they understand bilingualism as double monolingualism and linguistic purism as the rational option (Fallas, 2016; Fallas & Dillard-Paltrineri, 2015). Krista (39 years old), Linda (37 years old), and Alex (38 years old) agreed to collaborate in this research, in which I engaged with them in a series of critical dialogue sessions (Marchel, 2007) over the course of a semester; the premise being that dialoguing collaboratively and collegially would assist them in examining the language ideologies shaping their stances toward the heteroglossic perspective translanguaging is based upon.

Both Krista and Linda hold a bachelor's degree in TEFL and a master's degree in second language education whereas Alex holds a bachelor's degree in EFL and a master's degree in literature. At the time this study was conducted, these instructors had worked as language educators in the EFL Department in question for 6–8 years. Krista and Linda learned English in the BA and MA programs they completed while Alex started learning it in a private bilingual elementary school. It is worth mentioning that prior to this study, I had noticed that all four of us would informally engage in communication in ways that transcended language boundaries. That is, we oftentimes found ourselves translanguaging in the hallway or outside of campus, which came as a surprise to me given that they had previously expressed disagreement with translanguaging. As I noted earlier, this tension between their articulated and embodied ideologies led me to engage in the present research on their ideological stances.

4.2 Data Collection and Analysis

Given that ideologies are deeply entrenched and often invisible, I resolved to use critical dialogues, as these encourage educators "to examine underlying biases and assumptions that influence many important aspects of educational practice" (Marchel, 2007, p. 1). The value of critical dialogues lies in that "educators discuss teaching incidents and challenges with their peers in order to scrutinize personal experience and to avoid biased interpretations and actions in teaching" (p. 2). In this process, educators engage in collective inquiry in ways that promote constant reflection and reshape school culture (p. 2). Based on Freire's critical pedagogy and Vygotsky's sociocultural theory, critical dialogues have the potential to enable educators to engage in transformative thinking and practice and to pay "particular attention to ... patterns of power and privilege" that can be easily overlooked (Marchel, 2007, p. 2), especially amidst institutional pressures that instructors are exposed to.

To engage in critical dialogue with the instructors, I followed Marchel's (2007) four-step model. First, we discussed definitions of critical dialogue and the benefits it offers: "examination of thinking in order to make the best educational decisions for all students" (p. 5). Second, we discussed the stumbling blocks commonly encountered when engaging in critical dialogue: the blinders of assumption, the fallacy of intuition, and the rush to give advice. Third, I modelled an instance of critical dialogue for the instructors to better understand the practice. Finally, once they understood the dynamics of critical dialogues, we started having sessions about their postures regarding translanguaging. During the first session, we discussed the work of García (2009) and Li (2011). For the second critical dialogue session, they were commissioned to observe particular aspects of their classrooms related to their own and their students' language practices. For the third session, they were asked to experiment using translanguaging in their own classes. The last session revolved around whether they noticed any changes regarding their postures toward translanguaging and if they would implement it in their classrooms on a regular basis. Sessions were conducted using a discussion guide but were also open to instructor-initiated questions as well. It is also worth mentioning that although I specified that we could engage in translanguaging during these sessions, the instructors mostly participated monolingually in English.

I transcribed the 4 h of recorded data, which I later analyzed using inductive coding and focused coding. On the one hand, inductive coding enabled me to trace instances of instructors' articulation of their ideological stances and instances of narratives revealing their struggle to balance personal, institutional, and societal ideological orientations. On the other hand, focused coding allowed for the construction of an ideological stance profile for each instructor and also for the identification of major concerns causing them to develop ambivalent stances toward translanguaging. These concerns revolved around the potential complications instructors would face for incorporating translanguaging in their classrooms within an institution that endorses language separation. By and large, coding the data also helped identify moments of awareness of the ideologies underlying their posture and whether such awareness enabled them to re-assess their own postures and envision alternative teaching practices.

4.3   Researcher Positionality

As regards my own positionality, I am a Latino, Costa Rican, male, first generation university faculty, with an academic background in teaching English as a foreign Language (TEFL) and applied linguistics. Further, I am a fluent trilingual speaker of Spanish, English, and Portuguese, who has worked as an English language instructor and teacher educator for the last 17 years. Throughout my college years, an English-only classroom policy prevailed, to the point that transgressions on the boundaries of English as a named language were highly discouraged and taken as evidence of lack of proficiency. In retrospect, being limited to staying within language boundaries negatively impacted my own self-efficacy beliefs and my confidence in my bilingualism. Fortunately, encountering the concept of translanguaging and the scholarly work framing it (e.g. García, 2009; Otheguy, García & Reid, 2015) early in my career as a EFL instructor largely changed my own ideological orientations and classroom practices. By and large, this personal experience led to conduct a series of studies on tranlanguaging and this investigation on how critical dialogues centered around the construct of translanguaging could potentially help instructors in balancing and negotiating circulating language ideologies.

5   Discussion of Findings

On the whole, while the three instructors acknowledged that students habitually translanguage for different purposes and are somehow receptive of the practice under some conditions, not all three interpreted their own translanguaging in the same way for reasons that reveal broader institutional and societal pressures and ideological orientations. In this section, I first describe instructors' ambivalent ideological orientations and how their stances slightly shifted over the four critical dialogue sessions. Subsequently, I discuss the institutional and societal ideological orientations shaping the participating EFL instructors' stances to translanguaging, while also underscoring the fact that they do not passively give in to such orientations but agentively negotiate and appropriate them. I conclude by briefly referring to the affordances of engaging in collaborative and collegial reflection upon language ideologies.

5.1 Linda's Ambivalent Ideological Stance

From the onset, Linda was emphatic that she used English-only in class since beginning levels because students' exposure to as much English as possible was of utmost importance. She explained that she would address her students in English-only even when she ran into them in the hallways and off campus. As we moved along the sessions, however, she started to reveal that she did not mind her students' in-between-tasks translanguaging but had an issue with her own translanguaging. At points, she would defend language separation as a good teaching practice while at others she would explain that she used translanguaging to give grammar examples or explain vocabulary. As she reflected upon her classroom practices, she confessed that translanguaging is natural on the part of the students and on her part when mediating the learning of grammar and vocabulary. Beyond those limits, however, she would engage in policing practices in subtle ways, as she reported.

At times, as she recounted, when students needed to know the meaning of a word and her explanations did not suffice, she would have students translanguage until they arrived at the exact meaning, so as to avoid translanguaging herself. Ironically, while she thought that by engaging in this dynamic she avoided translanguaging, she was actually translanguaging in that she fluidly drew from her linguistic repertoire to respond accordingly and help students arrive at the meaning of the word in question. On the last session, Linda stated that her view of translanguaging had changed for both her students and herself, to the point that she started translanguaging in class beyond the grammar and vocabulary realms, without feeling unprofessional. Repeatedly throughout the sessions, she stated that ideologies of language separation were difficult to undo, given departmental pressures.

5.2 Alex's Ambivalent Ideological Stance

Alex was quite an exceptional case, as she did not have a background in TEFL. According to her, she translanguages when teaching grammar, but we later learn that she also translanguages when teaching literature. As we progressed along the sessions, Alex felt comfortable enough to reveal that she uses bilingual materials in her courses as part of her teaching. Unlike Linda, Alex explains that her students translanguage not only to transition between tasks but also to negotiate meaning within tasks. According to her, she feels at ease with her students' translanguaging, but a contradiction later arises.

During one session, she ascertains that she is more open to beginner students' translanguaging. To her, low proficiency students translanguage when they are struggling with English while more proficient students engage in the practice unconsciously. During another session, however, she explains she tries to force struggling students to stay on English and overlooks high achieving students' translanguaging, thereby constructing translanguaging as a crutch for the former and as a license for the latter. During her grammar classes, translanguaging serves as a tool to show them that languages are flexible and evolving communication systems. In the last session, Alex confesses that knowing there is a theory behind translanguaging makes her feel better about her teaching. Also, she explains that she understands keeping the entire class in English gives professors a sense of 'professionalism' within the department; a concern that all three instructors verbalized.

5.3   Krista's Ambivalent Ideological Stances

Among the three participants, Krista was the one instructor who had the hardest time envisioning translanguaging in her class. As she explains, her students translanguage in-between tasks or when she is not around to help, but she does not. Her discomfort with her own translanguaging was clear in one session in which she used a phrase in Spanish and immediately corrected herself by providing the English translation. Krista does not feel angry about her students' translanguaging, but whenever she hears Spanish -she reports- she turns around to see who is speaking and gives them subtle hints ("your Spanish is so beautiful!"). According to Krista, students' translanguaging normally serves as her cue that students are done with their task and she proceeds with the next one. In session two, she acknowledges that her students' translanguaging frustrates her and that the critical dialogues have made her think more about the reasons behind her irritation. During another session, Krista explains that while completing her TEFL degree she was taught that Spanish should not have a place in the EFL classroom, which is why she feels uncomfortable when she translanguages.

On the flip side, she confesses that she has learned that "the best way, but maybe not the right way," is to translanguage, especially when teaching lower proficiency students. For session three, instructors were encouraged to experiment with translanguaging in their classes. As she explicates, she failed at incorporating translanguaging because students are used to translanguaging in-between tasks but not as part of class instruction. As she stated, "A teacher's translanguaging is not normal and the students' reactions is the best proof that I have." She asserted that it was students' reactions to her translanguaging that pushed her to stay within the boundaries of English as a named language. During the last session, Krista reports that her view of students' translanguaging changed, but that her feelings toward her own translanguaging did not. She states she would not include translanguaging in her lesson plan, as she thinks translanguaging happens spontaneously on the part of the students but is not a practice she would include as part of her methodology or in her lesson plan.

5.4 Instructors' Balancing of Ideological Stances

Since the first critical dialogue session, the three instructors' ideological stances toward translanguaging were ambivalent in that they opposed to the practice but would indicate situations under which they would make exceptions. Although their stances slightly shifted and became more open to the practice, their stances still remained ambivalent. Yet, their ambivalent ideological stances should be understood as resulting from multiple pressures: loyalty to academic formation, institutional expectations, and broader concerns about the professional prestige English affords.

During sessions two, three, and four, instructors were invited to reflect about their postures toward translanguaging and dynamic bilingualism in general, and the most frequently referenced reason underlying their stance was the impact their academic formation had on them. When probed about their posture, Linda and Krista frequently stated they were implicitly and explicitly taught in their TEFL teacher preparation programs that language separation is a good practice, as evident in excerpts 1 and 2 below. And yet, they did not thoughtlessly follow language separation. In their experience as EFL instructors, they had realized that there were occasions in which dynamic use of language made sense and was productive. This suggests that they do not mindlessly adopt the language ideologies pushed down on them but reconfigure them in the face of their own classroom experiences.

Excerpt 1[1]
Linda: …They are learning English, so they're supposed to use English in the class…
Interviewer: "They're "supposed" says who?
Linda: To practice
Interviewer: But says who?
Linda: My professors when I was a student…

---

[1] Boldfacing indicates emphasis, capital letters indicate loudness, and ellipsis indicate pauses. Laughter is indicated in parenthesis.

Excerpt 2

Krista: … with this group I learned that sometimes the best way, maybe not the right way, but the best way for them to really get it, specially grammar, would be to go back to Spanish.

Interviewer: And why do you make that difference between the best way and the right way?

Krista: Because I would say, if you ask **me**, based on what I learned, the right way would be to have them understanding in English.

A second recurring concern that held them from more fully embracing translanguaging was a fear of being labeled 'unprofessional' for enacting practices that countered the department's ideological orientation. On one session, Linda described how using multilingual texts and clips made her nervous (excerpt 3 below). When asked about why she found herself having to justify her choice of materials, she stated that she did not want her students to go around saying she uses materials in Spanish when the goal of the department is to expose them to English-only input. Similarly, Alex stated that although she had always used translanguaging, she now feels better because she knows she is not breaking the rules and that there is a theory behind how she uses language in class (excerpt 4 below). The instructors' concerns around breaking the rules and looking professional suggest that departmental pressures to accommodate to certain language separation and language policing practices is so pressing that instructors struggle to break away from the existing English-only regime and embrace heteroglossic views. A final less frequently recurring concern revolved around the prestige that is connected to English. As the instructors coincided, at the departmental level, there is a tacit understanding that speaking English-only in class grants instructors more prestige (excerpt 5 below). Interestingly, the prestige argument fueling language separation also speaks back to ideologies of standard language and mother tongue ideologies in that they reference particular ways of speaking (formal) by particular kinds of people (native speakers).

Excerpt 3

Linda: Yeah, and I justify myself because …like a… 100% of the time what we do is that we bring material in English, we always try to look for …for… it doesn't really matter what the topic is, you always look for information in English, again, because they are learning it, because we're trying to help them, like to be surrounded (laughter) by English texts, videos, music, anything; and that …that was the reason why I thought: I better tell them because I don't want them going outside saying that we're watching videos in Spanish because someone is gonna get angry at me because I'm doing it.

Excerpt 4
Alex: Well, I don't, I haven't changed my mind because that's how I felt
  before.... I feel more at ease in the sense like, uhhhh, it's not breaking the
  rules, I never felt bad when I did it, but I always, I mean I thought it was
  okay, but now I feel more comfortable because there's like theory behind it
  [everyone laughs].

Excerpt 5
Linda: The same... the same ideas that we had back when we were students
  that Spanish is not okay, because you're an English professor, you are
  expected to speak perfect English.
Krista: I think it's a matter of prestige.

As evident in the critical dialogues, while some would argue the instructors'
ambivalence in their ideological stances may be the result of no or partial awareness,
it is clear that their postures are shaped by the language ideologies embedded in the
teacher preparation programs the completed, the EFL Department they work for, and
the broader society within which they situate themselves. This suggests that future
endeavors to assist these language instructors -and others- in further examining their
ideological stances and challenging circulating language ideologies should address
this intricate multi-scale ideological landscape within which they operate. These
three scales (personal, institutional, and societal) are filled with language ideologies
that are in dialogic relationship, affecting and shaping one another. Inevitably, EFL
instructors navigate such scales and are in turn shaped by them. Needless to say,
instructors do not thoughtlessly embrace these ideologies. As evident in this study,
the instructors only partially gave in to existing pressures, as they negotiated circulating ideologies and applied them in ways that made sense within their contexts.
And yet, the multiplicity and contention of circulating ideological orientations makes
providing opportunities for EFL educators to engage in collaborative collegial
reflection even more important, since it would allow EFL instructors to discuss the
struggles they face as they balance the needs of the students, their own needs for a
stable job and a sense of professionalism, and the demands of the institutions.

6   Lessons Learned

As evident in the present study, the three instructors displayed ambivalent stances
toward translanguaging. Although their postures toward translanguaging shifted,
the language separation ideology still dominates their ideas about language teaching

and learning. Despite this seemingly impossible implementation of translanguaging, these three teachers do acknowledge some of the virtues of translanguaging. All three can see the pedagogical value of translanguaging when teaching certain topics, even when their academic formation and departmental inclinations dictate otherwise. Linda states that translanguaging spaces could lower levels of anxiety in class but warns that these spaces would need scaffolding. Alex believes translanguaging could balance language power dynamics and sees translanguaging as a powerful pedagogical tool. Krista regards translanguaging as a spontaneous practice that should be exercised judiciously.

Interestingly, the two instructors who most struggled envisioning translanguaging in their classes -Linda and Krista- share a background in TEFL education. Alex, on the other hand, was already opening translanguaging spaces in her class prior to the critical dialogue sessions. Her already positive stance toward translanguaging speaks to how her academic formation (M.A. in literature) may have impacted her ideological stance and her interpretation of departmental unfavorable views of translanguaging. That is, not having been exposed to narratives and ideologies common to TESOL and TEFL programs, Alex had not been indoctrinated into the ideologies of strict language separation, linguistic purism, and bilingualism as double monolingualism. This points to the need for TESOL and TEFL teacher education programs to be reconfigured so that future language educators become more critical of societal and institutional ideologies and the pressures these exercise on them.

As clear-cut as the instructors' stances might appear to be, they struggle to accommodate or resist pressures to abide by language ideologies that frame translanguaging as undesirable and language separation as good practice. On the whole, these instructors have to navigate, negotiate, and contest a complex multi-scale landscape in which institutional/societal ideological orientations and their own lived ideology experiences collide. While they hesitate to fully leverage translanguaging in their teaching, data show that they sometimes do translanguage and see how translanguaging can be utilized as an effective pedagogy and tool to counter hegemonic ideologies privileging language separation. The inconsistencies in how they articulate and embody their language ideologies are further evidence of the ideological work they engage in as they balance layers of circulating ideologies. Arguably, increased awareness of these points of ideological tension can open up spaces for critical self-reflection and transformation.

7 Final Remarks

While many involved in bilingual education have collected evidence of the benefits of translanguaging, progress in this regard continues to be slow. The ideologies herein discussed are so entrenched that they seem to be the only way to envision EFL education in the department in question. In the daunting task of disrupting these language ideologies, engaging in critical dialogues with those instructors who oppose translanguaging constituted an important step forward. Such dialogues helped these instructors become more aware of the language ideologies shaping their stances toward translanguaging, conscious of the institutional pressures imposed on them, and able to assess if these ran counter to the dynamic and fluid nature of languaging of emergent bilinguals.

Flores et al. (2018) caution, however, that working toward changing individual instructors' language ideologies will not suffice, as these ideologies are a reflection of broader social and institutional stances. As these scholars assert, we must work to disrupt those broader institutional and societal ideologies before we can see substantial transformations. Although I agree with challenging institutional structures, I still see potential in working collaboratively and collegially with individual instructors to interrogate the broader institutional and societal contexts. As evident in this study, Linda, Alex and Krista examined the ideology of language separation, as they discussed other ways of doing EFL education, even against their desire for institutional prestige/status and acknowledgment as professionals. Our critical dialogues served as spaces to share how the ways they are teaching help or hinder their students' learning. These instructors found in our critical dialogues the validation that breaking away from language separation ideologies is a timely endeavor alongside the acknowledgment of the hurdles that such task poses.

These EFL instructors can further build their agency to challenge institutional ideological orientations as they work collaboratively and collegially around the tensions that arise from interrogating institutional structures (Palmer, 2018a, 2018b). This endeavor, nevertheless, necessitates that they be willing to address the tensions that arise from problematizing the status quo and the ideologies shaping their own teaching practices. To conclude, as more EFL instructors in this department find opportunities to develop their agency, they can come together to reconfigure their programs and/or departments in ways that better respond to the need for sociolinguistic justice in EFL education: translanguaging being a reasonable entry point by way of which they can engage in much-needed problematization of language ideologies.

References

Alim, H., Rickford, J., & Ball, A. (2016). *Raciolinguistics: How language shapes our ideas about race*. New York, NY: Oxford University Press.

Blommaert, J. (1999). *Language ideological debates*. Berlin, Germany: Mouton de Gruyter.

Creese, A., & Blackledge, A. (2010). Translanguaging in the bilingual classroom: A pedagogy for learning and teaching? *The Modern Language Journal, 94*, 103–115.

Creese, A., & Blackledge, A. (2015). Translanguaging and identity in educational settings. *Annual Review of Applied Linguistics, 35*, 20–35.

Cummins, J. (2008). Teaching for transfer: Challenging the two solitudes assumption in bilingual education. *Encyclopedia of Language and Education, 5*, 1528–1538.

De Los Ríos, C., & Seltzer, K. (2017). Translanguaging, coloniality, and English classrooms: An exploration of two bicoastal urban classrooms. *Research in the Teaching of English, 52*(1), 55–76.

Durán, L., & Palmer, D. (2014). Pluralist discourses of bilingualism and translanguaging talk in classrooms. *Journal of Early Childhood Literacy, 14*(3), 367–388.

Fallas Escobar, C. (2016). Challenging the monolingual bias in EFL programs: Towards a bilingual approach to L2 learning. *Revista de Lenguas Modernas, 24*, 249–266.

Fallas Escobar, C., & Dillard-Paltrineri, E. (2015). Students' and professors' conflicting beliefs about translanguaging in the EFL classroom: Dismantling the monolingual bias. *Revista de Lenguas Modernas, 23*, 301–328.

Flores, N. (2014). Let's not forget that translanguaging is a Political Act. *The Educational Linguist, 2014-7.*

Flores, N., Lewis, M. C., & Phuong, J. (2018). Raciolinguistic chronotopes and the education of Latinx students: Resistance and anxiety in a bilingual school. *Language and Communication, 62*, 15–25.

Flores, N., & Schissel, J. (2014). Dynamic bilingualism as the norm: Envisioning a heteroglossic approach to standards-based reform. *TESOL Quarterly, 48*(3), 454–479.

Gal, S. (1989). Language and political economy. *Annual Review of Anthropology, 18*, 345–367.

Gal, S. (1998). Multiplicity and contention among language ideologies. In B. Schieffelin, K. Woolard, & P. Kroskrity (Eds.), *Language ideologies: Practice and theory* (pp. 317–332). New York, NY: Oxford University Press.

García, O. (2009). *Bilingual education in the 21st century: a global perspective.* Malden, MA/ Oxford, UK: Wiley/Blackwell.

Garcia, O., & Sylvan, C. E. (2011). Pedagogies and practices in multilingual classrooms: Singularities in pluralities. *Modern Language Journal, 95*(3), 385–400.

García-Mateus, S., & Palmer, D. (2017). Translanguaging pedagogies for positive identities in two-way dual language bilingual education. *Journal of Language, Identity & Education, 16*(4), 245–255.

Gort, M., & Sembiante, S. (2015). Navigating hybridized language learning spaces through translanguaging pedagogy: Dual language preschool teachers' languaging practices in support of emergent bilingual children's performance of academic discourse. *International Multilingual Research Journal, 9*(1), 7–25.

Grosjean, F. (1996). Living with two languages and two cultures. In I. Parasnis (Ed.), *Cultural and language diversity and the deaf experience* (pp. 20–36). Cambridge, UK: Cambridge University Press.

Hornberger, N. (2005). Opening and filling up implementational and ideological spaces in heritage language education. *The Modern Language Journal, 89*(4), 605–609.

Irvine, J. T., & Gal, S. (2000). Language ideology and linguistic differentiation. In P. Kroskrity (Ed.), *Regimes of language: Ideologies, polities, and identities* (pp. 35–84). Santa Fe, Mexico: School of American Research Press.

Kroskrity, P. (2006). Language ideologies. In A. Duranti (Ed.), *A companion to linguistic anthropology*. Malden, MA: Blackwell Publication.

Li, W. (2011). Moment analysis and translanguaging space: Discursive construction of identities by multilingual Chinese youth in Britain. *Journal of Pragmatics, 43*, 1222–1235.

Lippi-Green, R. (2012). *English with an accent: Language, ideology, and discrimination in the United States.* London, UK: Routledge.

Makoni, S., & Pennycook, A. (2007). Disinventing and (re)constituting languages. *Critical Inquiry in Language Studies, 2*(3), 137–156.

Marchel, C. A. (2007). Learning to talk/talking to learn: Teaching critical dialogue. *Teaching Educational Psychology, 2*, 1–15.

Martínez, R., Hikida, M., & Durán, L. (2015). Unpacking ideologies of linguistic purism: How dual language teachers make sense of everyday translanguaging. *International Multilingual Research Journal, 9*(1), 26–42.

Ortega, O. (2014). Ways forward for a bi/multilingual turn in SLA. In S. May (Ed.), *The multilingual turn: Implications for SLA, TESOL and bilingual education*. New York, NY: Routledge.

Otheguy, R., García, O., & Reid, W. (2015). Clarifying translanguaging and deconstructing named languages: a perspective from linguistics. *Applied Linguistics Review, 6*(3), 281–307.

Palmer, D. K. (2018a). Introduction to the special issue: Teacher agency and "pedagogies of hope" for bilingual learners (in a brave new world). *International Multilingual Research Journal, 12*(3), 143–144.

Palmer, D. K. (2018b). Supporting bilingual teachers to be leaders for social change: "I must create advocates for biliteracy". *International Multilingual Research Journal, 12*(3), 203–216.

Palmer, D. K., Martínez, R. A., Mateus, S. G., & Henderson, K. (2014). Reframing the debate on language separation: Toward a vision for translanguaging pedagogies in the dual language classroom. *The Modern Language Journal, 98*(3), 757–772.

Sayer, P. (2013). Translanguaging, TexMex, and bilingual pedagogy: Emergent bilinguals learning through the vernacular. *TESOL Quarterly, 47*(1), 63–88.

Schwartz, M., & Asli, A. (2014). Bilingual teachers' language strategies: The case of an Arabic-Hebrew Kindergarten in Israel. *Teaching and Teacher Education, 38*, 22–32.

Skutnabb-Kangas, T. (2009). *Social justice through multilingual education*. Bristol, UK: Multilingual Matters.

Woolard, K. A. (1998). Introduction: Language ideology as a field of inquiry. In B. Schieffelin, K. Woolard, & P. Kroskrity (Eds.), *Language ideologies* (pp. 3–47). New York, NY: Oxford University Press.

Chapter 16
Effects of Teachers' Language Ideologies on Language Learners' Translanguaging Practices in an Intensive English Program

Laila Aghai, Peter Sayer (iD), and Mary Lou Vercellotti

Abstract This chapter presents the results of a qualitative case study conducted in a university-level Intensive English Program (IEP) in the U.S. The study focused on documenting the ESL teachers' language ideologies and the ways in which they encouraged or restricted translanguaging in their classes. The participants were three English as a second language (ESL) teachers working with beginner and inter-mediate levels in an IEP with L1 Arabic-speaking students. At a program level, there was no explicit language policy for teachers to follow (e.g. only English or allowing language mixing) at the IEP. Classroom observations and interviews with teachers indicated that participants had three different orientations that framed their understanding of what the role of the students' native language should be, and to what extent translanguaging would help or hinder their learning of English: *translanguaging-as-a-problem*, *translanguaging-as-a-natural-process*, and *translanguaging-as-a-resource*. The findings provide evidence that the teachers' orientations were influenced by their language ideologies and their beliefs about what was the appropriate role of certain translanguaging strategies.

Keywords Language ideologies · Language as a resource · Language as a barrier · Classroom language policy · Translanguaging · TESOL

L. Aghai (✉)
Department of Teaching, Leadership & Professional Practice, College of Education and Human Development, University of North Dakota, Grand Forks, ND, USA
e-mail: laila.aghai@und.edu

P. Sayer
College of Education and Human Ecology, The Ohio State University, Columbus, OH, USA
e-mail: sayer.32@osu.edu

M. L. Vercellotti
Department of English, Ball State University, Muncie, IN, USA
e-mail: mlvercellott@bsu.edu

© Springer Nature Switzerland AG 2020
Z. Tian et al. (eds.), *Envisioning TESOL through a Translanguaging Lens*, Educational Linguistics 45, https://doi.org/10.1007/978-3-030-47031-9_16

345

1 Introduction

This chapter starts from the premise that students learning an additional language are inclined, by the nature of second language (L2) learning, towards translanguaging. All language teachers therefore, face the question of how to organize students' natural tendency towards translanguaging. What guides their decision-making towards translanguaging, the classroom language policy, often depends largely on the teachers' own language ideologies (Palmer, 2011; Razfar, 2012; Sayer, 2013). Here we focus on how ESL teachers' language ideologies influence the way they treat their students' translanguaging in an Intensive English Program (IEP). The study is organized around two research questions:

1. How do teachers' ideologies of translanguaging interact with their teaching strategies?
2. How do teachers' language ideologies influence the students' translanguaging in the classroom?

We begin by discussing how language ideologies connect with the teachers' views of translanguaging, and review work done in the area of translanguaging in the language classrooms. We then look at the approaches to translanguaging of teachers working with L1 Arabic-speaking students in beginner and intermediate levels in an IEP based at a large public university in the southern United States. Examples presented from classroom observations and interview data illustrate that teachers in the study tended to adopt one of three predominant views towards language mixing: *translanguaging-as-a-problem*, *translanguaging-as-a-natural-process*, and *translanguaging-as-a-resource* (Hult & Hornberger, 2016; Ruiz, 1984). The analysis of the data indicates that each of these views is mediated through dominant ideologies of language, but also strongly informed and shaped by the teacher's considerations of what will best facilitate her students' L2 acquisition, the teacher's understanding of what constitutes "good" L2 pedagogical practices, and even the teacher's own language learning background and relationship to bilingualism. In turn, the study reveals that the teacher's stance towards translanguaging facilitates or limits the types of learning strategies the students use.

In this study, we drew on García & Li Wei's (2015) definition of translanguaging as well as the related concept from Canagarajah (2013) of *translingual practice* to refer to the various ways that ESL teachers and students use – and mix – their linguistic repertoire in the classroom as a means of supporting their learning of English. These may include intentional strategies, such as identifying a cognate, or more generally the bilingual sense-making that García and Li Wei (2015) explain is common amongst language learners. Canagarajah (2013) adds that "translinguals adopt a functional orientation to communication and meaning [...] What is important is not the English variety used or the level of formal proficiency, but the ability to 'deliver'" (p. 181).

From the teacher's perspective, Canagarajah (2013) refers to the *translingual competence* as the ability to view their students' translanguaging in the ESL classroom as a valuable resource. Therefore, in order to develop translingual competence, educators must come to an understanding of how to treat the various languages that exist in the classroom as a mediating tool and create teaching strategies that result in effective instruction. Although translanguaging is, on the one hand, a very natural practice for students to engage in; on the other hand, teachers often need to figure out "how to" implement translanguaging strategies that are intentional and deliberately used for sense-making within the classroom. Furthermore, students' translanguaging may be incidental and spontaneous, but it is the teachers' responsibility to guide their students' translanguaging. In this study, we look at the ESL teachers' views towards students' translanguaging in the classroom because it reveals the ideologies guiding their teaching practices.

We have referred to the participants' use of Arabic as L1 and native language in this study. While this is true in the sense that the teachers – and the students themselves – see them as "native speakers" of "Arabic", we are well aware that within translanguaging framework, the terms L1, L2, and native language are problematic. Ortega (2019) explains "languages are often identified and treated by speakers as labeled and separate at the conscious level" (p. 31). In referring to the L1, native language, and L2 within this chapter, we aim to reflect different perspectives of the teachers on translanguaging, and how each perspective represents the participant's language ideologies. For instance, while the teacher with a monolingual approach to language teaching, separated Arabic and English as L1 and L2 and viewed English or the target language as superior (translanguaging-as-a-problem), the teachers who viewed both Arabic and English as part of their students' integrated linguistic repertoire regarded their students' translanguaging as a meaning-making process (translanguaging-as-a-resource). Therefore, our own reference to "Arabic" and "English" (we forgo the scare quotes), is done with the understanding that we are both representing our participants' own use of the terms, as well as a move of strategically essentializing them as named languages in order to be able to analyze the ideological stances of the teachers. We also recognize that what the students and teachers are referring to as "Arabic" likely includes a wide range of linguistic practices associated with Modern Standard Arabic, the students' local or national vernacular, and classic Arabic. Likewise, the designations "L1" and "L2" are being used in the chronological sense to refer to those elements of language that were acquired in childhood and those learned subsequently in adulthood. In sum, we follow the convention of using Arabic (L1) and English (L2) as separate languages for the sake of simplicity and to facilitate the discussion below, even while recognizing the polemic nature of doing so within a translanguaging perspective.

2 Translanguaging and Language Ideologies

Our investigation of the relationship between the teachers' views of translanguaging and the strategies and types of practices the students engage in is framed through the lens of *language ideologies* (Kroskrity, 2004; Silverstein, 1979; Woolard &

Schieffelin, 1994). Language ideologies are "sets of beliefs about language articulated by users as rationalization or justification of perceived language structure and use" (Silverstein, 1979, p. 193). In other words, language ideologies that teachers subscribe to will shape (often encouraging or limiting) the students' translanguaging practices.

Teachers' beliefs and attitudes towards language and instruction, and the connection to language mixing, have been studied by many scholars (Gkaintartzi, Kiliari, & Tsokalidou, 2015; Palmer, 2011; Razfar, 2012; Sayer, 2012; Young, 2014). Sayer (2012), documented how the classroom language practices of English teachers in Mexico were strongly influenced by their particular ideologies of language. He also argued that there is not a simple relationship between a language ideology that a teacher holds and a corresponding language practice, but rather "language attitudes may reveal only one of several divergent and competing ideologies that can exist in a community and influence language practices" (p. 133).

The positive role that translanguaging plays has been studied extensively in bilingual education (García, 2009; García & Li Wei, 2015; Sayer, 2013). Palmer (2011) examined bilingual teachers' beliefs and attitudes towards language and teaching and asserted that teachers' language ideologies are directly related to their personal history and lived experiences. She also argued that teachers' language ideologies often become the basis of de facto classroom language policies. That is to say, in the case of translanguaging, a teacher's beliefs towards language mixing become the policy through which they make decision about the language practices in the classroom, both her own and her students, and either encourage or discourage translanguaging. This view of classroom language policy is what García meant when she stated that "different languages and standards are imposed as a result of an ideology" (p. 86).

In classrooms where translanguaging is supported by a teacher ideology that endorses a flexible view of languages, the practice of language mixing creates a *translanguaging space* (Li Wei, 2011). Li Wei explains that these discursive spaces provide the opportunity for multilingual speakers to negotiate their ideologies, values, beliefs, and life experiences:

> Translanguaging is both going between different linguistic structures and systems, including different modalities (speaking, writing, signing, listening, reading, remembering) and going beyond them. It includes the full range of linguistic performances of multilingual language users for purposes that transcend the combination of structures, the alternation between systems, the transmission of information and the representation of values, identities, and relationships. (p. 1223)

Thus, a classroom is a translanguaging space where students and teachers negotiate their culture, identity, and ideologies through multilingual language practices. Razfar (2012) stated that "when human beings engage in various language practices (e.g., narrative), they are simultaneously displaying their beliefs about the nature, function, and purpose of language" (p. 63).

While scholars have noted that many bilingual teachers (e.g. in dual language programs) have ideologies that validate translanguaging, second and foreign language TESOL contexts with adult language learners such as the one we studied are still most often seen by teachers through a monolingual prism. Gkaintartzi et al. (2015) examined Greek teachers' attitudes towards immigrant students' use of the heritage language in the classroom. They demonstrated that "teachers' views reveal their teaching strategy in the classroom" (p. 66), and that they frequently include ignoring the use of the students' native language and actively discouraging or even prohibiting students' use of translanguaging strategies. Hence, when monolingual approach to teaching is part of a teacher's language ideology, it influences the classroom policy and teaching strategies and as a result English-only rules may be implemented in the classroom.

The monolingual ideology amongst ESL teachers has often been supported by work in second language acquisition (SLA). SLA scholars have generally taken the view that there is a clash between using the L1 and L2 that will result in negative transfer, and reduce the amount of exposure and students' opportunities to practice the target language (Duff & Polio, 1990). Cook (2001) reexamined the view that L1 should be prohibited in the classroom and stated that "like nature, the L1 creeps back in, however many times you throw it out with a pitchfork" (p. 405). On the other hand, when ESL teachers have translingual competence, they view various forms of translanguaging as useful for sense-making, negotiation of meaning, and communication regardless of the individuals' language proficiency. Hence, Canagarajah (2013) maintains that teachers should strategically incorporate students' translanguaging in the classroom activities.

In sum, ESL teachers are the agents who shape and influence their students' translanguaging practices by encouraging, ignoring, or prohibiting them from translanguaging in the classroom. In order to understand how ESL teachers' ideologies impact their teaching strategies, and ultimately the students' ability to use translanguaging to support their L2 learning, we adopted the classic framework: language as a problem, language as a right, and language as a resource, which was first introduced by Richard Ruiz (1984). Hult and Hornberger (2016) explained that the orientations, which are the three main types of language ideologies, "have been widely used to inform the analysis of language policy and planning" (p. 31). This framework allowed us to analyze how the three focal teachers' views of translanguaging represented distinct ideologies, relative to the degree of translingual competence each teacher had their beliefs about the positive/negative role that the L1 could play in L2 learning. To combine the Ruiz (1984) orientation framework with our analysis of the teachers' views of translanguaging, we renamed the ideologies: *Translanguaging-as-a-problem*, *translanguaging-as-a-natural-process*, and *translanguaging-as-a-resource*. In what follows, we describe each teacher's ideology of translanguaging, her/his rationale, and how each view impacted their pedagogical strategies for L2 teaching.

3 Method

The data presented in this chapter are drawn from a larger study of ESL students and teachers conducted in an Intensive English Program to examine the role of L1 in ESL teaching, and the effectiveness of monolingual or "English-only" policies in IEP classrooms (Aghai, 2016).

3.1 Research Design

The methodological framework for this research is a multiple case study approach. In order to better understand how teachers' language ideologies influence their teaching strategy, three focal ESL teachers were selected from the larger group of teachers who participated in the study. The teachers were selected because, based on the analysis, they had different views towards the utility of the L1 for L2 learning, and each espoused a different ideology of translanguaging. Each focal teacher was treated as an individual unit of analysis and thus, an individual case. For each case or each teacher, the language practices of the ESL teachers were examined through class observations and interviews. As Dörnyei (2007) suggested "the case study is not a specific technique but rather a method of collecting and organizing data so as to maximize our understanding of the unitary character of the social being or object studied. In many ways, it is the ultimate qualitative method focusing on the 'Particular One'" (p. 152). Therefore, three ESL classes were observed, the teacher-student interactions were audio-recorded, and the ESL teachers were interviewed.

3.2 Research Site and Participants

Data for this study were collected at an Intensive English Program (IEP) at a university in the U.S. The goal of the IEP was to provide academic English to international students and prepare them for colleges and universities in the U.S. The courses that were offered in the IEP included reading, writing and grammar, oral communication, and TOEFL. There were five different levels in the IEP, from beginner to advanced, and the students' proficiency level was determined by administering the placement test when they first entered the program. Most of the students came from Arab countries such as Saudi Arabia, Kuwait, United Arab Emirates, Jordan, and Bahrain.

Of the three focal teachers, Valorie taught the level one (beginner) oral communication course, Nasser taught the level one (beginner) writing and grammar course, and Sally who taught level three (intermediate) oral communication course. Table 16.1 shows the teachers' background.

Table 16.1 ESL teachers

Pseudonym	Gender	Native language	Second language	Level of education	Years teaching
Valorie	Female	Spanish	English	M.A-TESL	6
Nasser	Male	Arabic	English	M.A-TESL	2
Sally	Female	English	French	M.A-TESL	10

All the teachers held a master's degree in teaching English as a second language, and they were bilingual. While Sally was a native speaker of English, Nasser and Valorie spoke English as a second language. Nasser and Valorie spoke Arabic and Spanish, respectively, as their native languages, and Sally spoke French as a second language.

3.3   Data Collection

The classroom observations were the first component of data collection. The classroom observations took place during the Spring semester. Each ESL class was observed for 4 weeks. The oral communication courses were 2.5 h per session and the writing and grammar courses were 2 h per session. Because Dörnyei (2007) explains that "highly structured observations involve going into the classroom with a specific focus and with concrete observation categories" (p. 179), the class observations were semi-structured and provided us the opportunity to observe the teachers and students' interaction with the classroom context.

The teacher interviews were the second component of data collection. The interviews were conducted after the class observations were completed because we wanted to examine the teachers' translingual competence and their degree of awareness when it came to their students' translanguaging in the classroom. The interviews were semi-structured and open ended, following Dörnyei (2007), who suggests that this approach is suitable once the researcher has a solid overview of the phenomenon in question through observations. Our goal was to be able to ask follow-up questions while they responded to the interview questions and ask questions regarding the instances where students were translanguaging during the classroom observations.

3.4   Data Analysis

For data analysis, the teachers' interviews and their interactions during the classroom observations were transcribed. Next, the transcriptions were coded based on Saldaña's (2013) coding methods and Gee's (2011) discourse analysis tools to obtain a deeper understanding of the teachers' ideologies towards translanguaging. To identify patterns and categories within the dataset that could be relevant to the research questions in this study, we followed three of the first cycle coding methods described by Saldaña (2013, p. 59): categories: (a) structural coding, (b) descriptive coding, (c) values coding. Since the interview was semi-structured, we utilized structural coding to identify the themes of the questions and answers. The conceptual phrases focused on teaching strategies and the role of translanguaging in the classroom. Next, descriptive coding was utilized to create a topic or name for each section of the classroom interactions and interview responses. Since the teachers' interviews were focused on their language ideologies and their perception of monolingual assumption to language teaching, values coding method was used to understand the attitude of the teachers towards their students' translanguaging. After coding the interview transcripts and classroom interactions, we utilized Gee's (2011) discourse analysis tools to analyze the interview responses, focusing on The Vocabulary Tool, The Context is Reflexive Tool, The Significance Building Tool, The Identities Building Tool, The Relationships Building Tool, and The Connection Building Tool.

4 Three Views of Translanguaging

The analysis revealed that each of the three focal teachers took a distinct view towards students', and their own, translanguaging. The views represented a progression from active resistance of translanguaging as a negative (Sally), to acceptance of translanguaging as inevitable but largely natural (Nasser), to the leveraging of translanguaging as a tool for teaching and learning (Valorie). We labelled these *translanguaging-as-a-problem, translanguaging-as-a-natural-process,* and *translanguaging-as-a-resource.* While each teacher's ideology fit the general category, the practices and stated rationales for their views were nuanced and showed that within each view there are embedded various considerations, all framed by language ideologies, but taken up and practiced by each teacher in different ways. Since the teachers were not familiar with the term "translanguaging", during the interviews, teachers variously used and talked about the L1, L2, native language, mixing, and target language to refer to their students' translanguaging in the classroom. We remind the reader that we are using the terms L1, native language, and L2 to discuss students' linguistic repertoire and the languages that they have acquired in childhood and adulthood. However, depending on the teachers' language ideologies, the terms L1 and L2 can bear their traditional meaning in monolingual approaches to language teaching.

5 Sally: Translanguaging-as-a-Problem View

The first question we asked Sally was whether she viewed her students' translanguaging as a valuable resource in the classroom. She responded:

> I think it could be a crutch as they get higher, but at a lower level I think it's an absolute necessity. You know how much quicker you can help a student understand a language if you give it to them in the original language versus pictures? I mean, it could take forever, but if you have a student who can explain it, it seems to me like it's better. Although I have heard that often times the definition or whatever is given is not always correct.

However, she also stated that her students "never" use their L1 in her class because she does not allow them to use their native language. Sally said that "maybe it happens in other classes but not in my class." She posited that "since this is an oral communication class and students mostly give presentations, they do not feel the need to rely on their native language so much." Sally added, "I am sure it happens more in grammar and writing classes."

Nevertheless, after the third class observation, Sally said that because she was being observed, she had noticed that her students do use translanguaging during group activities. Since Sally had mentioned earlier that her students did not use their native language in her class, we were interested in knowing whether she hadn't noticed it due to her lack of awareness or her monolingual perspective towards language teaching which encourages teachers to ignore students' L1. The way Sally framed translanguaging, essentially as a crutch which – if it were relied on too much – would hinder students' L2 learning, led us to conclude that she understood her teaching largely through a monolingual lens and viewed translanguaging as a problem.

Our analysis with Gee's (2011) Vocabulary Tool focused on how key illuminating terms the teachers used were clustered, like "crutch." The idea that L1 use is a crutch for students with high proficiency but a necessity for students with low proficiency level in English is consistent with a view that developing greater L2 proficiency means avoiding use of one's L1. In the work on code-switching, "crutching" is also used to refer to how bilinguals compensate for a lack of proficiency in one language by relying on the other (Zentella, 1997). Clearly, the term "crutch" has a negative connotation, implying that students with high proficiency level rely on their native language when it is not really necessary. Sally pointed out that at higher levels, translanguaging could prevent students from forcing themselves to use the target language. Thus, by choosing the word "crutch", Sally is framing the students' use of their native language at the upper levels as a deficit: something that is preventing them from walking on their own in the L2.

Furthermore, Sally stated that the ESL and EFL context differ from one another, and students who are learning English as a second language in the U.S. are more exposed to English than students who learn English as a foreign language.

> [Studying in an ESL rather than EFL context,] I think they are getting so much immersion whether it's in the classroom or… not that I don't think it's going to affect that much. I think if they are very willing to quit using their native language, they'll progress more quickly, but I just think it would be difficult to stop it.

Sally is justifying some minimal amount of L1 use on the grounds that students get enough exposure to the target language in an ESL setting. Sally's position seems to reflect the common concern that L1 use limits learner's success by reducing their exposure and practice (cf. Duff & Polio, 1990). Although Sally thinks that ESL students in the U.S receive enough exposure to the target language, she suggests that if students can be weaned off or forced to quit using their L1, they will become proficient more quickly. Sally's suggestion implies that she has a monolingual perspective towards language learning which is minimizing or eliminating students' translanguaging in the classroom.

We also asked Sally if she allowed her students to translate the newly taught concepts during group activities or use bilingual dictionaries in class. She had conflicting ideas regarding this type of translanguaging, as a translation strategy that students can use. First, she stated that she only allows her students to translate in class if they are confused, but then she added that the exercises that are given in her class are designed specifically to help students with learning the target language without having to resort to using the L1.

> The whole point of a classroom activity is to use the [target] language. So I only allow the [L1] language when it's trying to explain something and most of the time I can explain it [in English] and the students understand it, but if for some reason they are very confused and someone says it in their own language and they go oh! Then I think it's okay, but the whole point of all of my exercises would be to have them use the language. I think it would be very detrimental. The only time I allow the first language in the classroom is for explanation. That's the only time allowed.

As Cook (2001) and Auerbach (1993) point out, teachers with a monolingual ideology generally see students' L1 as the last resort, especially when they have not been successful in explaining the new concepts in English. Likewise, Sally only begrudgingly accepted her students' translanguaging in order to help a classmate who was confused.

Sally explained that the students' translanguaging is only useful for explanation and if it is used for any other purposes, it would be "detrimental". Her characterization of translanguaging as being potentially detrimental again underscores her belief that the best approach to L2 teaching is one that takes a monolingual approach to L2 learning. Sally's fear of overusing students' native language leads her to believe that if students' native language is used during classroom activities, it will affect their learning negatively because it will minimize the L2 exposure and maximize the L1 which is against monolingual views of language teaching. Sally viewed her students' translanguaging as the last resort, and she did not perceive it as a technique or a teaching strategy that could be used deliberately for negotiation of meaning and sense-making. Clearly then, Sally's approach represented a translanguaging-as-a-problem ideology, which holds that language mixing and L1 use anywhere beyond the most beginner levels hinders L2 learning and should be actively discouraged by teachers. As we will see, this represents one end of the continuum of teachers' ideologies of translanguaging. Nassar and Valorie's views represent other, more positive, positions.

6   Nasser: Translanguaging-as-a-Natural-Process View

Nasser was the only teacher in the study who shared the L1 of the majority of his students (Arabic). We also found that, overall, his views towards translanguaging seemed to represent an intermediate point between the "problem" (Sally) and "resource" (Valorie). When asked whether he allowed his students to use their L1 or mix languages in class, he asserted that students' native language can be used for solving problems and saving time. Hence, in his view both students and teachers can benefit from translanguaging. He also articulated his belief that teachers who share the students' native language are more sensitive to their needs because they understand the process of learning a second language, and the challenges that their students may face during this process.

> In my opinion it's okay to have a teacher who speaks the students' first language because he can actually help them. Because [a] long time ago he used to make the same mistakes the students make, and when the students communicate with their classmates in Arabic, they can solve some problems or difficulties when they speak Arabic to their classmates. But again if you want to improve your English, you should speak in English. But Arabic can help them as well. So if they don't understand something they can ask one of their classmates and get help.

Nasser explained that the shared experiences between the students and the teacher have a positive effect on their learning, and teachers who are second language learners themselves have a better understanding of the students' learning process. They are also more conscious of the difficulties that students may face when learning a new language. Moreover, he believed that when students are able to collaborate and share in their native language, they will improve their language skills. As Cook (2001) found, students' L1 can be utilized "to provide a short-cut for giving instructions and explanations where the cost of the L2 is great, to build up interlinked L1 and L2 knowledge in the students' minds, and to carry out learning tasks through collaborative dialogue with fellow students" (p. 418). Cook stated that not only the student-student interactions are more meaningful when they are done in the native language, but also teacher-student interactions are more focused on using their knowledge about the language to make sense of what goes on in the classroom. Nasser added that translanguaging is a "natural occurrence" not only for learning a second language, but also for communicating with students who share the same native language.

> You can't ban the students from speaking their first language. A large number of our teachers here in the IEP told their students 'don't speak Arabic', but the students speak Arabic anyways. In my master's program we had students from China. They speak English fluently, but when they worked together, they spoke Chinese. When I worked with some Saudi classmates, in our [masters] program, we spoke Arabic. We speak English fluently, but we used Arabic. We code switched because it was unnatural to speak in English when you are speaking with someone who shares your native language.

Nasser stated that regardless of the speaker's proficiency in a second language, when students share the same native language, they will speak in their L1 rather than the language being learned. Nasser provided the example of his classmates in the master's in TESOL program and stated that even in the graduate school where students are highly proficient in English, Arab students speak in Arabic in class. Nasser suggested that the same scenario holds true for IEP students: even if teachers prohibit them from translanguaging in class, they will naturally choose to translanguage to work through assignments and resolve problems.

Nasser also stated that communicating in a language other than the speakers' L1 is "unnatural" even among advanced language learners or those who have mastered English as a second language. Nasser's use of the word "unnatural" contrasts with Sally's "crutch view". While Sally perceived students' native language as a "crutch" and framed the students' translanguaging at the upper levels as a deficit: something that is preventing them from walking on their own in the L2, Nasser viewed translanguaging in the upper levels as a spontaneous occurrence that is expected from students who share the same native language. Nasser further explained that teachers cannot prevent students from translanguaging.

> I think even if you tell your students not to use their first language, when they need their first language, they will still speak in their native language. When students work as a group or when they work in pairs, it's a good thing for them to use Arabic. Because as I told you level one students, who don't speak English fluently, cannot communicate with Arabic speaking students in English. So it's much better to have stronger Arabic speaking students help the weaker students.

Allowing students to utilize their native language to increase their comprehension in the L2 will help them become more aware of how they can draw from their linguistic repertoire to assist them with learning the L2. As Lucas and Katz (1994) observed, using students' native language has "psychological benefits in addition to serving as a practical pedagogical tool for providing access to academic content, allowing more effective interaction, and providing greater access to prior knowledge" (p. 539). Nasser asserted that students have more difficulty with grammar, and he has seen his students translanguage in writing and grammar classes more frequently. He stated:

> I think in speaking classes students can communicate in English even though they don't speak fluently, they can use body language. But the grammar in English is completely different from the grammar in Arabic. So that's why I think the English grammar sometimes confuses Arabic speaking students and they have a hard time communicating in English in grammar classes.

While Nasser believed that translanguaging is a natural process, he explained that in certain classes, students translanguage more frequently for sense-making. For instance, grammar and writing classes are more difficult for Arab students, and therefore, they translanguage to make sense of the sentence structure and grammar items that do not exist in Arabic. In the next section, we will discuss a contrasting view of translanguaging.

7   Valorie: Translanguaging-as-a-Resource View

Valorie positioned herself at the other end of the ideology of translanguaging continuum from Sally, as she consistently expressed her view that students' use of L1 and language mixing is a resource that support learning English. When Valorie was asked what the role of the students' L1 was in L2 learning, she asserted that the students' native language plays an important role in teaching them a second language. Valorie explained that although sharing the L1 between teachers and students can be helpful in some cases, there are other factors that are crucial in students' L2 learning process.

> Do I think [that the teacher] knowing the [students'] L1 is important? Maybe in some cases it helps, but it's not all that important. The best thing is to have an understanding of their culture. Having knowledge of what their educational experience has been, valuing their native language, and allowing them to use their language when necessary. I know a lot more about the Arab world now than I did 2 years ago, and I'm more successful now with [my students] because I understand their history, their educational history. So I can bring in examples that are more powerful tools than me having the knowledge of their L1. I think that my life experience helps me a great deal. It's not just being bilingual though. It's being an immigrant and having this very hard experience with learning a second language, with the culture, with economic situations.

Valorie stated that her experience as an immigrant and second language learner has made her more sensitive to her students' educational needs. Valorie believed that when teachers are aware of their students' educational background, they are able to create methods and strategies in the classroom to help their students learn better. Valorie explained that since her Arab students enjoy speaking, she combines other skills such as reading and writing with speaking to make the activities more interesting for her students.

Valorie acknowledged her students' language practices by taking their topics of interest into consideration and including them in her class activities. Valorie's sensitivity to her students' culture indicated that she possesses a high degree of translingual competence (Canagarajah, 2013). Although Valorie did not share her students' native language, her classroom was an example of a "translanguaging space" where students from different language backgrounds are able to translanguage by using their background knowledge and the language being learned in class (Li Wei, 2011).

When we asked Valorie whether she allowed her students to translanguage in the classroom, she responded that teachers should know when to allow their students to draw upon their linguistic repertoire and when to redirect their attention to the target language. For her, there is a balance to be struck between pushing students to use English as much as possible with looking for ways to support students' translanguaging strategies:

> If I catch my students speaking in Arabic all the time or Spanish all the time, then of course I go around and I say you know ladies or gentlemen our primary goal here is to learn English. Let's practice. This is your safe environment. Please don't be afraid to make mistakes. And so I try to push them to speak as much as possible. But I don't ever tell them it

is no other language than English in this class. I would never say that. I say let's try to speak English the majority of the time. I understand if you have difficulties. I understand if you need a translation. That's fine but again I just make it known that it is the place for them to practice. This is the time they should be speaking English, but if you need to use your L1, if that is the best way for you to understand it, by all means do so. I encourage them to explain it to their classmates in their native language. A lot of them translate and I allow them to use translators. I sometimes google the definition in their language and show it to them. I also tell them make a vocabulary journal and write the vocabulary definition in both English and their native language.

Valorie created an environment for her students where they could translanguage freely. Unlike Sally, who discouraged students' translanguaging which she saw as a barrier to L2 learning, or Nasser who had an accepting but more passive approach, Valorie had an active role by encouraging her students to use translation dictionaries and assisting them in finding the definition. This is a good example of what (García & Li Wei, 2015) refer to as teachers "authorizing the translanguaging norm" (p. 237) in their class by establishing a translanguaging space where students can use their L1 freely for educational purposes. Although Valorie expected her students to speak in English, she recognized that her students will employ translanguaging to aid in comprehension, clarification, explanation, and understanding of new concepts. Thus, her goal was to create an environment or a "shared space" (Canagarajah, 2013, p. 39).

Furthermore, Valorie stated that while teachers should provide guidance and feedback when students translanguage, there are times when teachers should allow their students to express themselves in their native language.

One day a student was speaking about his wife and children in Spanish. He was very concerned because his wife was sick and the doctors thought it might be cancer. He was planning to go back to his country. My supervisor saw me speaking in Spanish and came to me after class and said, "Do not speak in Spanish! This is their only chance to practice their English," but it was after class and since the student was sharing a personal story, it didn't seem right to speak in English. You know, it wasn't the right time to ask him to speak in English.

Like Nasser, Valorie articulated her view that there is a time and place for the students' L1 in the classroom, and that teachers need to identify those moments and allow their students the spaces for translanguaging. Valorie believes that teachers need to act as facilitators and identify the teachable moments. However, they should also know when to require their students to use a specific language. The example that Valorie provided indicates that she is aware that there are certain situations where students should use their native language freely, and teachers should not interrupt them or ask them to switch to English. Moreover, the students' translanguaging practices are not limited to student-student interactions and classroom activities, and translanguaging is not only a spontaneous occurrence, but rather can be a strategic, systematic, and planned phenomenon.

8 Summary

As discussed in the findings, the three ESL teachers had different views regarding their students' translanguaging. These views represented different ideologies of language about how monolingual or multilingual ESL classrooms should be, and these ideologies in turn shape the teachers' pedagogical approaches and the students' interactions in the classroom. Drawing on Ruiz's (1984) three orientations to language planning, we labeled these ideologies as translanguaging-as-a-problem, translanguaging-as-a-natural-process, and translanguaging-as-a-resource. Each of these teachers embodied an ideology of translanguaging along a continuum from, on one end, a monolingual approach which actively discouraged translanguaging as a barrier to L2 learning, and to on the other end a flexible multilingual approach which endorsed students' spontaneous translanguaging as a resource for learning and attempted to leverage it strategically to support students' learning.

Sally had adopted a monolingual approach towards language teaching and did not participate in her students' translanguaging. One of the misconceptions in the monolingual approach is that to achieve communicative success "uniformity and sharedness" should exist (Canagarajah, 2013, p. 75). Sally chose to ignore or prohibit her students from translanguaging. When language teachers have a monolingual approach to language teaching, "different languages and standards are imposed as a result of an ideology" (García, 2009, p. 86). Although the IEP did not follow a strict English-only policy, the teachers implemented their own rules in the classroom when it came to the extend which students were allowed to translanguage.

The second teacher, Nasser believed that translanguaging is a natural process. However, he did not provide any guidance or feedback. Canagarajah (2011) explained in his study, educators might assume that "translanguaging is so fully developed among multilingual students in their home and community contexts that there is nothing further for the school to add, other than provide a context for it to be practiced" (pp. 8–9). While Nasser was not entirely passive, nor was as active and involved as Valorie in promoting his students' translanguaging, and he did not pursue the pedagogical potential of translanguaging in his own teaching. He reiterated that translanguaging occurs when there is shared language among students, and stated simply that when students want to make sense of the differences that exist in two languages, they translanguage. Although he was aware of his students' translanguaging and did not prohibit them using it, he did not provide feedback to his students and was a listener.

The third teacher who viewed translanguaging as a resource was Valorie. She believed that translanguaging had a time and place in the classroom. She was involved in her students' translanguaging by asking them to write in Arabic and report back in English, create a vocabulary journal that was written both in Arabic and English, use Arabic words in their writing to discuss a concept or cultural practice, and guided her students' translanguaging. Therefore, she had created a "translanguaging space" by turning her students' translanguaging into a learning opportunity (Li Wei, 2011). Her students' translanguaging seemed spontaneous but her guidance and feedback was done deliberately and strategically.

The observational data indicate that a teacher's orientation and the extent to which she or he sanctioned or encouraged translanguaging had a profound effect on the types of learning strategies the students used. Students who were in the class where the teacher viewed translanguaging as a problem used their native language mainly for clarification but were aware that they should not be heard by the teacher. Students who were in the class where the teacher viewed translanguaging as a natural process or as a resource, used translanguaging as a strategy and not only did they communicate with their classmates, but also communicated with their teacher. In other words, students' translanguaging shifted from clarification to sense-making, and successful communication depending on their teachers' view of translanguaging.

9   Conclusion and Implications

The teachers' orientations were influenced by their language ideologies about what was the appropriate role of certain translanguaging strategies. In the case of the focal teachers, this was at least partially shaped by their own learning history and identities as immigrants or speakers of a shared minority language. Teachers with a monolingual approach to language teaching showed resistance towards language strategies and approaches that were against their beliefs and language ideologies. While they might not be aware of this resistance, they tend to justify their language practices by stating that they want their students to have more language exposure, or by insisting that the ESL classroom is the only place that they can practice and improve their English.

The data from Valorie and Nasser indicate that even if teachers share the same native language with their students, their language ideologies will affect their students' translanguaging in the classroom. In other words, translanguaging goes beyond shared language systems and instead it is focused on understanding how each language could be used for a specific purpose to expand meaning making. Also, being a second language learner or having a similar experience as the ESL students, will not automatically increase the teachers' "translingual competence" (Canagarajah, 2013).

As seen in this chapter, all the ESL teachers had a master's degree in TESOL and spoke a second language, but had differing language ideologies and translingual competence. This shows that translanguaging is a concept that needs to be introduced in the teacher education and MA-TESOL programs. Teachers who possess translingual competence are more aware of their students' language needs and are more involved in their students' translanguaging. By the same token, they recognize that translanguaging has a "time" and "place" in the IEP classroom, and that teachers should be aware of the instances where translanguaging is helpful and leads to meaning-making and successful communication. Thus, teachers need to learn how to consciously select instances where translanguaging can benefit students, and guide them through their translanguaging.

The findings of this study suggest that teacher education needs to engage teachers with reflection on the connection between their own language ideologies and the multilingual practices of their students. Since teachers' language ideologies play an important role in the way they view their students' translingual practices, the first step in adopting a translingual approach to language teaching is to develop the teachers' translingual competence. When teachers possess translingual competence, they are able to recognize when and how their students' languages should be used in the classroom. Thus, the teacher training programs, TESOL workshops, and professional development sessions should train the ESL teachers how to treat the various languages that exist in their ESL class.

References

Aghai, L. (2016). *Translingual practices in the second language classroom: A comparative case study of ESL teachers in an Intensive English Program.* Unpublished doctoral dissertation. University of Texas at San Antonio, USA.

Auerbach, E. R. (1993). Reexamining English only in the ESL classroom. *TESOL Quarterly, 27*, 9–32.

Canagarajah, A. S. (2011). Translanguaging in the classroom: Emerging issues for research and pedagogy. *Applied Linguistics Review, 2*, 1–27.

Canagarajah, S. (2013). *Translingual practice: Global Englishes and cosmopolitan relations.* New York, NY: Routledge.

Cook, V. (2001). Using the first language in the classroom. *The Canadian Modern Language Review, 57*, 402–423.

Dörnyei, Z. (2007). *Research methods in applied linguistics.* Oxford, UK: Oxford University Press.

Duff, P. A., & Polio, C. G. (1990). How much foreign language is there in the foreign language classroom? *The Modern Language Journal, 74*(2), 154–166.

García, O. (2009). *Bilingual education in the 21st century: A global perspective.* Oxford, UK: Wiley-Blackwell.

García, O., & Wei, L. (2015). Translanguaging, bilingualism, and bilingual education. In W. E. Wright, S. Boun, & O. García (Eds.), *Handbook of bilingual and multilingual education* (pp. 223–240). Malden, MA: Wiley-Blackwell.

Gee, J. P. (2011). *How to do discourse analysis: A toolkit* (2nd ed.). New York, NY: Routledge.

Gkaintartzi, A., Kiliari, A., & Tsokalidou, R. (2015). Invisible bilingualism_ invisible language ideologies: Greek teachers' attitudes towards immigrant pupils' heritage languages. *International Journal of Bilingual Education and Bilingualism, 18*(1), 60–72. https://doi.org/10.1080/13670050.2013.877418

Hult, F. M., & Hornberger, N. H. (2016). Revisiting orientations in language planning: Problem, right, and resource as an analytical heuristic. *Bilingual Review/Revista Bilingüe, 33*(3), 30–49.

Kroskrity, P. V. (2004). Language ideologies. In A. Duranti (Ed.), *A companion to linguistic anthropology* (pp. 496–517). Malden, MA: Blackwell.

Lucas, T., & Katz, M. (1994). Reframing the debate: The roles of native languages in English-only programs for language minority students. *TESOL Quarterly, 28*(3), 537–561.

Ortega, L. (2019). SLA and the study of equitable multilingualism. *Modern Language Journal, 103*, 23–38.

Palmer, D. (2011). The discourse of transition: Teachers' language ideologies within transitional bilingual education programs. *International Multilingual Research Journal, 5*, 103–122. https://doi.org/10.1080/19313152.2011.594019

Razfar, A. (2012). Narrating beliefs: A language ideologies approach to teacher beliefs. *Anthropology and Education Quarterly, 43*(1), 61–81. https://doi.org/10.1111/j.1548-1492.2011.01157.x

Ruiz, R. (1984). Orientations in language planning. *NABE Journal, 8*, 15–34.

Saldaña, J. (2013). *The coding manual for qualitative research methods* (2nd ed.). Thousand Oaks, CA: Sage.

Sayer, P. (2012). *Ambiguities and tensions in English language teaching: Portraits of EFL teachers as legitimate speakers*. New York, NY: Routledge.

Sayer, P. (2013). Translanguaging, TexMex, and bilingual pedagogy: Emergent bilinguals learning through the vernacular. *TESOL Quarterly, 47*(1), 63–88.

Silverstein, M. (1979). Language structure and linguistic ideology. In P. R. Clyne, W. F. Hanks, & C. L. Hofbauer (Eds.), *The elements: A parasession on linguistic units and levels* (pp. 193–247). Chicago, IL: Chicago Linguistic Society.

The common European framework in its political and educational context. (n.d.). Cambridge, UK: Cambridge University. Retrieved from: http://www.coe.int/t/dg4/linguistic/source/Framework_EN.pdf

Wei, L. (2011). Moment analysis and translanguaging space: Discursive construction of identities by multilingual Chinese youth in Britain. *Multilingual Structures and Agencies, 43*(5), 1222–1235.

Woolard, K. A., & Schieffelin, B. B. (1994). Language ideology. *Annual Review of Anthropology, 23*, 55–82.

Young, A. S. (2014). Unpacking teachers' language ideologies: Attitudes, beliefs, and practiced language policies in schools in Alsace, France. *Language Awareness, 23*(2), 157–171. https://doi.org/10.1080/09658416.2013.863902

Zentella, A. C. (1997). *Growing up bilingual: Puerto Rican children in New York*. Malden, MA: Blackwell.

Chapter 17
Translanguaging as Transformation in TESOL

Peter Sayer (iD)

Abstract Language classrooms are multilingual spaces. While policies and pedagogies in the classroom may strive to circumscribe linguistic boundaries and define languages as separate entities, the task that students set themselves to in expanding their language repertoires is, by its nature, one that calls for multiples languages to coexist and comingle in physical and mental spaces. For this reason, in a few short years the concept of translanguaging has captured the attention and imagination of TESOL educators. Popularized in the field of bilingual education (García 2009), translanguaging has resonated strongly in TESOL because it allows us to bring together several related concerns and see them as different facets of the same conceptual and pedagogical challenge. The concept of translanguaging captures the overall move in the field of TESOL from a monolingual to plurilingual orientation. Translanguaging, therefore, is not about adding another layer to the cake of TESOL methods, but rather about bringing together these perspectives to transform TESOL in a way that truly recognizes and builds upon students' existing and emerging linguistic repertoires. The chapters in this volume provide an excellent representation of translanguaging work across the geographical diversity of TESOL contexts, as well as its diversity in terms of school settings, ages, levels, purposes, and pedagogical approaches.

Keywords Language ideologies · Social justice · TESOL postmethod · Stance-design-shift framework · Bilingual education · Language teacher education

Language classrooms are multilingual spaces. While policies and pedagogies in the classroom may strive to circumscribe linguistic boundaries and define languages as separate entities, the task that students set themselves to in expanding their language repertoires is, by its nature, one that calls for multiples languages to coexist and comingle in physical and mental spaces. For this reason, in a few short years the

P. Sayer (✉)
College of Education and Human Ecology, The Ohio State University, Columbus, OH, USA
e-mail: sayer.32@osu.edu

© Springer Nature Switzerland AG 2020
Z. Tian et al. (eds.), *Envisioning TESOL through a Translanguaging Lens*,
Educational Linguistics 45, https://doi.org/10.1007/978-3-030-47031-9_17

concept of translanguaging has captured the attention and imagination of TESOL educators. Popularized in the field of bilingual education (García, 2009), translanguaging has resonated strongly in TESOL because it allows us to bring together several related concerns and see them as different facets of the same conceptual and pedagogical challenge. These include the earlier ideas of pedagogical code-switching (Jacobson & Faltis, 1990), the role of the L1 in English teaching (Storch & Wigglesworth, 2003), the multilingual turn in SLA and L2 teaching (May, 2014; Ortega, 2013), and the increased sensitivity to issues of identity and social justice (Flores, Spotti, & García, 2017; García & Leiva, 2014). As Sembiante and Tian (Chap. 3) argue, the concept of translanguaging, therefore, captures the overall move in the field of TESOL from a monolingual to plurilingual orientation (Taylor & Snoddon, 2013, and cf. Hall Chap. 4). Translanguaging, therefore, is not about adding another layer to the cake of TESOL methods, but rather about bringing together these perspectives to transform TESOL in a way that truly recognizes and builds upon students' existing and emerging linguistic repertoires.

The contributions in this volume have set out to explore the possibilities of envisioning language mixing in TESOL classrooms through a translanguaging lens. The chapters, taken together, provide an excellent representation of translanguaging work across the geographical diversity of TESOL contexts, as well as its diversity in terms of school settings, ages, levels, purposes, and pedagogical approaches. The chapters have addressed these aspects of translanguaging as a theoretical framework for informing TESOL, as an orientation for teacher education, and as a pedagogical tool in the classroom.

1 Theorizing Translanguaging in TESOL

The genesis of translanguaging came from a practical problem in bilingual education: how should the use of languages be organized in language classrooms? This question arose from the practical concern in bilingual settings of protecting and promoting the use of the minoritized language. Initially, the focus was on determining the allocation of languages for certain functions, and the effectiveness of techniques, such as translations, that required students to explicitly connect meanings across languages. García (2009) developed translanguaging by theorizing its role in a broader conceptualization of language in bilingual education. In her work, translanguaging is an instantiation of a flexible, heteroglossic approach. It is explicitly a critical, post-structural view of language that challenges not only the linguistic boundaries separating languages in classrooms, but also the notion of languages as discrete entities. As we take up translanguaging in TESOL, we need to recognize how the theorization of translanguaging constitutes a radical challenge to much of conventional thinking in our field. As reflected in the chapters in the three parts of the volume, the move towards embracing translanguaging poses some theoretical "problems" as we try to productively incorporate flexible multilingualism into TESOL: the named language problem and the using multilingual resources versus "good English" problem.

1.1   The "Named Language" Problem

Translanguaging does not only seek to call out the separation of language or erase boundaries between languages, it seeks to call into question the existence of languages as discrete linguistic entities. Languages, the argument goes, are not separate from one another in the objective sense; what we name as "English" or "Chinese" or "Zapotec" and think of as distinct languages are social constructions based on historical, cultural, and political considerations (Makoni & Pennycook, 2007). The linguistic evidence that there must be distinct languages – dictionaries, reference grammars, works of literature – reifies the objective fact of language X, but a dictionary is also a social artifact, produced for a particular social purpose. As Zentella (2007) points out from a perspective of anthropolitical linguistics, at issue isn't whether there is any objective truth to language boundaries (there isn't), but rather whose purposes are served by policing and enforcing language borders.

The nagging existential question – *is there really such a thing as English?* – is obviously problematic for TESOL, given that its purpose is very clearly to promote the teaching and learning of a language called English. And yet applied linguists applying post-structural lenses have been grappling for quite some time with echoes of this same problem in other, related guises. In the 1980s, Kachru (1986) introduced the idea of *World Englishes,* and described how the fracturing of English was giving rise to the "nativization" of English in various parts of the globe, and distorting the traditional distinction between ESL and EFL settings. Likewise, as work in World Englishes brought the ownership of English under scrutiny, the validity of the concept of native speaker itself was problematized (Faez, 2011). Other applied linguistics have argued that the rise of global English was not a happy accident, a fortuitous by-product of increasing globalization, but was itself an intentional effort aligned with neoliberal political and economic interests (Pennycook, 1994; Phillipson, 1992; Sayer, 2015).

And yet, this radical deconstruction of languages and the challenge to the hegemony of global English poses a significant problem for English educators. Sembiante and Tian (Chap. 3) explain the "English (E)" of TESOL has been "traditionally conceptualized [in our field] under a structuralist notion as an objective fact possessed by native speakers or a prescriptive system of syntactic, semantic, morphological, and phonetic rules" (p. 52). On a surface level, we can put "English" in scare quotes to acknowledge that, like all named languages, it is a social construction. Seltzer and García (Chap. 2) adopt the convention of *English with an asterisk, following Lippi-Green (2013) who on referred to *SAE to remind readers that

Standard American English is social invention. However, even though translanguaging defies the structuralist orthodoxy of language, we also must recognize that *English – in particular its standard varieties – is a social construction that does have real world consequences for us as teachers and students.

1.2 Using Multilingual Resources Versus "Good English" Problem

The embrace of translanguaging as a critique of the monolingual approach therefore needs to be balanced by the recognition of the social consequences for many students of learning or not learning "good" English. The focus of much of the early work in sociolinguistics from a code-switching perspective was to validate languaging mixing as a socially and linguistically legitimate language practice, since language mixing has historically been stigmatized because it indexes laziness and lack of education (cf. Zentella, 1997). Likewise, in language classrooms, the L1 has generally been regarded as at best a crutch and at worst an impediment to L2 learning. In the SLA cannon, the L1 is a source of transfer (often negative transfer, or interference), and the use of the L1 was seen in a subtractive sense, as diminishing the amount of exposure and opportunities for L2 practice.

The chapters in this part, and throughout the volume, emphasize that a translanguaging approach takes as its starting point learners' multilingual repertoires, and aims to leverage these as resources for learning English. Sembiante and Tian (Chap. 3) characterize this as a "shift from prioritizing the teaching of English language to employing emergent bilinguals' fluid language practices in support of their English learning" (p. 55). In his representation of TESOL methods, Hall (Chap. 4) explains the alignment of a translanguaging orientation with the emergence of postmethod discourses (Kumaravadivelu, 2012). However, he argues that expert ESOL teachers have long deployed learners' full linguistic repertoires into their classroom. The difference, he maintains, is that within a postmethod approach, "opportunities exist to recognize and value more fully teachers' own theorizing about, and insights into, the affordances that translanguaging offers in the classroom" (p. 85). This not only moves the needle in terms of validating multilingual pedagogies as "best practices," but also has the potential to reduce the gap between theory and practice by recognizing the implications of the real-world understandings of expert practitioners. Seltzer and García (Chap. 2) illustrate how one experienced teacher's practice of translanguaging connected the levels of *stance,* her philosophy towards working with emergent bilinguals, her *design* (organization of the physical and curricular space), and her *shifts,* the moment-by-moment "moves" that teachers make within a translanguaging design. This framework is taken up by authors of several of the chapters in the second part.

2   Translanguaging in TESOL Teacher Education

The six chapters in the second part address how translanguaging is being taken up and incorporated into TESOL teacher education. For many of the same reasons outlined above, that translanguaging represents a theoretical challenge not only for monolingual teaching approaches but also for the conceptualizations of language upon which they are based, the concept of translanguaging is a difficult one for many pre- (and in-) service teachers to build a coherent understanding of. This is due to its complexity, but also because translanguaging actively resists reduction and essentializing into a neat set of steps or binaries. Several of the chapters in this part illustrate how teacher educators have attempted to deal with this complexity by framing translanguaging through ideology, social justice, and identity.

Deroo, Ponzio, and De Costa (Chap. 6) echo Hall's (Chap. 4) argument that a central goal of language teacher education should be to counteract the pervasive ideologies of monolingualism in TESOL. They explain that successfully integrating translanguaging into a language teacher preparation course involves creating opportunities to explicitly engage candidates' existing language ideologies. They lay out an alignment of Howard and Levine's (2018) language teacher learning framework and García, Johnson, and Seltzer's (2017) translanguaging pedagogy framework (stance, design, shift). This is highly instructive, since it illustrates how, for example, teacher support of students' translanguaging is an instantiation of an asset-based orientation to students' diverse linguistic and cultural resources. Robinson, Tian, Crief, and Lins Prado (Chap. 7) also use the *stance-design-shift* translanguaging pedagogy framework, but they root it in a teaching English for justice model. This entails teachers being able to "(1) recognize practices and structures that sustain inequalities (2) critique status quo practices and structures that sustain inequalities and (3) engage in practices that support all learners" (p. 139). Candidates' understanding of translanguaging was developed in relation to their awareness of connections between language, culture and power. In both chapters, the authors maintain that translanguaging represents a form of *praxis* in language teacher education; that is, the space (conceived as either a critique and re-examination of ideology or of power/social justice) where the synthesis of theory and practice is realized.

Turner (Chap. 9) likewise illustrates the creation of praxis in teacher professional learning in Australia with a group of highly experienced generalist teachers. In her conceptualization, *identity* becomes the locus of building teachers' understanding of translanguaging. She describes how this was accomplished through the affirmation of students' bi/multilingual identities, premised on a move from seeing students' identities as multilingual *being* to a view of students *doing* multilingual languaging. This is an important insight, since it not only succinctly captures the important connections between stance-design-shift components of translanguaging pedagogy, it also reflects the language as social practice aspect of translanguaging (and identity), in which we better understanding languaging as a verb, instead of a noun.

   Several chapters underscore the need to for teacher educators to approach trans-languaging and teacher preparation with honesty and humility. Andrei, Kibler and Salerno (Chap. 5) use narrative inquiry to approach this topic with a great deal of candor: translanguaging is complicated on several levels, and presenting the concept in a way that not only makes sense but is also relevant to teacher candidates is difficult. Andrei acknowledged that her own imperfect understanding of translanguaging made her first attempt to introduce it into her TESOL teacher preparation course as much of a learning experience for her as for the students. However, the fact that some of the students pushed back also underscores the importance of "practicing what we are preaching": creating a learning environment where ideas can be contested, discussed, and co-constructed is a hallmark of a translanguaging classroom. This sentiment was echoed in Morales, Schissel and López-Gopar (Chap. 8). They used participatory action research to document how the teacher educator (Morales) used translanguaging as an entry point to re-thinking his approach to embracing multilingualism, indigeneity, and the sociocultural context of his students in an EFL class for future English teachers. In doing so, he confronts a very practical issue of translanguaging and language teaching: how do we assess students' progress in English in a way that is consistent with a translanguaging approach?

   The contributions of Morales et al. (Chap. 8) and Lau (Chap. 10) address the practical difficulties of collaborative projects with teacher educators in "peripheral," post-colonial contexts. Lau describes both the promise of incorporating translanguaging as part of the project of decolonization in post-colonial Malawi, while also recognizing the complexity of the role of English in global discourses on the quality of education and world citizenship. The chapter reminds us that although ideologies of monolingualism and English hegemony are pervasive in many countries, they also take on very particular forms and meanings within local ecologies of language. She observes that "researchers on international development also need to exercise vigilance and humility in our understanding of what decolonization means to local communities [...] and how our new theories and insights on language and language education [like translanguaging] might facilitate or hinder local agentive efforts to find creative solutions to make do with varied severe socio- political and economic demands" (p. 222).

3   Translanguaging in TESOL Classrooms

The main themes that emerge across the chapters in part two – ideology, social justice, and identity – are also present in the six chapters in the final part. In this part, the authors portray teachers' efforts to leverage translanguaging productively to support learning goals. Taken together, the chapters give us a sense of the relevance of translanguaging for teachers' practice (and possibilities for reflecting on their practice) across a breadth of TESOL contexts. These include a content-language integrated (CLIL) model in Dutch kindergarten and primary classrooms

(Günther-van der Meij & Duarte, Chap. 11), a high school content-based class for immigrant newcomers in the U.S. (Seilstad & Kim, Chap. 12), a task-based lesson in a secondary school in Vietnam (Seals, Newton, Ash, & Nguyen, Chap. 13), an English for academic purposes at a Canadian university (Galante, Chap. 14), a university EFL course in Costa Rica (Fallas Escobar, Chap. 15) and a university-based Intensive English Program in the U.S. (Aghai, Sayer, & Vercellotti, Chap. 16).

As content-based instruction (CBI), including sheltered instructional models and content-language integrated learning (CLIL) approaches have become more common, many teachers see this as natural opportunity to integrate students' language backgrounds. Since language is seen as the medium of content learning, and L2 acquisition as a by-product – albeit an intentional and carefully designed by-product – of content teaching, the ideologies of monolingualism and language separation may be less influential on pedagogy. This is the case for the two studies that examine translanguaging in CBI classrooms. Günther-van der Meij and Duarte (Chap. 11) describe an approach to organizing languages in a kindergarten program in the Friesland region of the Netherlands that uses a trilingual model (Dutch, Friesian, English). Both migrant and minority languages of pupils are acknowledged and used in education, next to the majority languages. Here, translanguaging becomes a cornerstone of a holistic model for multilingualism in education, and includes components of language awareness, language comparison, receptive multilingualism, CLIL, and language immersion. Importantly, they also provide a specification for teachers of the functions of translanguaging in the classroom, with aims and the types of functions that teachers can use according to their proficiency level. This is an important insight, since it is common for educators when learning about translanguaging for the first time to respond that translanguaging is something that will work for bilingual classrooms where the teachers shares the same languages with students, but not for classrooms with many different languages. In arguing for translanguaging in multilingual TESOL settings, we need to be able to show how translanguaging pedagogies can be successful and effective when teachers and students do not all share the same language backgrounds. To this point, Seilstad and Kim (Chap. 12) give a concrete example of the potential of translanguaging in a highly multilingual high school biology classroom for immigrant and refugee newcomers in the U.S. They illustrate how an "activity drew on translanguaging pedagogy in an English-centric space, resulting in presentations that decentered English and produced an unexpected moment that, while fleeting, destabilized the national/named divisions between languages and created a positive response between the students and [teacher]" (p. 270).

The multilingual turn in TESOL has prompted language educators to re-examine how translanguaging fits into (or transforms) other pedagogical approaches as well. While the fit between translanguaging and content-based approaches may seem like a natural one, other approaches, such as task-based language teaching (TBLT), were developed from a traditionally psycholinguistic/cognitivist (and hence monolingual) approach to L2 learning and teaching, and it is therefore less clear what the role of translanguaging could be. Seals et al. (Chap. 13) acknowledge that there is a theoretical tension between the concept of translanguaging, which is more aligned with sociocultural ideas of L2 learning, and the mainstream cognitivist SLA roots of TBLT, but they take what they term an "applied sociolinguistic approach" to translanguaging in TBLT. In a secondary EFL classroom in Vietnam, they argue that rather than viewing students as having to "resort" to using the L1 to complete a task, they show that students translanguaged during tasks in order to generate ideas, scaffold, and self-regulate their output in the L2. Likewise, Galante (Chap. 14) documents how translanguaging supports vocabulary instruction for students in a Canadian English for Academic Purposes program. She uses a classic method comparison design to document how pedagogical translanguaging can support vocabulary acquisition, a key element for EAP students. She reports that not only did students in the (experimental) TL group have significantly higher scores on the vocabulary test than students in the monolingual (control) group, but that "students in the translanguaging group engaged in meaning-making across languages and took an active role in language learning" (p. 293).

Fallas Escobar (Chap. 15) and Aghai et al. (Chap. 16) look at the connection between teachers' ideologies of language, their pedagogical approaches, and the possibilities of translanguaging. In these chapters, the main aim is to examine how language teachers' ideologies, or *stances,* frame their approach to multilingualism and/or language separation in the classroom. As Fallas Escobar acknowledges that teachers' stances reflect broader social and institutional language ideologies (cf. Chaps. 2, 3 and 4 in the first part), but that the concept or even the term *translanguaging* can, in and itself, be a tool for teachers. Amongst the Costa Rican EFL teachers in his study, he explained that the initial anxiety or resistance one teacher had to her own acceptance of language mixing in her classroom, and the idea that perhaps translanguaging is a tool for some students but not for others ("struggling students"), was overcome when she realized: "So there is a theory behind what I do…" (p. 340). He described the stances amongst his teacher participants as: translanguaging as a conscientious choice, translanguaging as a political act, and translanguaging as a spontaneous but judicious practice. Likewise, Aghai et al. (Chap. 16) showed that the three focal instructors at a U.S. university-based Intensive English Program with Arabic-speaking students had distinct stances towards translanguaging. Drawing on Ruiz's (1984) language orientations framework, they described the teachers' stances as: translanguaging as a problem, translanguaging as a natural process, and translanguaging as a resource. In both studies, the authors suggest that the concept of translanguaging stance can be transformative because it allows teachers to reflect on their practice through a lens of language ideologies.

4   Future Directions and Challenges for Translanguaging in TESOL

Where do we go from here? At the outset, we stated that the goal for this volume is to contribute to pushing translanguaging into TESOL across a range of contexts and exploring the transformative potential of translanguaging for TESOL. The chapters provide accounts of teachers in diverse settings creating multilingual spaces that allow students to draw on their translanguaging resources in multiple forms to support their learning of English. We believe that, collectively, the chapters in this book provide convincing evidence that translanguaging is a central theoretical concept and pedagogical tool in the multilingual turn in TESOL. Translanguaging blurs linguistic boundaries, and its potential to inform and transform pedagogical practice extends across national borders, cultural contexts, learners' ages, language backgrounds, and instructional methods. In thinking about future directions for translanguaging in TESOL, there are three main take-aways from this volume: the place of translanguaging within the current state of TESOL (post)methods, the social justice orientation of translanguaging, and translanguaging as an ideology of language.

4.1 Translanguaging and TESOL Methods

The volume has invited us to think about how translanguaging should be integrated into our classroom practice. What is the "fit" between a given teaching method and using a translanguaging approach? The chapters provide examples that translanguaging can work with a range of approaches, from content-based instruction (Seilstad & Kim, Chap. 12), to English for Academic Purposes (Galante, Chap. 14), to task-based language teaching (Seals et al., Chap. 13). Hall (Chap. 4) locates our move to translanguaging as coinciding with the postmethod condition of TESOL. In figuring out the practical aspects of translanguaging pedagogy in a given classroom, we will do well to remember the reason we moved beyond our methods fetish is because we arrived at an understanding of language teaching not as a series of steps or a recipe to be followed, but as a flexible set of techniques and strategies, informed and guided by communicative principles. Here, the notion of *translanguaging shifts* captures the idea that translanguaging should not be reduced to a method, but rather is a set of related strategies that embodies the principles of flexible multilingualism. These can be planned as part of the *design*, such as the multilingual early grade curriculum in the Netherlands (Günther-van der Meij & Duarte, Chap. 11) described, or can be the openness to leveraging the ah-hah! moments that can magically arise within translanguaging spaces, such as the hummingbird example in Seilstad and Kim's (Chap. 12) biology lesson.

4.2 Translanguaging Is a Social Justice Orientation

A theme that runs across the chapters in this volume is that translanguaging is, at its heart, an orientation to language teaching that is rooted in social justice. This is to say, as TESOL educators we should strive to have our work contribute to creating greater social equality. This is certainly true for immigrant students (cf. Seltzer & García, Chap. 2; Seilstad & Kim, Chap. 12), whose linguistic and cultural identities are frequently marginalized. But it is also true for international students (cf. Galante, Chap. 14; Aghai et al., Chap. 16) who have access to significant socioeconomic resources but may nonetheless be positioned as minorities. This is not to say that a translanguaging lens views the struggles and marginalization of all groups the same. We need to recognize important differences between groups with different types of social and cultural capital. Sembiante and Tian (Chap. 3) remind us that the concept of translanguaging originated in bilingual education, which historically has been oriented towards the development of multilingualism as part of the struggle for civil rights and social justice for minoritized peoples.

The foregrounding of social justice aspect of translanguaging is most clearly articulated in the translanguaging social justice framework proposed by Robinson et al. (Chap. 7), but is exemplified in all the chapters. Two chapters (Turner, Chap. 9; Lau, Chap. 10) illustrate that translanguaging pushes our field to move beyond "learning English = access to linguistic capital for success" narrative that has driven the (neoliberal) argument for the importance of TESOL. The authors connect English language education to projects of decolonization and language maintenance. On the one hand, this argument is paradoxical given the history of TESOL and the rise of global English and neoliberalism. On the other hand, this is precisely why as scholars we are excited by the possibilities of translanguaging to contest and transform the prevailing discourses within TESOL. We would argue that future work on translanguaging in TESOL must remain firmly grounded within this social justice orientation.

4.3   Transforming Language Ideologies in TESOL

In the past decade, we have become more aware of how language education as field is strongly shaped by language ideologies (Deroo et al., Chap. 6; Sayer, 2012). Native speakerism, standard English, global English, testing and certification regimes, have all been powerful discourses that define the purposes and goals of TESOL. One unfortunate effect of this has been the Othering of the people TESOL is meant to serve (let's not forget, the "O" in TESOL stands for other). As Alan Luke (2004) observed: "TESOL is a pedagogical site and institution for educating the racial and linguistic Other" (p. 25). While the field has been largely constructed around dominant language ideologies, in translanguaging we see a discursive space to resist and push back against these ideologies (cf. Li Wei's [2011] notion of *translanguaging spaces*).

Translanguaging as a linguistic ideology of resistance is captured in the notion of *translanguaging stance*. As Seltzer and García (Chap. 2) point out, this is the philosophy that teachers bring into their work with students. It should, as explained above, embrace the social justice aspects of language education. However, as the chapters illustrate, a translanguaging stance incorporates other aspects of multilingual approach to TESOL as well. For Lau (Chap. 10), it includes engaging participants with the broader discourses of English and development and progress in Africa.

A translanguaging stance then, is also a potential space for teachers to interrogate their own practice. As the chapters in Part II illustrate, translanguaging is a powerful tool for teacher professional development. For Andrei et al. (Chap. 5) and Fallas Escobar (Chap. 15), explicitly engaging teachers in discussions on their pedagogical stances allowed them to reflect on, become aware of, and shift the mindsets towards the students' multilingualism. However, Andrei et al. (Chap. 5) note that although the draft version of the TESOL professional standards specifically mentioned translanguaging amongst the knowledge of language processes that teacher candidates should demonstrate, the final version omits translanguaging (but still specifies "interlanguage and language progressions", p. 6). This indicates that the there is still work to be done in pushing ideologies of multilingualism into the TESOL mainstream. A counter example can be found in Günther-van der Meij and Duarte's (Chap. 11) description of the early childhood language curriculum in the Netherlands, where translanguaging is used as a way not only of promoting students' plurilingualism, but of embracing and building bridges between language majority and minority communities. Future work should draw on this perspective, that sees translanguaging as a stance that resists dominant ideologies of language, but seeks to make connections between the diverse identities of students.

References

Faez, F. (2011). Are you a native speaker of English? Moving beyond a simplistic dichotomy. *Critical Inquiry in Language Studies, 8*(4), 378–399.

Flores, N., Spotti, M., & García, O. (2017). Conclusion: Moving the study of language and society into the future. In O. García, N. Flores, & M. Spotti (Eds.), The Oxford handbook of language and society (pp. 545–551). Oxford, UK: Oxford University Press.

García, O. (2009). *Bilingual education in the 21st century: A global perspective*. Malden, MA: Wiley-Blackwell.

García, O., Johnson, S. I., & Seltzer, K. (2017). *The translanguaging classroom: Leveraging student bilingualism for learning*. Philadelphia, PA: Caslon.

García, O., & Leiva, C. (2014). Theorizing and enacting translanguaging for social justice. In A. Blackledge & A. Creese (Eds.), *Heteroglossia as practice and pedagogy*. Dordrecht, The Netherlands: Springer.

Howard, E. R., & Levine, T. H. (2018). What teacher educators need to know about language and language learners: The power of a faculty learning community. In C. T. Adger, C. E. Snow, & D. Christian (Eds.), *What teachers need to know about language* (pp. 143–176). Bristol, UK: Multilingual Matters.

Jacobson, R., & Faltis, C. (Eds.). (1990). *Language distribution issues in bilingual schooling*. Clevedon, UK: Multilingual Matters.

Kachru, B. (1986). *The alchemy of English*. Urbana/Chicago: University of Illinois Press.

Kumaravadivelu, B. (2012). *Language teacher education for a global society*. London, UK: Routledge.

Luke, A. (2004). Two takes on the critical. In B. Norton & K. Toohey (Eds.), *Critical pedagogies and language learning* (pp. 21–29). Cambridge, UK: Cambridge University Press.

May, S. (Ed.). (2014). *The multilingual turn: Implications for SLA, TESOL and bilingual education*. New York, NY/London, UK: Routledge.

Ortega, L. (2013). SLA for the 21st century: Disciplinary progress, transdisciplinary relevance, and the bi/multilingual turn. *Language Learning, 62*(S1), 1–24.

Pennycook, A. (1994). *The cultural politics of English as an international language.* London, UK/ New York, NY: Longman.

Phillipson, R. (1992). *Linguistic imperialism.* Cambridge, UK: University of Cambridge Press.

Ruíz, R. (1984). Orientations in language planning. *NABE Journal, 8*(2), 15–34.

Sayer, P. (2012). *Ambiguities and tensions in English language teaching: Portraits of EFL teachers as legitimate speakers.* New York, NY/London, UK: Routledge.

Sayer, P. (2015). "More & earlier": Neoliberalism and primary English education in Mexican public schools. *L2 Journal, 7*(3), 40–56.

Storch, N., & Wigglesworth, G. (2003). Is there a role for the use of the L1 in an L2 setting? *TESOL Quarterly, 37*(2), 760–770.

Taylor, S. K., & Snoddon, K. (2013). Plurilingualism in TESOL: Promising controversies. *TESOL Quarterly, 47*(3), 439–445.

Wei, L. (2011). Moment analysis and translanguaging space: Discursive construction of identities by multilingual Chinese youth in Britain. *Journal of Pragmatics, 43*(5), 1222–1235.

Zentella, A. C. (1997). *Growing up bilingual: Puerto Rican children in New York.* Malden, MA: Blackwell.

Zentella, A. C. (2007). 'Dime con quién hablas, y te dire quién eres': Linguistic (in)security and Latino/a unity. In J. Flores & R. Rosaldo (Eds.), *A companion to Latino/a studies* (pp. 25–38). Malden, MA: Blackwell.

CPSIA information can be obtained
at www.ICGtesting.com
Printed in the USA
LVHW082259130121
676439LV00005B/61